FROM MOON GODDESSES TO VIRGINS

From
M⚭n Goddesses

PETE SIGAL

to Virgins

THE COLONIZATION

OF YUCATECAN MAYA

SEXUAL DESIRE

UNIVERSITY OF TEXAS PRESS,
AUSTIN

Requests for permission to reproduce material from this work should be sent to Permissions, University of Texas Press, P.O. Box 7819, Austin, TX 78713-7819.

♾ The paper used in this book meets the minimum requirements of ANSI/NISO Z39.48-1992 (R1997) (Permanence of Paper).

LIBRARY OF CONGRESS CATALOGING-IN-PUBLICATION DATA

Sigal, Peter Herman, 1964–
        From moon goddesses to virgins : the colonization of Yucatecan Maya sexual desire / by Pete Sigal.
            p.   cm.
        Includes bibliographical references and index.
        ISBN 0-292-77744-2 (cloth : alk. paper) — ISBN 0-292-77753-1 (pbk. : alk. paper)
            1. Mayas—Mexico—Yucatán (State)—Religion.   2. Mayas—Mexico—Yucatán (State)—Sexual behavior.   3. Mayas—Mexico—Yucatán (State)—Psychology.
    F1435.3.R3 S54   2000
    306.7'089'974152—dc21

                                                                    00-023488

FOR RICK AND BOOH

CONTENTS

LIST OF ILLUSTRATIONS

PREFACE AND ACKNOWLEDGMENTS

In 1517 a conquest expedition left the island of Cuba on its way to Yucatán, a peninsula southwest of Cuba and southeast of what was to become central Mexico. This group failed in its attempt at conquest, but not before one of its members, Bernal Díaz del Castillo, was able to make a series of observations. Díaz, writing his recollections decades later, remembered the people of Yucatán primarily as a deceitful and hostile group who used priests to engage in threats and even to kill people. Yucatecan people, according to Díaz, celebrated sodomy, practiced human sacrifice, and enslaved men, women, and children.[1] After several brief expeditions around the coast of the peninsula, the Spanish went on to conquer central Mexico before they returned, and in the 1540s they finally conquered much of Yucatán.[2]

Yucatán of the early sixteenth century was populated by a group of the descendants of the people responsible for the religious/urban centers and pyramids most often associated with the Maya. Most of these centers emanated from the Classic period (A.D. 250–900), although several of the Yucatecan sites (Chichén Itzá and Mayapán, for example) were used primarily during Postclassic times. The Maya, however, by the time of the Spanish conquest, had abandoned the major sites and had settled into independent farming communities. Still, they maintained a society with significant social stratification.[3] This Maya society was divided based on class, ethnicity, and lineage, a fact that did not escape its would-be conquerors.

Given Díaz's moral objections to certain aspects of Maya culture, one might think that the Spaniards would have placed great emphasis on changing these elements. Yet this was not entirely the case, and a complete spiritual and cultural conquest never took place.[4] Instead, the Maya ethical system in place at the time of the conquest changed dramatically, but in a manner that Díaz and his fellow Spaniards could not have predicted. The Maya ethical system changed into a hybridized form, one in which the two systems (Maya and Spanish) mixed to create something which did not replicate either of the prior two. The new hybridized ethical system was based on broader cultural changes: the ways in which Maya people made sense of their world were colonized and forever altered.

This book analyzes the hybridization of one complex element of this culture: sexual desire. For the Maya sexual desire was placed in a cultural framework centered around ritual. The rituals as a whole promoted warfare and sacrifice to maintain the gods. For the Spanish sexual desire was placed in a cultural framework related to sin. The hybridization of these two frameworks did not allow sex to be connected to sacrifice; nor did it subsume sex under the rubric of sin. Instead, for the colonial Maya, sex became connected with a cultural system related to the shedding of blood, the maintenance of lineage, and the connection with supernatural forces. While this system certainly related closely to concepts of sacrifice and sin, the very definitions of these elements were changed by the centuries of colonization and hybridization.

This book is the first manuscript that I know of to use Maya-language documents in order to study sexual desire. The discussion is framed around a series of texts, mainly written by seventeenth- and eighteenth-century Maya nobles, which were intended to show the history, religion, and philosophy of the Maya communities in Yucatán. In every case I find that the texts discuss, both directly and metaphorically, the genders, bodies, and sexual desires of the Maya peoples, often distinguishing the thoughts and actions of the people inside the local community from those of all others. Preconquest Maya ideas were used by individuals, lineage groups, and communities to gain various advantages over others. The same took place during the colonial era, although the context changed. The arguments were sexualized debates about political, social, cultural, and economic issues. I argue that by the late colonial period Maya sexual ideas, fantasies, and fears had changed dramatically. The alterations which took place were the results of a colonialism dominated by the force of hybridity (the development of something, in this case a culture, from the mixing of two other things where the resulting mixture was a new element —not just a structure which had some of the qualities of each of the other two), rather than a complete repression of Maya culture.[5]

This book is organized around various aspects of desire and power. I strive both to give the reader an introduction to Maya ways of describing sexual desire and to create an understanding of the ways in which sex in general has been constructed. The reader may understand these dual purposes more adequately in each chapter, where theoretical models are critiqued on the basis of Yucatec examples.

The first two chapters are designed to introduce the material and orient the reader. The first chapter, "Searching for the Moon Goddess," provides an overview, focusing on the theoretical and methodological contexts for this study. The second chapter, "Religion and Family," provides the reader with an analysis of these two aspects of Maya culture. This chapter is designed to present the reader with the central elements of colonial Maya society which related to sexual desire. The context of Maya sexual desire during the colonial period was both a hybridized religion and a family structure based on preconquest Maya ideas of extended lineage groups and Catholic ideas of the smaller family unit.

Chapters 3 through 5 more specifically present the context and "reality" of Maya sexual desires during the colonial period. Even though this entire manuscript focuses more on mental processes than on behaviors, these chapters provide an analysis of the ways in which Mayas and Spaniards viewed what they perceived to be actual sexual acts. These chapters thus analyze elements of the struggle (related to sexual perceptions) between colonial rule and Maya tradition which led to the strategy of hybridization. Chapter 3, "Framing Maya Sexual Desire," relates the cultural frameworks of sin and warfare to sexual ideas. Chapter 4, "Fornicating with Priests, Communicating with Gods," analyzes the textual discussion of actual sexual acts. It begins with the topic of "strategic inversion," presenting a case made against four "fornicating priests," and goes on to discuss differences and similarities between Spanish and Maya ideas. Chapter 5, "The Unvirgin Virgin," discusses in detail the colonial coding of the Virgin Mary, of the Moon Goddess, and of virginity itself. In this chapter I deconstruct the Maya concept of virginity to make a series of points related to hybridity and conceptual translation.

Chapters 6 through 9 shift the focus somewhat from daily sexual activities and perceptions to ritual processes. The signification of ritual activity allows me to present the relationship that I have found between various rituals and the colonial coding of Maya sexual desire. It is in these chapters that the reader will find an analysis of colonial Maya fantasies and fears. For it is here that I am able to reconstruct rituals in such a way as to promote some understanding of Maya imaginations. Chapter 6, "Gender, Lineage, and the Blood of the Rulers," analyzes the relationships between political power and blood, showing the ways in which human sacrifice and kinship rituals presented gender to the Maya people. On these ritual occasions the Maya leaders showed the ways in which they imagined masculinity, femininity, and sex. Chapter 7, "Blood, Semen, and Ritual," emphasizes bloodletting and penis piercing. These rituals were related to the power of the shamans and curers, who presented to the people some fantastic and some frightening scenes which no doubt influenced the imaginations of the Maya. Chapter 8, "Transsexuality and the Floating Phallus," analyzes implications of transsexuality in the texts, particularly discussing the position of the phallus as a ritualistic signifier of the power of gender and sexual desire. Here Maya fantasies were presented as transsexual, and the Maya utilized transsexuality as a metaphor to explain the world. Chapter 9, "Ritualized Bisexuality," discusses the ways in which bi-eroticism and pederasty marked the political and religious texts. The rituals described here gave the Maya the opportunity to fantasize about bisexual desires but more often presented to them the fear of rape. These chapters, although focusing on fantasy, also show ways in which the fantasies (almost exclusively postconquest) were influenced by colonialism and hybridity.

Chapter 10, "Finding the Virgin Mary," offers some concluding remarks on the relationships between sexual desire and colonial Maya cultural histories. The first and last chapters decode the symbolic irony of searching for the sign of the Moon Goddess and finding in her place the sign of the Virgin Mary.

Yucatecan Maya leaders understood and used Spanish/ Christian concepts of proper and improper behaviors. Maya nobles took these notions and applied them both to their own histories and to their ongoing disputes with individual Spaniards and other Maya nobles. They also interpreted Spanish/ Christian ideas related to proper sexual and gender roles in ways that undermined many of the foundations of those very ideas. In this book the reader will see that the Virgin Mary was reinscribed as a "virgin" goddess who had sex with many other gods. Mayas and Spaniards engaged in struggles over definitions, cultural and political structures, and behaviors themselves.

·   ·   ·

In September of 1991, after years of searching for the right research project, I approached James Lockhart and told him that I would like to work with him and study the colonial Maya peoples. He asked me why I wanted to be a student of the colonial period. I told him of my interest in culture and specifically in cultural change. He nodded his head, suggesting to me that he was interested, but that I was no different from anyone who had come to him before. I then told him my central interest: I wanted to research sexuality among the colonial Maya in order to gauge the sexual changes and continuities that take place when different cultural groups come into contact with each other. Jim showed me his excitement, an excitement for the field that I would see him express time and again; an excitement that is invigorating for graduate students. He told me that we should get to work right away, that this was one of the hot topics in the field. So this work first and foremost acknowledges the contributions of James Lockhart. He was the person who really introduced me to the field, training me in Nahuatl and encouraging me to expand my knowledge of Yucatecan Maya. I also thank both Jim and Maryann Lockhart for providing me with encouragement throughout and after the dissertation process.

Ellen DuBois made sure that I always had support at UCLA. She has fostered an excellent academic environment, bringing in graduate students interested in the study of gender and sexuality. She has supported me through many difficult times, and she has always encouraged me to continue my work. Ramón Gutiérrez has provided me with the support necessary to understand many of the theoretical issues. He has been able to connect my knowledge of sexuality with the situation of colonized peoples. The late E. Bradford Burns constantly held my interest and provoked my mind. His commitment to the people of Latin America was admirable. Charles Sackrey's support and encouragement led me to go to graduate school.

I wish also to thank the many others—academic colleagues and close personal friends—who have given me great support both by encouraging my scholarship and by helping me maintain my mental health: Barbara Bernstein, Bob Craig, Chris Ehrick, Arawn Eibhlyn, Gar, Kimberly Gauderman, Jim Green, Rebecca Hensler, Richard Iosty, Kaci Joy, John Kirkland, Jorge Klor de Alva, John O'Brien, John Peeler, Shela Patel, Bonnie Poteet, Matthew Restall, Earl Shorris, Moshe Sluhovsky, Lisa Sousa, Jayne Spencer, Paul Sussman, Kevin Terraciano, Richard Trexler, Andrea Tyndall, and Ericka Verba. I wish also to thank the staff and faculty of the history departments at UCLA and St. Cloud State University for their kind support. My current colleagues at California State University, Los Angeles, have been extraordinarily supportive. My students at UCLA, at St. Cloud State University, and now at Cal State, L.A., have provided me with great encouragement and hope. I want to thank my family for all that they have done for me. They have provided me with emotional and financial support to get me through difficult times.

I acknowledge UCLA's Latin American Center for providing me with two research grants, allowing me to travel to New Orleans and Mérida. I also acknowledge the history department and Mrs. Heyman for providing me with the Ira Heyman Dissertation Grant. The staff at the Latin American Library of Tulane University was extremely helpful. The staff at all of the archives in Mérida and the Archivo General de la Nación in Mexico City similarly led me to important documents. Likewise, the staff at Harvard University's Tozzer library, particularly Greg Finnegan, was very supportive.

Finally, this work is dedicated to Rick and to Booh. Many friends and colleagues have died in the time it has taken me to write this book. Rick's support and love always was incredible, and my love for him remains strong. I wish he could have lived to read this work. Booh has lived through this with me, and he has supported me throughout a long and arduous process.

NOTES ON TRANSCRIPTION
AND TRANSLATION

TRANSCRIPTION DILEMMAS

In the matter of transcription, I have, except where noted, transcribed all of the texts from the original or a photocopy of the original. As to the actual letters of the words, I have great faith in the transcriptions. The calligraphy of older Maya texts is in general readily legible. The transcriber does, however, face three central problems. First, the varying phonetic repertoires of Maya and Spanish provided the indigenous writers doing the texts with some challenges. In writing Spanish words, they would often change letters, leaving out the letter for a sound not in Maya and putting in the letter for its closest approximation in their own repertoire. Since the Maya heard no difference between sounds they had and sounds they lacked, they were prone to write some of the letters signifying exotic sounds even for their own sounds, a process often called hypercorrection, as in writing *fel* for *pel*, "vagina," even though Maya had *p* and lacked *f*. As a result, Spanish words are sometimes hard to recognize in Maya texts, and without the support of a recognizable root, one may even read the letters wrong.

A second issue for the transcriber is the fact that the Maya were not consistent in their manner of dividing strings of letters. In some sections of a text there may be spaces between the words almost as in modern writings. In another section the spaces may be in the middle of words. To this day, word division in Maya writing is not fully standardized. Since Maya roots generally are constructed on the model of consonant-vowel-consonant, I can usually discern the roots, distinguishing them from the set of affixes associated with them, and thus arrive with some certainty at the words.

A third problem is that older Maya texts had no punctuation, making it difficult for the transcriber to figure out where an utterance begins and ends. In several cases I have transcribed passages differently from Munro Edmonson because of these last two issues. We find different boundaries for words and put the beginning and ending of certain passages at different places.

In my transcriptions I have attempted to be as faithful as possible to the originals. I have followed standard formats for these types of transcriptions in ethnohistorical texts, placing the transcriptions next to the translations. I have allowed the text to run on in the original format, dividing it only where necessary for the reader to be able to follow the relationship between the transcription and translation. I have written glottalized consonants as the Maya wrote them, with a strike-through feature, as follows: *ch̵, p̵*. The Maya wrote the glottalized *ts* as a backwards *c*, and I have reproduced this convention. In some cases, the glottalized consonants were written as double consonants, such as *pp*. The glottalized *t* most often was written as *th*. The Maya term *yetel*, "and," most often was written as ꝡ.

THE ACT OF TRANSLATION

I must note that the translations of the documents, while generally very strong and always justifiable, are somewhat tentative. While all of the relevant translations related to the human body, gender, and sexual acts are extremely solid, some of the broader translations are based more on interpretation of the language. Wherever I have questions about the translations, I have provided the reader with a note explaining the circumstances. Except where otherwise noted, I have translated all of the documents myself in order to give the most accurate translations possible. However, in all cases I have compared my translations to those of other scholars, and in some cases I have rectified my translations accordingly. As the texts that I use are extremely complex, there is no way to provide complete definitive translations at this time.

Throughout this manuscript I have attempted to provide the reader with the most accurate possible transcriptions and translations of the Maya language texts. I have put a major effort into the task, working over the texts repeatedly, and I have consulted all known previous translations. Nevertheless, translating colonial Maya documents into English is a tricky affair. Work with the hieroglyphic writing and with the modern spoken language is perhaps more advanced for Maya than for any other Mesoamerican language family, but the same is not true of philology based on texts set down in alphabetic script in the centuries after the conquest. Scholars hardly know the general grammar of those times, much less the specific grammars of the genres in which the writing was done. William Hanks has pointed out some grammatical deficiencies in translations done to date,[1] but even when translators are aware of the problem, they cannot always easily overcome it. The obscurity extends to the vocabulary itself. Some of the documents studied in this work, particularly the Books of Chilam Balam and the Ritual of the Bacabs, are quite arcane, using some words found in no dictionary and others in senses not otherwise attested. Their language is extremely complex and metaphorical, consciously veiled. I have no doubt that much further progress will be made in the translation of these and other older Maya texts and that as that process goes on, it will be seen that I have committed some errors of translation. I have, however, done everything I could, and I present the versions here as at least comparable in quality to others that have been published. Throughout, I have tried to remain aware of the uncertainties. Indeed, I have omitted some very interesting texts because sufficient certainty could not be attained. When I am aware of problems in passages of my own translations, I have discussed them in the endnotes. In a few cases a particular word or line has baffled me to such an extent that I have used another scholar's translation as a last resort. Such instances are always noted. I have given maximum attention to accuracy in matters of the central terminology related to the body, gender, and sexual desire.

Of the grammatical problems I have faced, I have been especially aware of those related to the possession of nouns.[2] Maya uses possessive prefixes profusely. In the texts it is often by no means obvious to whom or to what the prefix refers, and in some cases no candidate for the possessor is on the textual horizon at all. The texts reduce the indication of the possessor to a minimum, writing *y-* for *u y-*, "his/her/its, their," and leaving out the *-ob* plural more often than not even when the possessor is both plural and animate. Only the context can determine the number of the possessor and in some cases even the person. Hence there are many uncertainties involved in identifying the referent of a possessive prefix.

Another problem I have faced repeatedly is the large number of verbal roots without inflection in the texts. Some can be accounted for as preterits, imperatives, hypothetical or unrealized forms, or even interpreted nominally, but there still seem to be too many of them, and they are very hard to interpret. I cannot avoid the feeling that verbal inflection, especially temporal marking, as it appears in older written Maya, does not correspond very well with the descriptions found in the Maya grammatical texts.[3]

At the level of syntax and stylistics, the issues are many. Munro Edmonson states that the couplet is the primary device used in the Books of Chilam Balam.[4] Hanks does not share Edmonson's opinion,[5] and I have shown above that the Maya used many other devices in their writing. One's opinion on this matter affects translation substantially.

FROM MOON GODDESSES TO VIRGINS

ONE　Searching for the Moon Goddess

As students of the Maya begin their course of study, they notice in the Dresden Codex, a Yucatec Maya manuscript written before the Spanish conquest, at least one figure that appears to many of them a bit out of place. There she is, a female figure engaged in what we are told were sexual acts with several others. We also are told that this female figure was a representation of the Moon Goddess, and indeed she was pictured in enough other places that we know this to be accurate (see Fig. 1.1). The Moon Goddess had sex with other gods, and we are told that in doing so she was able to reproduce and thus to create the Maya people. Who was this Moon Goddess, and what did she mean to the various people we call the Maya? How did her meaning change during the colonial years? As I began my journey into Maya studies, these questions loomed large. I have found that the Moon Goddess was a central signifier of Maya self-identity, gender, and sexual desire.

This book is a study of desire and power. Why did the Maya desire the Moon Goddess, and how, during the years of Spanish colonial rule, did they come to desire the Virgin Mary? The Moon Goddess and the Virgin Mary both were encoded figures that signified many things related to religion, gender, and sexuality, to name but three. This book reconfigures these codes and

FIGURE 1.1   The Moon Goddess inside
a glyph of the moon. From Linda Schele
and David Freidel, *A Forest of Kings: The
Untold Story of the Ancient Maya*, copyright © 1990 by William Morrow and
Company. Reprinted by permission of
William Morrow and Company.

then focuses not on the Moon Goddess and the Virgin Mary themselves, but
rather on what they, as encoded figures, had to say about sexual desires.[1]

The present work is about the Maya of the seventeenth and eighteenth
centuries in late colonial Yucatán. These centuries represented a time of significant change for the Maya people. Recovering from the demographic collapse (due to disease) of the sixteenth century, the Maya were attempting to
rebuild a society that had never entirely been destroyed.[2] At the same time,
with the economy of the Spanish colonizers in an upswing, more demands
were placed on the people as a whole.[3] They came into more daily contact
with non-Maya people.[4] The Maya during this time period produced a large
number of documents in the Roman alphabet and the Maya language. Spaniards in Yucatán also produced a significant number of texts that related directly to Maya history.[5] These texts presented a picture of a dynamic, changing, and rather tense society. The tensions were representative of the changes

which were taking place regarding sex and gender, the Moon Goddess and the Virgin Mary.

TO DESIRE THE MOON GODDESS

I AM MOON, born to rule, to provide my people with the appropriate life. I do this through my statement of the Maya Word (*maya-than*),[6] and through my role as mother of all. As I give birth to the leaders of the world, I present the people with a chance to survive. Without me survival is impossible, for it is I who provide the appropriate lineage to the nobles, those who will allow for the communities to continue to exist. Indeed, as Moon, I will provide light to guide the way of the people as they traverse the night skies. When I am angry I will not appear, and the people will need to provide me with some elements for my sustenance.[7] I am a goddess, and all will provide me with the respect to which I am obliged.[8] I am goddess of all life processes, of birth, disease, marriage, and death.

As a child I engaged in youthful sexual experimentation in order to learn my role in society. When I grew to an adult, my role became more clear as I ascertained what was needed to enable my people to survive. When the Sun began to court me, he gave me many precious gifts,[9] and my power increased. I am married to the Sun and, despite my tumultuous relationship with him, I remain the mother of my people, more powerful than even my husband. At one point I ran off with the King Vulture. The Sun, angered by my behavior, dressed himself in a deer skin and pretended to be dead. He sent a blow fly to attract a vulture to the dead deer. Once the vulture arrived, the Sun forced him to take him to the King Vulture's palace, where the Sun made me return with him (see Fig. 1.2).[10] Despite this outrage, my power has not been abated, and I continue to engage in marriages[11] with many of the gods. I shall be worshipped as Ix Chel, the Moon Goddess of my people.[12]

The story of the Moon Goddess was replete with important codes for Maya society. It provided the nobles with legitimacy, developed an important story about the mother, inspired moral stories related to deception, gave one ethnic group a symbol to colonize others, and suggested a story if not a method

FIGURE 1.2   The Sun God and a vulture. A Maya myth current since Classic times, in which the Sun God tricked a vulture into bringing him to the palace of the King Vulture, where he retrieved his wife. From Norman Hammond, *Ancient Maya Civilization*, copyright © 1988 by Rutgers, The State University. Reprinted by permission of Rutgers University Press.

of resistance. It was a tale of colonialism and an anticolonial struggle, all rolled up into one, and all centered around particular concepts of gendered performance and sexual desire.[13]

As the story goes, the Moon Goddess reproduced Maya lineages which were associated with her own community, a group among the Itzá,[14] perhaps the people of Cozumel.[15] From this base, the Moon Goddess was to expand her geopolitical power. By engaging in many sexual acts with the other gods, the Moon Goddess was able to reproduce many lineages and assert control over other communities. These acts, in fact, increased the Moon's power over the various Maya peoples. For peoples so concerned with lineage,[16] any of the Moon Goddess's reproductive sexual acts became a primary element in an Itzá colonialism. But how did she convince the other gods to engage in sexual acts with her? The ethnic groups that created those gods certainly wanted to maintain their power over their own communities. They wanted to continue to establish this power in local gods and goddesses. This allowed them to maintain a certain sense of authority. But in the end many of the gods were shown engaging in sexual acts with the Moon Goddess, thus allowing her to be positioned as the mother goddess for almost all of the Maya peoples. She became, for a while, perhaps the most powerful god of all, surpassing the power of the Sun.[17]

There are six parts to this tale that are relevant to a deconstruction[18] of the power of the Moon Goddess. These elements add up to the status of the Moon Goddess as a privileged signifier that represented the transformation of Maya society during the colonial years. The six parts of her story are central to the theoretical framework of this book. In sum, all of the changes in gendered presentation and sexual desire can be related to these six parts of the Moon Goddess story:

Part I: The Goddess of Life and Death

By declaring her ability to give birth and to destroy life, the Moon Goddess was represented as one who both was desired and feared.

Part II: The Mother

As the Mother Goddess, the Moon asserted her power through her children. The desire for her was one of respect for one's mother. This was used to assert nobility and privilege.

Part III: The Goddess of Sex

The sexual desires of and for the Moon Goddess allowed her to reproduce, making her into the mother goddess. These desires also asserted a classic Oedipal triangulation as the Maya writers of the Dresden Codex clearly intended to portray their own sexual desires for their mother goddess.[19]

Part IV: The Goddess of Colonialism

As the Moon Goddess was used by the Itzá to colonize the Maya region, she became a goddess of colonialism. Her reputed ability both to betray and to seduce helped her engage in colonial acts of domination.

Part V: The Goddess of Resistance

During the colonial years the Moon Goddess at times was used as a goddess of resistance, an assertion of traditional Maya (or Itzá) culture. Religious millenarian movements, while stronger in Peru than in Mesoamerica, maintained active resistance in the Mayan regions through the nineteenth century and until today.

Part VI: The Goddess of Hybridity

During the colonial years, more often than becoming a goddess of resistance, the Moon Goddess was conflated textually with the Virgin Mary, thus becoming a hybrid Christian symbol, recoded in such a way as to lose her original meaning, but also in such a way as to change the meaning of the Virgin Mary (and of Christianity itself).

The Virgin Mary Moon Goddess hybrid signified a colonial coding of gendered performance and sexual desire. This signification developed meaning only through the cultural matrix in which it existed. This cultural matrix was a colonial hybrid.

SEXUAL DESIRE

At the first class meeting of my sexuality in the Americas course, I ask my students one central question: "What is sex?" Many students find the question ludicrous (or at least surprising) as they consider the answer to be obvious. Yet, as we begin on the first day to analyze non-Western societies, the students quickly learn that the question is complex. The Maya considered various acts to be sexual, including many (e.g., anal and vaginal intercourse) that define sex in the modern West. For other acts (e.g., hugs and kisses), there is no evidence that the Maya would have considered these sexual, and for yet others (e.g., ritualized intercourse between humans and gods), there is no place in modern Western discourse.[20] The problem is that the boundaries of the answer to this question (what is sex?) are sociohistorically constructed.[21] The modern constructions of sexuality and sexual desire can be used to understand the colonial Maya only if we contextualize these analytical categories in terms of power.

Sexuality

I analyze the ways in which sexual desire was presented in the texts of the Maya of Yucatán, a colonized people. Two premises of this study are that sexuality is a socially constructed phenomenon, and that all sexual desires have been influenced by sociohistorical forces. People's desires are not simply based in biology and nature, but rather are influenced by the societies in which they live. Family, community, media, work, and politics all influence whether and what people seek for erotic fulfillment. Western society, since the nineteenth century, has developed taxonomies, lists designed to categorize what people do sexually, and, importantly, to make people believe that those sexual desires are internal to their senses of being.[22] The colonial Maya had no such taxonomic obsessions.[23] Nor did the Maya at the time of the Spanish conquest understand sexual behaviors and ideas in the same ways as their European conquerors, who were developing the notion of sexuality as a discrete category of experience.[24] The sociohistorical creation of sexuality as an ingrained identity based on a set of shared experiences was a complex process, and the Maya did not view sexual desire with the same types of taxonomies as either modern Western (categorizing people as either homosexual or heterosexual)[25] or early modern European (classifying acts as sinful or nonsinful, and within certain parameters, basing identities on these acts)[26] peoples. Although there were many similarities in these understandings, the Mayas and Spaniards approached sexual desire in very different ways because of their different historical experiences.

Desire

The concept of desire is used here for the purpose of elucidating particular aspects of Maya society and culture. Many scholars from several different disciplines, at least since the days of the classical Greek philosophers, have debated the importance and meaning of desire, a broad analytical category which describes the state of mind needed for a person willingly to commit a wide variety of actions. But desire here does not and cannot mean a set of feelings free from power, free from the political, economic, social, and cultural implications of any such thoughts in any society.[27] Desire is part of the societal codes created in order to develop meanings out of people's thoughts and actions.

Colonial and colonized desires related directly to conceptions of sexuality and libido in that the colonial construction of hybrid desires in fact created the sexual desires of the colonized. This is not to say that the colonized did not have desires of their own. Nor is to say that such desires were constructed only by the process of conquest and colonization. Rather, sexual desires did not (and do not) exist without social constructs, and these social constructs during the colonial years were by definition colonial. Many colonial desires (to defeat the opponent, to extract wealth, to differentiate colonizer from colonized, to alter the colonized in a variety of ways) were scripted onto the human body along with sexual acts.[28]

Power

Scholars in this postmodern age almost incessantly debate questions of power: what is it, who holds it, how is it constituted, and how is it deployed?[29] The texts that I discuss in this manuscript were colonial productions, and thus were implicated in the creation and maintenance of a colonial society, so they were evocative of colonial power. This, of course, does not mean that the texts (mostly written in the Maya language) were *intended* to support the power of the colonizers. Instead, the texts were part of the colonial framework; they were cultural productions within a broader colonial cultural matrix. Power is understood in this book as a mode of analyzing thoughts and actions utilized by people or groups in order consciously or unconsciously to gain dominance over the actions and thoughts of others.[30]

In a colonial society power is manipulated in a wide variety of ways in order for the colonizers to gain as much effective control as possible over the colonized. In that sense, hybridity, the mixture of cultural traditions, is formed as a result of colonial power and its interaction with the traditional power relationships of the dominated groups. Colonial hybridity formed sexual desires and acts which were no longer Maya, but nor were they Hispanic: they were formed by the interactions involved in colonial power relations.

COLONIAL MAYA SEXUAL ACTS

For the colonial Maya a person may have engaged in particular behaviors, but she or he most often did not receive a specific, unchangeable identity based on this behavior (at least until his or her death). Without such an identity, the concept of *the* homosexual or *the* heterosexual as a category of person was unimaginable. The Maya used homosexual sodomy to understand particular historical stories, and they condemned other groups because of a supposed endemic sodomy. They thus understood (or at least played out) a connection between sodomy and power, but not one between sodomy and identity politics. Identity in the Maya world was a highly ritualized affair. One's identity was based on one's relationship to the lineage, the political hierarchy, the community, and the gods. None of the colonial documents show any terminology used to separate heterosexuals from homosexuals. Rather, many show that sex was divided between appropriate sexual behavior, which maintained society, and excessive sexual behavior, which destroyed society. These were attempts at creating, understanding, and controlling desire and power through discourses of hierarchy and conquest.

The Maya, like other early modern peoples, did not discuss sexual behavior extensively, but they, like others, did leave evidence of a wide variety of sexual acts. The Maya at the time of the conquest knew of and participated in vaginal and anal (between men and women, men and men, and men and youth) intercourse, oral sex, masturbation, pederasty (with boys and girls), bestiality, and unspecified sexual acts between women. They engaged in sexual acts with gods and in ritualized sexual acts between shamans and other people.[31] They appear to have known of and participated in digital stimulation. The commoners were supposed to practice serial monogamy, and all but the higher levels of nobles engaged in monogamous marriage. Polygyny was the rule for kings and the higher-level nobles. Divorce was readily available for most of the population. The Maya had defined categories for adultery, incest, and rape.

COLONIAL MAYA SEXUAL IDEAS

This book does not attempt to reconstruct Maya sexual behavior, as any such reconstruction necessarily is problematic. A social historian might look at the criminal trials and Inquisition cases to understand more about colonial Maya behaviors. However, the documentation of these behaviors specifically focuses on those who fall outside of the perceived "norms."[32] Instead, I focus here on the cultural matrix behind the creation of the norms related to desires, fantasies, fears, and ideas regarding sex (and the elements with which sex was associated in Maya discourse). More than "what did the Maya do?" the two central questions for me are "what did the Maya think?" and "why did they think what they thought?" The analytical concept of the cultural matrix is important here, as it describes the underlying organizational principles present in a given culture. The cultural matrix of the colonial Maya was developed by a hybrid discourse.[33] This matrix was created through psychocultural and psychosocial processes in which Maya minds were altered: the very forms of Maya thinking were changed in this process.

The Maya at the time of the conquest did not devise a discrete category of sexuality which divided sexual acts from other elements of life. This, of course, does not mean that the Maya would not have understood the concept "sex." However, this concept was subsumed under a set of other ideas which related sexual desires to a panoply of things: bloodletting, curing ceremonies, communion with the gods, various forms of sacrifice, and warfare. The broader category for the Maya had to do with the creation of life (amidst the threat of death) through some sort of ritualized penetration. As the Maya were colonized, they were faced with a radical rupture of these activities and ideas, a rupture which created hybridization. Given this context the reader may legitimately ask how it is possible to understand "sexuality" among a people seemingly so far removed from the current Western notion of a sexual identity. Here I follow other historians and anthropologists in discussing the frameworks of sexual desire, rather than allowing the concept of identity to be the core of the analysis.[34] The acts cited here did not and could not correspond to modern Western notions of sexuality because the colonial Maya did not have a similar way of conceptualizing and categorizing sexual desire.

Ideas of gender for the Maya at the time of the conquest were related closely to their concept of sexual desire. Gender formed a category in which male dominance was the rule. The Moon Goddess's power did not extend to any significant power for women. And, in fact, much of her power was based on aspects of Maya life that were associated with feminine submissiveness. The Maya metaphorically gendered much of the world and the cosmos by asserting supposed male aspects as dominant and female aspects as submissive. Gendered culture and society thus had a strictly defined hierarchy.[35] However, gender in colonial Maya culture did not correspond to that of the contemporary West as genders and anatomical bodies did not always agree, particularly in ritual contexts. Gods often had two genders and occasionally changed from one to the other. The metaphorical language of the texts accentuated the gender dualism present in Maya religion.

Many of the Maya ideas portrayed throughout this book were unconscious formations, and thus the book is about the ways in which the culture interacted with psychological processes related to sexual desire. The reader should not get the idea that the Maya were less or more homophobic or sexist than people in the contemporary West. The Maya would not have understood these ideas as they simply did not develop cultural categories in the same way.[36] In general gender was strictly hierarchical and people were punished severely for gender and sexual transgressions. However, Maya unconscious formations of sex and gender were different from their European counterparts.

THE HISTORIAN'S METHOD

As a historian I necessarily rely primarily on written texts. Formerly many historians have suggested that scholars should use these texts to reconstruct the past. I do not believe that such a reconstruction is possible. Instead I propose, along the lines of some of the more recent cultural and political histories, that scholars provide a new corpus of knowledge based on an understanding of the uses of discourse, language, and texts.[37] Here I seek to deconstruct the codes, presented in the texts, which were used by those in power to maintain their power and by others to challenge that power.[38] I rely on ethnohistorical research and textual analysis to uncover the codes that the Maya (and any peoples with whom they had contact) used to make sense out of sexual desires. It is through the act of decoding that I have discovered relationships between sex and the other elements of desire and power that are discussed in this book.

I seek to understand many of the changes in meaning which took place during the colonial period. As writings related to gender, sexual desire, and the human body became infused with European ideas, I explore the development of those ideas. However, because I am more interested in the cultural matrices underlying sexual attitudes, I am not attempting to show linear changes in those attitudes themselves. I seek to discuss language, culture, and power, thus invoking some ideas related to the unconscious phenomena which occurred in Maya minds. These unconscious structures were developed through a colonial matrix designed to change and conquer indigenous minds. In this attempt, a colonial hybrid unconscious was formed.[39]

I am analyzing documents that primarily come from what has been termed "high culture." These texts were representative of the views of a sector of noble men. The narratives were infused with masculine upper-class power and privilege. In my analysis I work to understand how these power dynamics functioned. My method comes from anthropology, literary criticism, philosophy, and psychology as well as history. This method, while unconventional to historians, allows me to understand sexual desire.

The New Philology

One brand of cultural/social history that has been most influential in studies of the indigenous peoples of colonial Mesoamerica has been what James Lockhart has dubbed the "New Philology."[40] In this brand of work, scholars translate and reproduce indigenous-language documents for the reader.

Those documents then are categorized and interpreted. A scholar may use texts which were reflectively philosophical or which were more "mundane" notarial texts[41] to reconstruct various aspects of indigenous culture and society.[42] I use philology in order to introduce the reader to some Maya texts and to allow me to understand both the direct and most often less consciously reflective uses of language in some of the more mundane documents and the more metaphorical language of the broad array of historical and philosophical documents.

Postcolonial Studies

Studies of colonialism most recently have developed a methodology heavily influenced by both poststructuralism and cultural Marxist theory.[43] Postcolonial studies theorists argue that colonialism cannot be understood simply as an outside society attempting to destroy, dominate, and make dependent a conquered group. Debates about colonialism must go beyond the dualism of a domination/resistance paradigm. For if the Maya and Nahua peoples all unequivocally had allied with each other and resisted Spanish colonization,[44] it is unlikely that the Spanish would have been able to dominate the indigenous peoples as effectively as they did. The Spaniards developed a way of using and incorporating indigenous systems of meaning in their attempt at dominating the conquered groups. The same occurred with European conquests in Africa, Asia, and other areas of Latin America. The conquerors reinscribed traditional signs with new meaning. According to cultural theorist Homi Bhabha, describing the British colonization of India, the result of this reinscription is "the effect of an ambivalence produced within the rules of recognition of dominating discourses as they articulate the signs of cultural difference and reimplicate them within the deferential relations of colonial power."[45] Colonialism works primarily through disavowal and reinscription. "The trace of what is disavowed is not repressed but repeated as something *different*—a mutation, a hybrid."[46] The creation of this hybrid entity serves to colonize the cultures and minds of the colonized. For the Maya, this does not mean that the Spaniards ever established hegemony.[47] The Spaniards, however, were able to colonize the unconscious minds of many of the Maya so that desires, fantasies, and fears were altered.[48] In order to study these changes, I have chosen to use the deconstructive methods of postcolonial theory. As such, I understand the texts that I read as literary devices which I decode in order to represent the cultural matrix.

Gender Studies/Queer Theory

Recent works in gender studies and queer theory also have been influenced by poststructuralism. These works have shown that gender and sexual identities are constructed in a matrix of power relationships. Gender and sexual desire have been seen as "performative effects, unrealized potentialities," and other such signifiers.[49] Those gender studies scholars and queer theorists that have studied colonialism have found that Europe asserted fictions related to the ideas of "geographies of perversion" and that "white men are saving brown women from brown men." These theorists have recognized that colonialism was deployed partly as an assertion of white masculinity.[50] This book uses an analytical technique, advocated by gender studies scholars and queer theorists, that works to understand the ways in which gender and sexual desire have been deployed in texts.

Colonial Latin American historical studies until recently rarely touched on the subject of sexual desire,[51] and even more rarely were influenced by gender studies or queer theory. Anthropologists, however, have researched sexual symbols in several Latin American societies, and, more recently, historians, art historians, and literary critics have studied desire in a variety of contexts. It is only recently that the poststructuralist gender studies and queer theory influences have been felt in this field.[52] The research on sexuality has shown that sexual behaviors and desires historically have been given different meanings in Latin America than in the United States and Europe. Indeed, comparing the various works, one finds that the meanings given to sexuality in such a place as Mexico City are very different from sexuality in the Maya lowlands and the central Andean highlands.[53]

The Historian's Imagination

This section on historical methodology would be incomplete if I did not discuss the defining metaphors used in my work.[54] Defining metaphors, in Hayden White's terminology, are those that represent the historian's purpose of study. How does the historian relate his or her discourse to conditions of the present?[55] The metaphors used are relationships established between the historian's imagination, the historical evidence (documents), and the present interests of the historian. I theorize about the past, bring my defining metaphors and paradigms to the foreground, and I seek to understand my own use of texts as narratives.[56] I theorize about the ways in which sexual desire was

used as a trope in the texts under consideration.[57] I use my historical imagination on three levels that add to the methodology I describe here:

  1. Reading: The documents had particular purposes, and the Maya told
something about how they used these documents, but in order not to efface
the human faces behind the documents, in order not simply to place the Maya
writers in a framework that does not relate to Maya thoughts about their own
actions/writings, the historian must work to define the cultural matrix which
the texts display. As I read, I work consciously to develop and spell out the
metaphorical relationships that are presented in the texts.

  2. Telling: The historian necessarily tells a story, and that story is dependent only partly on the documents chosen. The historian uses his or her own
thought processes in telling the story. In a few places in this book, I invoke
the genre of fiction to establish a temporarily fixed model for explanation.
That genre is designed to help explain the conscious and unconscious moti-
vations behind the texts. The creation of these fictions is based on my reading of the language of these bodies of evidence.[58]

  3. Understanding: The historian attempts to understand particular issues
that she or he believes to be important. Those issues may be framed in ways
that have little importance to the subjects of his or her study. My choice of
topics has most relevance to analyses of sexual desire, gender, and power as
cultures come into conflict. I am working to understand the ways in which desire, power, discourse, and text worked to construct a cultural matrix around
which real people organized their thoughts and actions/writings regarding
sex. I am attempting to understand the ways in which desire and power are
connected, so it should be clear that my choice of topics was not arbitrary in
any way: it came out of my own desire to explain a set of issues.

Documents

Primary documents in Yucatecan Maya, supplemented by some relevant
items in Spanish, provide the source base for this book. The documents manifested a variety of strategies, often not conscious to the authors, which were
based on specific traditions and represented an effort to deal with the local
ethnographic situation.[59] The Maya-language corpus includes many testaments, petitions, bills of sale, and other formal notarial sources.[60] This group
of documents also includes several historical, medical, and religious ritual
texts, most of which were anonymous and undated. Over 1,700 Yucatecan
Maya–language documents now have been found.[61] These documents center

around the period 1770–1820,[62] although there are some sixteenth- and more seventeenth- and early-eighteenth-century texts.[63]

Most of the documents used here are seventeenth- and eighteenth-century historical and religious ritual documents. These vague dates are based on the language in the texts; the authors did not date the documents.[64] Even with these proposed dates, the texts present the problem of asserting change through time. As an ethnohistorian, I compare the use of sexual desire in the narrative to uses of sexual desire during other time periods and in other cultural contexts. While this alone does not allow me to analyze specific changes through time, I find many cases of general changes from preconquest to colonial to postcolonial times. Specific time changes are less important to me than the ability to theorize about the more general cultural changes of a colonized people.

Two sets of texts make up the bulk of the source base for this manuscript. The Books of Chilam Balam and the Ritual of the Bacabs are anonymous and undated, and they were written by Maya noblemen. The main advantage of using these texts is that, as they presented disagreements and challenges to particular leaders, they offered extensive reflection on the contestation of colonial Maya cultural norms. These texts reflected on the sexual desires, fantasies, and fears of leaders, nobles, commoners, outsiders, and gods. However, the distinct disadvantage of relying on these texts is that they represented the views of their authors. They contained little information about the cultural views of commoners.[65] However, I do not just portray the sexual rules that the elite distributed. Rather, I seek to deconstruct the language and arguments used in order to delineate the cultural values supported by the community, including those that were challenged by nobles and commoners.[66] In these documents Maya nobles described commoner sexual desires, which cannot be taken as factual notions of commoner desire, but rather must be understood as elements designed to stress stratification, difference, and, occasionally, sameness.

This book uses several of the Books of Chilam Balam,[67] extensive historical, philosophical, and prophetic texts.[68] The Chilam Balams were intended to record, for uses internal to the individual Maya community, much of their culture and history.[69] The Maya nobles likely used these texts to teach themselves the history of the community and the rules that they and the commoners were supposed to follow. Most of the Chilam Balams were unknown to the Spaniards, and they were kept in the individual communities. Most of them purported to cover long periods of time, but skeletal entries nominally representing the preconquest period became steadily more complete through the seventeenth and eighteenth centuries. For this reason the documents told more about the organization of late colonial culture and society than about preconquest social norms. From the language and format used, it is clear that the bulk of the Books of Chilam Balam were written during the eighteenth century.[70]

The Ritual of the Bacabs was a collection of highly ritualized medical/ religious texts in which the human body was presented as constructed from wood and stone. These esoteric texts were intended to accompany a shaman. The texts used magic and other types of medicine in order to cure the ill person. The curing rites maintained extensive ritualistic activity, related to the erotic, and placed great importance on the signs of blood, semen, and the phallus. Based on linguistic and structural similarities between this text, the hieroglyphic codices, and the notarial documents, it is very likely that this was another text authored by a series of notaries for the use of a particular community or group of communities. The texts intentionally were archaic, designed to represent preconquest rituals. Ralph Roys claimed that the texts were seventeenth- or eighteenth-century documents,[71] and Ramón Arzápalo Marín dated the texts to the late sixteenth century.[72] However, the intentional archaism of the texts recalls another two sets of documents, the Maya chronicles and Nahuatl false titles. These were seventeenth- and eighteenth-century land documents dated to the very early colonial period as a strategy to claim land ownership.[73] It is plausible that a similar strategy was being used here, although the rationale is unclear. The mid-colonial period (the seventeenth century) seems a likely time, when the Maya still remembered the oral traditions of the preconquest rituals (several of which could not be performed any longer), but also had some reason to write them down: memory of the rituals was being lost.

Other documents, including Maya-language songs, historical chronicles, and more "mundane" notarial texts, as well as Spanish-language religious and secular chronicles and histories, also are important to a study of sexual desire. The collection of Maya-language songs signified many cultural changes related to sex. The songs were written in the late eighteenth to early nineteenth centuries, although many appear to have been handed down through the centuries by oral tradition. They discussed many elements of Maya culture and focused on the symbols of the flower and virginity.[74] Petitions, baptism records, confessional manuals, prayers, and testaments all were used to make particular points about the relationships between sexual desire, kinship, property, and political power. Matthew Restall used the widest variety of these texts, and, among other things, he was able to analyze gender, sexuality, and kinship.[75] The work of Fray Diego de Landa, who was interested in wiping out "idolatry," discussed many Maya practices, including sexual and gender norms.[76] Other Spanish-language documents, including chronicles and histories used by the Spaniards, analyzed various relevant themes.[77]

The Hybridization of Desire

The late colonial period in Yucatán signified a time of cultural change amidst economic stagnation. Political and cultural power were negotiated in a system that developed hybridization. My analysis of a colonial Maya sexual culture shows that what happened was a tremendous mixture, a *mestizaje* of the mind as well as the body. It is only in this way that we can comprehend the importance of the Virgin Mary Moon Goddess hybrid. This figure was desired during the colonial period as a result not of the "new mestizo race," but rather because of the infiltration of colonialism and the attempt to understand, accept, assimilate, cope with, and resist colonial rule.

TWO   # Religion and Family

At the time of the Spanish conquest, Maya religious thought provided society with a rigorously ordered system. The Maya family unit, the household group, was part of an extended network of kin that was an orderly unit which derived from the gods. Religion asserted moral boundaries that were reified by the perceived actions of the gods. Family/household was the place within which much psychosexual development occurred. In this chapter I seek not to give the reader an overview of colonial Maya culture, which she or he can find elsewhere,[1] but rather to present the central aspects of religion and family that related to Maya notions of sexual desire. From preconquest to late colonial times, Maya religion and family were restructured in such a way that the Maya communities understood both a hybridized religious structure in which the Christian God, Jesus, the Virgin Mary, and the Catholic saints were among the many gods they worshipped, and a hybridized family which included a small discrete family unit within the extended lineage group.

RELIGION

Maya religious traditions at the time of the conquest were based on a system which contained many gods who were thought to have control over all aspects of life. The sacred world was seen as extremely powerful, and a series of priests had high official positions in the Maya hierarchy. The gods required the people to engage in significant amounts of warfare and a wide variety of types of sacrifice. In the early colonial period the Franciscans and other clergy who participated in instructing the Maya expressed dismay at Maya resistance to their instruction. The clergy wanted the Maya to accept a monotheistic system which prohibited idolatry and the practice of any type of blood sacrifice. They were only partly successful in this instruction.

Maya religious traditions contextualized sexual desire so much that most of this book analyzes religion and ritual. At the time of the conquest, the Maya believed that the gods engaged in sexual activity with each other in order to create the people. Some gods had many sexual partners, while others were relatively circumspect in their sexual activity. The Catholic clergy preached instead that there was just one God, and he did not engage in any sexual activity. Virginity, chastity, and monogamy were to be the main sexual values of the new religion. But the Maya altered these values to develop a mixed religious tradition.

Preconquest Religious Worship

From birth to death, the sacred sphere regulated life for the Maya people. Upon a child's birth, sacred diviners told kin what the child's life had in store for him or her. As the boy grew up, he was educated in religious lore. When he was old enough, he was trained in the community house, and he was taught the sacred aspects of warfare, farming, and hunting. The girl was trained in the household, and she was taught how to keep the domestic religious shrines. The gods regulated the harvest, so the survival of the group depended on divine intervention. Marriage was seen as a sacred religious ritual event. Death was marked by more religious ceremonies, and Maya ancestors were venerated as their spirits and bodies were thought to protect the household. After death, almost all people were thought to go to the underworld, while a few went to the heavens. The sacred world controlled life processes, and the sacred had a great amount of power over everything.

Maya religion at the time of the conquest had a ritually based structure which asserted social stratification. Nobles controlled the rituals and access to many of the gods. They ran the priesthood, and they were trained more extensively in religious lore. There are four aspects of preconquest religion that are analyzed here: gods, the priesthood, ceremonies, and the gendered structure.

1. GODS.   Based on preconquest codices and archaeological and epi-
graphic evidence, scholars have found that the Maya gods most often were
devised in groups of four, which could be considered to be separate gods or
one god. Among certain gods, each of the four parts was associated with its
own direction and color.[2] The four parts represented duality, as one part
signified the opposite of the other. For example, one part of a god might signify life, where another part could signify death. The god thus could represent Maya thoughts on the relationship between destruction and rebirth.[3]
This interpretation has been supported by evidence in the Books of Chilam
Balam, showing that these preconquest concepts were known to postconquest
peoples.

Several Maya gods are most relevant to this study.[4] Itzamna ("Iguana
House") was a central god, certainly among the most powerful at the time of
the conquest. This god had so many different aspects and so many different
names that he appears to have contained many of the other gods within him.
He was worshipped as god of the harvest, sun, earth, and rain. He was considered to be the creator of writing. In the colonial documents, he often was
associated with the Moon Goddess.[5] Kinich Ahau, the Sun God, the husband
of the Moon Goddess, was seen as something of a father god, at least to Maya
rulers. The rulers associated themselves with the Sun God as he represented
life, and he was believed to give them power.[6] The Bacabs were said to be four
brothers who held up the sky. They were the most clearly associated with the
four directions, four colors, and various elements of the Maya calendar. They
were vital during the colonial years, as they were mentioned extensively in the
Ritual of the Bacabs and in the Books of Chilam Balam. They appear to have
been important because they represented Maya astronomical and time calcu-
lations, which determined the course of life for the individual and the community.[7] The most important god for the purposes of this book was Ix Chel,
the Moon Goddess. From all characterizations she was a very powerful god.[8]

2. THE PRIESTHOOD.   Maya priests had an extensive hierarchy that was
linked to the political sphere. The *halach uinic* ("true man"), who was a regional political ruler, also had religious duties. Another man normally served
as a high priest, who had to train the other priests in writing, calendrical issues, divination, rituals, prophecy, and sacrifice. Under the high priest were a
series of priests who had different responsibilities. The priests were supposed
to be involved in the daily lives of all Maya people. They engaged in prophecies at births, presided over all the major ceremonies, engaged in curing rituals, and even came to the households to preside over some of the ceremonies

there. The priests decided when it was time to go to war, to plant crops, to harvest them, to marry. The priests were well respected and, no doubt, feared. Their hair was unkempt and their heads were smeared with blood. Priests fasted and refrained from sexual activity for periods before the major ceremonies. They were the ones who most often communed with the gods through prayer, autosacrifice, and hallucinogenic drugs. The priests thus were considered some of the most important people for community survival.[9]

3. CEREMONIES.   The gods needed some ceremonial worship and sacrifice in order to survive. The Maya kept idols of the gods, which were used in the ceremonies. These events took place in a wide variety of locations. The temples were considered the houses of the gods, and the most important ceremonies took place in and around these temples. Some ceremonies occurred in the fields, on hills, and under trees. Other events took place in caves, where particular gods were worshipped. More ceremonies occurred around the water supplies, the sacred cenotes. Finally, in the household, shrines were created and household gods were worshipped.[10]

The ceremonies involved a series of prayers which were designed to request various things from the gods. Most often the prayers requested material benefits, such as a strong harvest.[11] The prayers and ceremonies were intended to call upon the ancestors and the gods to protect the individual, the family, the lineage, and the community.[12]

In the more important ceremonies, sacrifices were offered to the ancestors and the gods. On most occasions the sacrifices offered were of one's own blood or of vegetable and inanimate products. On other occasions animals were offered. On some occasions, human sacrifice was performed. Most important for the purposes of this book were the offerings of human blood (which was related closely to the body and sexuality). The Maya believed that human blood was an important offering as it both gave birth to and fed the gods. Further, the sacrifice of human blood was one of the few ways in which people could commune with the gods. At major ceremonies related to the rulers, they would sacrifice their own blood primarily from tongues, ears, the fleshy part of arms, and penises. In most cases a stingray spine was used, and a large amount of cord (sometimes spiked) or grass was passed through the pierced holes. The blood then was placed in a bowl and offered to the gods. The iconography of this type of sacrifice made it clear that the Maya leaders believed (and wanted others to believe) that they engaged in a trance that opened up a gateway to the world of the gods.[13] It appears that the household ceremonies also involved blood sacrifice, but less documentation exists.[14]

Human sacrifice, while less common, did exist in Yucatán since Preclassic times. Heart excision appears to have been the most common type of sacrifice. Maya priests tied a captive down, and one priest then used an obsidian-bladed knife to penetrate the chest of the captive, after which he reached into the chest and tore out the heart, which then was offered in a bowl for the gods. Flaying, probably introduced in Postclassic times from central Mexico, was a form of sacrifice in which a captive was thrown by a priest from the top of a pyramid; other priests on the ground picked up the body and flayed (skinned) it, after which one priest wore the skin. Various forms of decapitation were used in human sacrifice, as well. Arrow sacrifice was a ritual in which a captive was tied to a post and a group of warriors danced around him, aiming arrows at his chest. They were to keep him alive as long as possible before killing him. Some captives were thrown into a cenote at dawn. They were supposed to go to the bottom of the pool of water and commune with the gods. If they survived through midday, they were released, but it appears that few survived as they were thrown into the water from about sixty feet up and often were bound. In many cases of human sacrifice, the bodies were divided up and the Maya then engaged in a small amount of ritual cannibalism. Noble war captives were considered the best people to be sacrificed, but commoners, slaves, and children also were killed.[15]

The human sacrifices were intended to be events in which the nobles and priests saved the community by offering the gods some blood for their sustenance. This was intended to be both a fertilization of the cosmos, which gave birth to the gods, and a noble spectacle which maintained community support and stratification.[16] The spectacle instilled in the Maya a fantasy of communication with the gods, a respect for the nobles for their willingness to shed their blood and the blood of their captives and slaves, and a fear among the people of their rulers and their gods.

This fear was portrayed in the underworld, a place to which almost all would go, but which all were supposed to dread. The underworld was the unknown, a place where gods to be feared resided.[17] The Maya saw the underworld as a place which "had animals, plants, inhabitants of various kinds, and a landscape with both natural and constructed features."[18] The Christian hell of fire and brimstone did not seem particularly relevant. Some select people went to the heavens, but this process had nothing to do with sin and atonement. According to Diego de Landa, "people who had hanged themselves went to . . . paradise; and there were many who in times of lesser troubles, labors or sickness, hanged themselves to escape and go to that paradise."[19] Warriors killed in warfare, people who were sacrificed, and mothers and children who died in childbirth went to the heavens. The ceremonies were designed to instill all the elements of fantasy, desire, respect, and fear for the sacred world. These ceremonies demanded compliance to the rules that the cosmos prescribed for the people.

Perhaps the most important aspects of these ceremonies to the Maya were those that marked space and time. Some events involved people walking the "ritual circuit," an area designed to mark off boundaries and signify the five directions (the movement was from the east, where the sun rose, to the north, the west, the south, and then the center, which, perhaps, was the direction to the Otherworld, the sacred space of the gods and the ancestors) which represented sacred space.[20] Time was considered a vital ordered piece of the world that gave meaning to life. Time was partly cyclical, and the Maya placed great emphasis on "demonstrating historical action as the inevitable result of cosmic and ancestral necessities."[21]

The spectacle of the ceremony, the performance of sacrifice, the maintenance of sacred space, and the ritual computation of time all were aspects that served to stratify society by legitimating the nobility. The spectacles and sacrifices served to show the community that the nobles were committed. The maintenance of sacred space and the computation of time served to show the community that the nobles had some specialized knowledge. These were vital elements in Maya community survival.

4. THE GENDERED STRUCTURE. Maya religion structured gender such that it presented the people with both a sense of gender parallelism and a sense of masculine power. While I will be discussing this gendered structure throughout the book, a few introductory comments are warranted. In the Maya mind, creation, as it was linked to reproduction, required both female and male aspects. So the sun was male and the moon was female; day was male and night was female. Many gods could change genders, and male priests who worshipped the Moon Goddess at her shrine in Cozumel climbed inside the very large idol, impersonating her.[22] The Maya had a sense of gender parallelism; they believed that male and female were complementary aspects, both of which were necessary for all creation.[23]

However, the Maya sense of gender parallelism within religion certainly was limited. Almost all of the priests were men. Women, except for older women, apparently were not permitted to enter the temples during ceremonies. Sacred water for ritual occasions was gathered from far-off places where it was believed to be untouched by women. Men participating in major ceremonies could not engage in any sexual acts and could not see women at all, sometimes for a period of several months. These men were said to not even be allowed to think of women.[24]

The gendered structure of religion was complex as women actively participated in many important religious ceremonies, but it usually was forbidden for them to enter the temples. Women provided many of the food offerings, and they even offered their own blood. But other offerings were supposed to be untouched by women. Clearly gender parallelism and male control and symbolic dominance over many religious functions did not conflict in Maya minds.

Colonial Maya Catholicism

When the Maya were colonized, one of the central things emphasized to them was that they had to convert to and learn Christianity. To the Maya this was no surprise, as they had always incorporated any conqueror's gods. What certainly was different was the concept that the Spaniards believed that the Maya had to give up their entire religion and adopt a monotheistic Catholicism. Still, as Matthew Restall has noted, this difficulty probably was overcome within the first couple of generations after the conquest.[25] Here I will consider four elements of colonial era Catholicism that paralleled those elements I discussed above: saints, community church hierarchies, public rituals (mass, feasts, and the making of testaments), and the gendered structure of the religion.

1. SAINTS. For the Maya, the appeal of a system of saints was immense. Preconquest Maya gods, in a way, could be and were transformed into Catholic saints.[26] The preconquest gods also played some role in the cult of the cross, the religious agent of the nineteenth-century Caste War.[27] The saints, however, did not simply signify the preconquest gods, as the Maya did not have much choice over which saint their community would adopt. Nor did they make the image (idol) of the saint, which first came from Europe, and later from Mexico or Guatemala. Nor could they have ignored the connection between the saints and the Spaniards.[28] But the Maya did give the saints dual identities by worshipping them in a way consistent with the worship of the preconquest gods. The Maya did not worship the saints for the particular properties attached to them in Catholic thought.[29] Most importantly, the saints represented the community. The local town believed the saints to be both their owners and their protectors. The saints signified intercommunity competition, as the group that had built the biggest church to house its saint was given great respect, and the saint of the community that had the most economic, political, and social power was revered throughout the region.[30]

The saints also were seen as controlling much of life within the community. Those people who owned the most impressive images of those saints were accorded great social status.[31] Feasts put on for the saints were sponsored by the nobles and allowed the commoners to see that the nobles were caring for the saints.[32] At these feasts and on other occasions, images of the saints were brought from the church and "installed under a temporary arbor or pavilion to witness the festivities."[33] The *cofradías* took charge of "feeding" the saints, and they used that responsibility to allow the saints to maintain many of the attributes of the preconquest gods. The saints could do good or bad things, and they were associated with the fate of the individual community. A well-fed saint would help the people, while a poorly fed saint would not.[34] Nancy Farriss notes that the saints, much like the preconquest gods, were unhappy if they were not fed and clothed properly.[35]

The saints were adopted eagerly by the communities, much more so than the concept of monotheism. The Christian God appears to have been seen as a distant figure who did not have much influence on the lives of the people.[36] The trinity does not appear ever to have been adopted as very important.[37] Jesus was important, but in many ways he was considered another of the saints.[38] The Virgin Mary, the most important Christian figure for my purposes, also was vital to the Maya communities. Yet she was venerated in the same manner as the saints. There were many images of the Virgin Mary, and households had her image alongside the image of the community saint. She was believed to be very important to the household but also to the community at large. She was one of the few "saints" who was worshipped throughout Yucatán. The Virgin, further, was adopted by the Maya in a significant way: in most of the eighteenth-century documents, Mary was not identified by name, but rather was identified only by the Maya phrase, *ca cilich colel*, "our holy lady."[39] The Virgin also was treated as a saint in the way her image was presented. "The Virgin would be displeased if her dress were allowed to become shabby."[40]

The relationship between the image and the saint is vital to understanding Maya postconquest religious beliefs. For the clergy, if the image was seen as actually being the saint, and that image was worshipped as such, then that worship signified idolatry. For the Maya the relationship was hardly so clear.

If the signifier was intended to be the image and the signified the saint, the Maya mixed signifier and signified into one. At least symbolically the Maya believed the image to be the saint.[41] However, the way in which the Maya related symbolism to "reality" in this case is unknown.

The saints, the Virgin Mary, and even Jesus allowed the Maya people to see Christianity as a polytheistic religion. The saints represented, owned, and protected the individual community, a notion which must have prevented a crisis in belief systems, as the Maya continued, for a time, to believe in the relationship between the individual community and its god. Christianity certainly altered Maya concepts, but the appeal of the system of saints for a polytheistic people is clear.[42]

2. COMMUNITY CHURCH HIERARCHIES.   From the perspective of the Catholic clergy, the Maya high priests had to be stripped of any power that they once had. The Catholic priests were to become the ones in charge of religious worship. But the community's priest most often was a distant person who could not come to the town very often. Even a diligent priest, and there were many who were not so diligent, simply had too much territory to be able to be present in the community for a significant amount of time.[43] Most of the religious duties thus were left to the priest's assistant, an indigenous man who had enough legitimacy within the group to get people to attend the ritual ceremonies. This powerful man was the *maestro cantor*, the person who taught the children, ran the catechism, registered births, marriages, and deaths, and, no doubt, often performed other types of religious services. He also worked closely with the man who ran the *cofradía*, the lay brotherhood of the Catholic Church.[44]

Within the *cofradía*, the Maya developed a hierarchy of indigenous people, which officially was separate from the religious and political hierarchies. In fact, however, as the *cofradía* quickly became a public function that was controlled by the community (in the Hispanic world it was a private religious group that solicited members from various sectors of the populace),[45] the lines between the three hierarchies were not so clear, and often the *batab* ("governor") of the community also was the head of the *cofradía*. While the Catholic priest appointed the officers in the religious hierarchy and the *cofradía* officials, there were, no doubt, many cases in which the priest just appointed whomever was recommended. The *cofradía* received significant support from inside the community, and it garnered a large amount of money and property.[46] The *cofradía* ran the various religious festivities, provided money for such things as candles in the church, and performed many of the religious functions when the priest was not present.[47] No doubt the officials of the *cofradía* and the leaders of the local religious hierarchy were nobles who before the conquest would have been priests.[48]

3. PUBLIC RITUALS.   Before the conquest, the public display of ritual activity was vital to the maintenance of the cosmos. Such a concern with public display was evident throughout the colonial period. However, the rituals themselves relatively quickly became primarily Catholic. Farriss's study of this phenomenon shows that during an early period some Maya religious leaders continued to worship preconquest gods, but the ceremonies, as they were necessarily hidden, did not serve their preconquest function of keeping the community together in large, meaningful rituals.[49] Instead Christianity was adapted to serve this function. The Maya did not simply stop worshipping the preconquest gods that had represented the community; rather, they gave these gods a sort of dual identity, "smuggling the idols" into churches. They then associated these idols with the Christian saints, giving them saints' names. This activity eventually replaced many of the old Maya rituals.[50]

For the Maya, mass was an important element of public ritual, but it is unclear how much of the Latin mass they understood. The Maya used the verb *il*, "to see," to describe their actions at mass.[51] Certainly in the early colonial period, few Maya would have understood the details of mass. As the colonial era progressed, however, the Maya developed a greater understanding. Several Maya petitions showed that the petitioners were concerned about not receiving proper sacraments.[52] As early as 1578, a petition noted that the priest gave mass "in a twisted fashion."[53] Some Maya testators wanted to have the priest perform a "sung mass," as this signified social status.[54] Further, the Books of Chilam Balam and other texts made it clear that some Maya understood much of what the priests said. In what was a relatively faithful translation, the Book of Chilam Balam of Ixil translated the story of Moses fleeing from the Pharaoh.[55] So while masses certainly at first were "seen" and not "heard," the Maya eventually understood much of what was being said.

The feasts for the saints served to maintain status in Maya communities. The small group of nobles in charge of any particular feast, most often those running the *cofradía*, would fund the ceremonies, and those with the largest ceremonies gained the most status. So the wealthier nobles invited not only all of the people of the community, but also the people from surrounding towns. The public displays were linked explicitly to the worship of the saints, and they indeed were grand spectacles. Further, some important Christian festivals like Holy Week were not particularly important to the Maya, while others, such as All Souls' Day (Day of the Dead), took on great importance. All Souls' Day was a time when ancestors could be worshipped.[56] Internal Maya control was important: petitions complained of priests seizing control over these festivals.[57] These events certainly served a similar purpose as the preconquest ceremonies.[58]

Restall, who has done an extensive study of Maya wills, has shown that the making of the testament was a public affair. While the will normally was dictated only a short time before death, the community officials and the notary almost always were listed as present. This public ceremony signified something about Maya inheritance (that it was seen as a public affair), but it also showed that the Maya concept of Christianity involved a public display of faith. The preambles to almost all of the wills were formulaic recitations of faith and piety. While these words, no doubt, in many cases were recited by the notary himself, Maya beliefs in some sense were represented by the terms. Many of the wills consisted only of this formula. There was no property to distribute, so the only reason for making the will was to express faith. Most of the testators requested burial in the church, another show of faith.[59] While these acts may have represented beliefs, they also signified social status.

4. THE GENDERED STRUCTURE.   Catholicism, even more than preconquest Maya religion, is and was male dominated. Certainly the Maya knew that God and Jesus were men. But since the Maya were more concerned with the saints (some of whom were female) and the Virgin Mary, some of this male dominance was mitigated. Moreover, women were required to attend church with the men, and girls received religious training with the boys.[60] While the gender parallelism of Maya preconquest religion did not apply, women had more access to some of the religious ceremonies.

A Few Considerations Regarding Postconquest Idolatry

Idolatry, or the practice of non-Christian religion, certainly existed after the conquest. However, the meaning and amount of that idolatry is a hot topic of debate for scholars. Farriss has said that many of the more gruesome acts (of human sacrifice) did take place.[61] Inga Clendinnen's view is that, while the sources overestimate the amount of idolatry and human sacrifice that was taking place, a significant amount of what was reported did occur.[62] Restall has argued that the idolatry which has been reported so sensationalistically in both colonial times and among modern scholars, largely was a figment of the Spanish imagination.[63] All of these scholars are referring to events which took place in or around 1562, when Franciscan friar Diego de Landa claimed to have found idolatry and human sacrifice. These events were documented by statements of Spaniards and confessions of Maya, many of whom had been tortured. But more documentation of other cases of "idolatry" exists.

Curing rituals, in which traditional Maya shamans presided over the cure and engaged magical spells, bloodletting, and other elements of traditional medicine, were common in Yucatán throughout the colonial period. Christianity had no equivalent for these rituals. The *ah men*, the shamans, survived the conquest (and exist today) probably because the Spaniards did not see them as high priests, and they did not see their occupations as under the purview of Christianity. The Ritual of the Bacabs and other sources, including testimony from present-day Mayan people, documented the existence of these curing rites well after the conquest.[64]

Other rites have had significant documentation. Some Maya, in caves, continued to give food offerings to gods. The rain gods continued to be worshipped significantly after the conquest, and they too were given offerings of food. Idols were smuggled into the churches, and songs, dances, and drums of preconquest origin were used in Catholic rituals.[65] No doubt this idolatry occurred because some Maya people believed very strongly that it would have been disastrous to ignore the preconquest gods.

Returning to the idolatry and human sacrifice which was alleged to have taken place in 1562, I have reservations about taking the confessions at face value. Some of this certainly, as Clendinnen has shown, represented the Spaniards' worst fears. The crucifixion, something that the friars had taught the Maya, was said to have been used in human sacrifice. The psychological trauma of a Franciscan friar hearing of such an event must have been immense. Both Clendinnen and Farriss argue that many Maya before the conquest believed that human sacrifice was vital for community survival, particularly through hard times. In 1562, with epidemics and famines, times were difficult. Additionally, the sacrifices were alleged to have taken place in caves, a traditionally important locale for human sacrifice.[66] Yet the public spectacle also was vital to the preconquest ritual. Certainly some of the participants in postconquest human sacrifice would have thought it was a pathetic imitation of the grand preconquest rites. Whether or not these events were figments of the clerical imagination, idolatry did take place after the conquest, but it most often was relegated to the margins of Maya society.

Religious Hybridization

As a strategy that would allow for more effective religious instruction, the Franciscans attempted to understand indigenous cultures. They believed that they had to use some element of hybridization as a way of altering the Maya belief system. Landa's methodology was important in this regard, as he was a central representative of the Franciscans in Yucatán. He understood the Franciscan mission as an attempt to instruct and learn about the Maya as well as to eradicate human sacrifice and other elements of idolatry.[67] The rationale behind his study of indigenous ways was that such a study would allow for more effective religious instruction. This information was used to relate Christian ideas to similar Maya concepts. This was an act of ritualistic translation.

Hybridization thus was a strategy of colonialism, but it also allowed for survival of some preconquest elements of Maya religion. The idols worshipped in the church were used to make sure that the gods would hear Maya prayers. The saints were used to celebrate the community and the gods. The idols worshipped in the caves were given saints' names so that the Maya could see them as part of Christianity. Christian prayers were recited to the rain gods. Festivals were used as spectacles of power. Jesus sometimes was seen as an equivalent of the Sun God. And, of course, the Moon Goddess was turned into the Virgin Mary. The hybridization was a sometimes conscious, sometimes unconscious maneuver that both allowed for the colonization of Maya rituals and minds and permitted the survival of some elements of preconquest knowledge and beliefs.

This change, of course, was not simple; nor was it easily accepted. The Maya of the first generation certainly suffered some psychological shock when they realized that they no longer were permitted to worship their gods. The psychological and cultural damage of such a change must have been immense: they were told that their entire system of beliefs was a sham. That system had included a worship of ancestors that was a way of dealing with death. After the conquest, with epidemics decimating the population, with Catholic priests telling the people that they no longer could worship their ancestors, many Maya must have gone into a profound state of despair and anger. Yet the hybridization of religion may have alleviated some of the despair, and much of the shock must have warn off sometime within the first few generations after the conquest.

FAMILY

The Maya traditional concept of family was of an extended family unit living and working together. This family unit, as part of the larger lineage group, was perceived to be vital for survival. The family also was the central place in which psychosexual development occurred. The child at the time of the conquest grew up in an atmosphere in which rigid sex segregation was maintained. The child's mother and other female relatives took care of the house and the plot of land around the house, tended to the cooking, and reared the younger children. The child's father and other male relatives went out of the house to work more distant lands, participate in political and religious rituals, and go to war. The male kin often were gone from the house for months at a time. Noble children were raised separately from the commoners, and noble boys were educated by the priests. After the conquest, some extended family units broke down due to disease and active intervention of the clergy, but many survived despite these hardships. Men were encouraged to stay home more often as they did not have to leave the household to go to war or to prepare as extensively for religious rituals.

The Household

In Maya terminology used during the colonial period, the household, *otoch*, was important, while no term representing the nuclear family existed. This does not mean that the Maya did not have a sense of family, nor does it mean that family was unimportant to them. Rather, the sense of Maya family was based at least partly on coresidency.[68]

Households at the time of the conquest probably were compounds which housed extended family groups. The commoner household in the seventeenth and eighteenth centuries appears to have included only one or two small dwellings on a single plot, but within those dwellings lived six to twelve people.[69] At the time of the conquest, the nobles owned the same types of houses, but the houses and plots were larger.[70] After the conquest, wealthier Maya nobles attempted to build Spanish-style houses but found the traditional Maya style more suitable.[71] The Maya do not appear to have had an equivalent of the *solar*, the Spanish-style house plot, but rather they had fields around the house area which were considered to be a part of the household's land. The *solar* was a concept which was adopted by the Maya soon after the conquest. Maya commoners at the time of the conquest appear to have had little in the way of furniture or valuables inside the house,[72] but Restall points out that, at least by the late colonial period, the testaments show that they did have a significant number of items which were European in origin.[73] The household was a unit that enclosed the extended family and provided members with material comfort.

The Extended Family

The extended family was part of the larger patrilineage group, the *chibal*, which remained important throughout the colonial years. The lineage group had been a bedrock of Maya society from Classic times. During that time, the kings sought to extend their power by taking control over the various lineage groups.[74] Patricia McAnany has shown that together with the colonizing kings existed a kinship system that was not as centralized and hierarchical. This system was based on kinship ties and on the worship of ancestors. McAnany has shown that kinship and lineage were venerated very strongly in Classic and Postclassic times. The people called upon their deceased ancestors to help them through difficulties. The ancestors were worshipped extensively in many, perhaps all, Classic communities.[75]

By the time of the Spanish conquest, there were no longer kings trying to control all of the Mayan area,[76] but the kinship system remained very strong. Restall shows that the *chibal* group was an important determinant of class, political status, marriage, naming patterns, and inheritance. It was one of the core units of Maya society.[77] During the colonial period, much property was viewed as being owned by both the individual and the larger lineage group, in some cases, no doubt, because the group worked the land.[78]

In many cases a large extended family, incorporating three generations, lived and worked together. The survival of this group of farmers depended on being able to mobilize a large number of male workers who could go to distant fields and forests to work the land. The Maya got these numbers of men by having a core of patrilineal kin that would work together.[79] The extended family had a very strict gendered division of labor, with women doing various things centered around the household and the household plot, and men in charge of the fields.[80] After the conquest Farriss notes that the clergy were strongly opposed to the living arrangements of the extended family, as they believed that such close quarters promoted incest. The clergy thus broke apart some household compounds.[81] Of course, with the limited number of clergy, and what would, no doubt, have been fierce resistance to the destruction of the extended family unit, it is likely that such clerical activity did not have a great effect on at least the more remote areas, and censuses have shown that a significant number of extended families lived and worked together in the late colonial period.[82]

The presence of the extended family in or near the household compound certainly had a significant effect on the relationship of a married couple and on the rearing of children. The extended family provided the married couple a support network but also limited their privacy. The extended family provided children with advice and comfort from a larger number of adults but also decreased their opportunities for independence.

Marriage

At the time of the Spanish conquest, monogamous marriage was the rule for commoners, while some noblemen had several wives and assumed the right to sexual use of their female slaves.[83] Most nobles and some commoners had arranged marriages.[84] After the conquest, arranged marriages were prohibited, and the nobles were required to have just one wife, although there is fragmentary evidence that some kept mistresses as sorts of wives through the eighteenth century.[85] Marriage patterns show that nobles attempted to marry other nobles throughout the colonial period.[86]

The primary marital rule that was in force at the time of the conquest was that one could not marry someone from the same *chibal*, the patrilineal group. But there do not appear to have been any restrictions on marrying someone from the same *naal*, the matrilineal group. The *chibal* marriage rule was broken at least occasionally by high-level nobles who presumably could find few suitable marriage partners.[87] But this was the central rule related to incestuous marriage, clearly in conflict with Spanish thoughts on the matter. Cross-cousin marriage was permitted, as these cousins came from different patrilineal groups, but were related by consanguinity. According to Church doctrine, such marriages were illegal.[88]

During early colonial times, after commoners married, the couple lived with the parents of the bride for two or three years, the husband's labor going to the bride's family as a bride price.[89] After this period the married couple took up residence with the parents of the husband, and the wife's labor was believed to belong to the patrilineal extended family group.[90] The wife had the protection of her kin group for the first few years, after which, if her husband became abusive, she still had the protection of others.[91] Clendinnen and Farriss have argued that this process was severely curtailed because of clerical interference and demographic collapse,[92] leading to great economic hardship for young married couples, but again this would not have been as much the case where the clergy were unable to break up the extended family complexes.[93]

In colonial times marriage took place at a much earlier age than had been the case before the conquest, partly because some of the clergy insisted that this would discourage "sexual immorality," but primarily because tribute obligations were structured in such a way that it was economically logical for couples to marry at a young age.[94] Those couples, if they were living on their own, still had to provide service to their parents at the same time they raised their children. No doubt this increased the obligations of the young married couples.[95]

Little information exists on sexual behavior within marriage. The friars attempted to regulate sex so that it occurred only in marriage, and only in one sexual position, but their effects are unknown. The Maya had a system whereby couples who found themselves to be incompatible could get divorced. After the conquest, of course, the Catholic clergy outlawed divorce.[96] On another level, the friars interfered with marriage to the benefit of women. They actively encouraged women and slaves to complain about sexual abuse and any other violations of their rights. This certainly was a more egalitarian view of rights than women had before the conquest.[97] Marriage patterns, duties, and rights all were altered by the Spanish conquest. Their alterations, however, do not appear to have radically changed Maya life.

Children

The Maya placed significant emphasis on the birth, growth, and education of children. An image of the Moon Goddess was placed under the bed to induce pregnancy and/or to ensure success during childbirth.[98] Upon childbirth in several Mayan areas, the child's umbilical cord was cut over an ear of corn. Then the bloodstained corn was preserved and the grains were planted during the appropriate season. The child was compared with corn, as this was the crop that to the Maya signified life.[99] At least among nobles, after the baby was born, two boards were tied to opposite sides of the child's head in order to flatten the forehead. Soon after the birth, a priest provided an astrological reading of the child's fate, and the childhood name was given.[100]

Before the conquest the child received a name that incorporated the matronymic of his or her mother and the patronymic of his or her father. After the conquest all people were given baptismal first names, which usually were combined with the father's patronymic.[101] Yet, as baptismal documents have shown, some Maya children received the mother's patronym. Apparently the Maya adopted the Spanish system, in which the child usually emphasized the father's patronymic, but occasionally used the mother's if her kin group was more socially influential (or if the child was "illegitimate").[102] The changes in naming patterns were important markers, as the postconquest child could not as easily find a relationship with distant matrilineal ancestors.

A modern Yucatecan practice, in which a girl at the age of three and a boy at the age of four are first carried astride the mother's hip, probably dates from preconquest times. This public ceremony asserts gender differentiation: the age difference is because the girl symbolically is associated with the three hearth stones, while the boy symbolically is associated with the four corners of the field.[103] "Baptism" was an important rite for the preconquest Maya. The ritual was an elaborate passage, which may have signified a puberty rite that launched children into adulthood. A lord sponsored this public community ceremony, in which offerings were given to the gods, and a feast ensued.[104]

After puberty, or perhaps a little before, according to Ralph Roys, Maya boys slept in a large public communal house (what Clendinnen calls a warrior house), where they also gathered for other activities. Roys, following Landa, claims that the youth brought prostitutes into this house. No doubt in this house the boys also learned about warfare, farming, and hunting. During the day, the boys most often were helping their fathers and other male relatives in the fields. The girls slept at home and spent most of their days in their houses with their mothers and other female kin.[105]

A particular priest was assigned the job of educating noble boys. This priest would teach them various aspects of religious ritual and the ways in which that ritual affected farming, hunting, and warfare. A few of these youth, those who were destined to become priests and political leaders, received more extensive training in history, religious matters, and writing.[106] After the conquest the clergy asserted that education was for all of the children: boys and girls, nobles and commoners. Of course the ones who received the most education still were the noble boys. The *maestros cantores*, the local religious leaders, were those who taught the classes.[107]

Orphans, of whom there certainly would have been many, received somewhat different treatment after the conquest than before. Before the conquest orphans often became dependents of nobles and lords, were sold into slavery, or were offered for sacrifice. But with the extended family group in place, the children considered orphans were those who had no close kin left. After the conquest Farriss notes that the Spaniards chose to take children whose parents had died, but who still had kin to take care of them. These orphans then were used as domestic workers in Spanish households or *haciendas*, or they were sold into slavery. The Maya complained bitterly that the Spaniards were taking children who were not orphans by their standards.[108] The Maya traditional standards of orphanage extended into the late eighteenth century, when a song was written about the poor orphans:

HACH CHIICHANEN CAA	I was very small
CIM IN NA CAA CIM IN YVM	when my mother died, when my father died.
AY AY IN YUMEN	Ay, ay, my Lord. . . .[109]
OU MAN LAIL KIN	This past day[110]
TIN HVN PPAT CEN	I had been left alone,
CAA TV HAN CH'AHEN	then I suddenly was taken,[111]
V BIZEN T NIN	and carried away
V PPEL OVL TV KAB	in a stranger's[112] arms. . . .
MIIX IN VONEL YAN	I have no relatives.
HACH CHEN TIN HVM	I am very alone. . . .[113]

The orphan, taken by a stranger (probably a Spaniard), emphasizes his or her sadness, a sadness compounded by the fact that she or he has no relatives left. Here the conflict in the system of meaning had a very cogent effect on the lives of individuals: the meaning of the term "orphan" was contested, and the Spaniards, who had more power, asserted their meaning as "truth."

The Hybridization of the Family

The Catholic clergy made a series of attempts at altering the family. Matrilineal descent was no longer as important as it had been. In some areas the extended family could no longer live on the same plot. Marriage was to be monogamous, divorce was not permitted, and concepts of incest were changed. Boys were to live with their parents instead of in a community house, and boys and girls were to be reared more similarly to each other than they had been before.

All of these alterations, instead of repressing and destroying the preconquest Maya family, actually formed a hybrid notion. As can be seen in inheritance patterns, the extended family remained committed to each other. In areas where this family could not live on the same house plot, they no doubt lived on plots that were near each other. While in some cases bride price no longer could be paid by the husband living in the wife's father's house, it probably was paid in less formal ways, through farming or other work-related activities. Cross-cousin marriages and divorces were strictly prohibited, but as Farriss has noted, some Maya resisted these prohibitions by engaging in what the clergy perceived as "illicit unions."[114] Children still were raised primarily in a sex-segregated environment (with regard to work), although they had to live together. These elements, when taken together, signified the hybridization of the family: the Maya postconquest family was neither the traditional Maya preconquest family, but nor was it the Christian European family.

REVISITING HYBRIDITY

The advent of Christianity and Spanish colonial rule altered both Maya religion and family. The religious structure, a very public discourse, was changed radically as the newly arriving clergy challenged all the foundations of Maya religion, which they termed "idolatry" and "devil worship." The family structure, in Spanish eyes a much more private system, was changed less radically as the clergy and other Spaniards were concerned with only a few aspects of familial arrangements, and they often had little access even to those few elements. Despite the differences in these two structures, the changes which occurred were related to each other through the colonialist system of hybridity. In both cases, changes took place which, despite clerical intent, primarily did not repress the old structures but rather resignified them with new meaning.

One more example of change relates to both religion and family and points to the process of resignification. The Franciscans attempted to mediate inside the family in order to achieve religious goals. Landa noted that children, after attending schools led by the friars, represented Christianity most effectively: "The children, after being taught, carefully informed the friars of idolatries and drunken orgies. They broke the idols, even those belonging to their own fathers. They urged the divorced women and any orphans that were enslaved (to *encomenderos* or Indians) to appeal to the friars. Even when they were threatened by their people, they did not cease doing this."[115]

The friars instructed the children and thus enabled the society to accept Christianity.[116] The chain of idolatry was supposed to break, and various behaviors were supposed to change. This disrupted some internal dynamics of Maya society. Yet one can find few documented cases of children informing on adults, and Landa likely was overestimating his success. The resignification of family and religion was the most relevant point here. The friars attempted to break filial obligations and to insert themselves symbolically in the position of "father." The old Maya concept of family was to be destroyed in favor of a new concept, that of the larger family of the Franciscan or Christian community. The friars were to use this concept of family and community to destroy old religious ceremonies and ideas. Yet, while the friars could teach the children, and thus insert themselves into the process of child development, they could not break the obligations that children felt toward their parents. While the friars could destroy traditional public idolatry and orgies, they could not repress the desire to see old gods within new saints; nor could they inhibit the process of feasting, which incorporated much of the meaning of the old ceremonies.

In each case mentioned in this chapter, meaning was altered by a process of hybridization. The meanings of family, childhood, marriage, religion, gods, priests, and ceremonies all were altered by colonialism. Hybridity meant that Maya traditions were renamed, but that, in the process of renaming, new and different qualities were given to all cultural structures. Two conflicting systems of meaning came into contact, and, as we will see throughout this book, the cultures resolved that conflict by hybridizing the systems of meaning, thus altering and colonizing the Maya world.

THREE   Framing Maya Sexual Desire

The colonial Maya deployed a system of categories
in order to distinguish a recognizable "Self" from
an equally recognizable "Other." Before the Spanish
conquest, the Maya people (particularly the nobles,
but also the commoners) worked to distinguish various ethnic groups, lineages within the ethnic groups,
individual city-states, and social classes; but with the
advent of Spanish colonialism, the effort at distinguishing Self from Other took a different turn.[1] The
Spanish colonizers asserted their own ideas of self-
identity, notions that were to be grafted onto the
Maya in various ways. The Europeans had methods
of categorizing class, ethnicity, gender, and sexuality that were different from
Maya ways of understanding Self and Other. This system of categories was
developed partly based on notions of gender and sexual desire.

In a colonial society one strategy used by colonizers in the attempt to establish hegemony is to assert difference. The establishment of a stable sense
of Self, contrasted with the necessarily inferior (and often exotic) Other, allows the colonizer to maintain a secure hierarchy. Similarly, some (noble)
members of the colonized group attempt to solidify the group's notion of Self
in order to maintain traditional privileges. The subaltern members of the
colonized group may attempt to maintain their own ideas of Self in order to

resist what they perceive as a difficult future under colonial rule.[2] For many people in both groups, assertions of difference are vital.

However, the colonizers, in order effectively to control the colonized population, necessarily attempt to control their cultures and thus their minds. To gain this control, the colonizers must attempt to alter the cultural matrix of the colonized in such a way as to make the colonized more similar to themselves (in order for hegemony to be established, the colonized must accept the legitimacy and/or necessity of the colonial system). In doing this the colonizers are in a sense working against the desire to assert stable notions of Self and Other. In fact, the colonizers use hybridity as a strategy: they place concepts related to the colonial culture in the cultural matrix of the colonized.[3] For the colonized, this strategy of hybridity has a different meaning: individual members may use such a strategy to reassert their privileges during colonial rule, and the collective group may use hybridity as a form of resistance.

At the time of the conquest, the Maya distinguished between themselves and outsiders based on the notion of the autonomy of the local city-state. Evidence suggests that, in earlier times, despite the presence of kings who claimed rulership over larger areas, both ethnicity and identity were localized.[4] Local ethnicity and pride combined with the presence of large ethnic groups attempting to dominate regions.

The Maya used warfare to distinguish between Self and Other in a variety of ways. Wars, until the end of the Spanish conquest, were very common. Warfare promoted the pride of the local ethnic group and the power of the local gods, and the winner of the war received tribute, slaves, and captives for sacrifice. In associating warfare with local pride, the Maya used their warriors to promote the differences between Self and Other, differences which metaphorically and symbolically were gendered and sexualized.[5] In each case, the Maya viewed the winning group as masculine and as penetrators in sexual acts. The losers were viewed as feminine and as those who were penetrated by the penises of the opposing warriors. This distinction formed one core of the cultural matrix around which the Maya organized their perceptions of sexual desire.

But the advent of colonial rule destroyed many of these distinctions. The metaphors of warfare remained present in colonial era documents, but primarily based on memory of past wars. Many cultural metaphors related to sexual desire shifted from concepts related to war to those related to sin. The idea that sex was sinful was itself a theory alien to the Maya, who believed sex to be related to creation, pollution, destruction, and power. But the advocates of sex as sin were powerful, and the Maya by the end of the colonial period understood the idea (at least, as we will see, in its altered form). This attempt to establish sin as the primary cultural matrix in which sexual desire was understood was an attempt at making the colonized Other more similar to the (idealized notion of the) colonizing Self.[6] The movement from sex as defined by warfare to sex as defined by sin was a movement toward a hybrid mixture of traditions.

DEFINING THE HYBRID CULTURAL MATRIX

Maya sexual desire was placed in the Maya-language historical and philosophical texts at many points. The writers implicated historical eras with particular sexual actions and desires. The Maya nobles claimed desire to be a problematic presence, one that could destroy society. Yet it also was a presence that could replicate society and make it grow. Those with sexual desires most often were those with power, those who could create and destroy the world. Desire was a powerful and dangerous force, a flow[7] which, when unleashed, could either destroy society or enhance life.[8] It had this power because desire could please or displease the gods, the nobles, and the commoners alike.

The cultural matrix which related to sexual desire was a metaphorical grid upon which culture was written. On this grid of conflicting ideas, experiences, and traditions, the Maya and their colonizers developed notions of what it meant to be a person and how the individual could interact with others and with nature. The conceptions of Self and Other formed a part of this matrix, and, most importantly, the culture defined the basic category of personhood.[9] For the Maya, the person came into existence and had an identity based on his or her local ethnic group, lineage, and relationship with the gods. For the Spaniards the person came into existence and had an identity based on his or her local ethnic group, lineage, nation, and relationship with the Christian God. The similarities between these two notions are obvious, but the differences are more instructive. These differences can be understood through an analysis of some of the central categories of personhood: much of Maya preconquest identity was centered on the individual's symbolic relationship with the warrior, while much of Spanish identity was centered on the fact that all people were seen as sinners in the eyes of God.[10]

The matrix upon which Maya sexual desire was formed became a battleground during the colonial era. Christian clergy, Spanish seculars, Maya nobles, and Maya commoners all struggled over the meanings related to desire. It is an analysis of these elements that will show how the history of desire itself has been based on intrusions, interruptions, and battles which have changed the very foundations of desire.[11]

SEX, GENDER, AND WAR

In the period preceding the sixteenth century, the Spaniards fought many wars, and the Maya reportedly were in a state of endemic warfare.[12] In both the European and Mesoamerican cases, war was seen as a central component of life, one which a man most often could not avoid. Historians have shown that war has had a wide variety of meanings and purposes,[13] and indeed, the Maya and Spaniards had different ideas about the meanings of warfare and conquest.[14]

Symbolically, metaphorically, and on the field, war was an event that marked both sexual desire and gender.[15] While both Mayas and Spaniards developed a sexualized discourse around war, various elements of that discourse made it difficult for one group to understand the other. When comprehension did take place, of course, the two groups were on opposite sides of the battlefield, making their differences irreconcilable.

Richard Trexler's groundbreaking work on the topic, *Sex and Conquest*, definitively establishes a connection between war, gender, and sexual desire. Trexler shows that the Spaniards often feminized their enemies in warfare by declaring them sodomites, pederasts, and effeminates. At other times the conquerors stated that the group in question was free of sodomy and bestiality. Such a declaration made the conquest seem an even more vigorous exercise ("It takes a real man to conquer a real man"). This connection between gender, sexual desire, and warfare was not limited to Europeans. Trexler presents most of the indigenous peoples as groups that prized the extreme masculinity of the warrior. Losing warriors were degraded as effeminates who had been sodomized by their enemies. The causes of victory were seen as both supernatural and natural masculine prowess. Importantly, these elements of warfare allowed both Europeans and indigenous Americans to construct particular ideas of the differences between masculinity and femininity.[16]

Spanish Warfare

The Spanish ascribed particular peoples with sexual habits which were seen as unnatural. By so ascribing, they were able to distinguish themselves from the "other races."[17] The Spanish use of sodomy, transvestism, and transsexualism to show the degeneracy of the indigenous peoples was immediately apparent from the conquest narratives.[18] These charges were used strategically in order to assert the superiority of one race over another.[19]

The Spaniards, in their development of the powers of warfare and conquest, had particular preconceived ideas about Maya sexual behaviors. Trexler stresses the context of this history by noting that the Spanish understood a relationship between sexual behavior and conquest. They often raped both men and women among the conquered groups. The conquerors developed different, sometimes conflicting ideas regarding the relationships between gender status, sexual desire, and war. Some believed endemic sodomy and transvestism to be a characteristic of all the conquered groups. This showed Europeans that the conquered peoples were less civilized than their conquerors. Others stated that the group under discussion (e.g., Inca society) was free of sodomy and bestiality. This accomplished the feat of portraying that society as noble. Such a declaration made the conquest seem an even more impressive accomplishment, as well as allowing for a discourse of progressive enhancement of society where sodomites and pederasts only were present in the lowest of the societies (thus allowing the Spaniards to distinguish between the various conquered groups).[20] Such a practice also allowed the Spaniards (and other Europeans) to develop a "geography of perversion," emphasizing a purported relationship between the environment and sexual activity.[21] Eventually, the idea of such a relationship was discarded in favor of the concept of a "deviant" sexual minority present in most or all societies. This new idea at least partly was based on colonial experiences and attempts to distinguish a "superior race" from the mass of humanity.[22] The Spaniards, in asserting the presence or lack of sodomy as an important element in the conquest, were presenting the people with a particular notion of social development. In believing sodomy and transvestism to be present in some or all "less civilized" societies, the conquerors supported a gender ideology in which sodomy and effeminacy were seen as inferior.

European goals in asserting the masculinity or femininity of the conquered group were complex, and they were made more complicated by the fact that many of the Spaniards were fighting with each other, primarily for economic and political reasons. Spanish chronicles, which outlined the wars of conquest and the initial sightings of the indigenous peoples, contain some information about the chroniclers'[23] perceptions of indigenous sexual behavior.[24] Peter Martyr, an early official historian working with the Spanish crown, wrote in 1516 about the conquest of Panama: "Vasco [Nuñez de Balboa] found [the house of a *cacique*][25] full of nefarious lechery: he found the *cacique's* brother in women's clothes, and many others were also adorned that way. According to the testimony of the citizens, these men were reserved for licentious uses. Thus he [Nuñez de Balboa] ordered them thrown to the dogs, killing some forty."[26] The chroniclers treated much indigenous sexual behavior with great disdain. They certainly said little about the meanings that the indigenous people attached to such behavior. These descriptions represented political and material strategies related to cultural sightings which touched off particular reactions in Spanish imaginations.

In the chronicles of Yucatán, there were few similar texts. Bernal Díaz del Castillo, speaking of his first expedition to Yucatán, stated that they found "many clay idols, some looking like faces of demons and other figures looking evil in such a manner that the figures appeared to be committing sodomy: some shadowy figures of Indians with others."[27] The narrative here intended to legitimize particular actions: the destruction of the idols. Díaz wrote his chronicle, significantly after the conquest, in order to dispute assertions which, in Díaz's view, gave Hernando Cortés too much credit for the conquest of Mexico, and hence gave his descendants too much wealth and prestige.[28] The text used sexual acts in an attempt to assert the political strength of the author and other conquerors.

This Spanish discourse was a gendered account of warfare. The Spaniards feminized their enemies in order to assert social distance between themselves and the Other. The Spanish had engaged in this practice during wars in Europe and north Africa as well. In the fourteenth and fifteenth centuries, contact with other European countries and with the Moors led to theories of endemic sodomy in other ethnic groups. This concept was a gendered notion of power: the Other was presented as more effeminate, and thus weaker than the Self. The practice of rape during war, in addition to giving conquering armies a sexual outlet, was designed to denigrate and feminize the enemy, declaring that enemy to be unable to protect the women and even the men of that society. The concentration on the Other in Asia, Africa, and Europe delimited certain sexual boundaries where the Spanish saw themselves as sexually, socially, and culturally superior.[29]

This was the baggage that the conquerors brought with them to the Americas. They then engaged in similar actions, and, as noted above, feminized enemies, discussed endemic sodomy, and engaged in the practice of rape.[30] In this way they were able to establish a social and cultural distance between themselves and the indigenous populations. In this conceptualization, the masculine figure proved himself by defeating others, both in the battlefield and in bed. The sexual component of such actions was important to the Spaniards.

Several narratives of the period asserted valor through both warfare and the conquest of women.[31] In this sense the conquest of the Maya effeminized them in the eyes of those engaging in battle, and in the Spanish cultural framework as well.

Maya Defeat

This sense of the meaning of warfare was not lost on the Maya. They tended to feminize enemies, stressed masculinity through the successful warrior, and directly connected masculinity with sexual desire.[32] However, the Maya sense of war did not feminize the defeated society in the same way as the Spanish. Instead, the Maya promoted a notion of the masculinity of the defeated warrior as representative of the defeated gods.

The Book of Chilam Balam of Tizimin presents an account of warfare which Munro Edmonson appropriately calls the Flower Katun.[33] The text explores the relationships of both time and the flower to various life processes and emphasizes a Maya approach to understanding the reasons for defeat and destruction:[34]

ychil ah buluc ahau ca liki ah musen cab kaax ix u uich oxlahun ti ku maix yoheltahob u kaba cilich citbil lai u kaba yalahob. . . . oxlahun ku ti bolon ku ca emi [kak] ca emi tab ca emi tunich y chee ca tali u baxal che y tunich ca ix kuchi oxlahun ti ku ca paxi u pol ca lahi u uich ca tubabi ca colpahi canhel y ho sabac ca chabi ix kukil ix yaxum u puyem sicil u puyem top u tepah u yinah yax bolon ɔacab ca bini tu y oxlahun tas caan ca cul hi u maɔil y u ni u baclil ca bini u pucsikal tumenel oxlahun ti ku ma ix yoheltah bin ci u pucsikal u uil lae ca hut la hi ix ma yumob ah numyaob ix ma ichamob cuxanob ix ti manan u pucsikal ca mucchahiob tu yam sus tu yam kaknab hun uaɔ hail ti uchi u col canhel. . . . hokciob nicte lae ah con mayelob lai u na nicteob hokci yuɔub ah kin yuɔub ahau yuɔub hol can lai u cuch nicte ahau ca emi. . . . maix yoheltahob yemel u keban pop kuchi tu than cuchi nicte ix u pop nicte ix u kan che sauin culic sauin u luch [sauin] u lac sauin u pucsikal sauin u chi hach co u coil u than ti y ahaulil tu kinil. . . . sip u than ti culic sip u can kaxan u uich ti culic cha u cah tza u cah pop culic tu y ahau lic tuban u yum tuban u naa maix yohel uyum mehente maix yohel u na sihese halil yan ti ni yak. . . . ca ix sati yol ca ix sati yik ca chaci u cal u hich u cal tuba tu hunal sip u than ah bobat lae si pix ah kin lae sisip ahau sipob ix hol can lae ti haulahi tu thubob ti noclah chimal ti noclahi nab te lahun

yal yah ual uincob ix ca ual hi maix ti yoltahob u talel u ɔocol u than. . . .
u ɔahob ix u tan ti lomol nicte ix cimci. . . . numya u yal u mehen ah num
ytza ma cetel bin ɔocbal nicte uinicil nicte katun ichil christianoil uale

During 11 Ahau, Ah Musen Cab[35] arose to tie the faces of the thirteen
gods, but they did not know their names. "Holy father,"[36] that's the
name he called them. . . . The thirteen gods said to the nine: "Let fire,
rope, stones, and wood descend."[37] Then came the beating of the wood
and the stones. Then the thirteen gods arrived and they beat their
heads, and slapped their faces, and the year bearers[38] and Ho Sabac[39]
were spat upon and snatched away. The quetzal and bluebird were
taken, crushing their covering, crushing their flower and wrapping the
seed/semen[40] of the first Bolon Dzacab,[41] who went to the thirteen
levels of the sky.[42] Then they cut their skin[43] and their septums, and
then their hearts, because of the thirteen gods, but they did not know
what was happening. The heart of the moon was then dropped and
flattened. The fatherless, the miserable, those without husbands or
living protectors, and those without hearts were buried in the waves
of the sand and the sea. There was a torrent of water released by the
year bearers. . . . The flowers and water sellers[44] appeared. Thus the
house of flowers appeared. The blossom of the priest, the blossom of
the lord, the blossom of the soldier is the burden of the flower lords
as they descend. . . . Although they do not know them, the sinful mats
descend and arrive at the statement bearing the flower, the mat of the
flower, the yellow tree.[45] Deceit[46] is seated. Deceit is its gourd. Deceit
is its plate. Deceit is its heart. Deceit is its mouth. The great insanity
of the lordship: his words were insane at the time. . . . The words of
[the one] seated [in office] are to blame. His tale is to blame. The face
of the one seated is tied as he carries and demands his mat. He sits as
their lord as if forgetting his father, forgetting his mother. He does
not know the father who bred him. Nor does he know the mother who
gave birth to him. In truth, he was born by nose and tongue. . . . Then
they lost their hearts and they lost their breath. They cut and tied
their own throats, by themselves. The words of the prophet, the priest,
the lord, and the soldiers were to blame. They rested in the bottom of
their hammocks, dropping their shields and dropping their lances to
the ten children, the enemy people. They turned their backs and they
did not know about the coming of the end of the world. . . . They came
into the presence of the stabbing flower and died. . . . The children of

men and women were miserable and suffering. The Itzá were not sufficient to end the flower people, the Flower Katun, when Christianity returned.[47]

The narrative relates part of the rationale behind war: the struggle of the supernatural. This is one of many discussions of war in the Books of Chilam Balam. This story, likely recounted in the eighteenth century, mixes Christianity with preconquest gods and wars. The war being fought is ritualized as the classic fight between the thirteen gods of heaven and the nine gods of the underworld. At the same time, this war could have signified the Spanish conquest and/or a war taking place between several Maya communities. In this sense, the document is a hybrid, combining many elements of the two cultures. As the fighting began, the people spat upon the thirteen gods, who then lost the war, which presaged the destruction of the world. The narrative shows that the people should have listened to the omens.

The masculinity of the defeated Maya peoples, however, was saved through the rituals of human sacrifice. The text depicts the warriors quite literally tearing the body apart, cutting the skin and then the septum, and finally the heart. The sacrifice signified a process of death and rebirth in the community whereby the people themselves moved from one era to another. Sacrifice was intended to mark time and survival by placating the gods and, in the flood scene, human sacrifice was seen as creating life and ensuring survival.

The flower and the existence of human sacrifice represented the masculinity of the warriors. In this case, the local warriors could not defeat their opponents and thus symbolically lost their masculinity, which could only be recaptured through sacrifice. Warfare in this sense was seen as the proof of one's masculinity and the power of one's gods.[48]

The flower, a complex symbol discussed below, signified to the Maya a sense of sexual penetration. The flower that won the war was seen as the successful penetrator and the worthy leader. The flower lords here could not protect the community because they did not understand that the "ten children"[49] came to defeat them. The flower then became a "stabbing flower," an enforcer and a penetrator: in stabbing, this flower was able to defeat the community and symbolically feminize (penetrate) the warriors. Yet this stabbing flower also was seen as a creator, allowing the community to be reborn. The flower both killed and created life as the flower lords forgot to complete their obligations. And the narrative ends by showing that the flower people survived, stressing the relationship between the flower and life.

Sexual desire was used as part of the text, symbolically allowing the people to connect this desire with warfare. Bolon Dzacab's seed, translated from *inah*, was both the seed from which the flower emanated and the semen which came from Bolon Dzacab himself. This god often was seen as the creator of the universe in the Maya world, so his semen was a powerful force of creation. Sexual desire here stood for the development of life but also for destruction, for it was the sacrifice of Bolon Dzacab's seed that initiated the end of the world. Bolon Dzacab, as the penetrating, penetrated, and defeated god, ushered in destruction. But in the Maya cyclical sense of the world, this destruction then led to creation. Sexual desire, even when the people were defeated and penetrated, allowed for their eventual rebirth and survival.

The narrative further relates these desires to warfare through the concept of illegitimacy. The lord was insane and blameworthy because of his lack of legitimacy, and the fact of illegitimacy was the central reason for the battle between the heavens and the underworld. The leader of the community faced insults, as the narrative insists that he was a commoner, and thus unqualified for office. He did not know either of his parents, suggesting that he was both illegitimate and unwanted. This reference was intended to show the excess of commoners: from the perspective of the nobles, commoners did not know their lineage, and thus necessarily were born out of illicit unions. But the narrative takes the insult further: this lord was not born in a normal manner, but rather through acts related to the nose and the tongue. The narrative uses these particular body parts to suggest the excesses of commoners, perhaps connecting those excesses to sexual acts leading to the birth of the illegitimate ruler. The nature of these sexual acts was incomprehensible to the nobles writing this document and, of course, that is the point.[50] The narrative shows that commoners engaged in procreative sexual acts that could not be comprehended by the proper human (noble) mind. The sexual desires of the commoners made them unqualified for leadership roles, and, when they took such roles, destruction and war were preordained. Illicit sexual acts caused war, and war caused unwanted feminization and forced sexual acts.

The Maya further supported this connection between sexual desire and warfare through the presence of the *nacon*, the war chief.[51] This figure was a key leader, probably second in command, of the local community. According to Diego de Landa, this person was chosen for a period of three years, during which time he was not permitted to engage in sexual acts with any woman,[52] even his wife. Further, he did not have women to serve him (limiting his contact with them), and he could not become drunk, nor could he eat certain meats.[53] The *nacon* was not permitted to have sex with or even have much contact with women because of perceptions of their polluting effects. If he had contact with women, his masculinity would be drained.[54] His masculine valor was needed in order for him to be the most effective war leader.

Sexual desire was constructed in this Maya universe at the time of the Spanish conquest as something which could destroy the community through its relationship with war. These desires, along with the improper behavior of the gods, led to Maya defeat, death, and destruction. This discourse was part of a Maya narrative technique which showed that all previous eras ended in disaster. Gender and sexual desire were part of the discourse, and were seen as important measures of a society's validity. The Spaniards similarly found gender and sexual desire to be important measures of a society's level of development.

Unlike the Spaniards, though, the Maya did not assert a stable sexual distinction between Self and Other. For the Maya, the losing side was the feminized side, and the loser could be the home community. The Spaniards, who certainly believed that their fighters lost battles partly because they were not masculine enough,[55] still asserted that the opposing side was, in the end, the more feminine one. Further, the Maya believed that war leaders needed to be free of feminine pollution, while the Spaniards were more interested in having their war leaders prove masculinity through the conquest of women. For both, however, the proper society, the winning society, asserted its masculinity through "appropriate" sexual desires and masculine prowess.

Conquest and the Flower

One element which stands out in the quote from the Book of Chilam Balam of Tizimin warrants extended commentary. The flower, which Maya writers related to life, death, war, the human body, sex, and sacrifice, was one of the most important symbols in the Maya texts. The flower was a sexualized object in much of this discourse, which connected destruction and war with sexual desire.

Above it was shown that the flower people ushered in their own destruction. The flower represented all of the people of the community (although it could have implied the nobility). The people needed protection from outsiders, and they should have received this protection from the nobles. The flowers here came to represent leadership, authority, war, and ritual.

A closer analysis of the position of the flower shows that it was a complex symbol which signified elements that at first glance are contradictory. The flower comes into the text on four occasions. First it is represented as something crushed by the forces of war. Here it is designed to show the presence of human sacrifice. Next, the flower (through the flower house and the flower lords) ushers in the illegitimate lord. Third, the flower enters the text as a "stabbing flower." Finally, at the very end of the text, the people are called "flower people" and the time period is called a "flower katun." Additionally, in the portion of the text not included here, the term "flower" is repeated many times, each time signifying either creation or destruction. On these occasions the flower is once a symbol of life, then a symbol of illegitimacy, next a symbol of death, and finally a symbol of existence (people and time).

Writing about the Nahuas, Miguel León-Portilla argues that the flower, combined with song, represented Nahuatl poetry, "a creative and profound expression which, through symbol and metaphor, allows man to discover himself and then to talk about what he has intuitively and mysteriously perceived."[56] The concept of the flower, to León-Portilla, represented the truth of self-discovery.[57] If León-Portilla's concept of truth is applied broadly, it has some pan-Mesoamerican validity. While the flower in Mesoamerican thought did not simply represent poetry, it did symbolize a certain ritual relationship with the supernatural which could be characterized as "truth."

The second central use of the flower in Nahua society was to describe a ritualized form of war: the flower war. This war was fought between two relatively equal opponents, and it was set up such that hand-to-hand combat was the main form of fighting. This combat was designed for the taking of captives for human sacrifice, but Ross Hassig points out that it clearly also was an attempt to weaken an enemy in order to prepare for an eventual regular war in which one side would attempt to subdue and subjugate the other.[58]

In both of the Nahua cases, as is supported by Maya uses of the idea of the flower, the term represented ritualized events: ritualized speech which took place regularly to teach people lessons, ritualized wars which were staged, ritualized battles between the gods. The flowers signified these rituals by presenting the people with a series of relationships which made sense in Mesoamerican dualism. The destruction of warfare created and maintained life by feeding the gods the blood of sacrificial victims and by ushering in a new time period. Thus, structured around the concept of warfare as a destructive and creative enterprise, the flower could signify life and death.

It is in the sense of this dualism that the flower related to sexual desire, another enterprise which, like war, destroyed and created life. Maya vase paintings which depicted explicit sexual activity regularly pictured the flower in order to emphasize the sex.[59] The word often used for flower, *nicte*, also was translated by the Motul Dictionary as "carnal vice and naughtiness of women."[60] In another case, from the Book of Chilam Balam of Kaua, the flowers spurted up as adultery was abundant, thus connecting the flowers with the excesses of society.[61] In the Book of Chilam Balam of Chumayel, the flowers similarly were associated with sexual desire, but in one text they signified the space in which acts could be performed:

u than Dios citbil ꜩ Dios mehenbil ꜩ D^s espiritu sancto santo xot kin lae santo juiçio tumenel ca yumil ti D^s bin minanac u muk caan ꜩ luum bin ococ ti christianoil nucuch cahob u cahal macnalob u nohochil cah max u kaba bay u cah tu yukul lay mehen cahob lae tu yukul lay ca petenil maya cu çamil maya patan licil ca ca kin uinicil tucal coil ꜫiꜫi mehenil tu xul ca sat mail ylil ꜩ subtalil cux yol ca mehenob tu nicteob

The word of God the father, God the son, and God the holy spirit was a sacred judgment[62] by our father, God. There will be no strength in heaven or on earth. The head towns, the settlements of people, the great people of the towns, called monkeys, will enter Christianity. Likewise for the community and all of the inhabitants.[63] All of this Maya land thus pays Maya tribute.[64] Becoming two day people, therefore crazy and lustful, the sons in the end lost their vision, shame, and discretion among their flowers.[65]

There are several possible interpretations of the space represented by the flowers in this text. The flowers may have been the lineages of the sons, which predated Christianity. The lineages, while they gave the sons life, somehow became contaminated and allowed the sons (nobles) to lose their vision because of illegitimacy. They also connected the sons to the social world, signifying blood ties. The sons, not prudently thinking about the future, became very lustful and had inordinate amounts of sex positioned on the flower. The sons brought shame to the flowers and to their lineages both by engaging in these sexual acts and by allowing the Spaniards to defeat them.[66] The flower here may have signified both the possibility for life and the possibility of destruction. The flower may have been a strategic space in the text which allowed for the commission of these acts.

Flowers, as ritualized symbols, often represented sex, war, and human sacrifice in these texts, showing metaphorical similarities for all of these elements. Such similarities related to the Maya conceptualization of sexual desire as a form of ritual penetration. If sexual activity was associated with penetration, then any type of penetration, whether by a sword during war or a knife or needle during sacrifice, may have related to such a construction. As we have seen, the flower had a ritualized relationship with the Maya system of duality, a system in which death created life. Sexual acts were represented in these texts as inherently destructive and creative at the same time. War and human sacrifice done on proper occasions and in the proper manner maintained the community through this same duality.

In a passage from the Book of Chilam Balam of Tizimin, the flower signified life itself, only destroyed by an illegitimate leader:

> *mayapan u heɔ katun ti uuc ahau ek chu uah u uich ti yahaulil tu pop tu*
> *ɔam amayte kauil u uich tu canil ti y ahaulil hopic ci u ɔocol u toppol ix*
> *bolon yol nic te ɔibal yol nic te nic teil uah nic teil haa y aal ɔam lic u halach*
> *uinicil bal cah ɔam lic ah kin ɔam lic ah bobat*

Mayapán was the seat of the *katun* in 7 Ahau. The west priest Chu Uah was the face[67] of the lordship on the mat and the throne. Amayte Kauil was the face of the sky[68] of the lordship which began and ended the sprouting of the nine-hearted flower, the painted-heart flower, flower food, and flower water [nectar]. He acted as the *halach uinic*[69] of the world, he acted as the priest, he acted as the prophet.[70]

In this passage Amayte Kauil destroyed society, but by destroying the flower, which signified life in addition to death. The flower had nine hearts, a painted heart, and it was related to food and water. Amayte Kauil was seen as illegitimate because of his destruction of the flower.

The desire for the flower was a desire for a particular kind of life. Society was maintained through the proper ritual roles of war, sacrifice, bloodletting, and sex when those acts strived to maintain the flower. The Mesoamerican flower was a symbolic representation of ritual and duality. The nobles spoke and wrote of the flower as a special element of society which was cause for an understanding of creation and destruction. For the Maya the flower was linked closely with the concept of penetration: something which, as we shall see, was to be feared greatly, but which also was something to be desired.

The Maya sense of warfare was represented both as a masculine endeavor under threat from feminine pollution and as a ritual of competitive sexual penetration which determined the course of society. Maya defeat stemmed from sexual activity, but rebirth was imminent, and it developed out of the sexual behavior of the gods and the duality of the flowers. Bolon Dzacab's semen maintained the flowers and the cyclical life of Maya time.

COLONIZING SIN

The context of sexual desire was to change during the colonial years as the clergy, particularly the Franciscan friars, attempted to put sex in what they perceived to be its proper place, under the rubric of sin. The charge of "sin" was a traditional Catholic method of control over Spaniards, indigenous peoples, and others. Encountering the Maya, the clergy faced a central problem when trying to implement their concept of sin: the Maya had no similar ideology.

In order to understand the sixteenth-century Catholic concept of sin, one must take into account three vital points. First, sin required some notion of free will. The individual had to be free to choose whether or not to sin. So, a baby who hit a priest had not sinned; nor had a person who mistakenly tripped and fell down in church. In both cases, sin would have been impossible as the individual did not choose to commit these acts. Second, confessing one's sins was based on the presumption that the individual would try not to sin again. Third, one had to confess one's sins before death, or one would risk purgatory and hell.[71]

Maya Sins

The concept of sin, intimately connected with sexual behaviors in Catholic thought, had different origins for the Maya. The word most often used for sin, *keban*, appeared in the documents with great frequency. It related to adultery and sodomy, but also to political corruption, social inequities, obesity, hunger, and various ritual improprieties. In many ways this looked like the Catholic idea of sin, but the concept had little to do with the central point of Catholic understandings of the term: intent. Landa, reporting on preconquest confessions, stated:

> The Yucatecans naturally knew when they had done wrong, and
> they believed that, because of evil and sin, they would receive death,
> disease, and torment; so they had the custom of confessing when
> such was the case. In this way, when through sickness or another
> cause they were in danger of death, they confessed their sins, and if
> they neglected it, their close relatives or friends reminded them; thus
> they publicly stated their sins: to the priest if he was there; or if not,
> to their parents, women to their husbands, and husbands to their
> women.[72]

If Landa was correct, then the Maya had a concept of sin similar to that of the Spanish. However, in writing his treatise, Landa had particular goals in mind: he wanted to absolve himself of any wrongdoing which he, other friars, or the Council of the Indies (he was writing while he was in "exile" in Spain) may have felt he had committed against the Maya in his Inquisition against them. He wanted to recruit more friars to Yucatán. Finally, he wanted to strengthen the position of the Franciscans relative to the other Orders, the secular clergy, and other Spaniards.[73] Certainly these goals colored his observations.

Landa may have believed at the time that the Maya concept of sin was similar to the Catholic concept. It is possible that he was reestablishing his prior optimism about the Christianization of the Maya people.[74] Let us read Landa's views a bit more closely: He clearly stated that the Maya confessed their sins when they feared death. This no doubt was relatively normal Spanish practice as well, but what did it say about the Maya? Either they knew when they had sinned, and they just confessed before death because that was when they felt the need to do so, or the illness caused them to believe that they had sinned. The difference is subtle, but vital to understanding the concept, for, if the latter is the case, then the Maya believed, like the Nahuas, that often illness and death befell a person because the gods were displeased. This did not mean that the person had sinned in the Catholic sense of the term, for the central components of control, free choice, responsibility, and repentance would not have applied.

The Maya did not believe that they had control over all of their actions. Although they did not believe entirely in fate, the quoted passages in the Books of Chilam Balam make it clear that the Maya believed in predetermined cycles of time. If one was born at a particular time, then one was predestined to have a particular fate.[75] If a leader led a society moving into a new period of time, then that leader necessarily was fated somehow to be removed from office at a specific time.[76] This lack of control and free will would make the Catholic concept of sin untenable: if a person did not exercise free will over whether to commit a particular sin, then confession, penitence, and absolution would not have the same effect.

Landa, although he did not analyze cognitive perceptions, understood sin in a different manner. The above passage continued: "The sins of which they commonly accused themselves were theft, homicide, of the flesh, and false testimony; in this way [by confessing] they thought themselves safe."[77] Landa's words again evoked a sense that the Maya may have thought of illness and death as markers of divine unhappiness as opposed to individual sin. The penalties for the supposed sins involved types of restitution: the man who had sex with another man's wife had to make some sort of arrangement with that other man or face death; the murderer provided money to, was enslaved by, or was killed by the relatives of the slain person; the thief paid back the amount stolen and was enslaved.[78] In each case the primary goal of the penalty was restitution, not repentance; nor was there a separate religious penalty for such acts.

Another striking element regarding Landa's statement is the public nature of confession. In fact, Maya confessions did occur in public, at the time of important rituals or when a person was ill. The confession was believed to have a protective effect on the community more than on the individual.[79] The confession allowed for community survival in the face of various threats; it appeased the gods. Hence, in the situation Landa described, family and friends had an interest in getting the dying person to confess. No doubt public confession also was a way of attempting to keep peace in the community by airing all disputes in front of priests and elders. Again, this had little to do with the Catholic notion of sin.

As noted in the last chapter, the Maya concept of the underworld and the Christian concept of hell were not synonymous, and a Maya person, while she or he could and would fear the underworld, in all likelihood could not avoid it. So the afterlife could not have served as a punishment for sins. I have proposed that the Maya notion of the power of the gods and fate precluded Catholic-like ideas of sin. The evidence in the preconquest period, however, is sparse. The proof of the Maya concept of sin lies in the colonial years, when the Franciscan friars, including Landa, expressed disdain for the Maya because of their disregard for the concepts of sin and repentance.

The Power of Sin as a Colonizing Force

The Inquisitors from the Office of the Holy Inquisition who tried the indigenous peoples in the Americas realized that these peoples did not have a clear grasp of the concept of sin. The crown found that Inquisitorial punishments of Indians were too excessive because the Indians did not know how to defend themselves or how to keep themselves from committing the "egregious sins" that led to Inquisitorial prosecution. This was one of many reasons that Indians were exempted from the Inquisition. Church and crown believed that indigenous peoples at the time were incapable of conceiving of the difference between appropriate and inappropriate behaviors.[80]

Louise Burkhart, in her research on Nahua morality, found that the Nahuas had a difficult time comprehending the concept of sin. The friars complained that the Nahuas rarely came to confession at all and, when they did come, they confessed such things as "dirt blew into my house and I failed to sweep it up," or "I fell down in public." Certainly one possible explanation for this phenomenon would be that the Nahuas were using the confessional to resist Catholic intrusion into their morals and values.[81] Another explanation, and the one that Burkhart finds more convincing, is that the Nahuas had a different concept of "sin" than did the Spaniards. The Nahuas believed that anything negative that befell them was the consequence of divine unhappiness. Thus, if dirt blew into one's house, then that person was facing the wrath of the gods. The reason behind that wrath was not always clear, and perhaps stemmed from the Nahua belief that the individual did not directly control his or her destiny.[82] For the Nahuas, when the friars and others attempted to impose a foreign concept of sin, they initially did not change their preconquest notions, but rather resisted by maintaining many traditional preconquest moral codes.

The Maya had a similar conceptualization of divine unhappiness. In the Books of Chilam Balam, every time a leader was conquered or a famine existed, whether or not the texts could find fault with the particular leader, the bad event was blamed on divine displeasure with the people.[83] The gods had control over the passage of life, and they exercised this control based on some knowledge that humans, even leaders, could not have.[84]

Following the conquest, however, as Burkhart notes for the Nahuas,[85] the moral dialogue which took place between the Spaniards and the indigenous peoples developed a new concept of deified displeasure, a concept related to the notion of sin. The disparity between this concept and preconquest Maya moral codes was manifested in what Inga Clendinnen has called a "confusion of tongues."[86] This notion, representing an initial stage of colonialism, shows that neither Spaniard nor Maya knew each other, but instead transferred concepts from their own system of meaning onto the system of meaning of the other.[87] When the clergy presented the Maya with the concept of sin, they believed that the Maya understood that idea, but they relatively quickly became dismayed when they found out that the Maya reinscribed the theory of sin with Maya moral codes.

The documents related to Landa's Inquisition against the Maya are most instructive in this regard. This Inquisition took place in 1562, after Landa and other friars claimed to have found significant evidence of human sacrifice.[88] In Landa's own testimony, he stated that he had met with several Maya leaders in the period immediately preceding the discovery of the sacrifices. He had found that these leaders were sacrificing food and drink to some "images" that they kept hidden, so he lectured them on the sinfulness of the activity, and then he pardoned them.[89] He further admitted that some of the very people whom he had lectured later were involved in the human sacrifices.[90]

Landa certainly believed that these people had been influenced by "demons" and by the priests of their traditional religion. They had engaged in these sacrifices in order to prevent famine and further illnesses, as had been predicted by these priests.[91] According to a wide variety of testimony (much of which was given under torture), the traditional priests had held secret ceremonies with other Maya leaders, and there they had engaged in the said sacrifices. These priests further told the Maya leaders to keep these sacrifices secret, and not to listen to the Catholic priests.[92] To Landa, these people knew exactly what they were doing.

The confessions told a somewhat different story: of people working to comprehend the world within their own system of meaning. Most of the indigenous peoples freely admitted to idolatry, as they did not believe that there would be a serious penalty for such activity.[93] The activities were appropriate when considered from the vantage point of Maya cognitive perceptions of the world. In the testimony that alleged human sacrifice, the participants knew that the friars would disapprove of the activity, but they claimed to do it anyway, apparently not primarily from fear of the traditional priests, but rather from a desire to prevent the gods from being unhappy.[94] Some of the sacrifices allegedly took place as crucifixions, which was not a traditional form of Maya sacrifice. The testimonies of these sacrifices thus were hybrid creations, but ones in which the lessons of Catholicism were used to promulgate activities condemned by the religion.[95] No doubt such sacrifices had a grave effect on the fantasies of Landa and the other friars.[96] The supposed sacrifices suggested resistance, not misunderstanding, and, as Landa clearly and perceptively understood, they pointed to the idea of the Maya priests that this sort of hybrid religious tradition could save the society.

In the end, many Maya leaders committed suicide to avoid being tortured by the Franciscans. The suicides themselves were sinful in the Spanish world, but not in the Maya. Before these events, Landa believed that he had given the Maya effective instruction on Christianity, but afterward he realized that many of the Maya thought about that instruction and hybridized it by placing traditional Maya codes inside Catholic ritual. Part of the reason for this was that before the conquest the Maya did not have a similar perception of religion, confession, and sin.

For the Maya to be taught the new framework for sexual activity, they had to understand the role of sin itself. The clergy attempted to teach them this role through stories, sermons, catechisms, and confessions.[97] Yet these members of the clergy claimed that they felt exasperated at the difficulty of making the Maya understand the concept of sin.[98] To the Franciscans, these difficulties emanated from the temptations of the devil. The friars did not understand that Maya mental processes made the people interpret sin in a different manner; it was not a case of simple misunderstanding. The friars were not able to account for the fact that the Maya did not see Catholicism and traditional Maya religion as mutually exclusive.[99] As such, the Maya tended to mix their traditional rituals with Catholicism, and they began to understand sin as part of a broader religious framework. So sin by the eighteenth century was defined as a set of activities which displeased the friars and the Christian God.

A passage from the Book of Chilam Balam of Tizimin described the relationship between sex and sin a manner which emphasized the hybrid:

> *hunac tzuc ti cab pen cech cal pach yani ti pulan yoc tulacali la u tucul tu kinil la u tucul ti akab u keban kin u keban akab u munal u pucsikal halach uinicob ah bobatob*

The land was very lustful.[100] There was excessive adultery which was carried and taken everywhere. Such were their thoughts by day; such were their thoughts by night. The sin of day and the sin of night enslaved the hearts of the *halach uinicob*, the prophets.[101]

The sins of day and night related back to the "excessive adultery." The word that I have translated as sin, *keban*, was, based simply on the decontextualized colonial translation, related to feelings of uneasiness rather than the commission of actions defined as wrong by religious authorities.[102] Here the wrong done could have been the feeling of uneasiness among the population because of the excessive nature of the sexual behavior. The excessive adultery was condemned as sinful through the idea of a sin committed all the time (in day and night). The narrative morally condemned the entire society, not an individual, for these sins. This condemnation had little to do with the intent of those committing the sins, and more to do with the effects of their actions upon society.

The document was part of the grander scheme of the nobles to use sexual license as a way of suggesting the illegitimacy of the commoners. The very next line in the text showed this genealogy, as "those without mothers and fathers" demeaned themselves and caused great destruction. This text intended to convince the reader that these sexual sins were the fault of the leaders of society (a historical leadership), and that society was destroyed because of these leaders. But, at the same time, the text hurled great insults against the commoners (who were "those without mothers and fathers"). The commoners demeaned themselves, informing a strategy which showed why they were unfit to rule: because they did not know the identities of their mothers and fathers, the commoners were incapable of effective self-rule. They were the products of illegitimacy and perhaps of the very adultery condemned here. They had nobody to protect them, at least not through filiation, so they had to seek nobles to protect them through alliance. The only way to do this was to support the legitimate nobles (those colonized by the Spaniards) and oppose the illegitimate nobles (those long dead as well as live commoners pretending to be nobles). Sin and history were used for politics. And commoner sexual desire was the illegitimate and destructive device that destroyed nobility and society.

By the eighteenth century, when this text was written, adultery fell into the category of sin, an idea certainly compatible with Catholicism. However, the sins of day and night related back to a preconquest notion that gendered day male and night female. This had been related to the idea of female danger in the act of creation: men were the creators of day (through the male sun); women were the creators of night (through the female moon). The moon and night were powerful and dangerous feminine qualities.[103] So while adultery here was sinful, the notion of sin that was presented was not simply a postconquest rendition of the term, but rather was an idea which was related to preconquest concepts of gendered creation. The hybrid formation of sin here was not what the friars had taught, but rather was a new form of understanding sex and sin.[104]

Even by the nineteenth century, the clergy still found it difficult to teach the Maya the basic concepts of Catholic ritual, and they had particular difficulty with the idea of sin. Late colonial sermons in the Yucatec language focused extensively on sin and repentance. In several cases, the priests interjected stories designed to teach the concept of sin, stories that clearly were intended to help cross the divide that had led to this "confusion of tongues."[105]

Other texts attempted to teach Catholicism through the use of a particular concept of "sin." The Book of Chilam Balam of Tusik was a (late-eighteenth- or early-nineteenth-century) document that the people of Tusik had hidden from the Spaniards. It, like the other Books of Chilam Balam, was an attempt to deal with issues inside of the community. It told of the conflict between the Christian God and the devil. In this case the author was introducing a moral story in which he told how the people of Tusik came to accept Catholicism. In so doing, he told a tale of the people, before accepting Catholicism, listening to the words of a deer, after which a certain person

> *ci yalabal cat yubah u than cehe cat bini ti y otoch cat yalah ti u chuplile ca a*
> *uohe te hach okom in uol tumen uchic in uuyic u than ceh binbin in cimes yn*
> *yum y in na hebac binel in cah in uutz cin tu sentenciail in keban maix in*
> *kat in cimes*

understood that which was said, the statement of the deer. He went home and said to his wife, "You know, my spirit is very gloomy because I heard the deer's statement that I will kill my father and my mother. But I am going to be good in the judgment of my sin. May I not want to kill them."[106]

Killing the father and the mother; had Oedipus really entered Yucatán by the eighteenth century? This clearly was the beginning of what Freud would determine to be an Oedipus complex (although with a twist: killing both the mother and the father). Here the father and the mother and the whole kinship line were replaced by the new kin of alliance: the Catholic priests.[107] In fact, it was Catholicism that saved this person. The son was to be good, and he asked the deer to allow him to escape this fate. He asked for the power of resistance, which he received, and he and the rest of the people accepted Catholicism and thus escaped the words of the deer. Here was the development of the individual subject as one who controlled his or her desires, an important aspect of the Catholic concept of sin. The son no longer accepted the words of the deer as his fate, but instead he recited an oration to Catholicism and the Christian God which prevented him from sinning. He had power over his actions, and his destiny was not predetermined. He became the subject of his own desires as opposed to the object of the desires of the deer, or so Catholicism would suggest. Yet, in fact, he was not in control of his own desires. Catholicism took over, and his desires still were not free. But this desire took an even more insidious turn: he was told that he was in control, but Catholicism told him what was sin and what was not.[108]

The confessionals and other more successful interventions into Maya norms proved to have a very strong effect in influencing Maya concepts of sin.[109] The hybrid conceptualization allowed the Maya to adapt to a new cultural phenomenon, colonialism. Many of these changes took place as the Maya nobles, attempting to retain their power as local elites, began to support various Spanish and Catholic cultural notions that they believed would enhance their positions. Additionally, many commoners, lacking access to political power and economic support in the Maya communities, left these communities for the Hispanic cities and most often adopted Hispanic culture only to bring that culture back to their kin. The alteration of Maya minds would not take place so easily, however, and hybridization became not just a strategy of the colonizers, but also an important piece of colonial resistance.

Sin was used as part of various strategies, some present inside the narrative, and some representative of larger changes in the power structure. The Maya, understanding the new hybrid concept of sin, revised old strategies and allowed for sin as a method of contexualizing sexual desire and other elements of culture. Sin was centered in a new concept of Self, a concept that encouraged the individual to believe that she or he was not predestined to commit certain acts. Now the individual subject would have to control his or her desires and was at fault when those desires were sinful. Catholicism and colonialism were able to use the concept of freedom of the individual to gain more control over that individual's actions and desires.

PERFORMING THE HYBRID

When colonial culture developed, the symbolic concepts of the warrior and the sinner came into conflict. As they struggled, the symbolism changed and altered the cultural matrix in order to develop a hybrid force. It was this hybridity that formed the desires discussed above, which were the results of the development and mixture of tradition and colonialism. Postconquest Maya desire was a particular mix of Spanish, Nahua, African, Mexican, and Maya conceptualizations of desire.

In essence, hybridity worked by, over time, altering Maya mental processes. Early in the colonial period both Spaniards and Maya believed that they clearly could distinguish Self from Other partly based on perceptions of gender and sexual desire. By late colonial times, a hybrid, specifically colonial, desire was created in which the Maya believed sexual desire to be formed in the hearts and minds of the warriors and in the ideas and perceptions of the sinners. Desire effectively had been reinscribed with new meaning, the meaning of the mixture. The reinscriptions discussed here primarily stemmed from the confusion of tongues present in colonialism.[110]

The documents discussed in this chapter, written in the eighteenth and early nineteenth centuries, represented late colonial adaptations to the cultural rules. For the Maya, sexual desire in the eighteenth century was not a misunderstood concept but rather was a concept placed in a hybrid cultural tradition. The warrior still was an important symbol in this understanding of desire, but the sinner was becoming more important. The mental processes of the Maya had changed to such an extent that they placed sexual desire in a different cultural matrix, one which combined sin and warfare.

In order to comprehend this concept of the hybrid matrix, I return to the figure of the Virgin Mary Moon Goddess. Once the Spanish conquest took place, the Moon Goddess retained much of her prior status, including her promiscuity and her ability to cure disease, but she underwent a name change. Her new name and identity, that of the Virgin Mary, was a name heavily invested with the power of the conquerors. But in what one may see as a rather unconscious usurpation of this power and privilege, the newly named goddess was claimed by the Maya people and invested with many of the qualities of the Moon Goddess. At the same time, however, the Maya began to be taught the story of the Virgin Mary in its traditional form. Maya mental processes were altered, and the new Virgin Mary, sexualized in a different way than her Spanish namesake, presented a story of Catholic morality. So the Maya neither maintained their traditions nor repressed them; they neither accepted the traditional Virgin Mary nor opposed her. They formed a hybrid figure, one with qualities which adhered to a new liminality, somewhere between a mother of Jesus and a goddess. The acceptance of the Virgin did not simply replicate the existence of the prior Moon Goddess: she did not survive; nor was she destroyed.

By the eighteenth century in Yucatán, the cultural matrix was altered such that the Maya viewed sin as an appropriate category within which to understand sexual desire. But sin did not exist simply by repressing the connections between sexuality, the Moon Goddess, and warfare. Instead, these connections themselves were reinscribed with new meanings. Between the sixteenth century and the eighteenth, a radical rupture had taken place, but this rupture had not destroyed the vestiges of Maya ways of knowing the world; it had developed a new cultural matrix with which to understand these ways of knowing.

FOUR

Fornicating with Priests, Communicating with Gods

During the colonial years, the Maya were able to use their interpretations of Catholic morality to assert control over members of their own communities and over Spaniards and others. Maya people used this understanding for individual and collective gains. Moreover, the Maya were able to develop a colonial moral code that was at once a creative enterprise, a repressive mechanism, and a resistance to Spanish intrusion. The Maya used rules and conventions of Catholicism, the legal system, and the political structure of the Spaniards. In effect, this was one central element that made colonial rule possible: the Maya used devices internal to the structure of the colonial state in order strategically to subvert the powers of certain officials. But in doing so, many Maya allied themselves with the colonial political system in a struggle in which that system was challenging Maya traditions.[1] The changing nature of colonial Maya sexual desire shows that desire and morality were altered by the infusion of a new culture.

HAVING SEX IN A CHURCH

The idea that sexual acts take place in the Catholic Church, particularly involving priests, is a very controversial topic in society today. This was no dif-

ferent during the colonial period, and both Mayas and Spaniards tried to exploit the situation.

ten cen ah hahal than cin ualic techex hebaxile a uohelex yoklal P^e torres p^e
dias cabo de escuadra P^e granado sargento yetel p^e maldonado layob la ma
hahal caput sihil ma hahal confisar ma hahal estremacion ma hahal misa cu
yalicobi maix tan u yemel hahal Dios ti lay ostia licil u yalicob misae tumenel
tutuchci u cepob sansamal kin chenbel u chekic ueyob cu tuculicob he tu yahal-
cabe manal tuil u kabob licil u baxtic u ueyob he p^e torrese chenbel u pel kakas
cisin rita box cu baxtic y u moch kabi mai moch u cep ualelob ix ɔoc cantul u
mehenob ti lay box cisin la baixan p^e diaz cabo de escuadra tu kaba u
cumaleil antonia aluarado xbolonchen tan u lolomic u pel u cumale tutan
tulacal cah y p^e granado sargento humab akab tan u pechic u pel manuela
pacheco hetun p^e maldonadoe tun ɔoc u lahchekic u mektanilobe uay cutalel u
chucbes u cheke yohel tulacal cah ti cutalel u ah semana uinic y xchup ti
pencuyute utial yoch pelil p^e maldonado xpab gomes u kabah chenbel padresob
ian u sipitolal u penob matan u than yoklalob uaca u ment utzil maçeuale
tusebal helelac ium cura u ɔaic u tzucte hetun lae tutac u kabob yetel pel lay
yaxcacbachob tumen u pen cech penob la caxuob yal misa bailo u yoli Dios ca
oc inglesob uaye ix ma aci ah penob u padreilobi hetun layob lae tei huni ma
u topob u yit uinicobe yoli Dios ca haiac kak tu pol cepob amen ten yumil ah
hahal than

I, the informer of the truth, tell you what you should know about
Father Torres, Father Díaz, squad corporal, Father Granado, sergeant,
and Father Maldonado. They say false baptism, false confession, false
last rites, false mass. Nor does the true God descend in the host when
they say mass, because they have stiff penises.[2] Every day all they think
of is intercourse with their mistresses.[3] In the morning their hands
smell bad from playing with their mistresses. Father Torres only plays
with the vagina of that ugly black devil Rita. He whose hand is disabled does not have a disabled penis. It is said he has up to four children by this black devil. Likewise, Father Díaz, squad corporal, has a
woman from Bolonchen called Antonia Alvarado, whose vagina he
repeatedly penetrates before the whole community, and Father Granado bruises Manuela Pacheco's vagina all night. Father Maldonado
has just finished fornicating with everyone in his jurisdiction and has
now come here to carry out his fornication. The whole community
knows this. When Father Maldonado makes his weekly visit, a woman

from Pencuyut named Fabiana Gómez provides him with her vagina. Only the priests are allowed to fornicate without so much as a word about it. If a good commoner[4] does that, the priest always punishes him immediately. But look at the priests' excessive fornication, putting their hands on these whores' vaginas, even saying mass like this. God willing, when the English come may they not be fornicators equal to these priests, who only lack carnal acts with men's anuses. God willing that smallpox be rubbed into their penis heads. Amen.

I, father, the informer of the truth.[5]

The Petition

This petition was received in the offices of the Holy Inquisition in 1774.[6] The anonymity of the petition as well as its rather shocking tone and explicit language set this text apart from all other known colonial era Maya documents. It therefore was not typical of its genre or representative of Maya thoughts on sexual behavior. Rather, the text is an example of a strategy in which the writer used the rules of Catholic morality to confront the priests. The text was at once both prudish (arguing that these sexual acts should not have taken place) and confrontational (taking a certain glee in using explicit descriptions). The writer turned the rules of Catholicism against the representatives of the Church. This text is central for my purposes, and the beginning of this chapter places this single narrative in its context, finding its genealogical importance. In this section I analyze the strategies implicit in the language of the document. A close deconstruction is necessary in order to understand the true mastery of this type of strategy.

This narrative was more than a functional piece, as in its context the petition told many stories about colonialism. It recovered much about Maya desire for the Spaniards, as well as Spanish desire for the Maya. The text told stories about the ways in which Maya people used disparate strategies in order to cope with Spanish rule. It told other stories about conflicts within Hispanic society. While our petitioner sounds like he left very little hidden, he actually hid much.

A close analysis of the petition will bring out many parallels with Franciscan thought[7] and show an area in which a cultural conquest perhaps did take place. The narrative was a conscious strategy in which the writer was attempting to gain some power over a situation which was not named. He began and ended the petition by describing himself as "the informer of the truth." He set up a situation which allowed him to remain anonymous, either for fear of retribution or to hide a connection with a member of the clergy, but still permitted his word to construct truth. Here the writer both placed the petition in the first person and demanded that the reader know that it was accurate. He represented himself as something of a courageous informant. The truth of the statement contrasted directly with the "false" baptisms, confessions, masses, and last rites performed by the priests. They were constructed precisely as the negation (*ma hahal*, "not true") of the element which the writer possessed (*hahal*, "truth"). These lines together strategized to convince the reader: a futile project, as I will show.

The statement about the "true God" again used the term *hahal*, in a common construction of a Maya reference to the Christian God. This legitimizing strategy referred back to the contrast between the writer and the priests. It also may have referred forward to the notion of Christ's body. The body here, represented as truth, did not descend in the host. Truth and the true God's body were lost with these priests because of their lack of truth and lack of celibacy. This body did not descend and was not eaten because the priests said mass while they had "stiff penises." These stiff penises likely related to the sexual acts of the priests. The mass was a false mass, one which did not allow access to the body of the true God. This lack of access to the host emanated from the stiff penises, *tutuchci u cepob*. The writer did not use the colonial Maya word translated as "erection," *thech*.[8] Instead he provided a description of the body part, which focused attention on the penis. Access to the host was denied because the priestly penis could not control itself.

The petitioner often chose to describe sexual acts by the sites where they took place. He did not use shorthand terms for sexual acts even when they existed in Maya. The priest "penetrated" the vagina of a woman.[9] Note that translations of sexual words were (and remain) quite imprecise. An accompanying Spanish translation simply used *joder* ("to fuck") for *lolomic*. But this translation used *joder* for several different sexual terms. The modern Maya use the term *top* (discussed below) in situations where mestizos might use the term *joder*.[10] The next line substantiated a similar point. Another priest "bruised" the vagina of a certain woman. The Maya *u pechic u pel* probably was some slang for having intercourse, but it could also have referred to rape or to some other violent sexual encounter. I cannot determine the precise nature of what it meant to "bruise Manuela Pacheco's vagina." Toward the end of the petition, the writer objected vehemently to anyone who had "carnal acts with men's anuses." Even these priests did not do that. The petitioner chose terms which related directly to the body parts involved in the sexual acts. Whether the vagina or the anus or the hand, the writer wanted to talk about the body parts in order to discuss the acts. It seems likely that the petitioner used these extended descriptions in order to maximize the insult to the priests.

All of these descriptions related back to Christ's body itself. The writer, beginning with his description of the priestly penises, used the narrative to show (however indirectly) that Christ's body was blocked by the bodies of the priests. Their bodies in a sense replaced Christ's body and forced the community to do without any communication with God. The petition demanded that the priests focus their energies on recalling the host and adhere to their vows of celibacy. This section of the petition was analogous to the Franciscan texts which demanded strong adherence to celibacy in order for the friars to maintain their ritual unions with Christ and God. Likewise the petition requested celibacy in order for the priests to regularize their union with Christ.

It is this desire for Christ that was most central to the petition. Whatever desires the Maya may have had before the conquest, by two centuries later, their initial desires had been displaced onto Christ and his body. This was an act of colonialism where the Spaniards and the clergy in particular had been able to convince at least some of the Maya to change their beliefs and even their desires. The text desired Christ's body as it demanded that the body descend properly in the host. It could not have done so if the priests were engaged in these sinful acts. Our writer had a close affiliation with and attraction to Christ's body. This body, then, signified a colonialist homoeroticism, present not just here but in any colonial system where the colonizers demanded that the people prostrate themselves before the body of a male god. Indeed, at least some of the men and women of the society displaced their desires onto the bodies of Christ and Saint Francis.

But, alas, this desire itself may have been a false notion. I do not know who wrote this petition. Nor is it possible to know what was "true" and "false" here. In such a petition to the Inquisition, the petitioner likely automatically would say that he wanted Christ to descend in the host. This was a good strategy for anybody requiring a favor from Catholic authorities. Nonetheless, as genealogy shows, the intent of the writer did not matter as much as the textual use:[11] here it was an entirely plausible assertion that this Maya community and its nobles desired the body of Christ.

But did they also desire the women with whom the priests were said to be having affairs? These women were mentioned immediately after the petition discussed the stiff penises. The word I translate as mistress came from *uey*, which the dictionary inscribed as "mistress, concubine, or girlfriend."[12] The context here showed the women as sexualized beings. The narrative only mentioned them through their sexual relationships with the priests. It began by positing these women as the recipients of priestly thoughts about intercourse. These women linguistically were possessed by the priests. Indeed, the women signified the violations of celibate thought and action which formed the central complaints of the petition.[13]

As the narrative continued, the writer feigned disgust at "the bad smell" of the priests' hands from "playing" with their mistresses. The word for play, *baxtic* or *baxtah*, also meant to "handle" or to "paw."[14] Here *baxtic* signified some type of play that involved pawing at somebody or handling her. The petitioner used *baxtic* in the very next line of the petition, saying that one priest played only with the vagina of a black woman. The writer used the smell of the priests' hands as a legitimizing technique in the petition. Their hands smelled of sex; therefore they must have been engaging in sex. The smell itself was a strategy designed to prove the validity of the claim. The writer also revealed the male hand as a sexual organ. The hand may have played with a vagina, an anus, or any other part of the women's bodies, but it certainly played with some parts of their bodies in a sexual manner. The smell of the hands was proof of sexual acts. And the petitioner toyed with this idea when he found that Father Torres had a disabled hand: this did not mean that he could not engage in sexual acts, for he did not have a disabled penis.

The hands and penises of the priests found that they were attracted to the women who signified the violations of celibacy. And who were these women? First was Rita, a black woman constructed as a "black devil." Next was Antonia Alvarado from Bolonchen, and finally Fabiana Gómez from Pencuyut. First they were described as mistresses (*ueyob*) and then as whores (*yaxcacba-chob*).[15] These women received the blame for taking the priests away from the community. The women were named as outsiders both ethnically and politically. As Maya women would have had Maya surnames, the narrative showed the women with the surnames Alvarado and Gómez as women connected with the Hispanic community. They were constructed (whatever the "truth" of their lineages) in the narrative as belonging to the outside. And they were seen as possessions of the priests. The black woman, Rita, also was constructed as an ethnic outsider and an enemy. The ethnic construction of woman as outsider also implicitly may have critiqued interracial sexual relations. In addition, Fabiana Gómez and Antonia Alvarado came from places constructed as outsider communities, Bolonchen and Pencuyut.[16] The narrative presented these as outsider towns, despite Spanish understanding of them as Maya, pointing to the centrality of the community in the determination of ethnic identity.[17] The narrative constructed the women as outsiders and enemies, as they belonged to the world exterior to the local group. These statements were an attempt to denigrate others through the utilization of a gendered construct. Gender was an element in a sexualized narrative that based itself on an insider/outsider dichotomy. The outsiders therefore were women who did not belong.[18]

The women were both the objects of the priests' attentions and those who lured the priests into sin. The priestly violations of celibacy were possible only because of these women and their vaginas. Their identities were based on their vaginas and their sexual relationships with the priests. They were the lure to priestly violations in both thought and deed.

There also was a note of jealousy on the part of the petitioner. Desire was displaced as the writer wanted more attention from the priests. He wanted the priests brought back inside the community. There was a homoerotic desire, however unconscious, on the part of the male members of the community, and the bodies of the priests themselves signified this desire. The priests had become outsiders to the community, and the petitioner wanted them to regain their status as insiders. He wanted the priests to penetrate the community and give him the attention given to the women.

The petitioner, clearly taking a certain glee in writing about the women's body parts, appeared also to be jealous of the priests. The narrative said explicitly that, if commoners were to do this, they would have been punished severely by the priests. So the text itself suggested that the people of the community wished to engage in these acts. They desired these women. This is, of course, a displaced desire, and it certainly was not the central desire of the text. But it signified the bi-eroticism of desire placed in the narrative. The local group desired the bodies of Christ, the priests, and the women, all differentiated and divided, but still all desired.

Class and colonial divisions were used in the sexual discourse as the term *masehual* (which translated as "commoner") was used to represent all of the Maya people. The term had a universalizing application, suggesting the poverty of all. It was a strategy designed to show that the officials should have taken pity on the community. Here the strategy displaced the desire for difference inside the community with a desire for difference from the priests. As the commoners desired the women, the narrative suggested that the whole community desired them (leaving aside, for now, the question of whether this desire could have been representative of the desires of Maya women).

There are parallels between the way women were discussed here and the role of women in Franciscan texts. The Franciscans, trained to view women as those who would lure them away from celibacy, found a text in which priests were lured away from their vows. The petitioner might have presumed that a good Franciscan, trained to regard women as dangerous, should not have allowed such a situation to take place. This complaint was contextualized by the desire for Saint Francis, a desire to gain access to the host or the true God or the body of Jesus through what might have been considered a superior order. This petition was a sexualized text which fit into a strategy of a struggle occurring inside the late-eighteenth-century Catholic Church.

Franciscan Concepts

The desires presented above were symbolic, and they require some context. This document was sent from a local Maya town to Inquisition officials. This particular Inquisition case, however, did not accuse these four priests of anything. The case involved a Franciscan friar, Manuel Antonio de Rivas, who was accused of various improprieties. The four priests (also friars) were involved actively in the case against Rivas. The case was about the contest then taking place among these clergy. Rivas was accused by Granado, one of the four, of making "heretical propositions." Rivas also was accused of the "nefarious sin" (sodomy), but this accusation disappeared early in the case. The document in question was part of the defense case, and it is likely that its production was influenced rather heavily by Rivas. The most likely writer certainly was a close ally or Maya aide of his.[19] I argue, however, based on one mistake in the description of Catholic ritual, that the friar himself did not write the petition. It is very unlikely that the friar would have used the term "true God" to describe the deity who would not descend in the host (it should have been Christ). This mistake shows that, while the petition was influenced heavily by the friar (who may have even witnessed its production), the actual words placed on the paper did not correspond directly with his thoughts.

The writer used a sexualized discourse to make a persuasive but unstated argument about his preference for Rivas over the others. The text used the Church's own sexual code to overcome the power differential between the community and the priests. This petition followed a genre of anticlerical petitions found among the Maya and the Nahuas. Both groups often stated that the priests violated their vows of celibacy, abused the confessional, and assaulted indigenous officials.[20] Most often, the petitioners demanded to receive the proper sacraments.[21] This genre shows that the authors of the petitions among both the Maya and the Nahuas understood many of the technical aspects of Catholicism extremely well.

This petition was not just an attempt to defend an errant friar. It was an attempt to show a great knowledge of and affinity for the Franciscan order.

The petitioner clearly knew a large amount about Catholic thought. He demanded that the priests not violate their own vows of celibacy. He understood that the priestly violations of these vows interfered with Maya access to the Christian God through the host. If the host was taken to be Christ's body, then this body may have been a symbol for the loss experienced by the community because of the priests' sins. The implicit request, that the officials remove these priests instead of the friar, played into the power struggle that was taking place. The explicit request, "that smallpox be rubbed into . . . [the priests'] penis heads," was an extreme version of the implicit request.

In the early to mid sixteenth century, the Franciscans developed a strong sense of their mission, believing the idea of instructing the Indians to have great biblical importance.[22] Relatively quickly, however, the friars became disappointed with many of the various indigenous groups.[23] By the late eighteenth century, the zeal of the early Franciscans was lost. But these later friars still found themselves engaged in strong combat both with the other orders and with the secular clergy. This combat included attempts at proselytizing in Yucatán, where many conflicts took place.

The Franciscans dominated the clergy in Yucatán for most of the colonial period. They engaged in many rhetorical battles with the Spanish settlers, particularly the more powerful *encomenderos* and political leaders.[24] The Franciscans often believed that they should have the charge of instructing the Maya people, and the dominance of the order showed their success. Probably because of Yucatán's relatively slow economic growth when compared with central Mexico, the Franciscans continued to dominate the territory throughout the colonial period. They were granted an exclusive right to establish their order in the entire area, and they successfully resisted challenges from the secular clergy. In the eighteenth century, the Franciscans still had exclusive control over a large number of parishes, and they held control over approximately 36 percent of the Maya people until independence.[25] While Nancy Farriss's research demonstrates Franciscan dominance of Yucatán, she also shows that by the late eighteenth century the secular clergy had gained a very strong foothold. The Franciscans and the secular clergy engaged in a battle for control.

I do not know if the petitioner or the nobles of his community understood much about the Franciscans beyond what was implied in the petition, but the narrative itself showed some relationship with Franciscan history. No doubt Rivas or another friar had trained the author of the petition and other local Maya leaders, giving them knowledge of this history and philosophy. The early part of the petition related to the body of the true God, here implying some confusion with Christ's body. This body could not descend in the host because the priests had engaged in mortal sin. Indeed, this itself showed a strong knowledge of Catholic thought on the matter. This contrasted strongly with perceptions of the Franciscan relationship to the bodies of Christ and Saint Francis, in which the friars, through Christ's body, following Francis, engaged in a mystical marriage with God.[26] Ramón Gutiérrez explains that the union between Christ and the friars was both erotic and painful. Christ on the cross was shown as torn between "joy and despair as he approached his Father."[27] While the soul engaged in a mystical union with Christ and God, one should recall that the union certainly was perceived as a chaste one.[28] The Franciscan friars understood their relationship as a chaste union with God, but one mediated by Christ's crucified body. Their relationship with Christ's body allowed them to recall that body in the host.

The petitioner here specifically complained that because of the sins of the clergy, the people of the community could not obtain the body of God through the host. God's (and perhaps Christ's) body was perceived as lacking in the ceremonies mediated by these priests. The relationship of the Franciscans to Christ's body should have suggested that a good Franciscan friar (at least the one defended in this case) would have obtained access to it. The Franciscan spiritual formation was an important element, even if unrecognized by (and perhaps unknown to) the petition's author, in the strategy of the text.

The early Franciscan texts demanded that the friars, like all Catholic clergy, engage in a rigorous celibacy. The chronicles of the Franciscan saints which were read by the friars in their training showed a very strong erotic connection both with women and with sexual self-control, as men exposed their bodies to "icy pools of water" in order to extinguish their passions.[29] Ecclesiastes stated, "more bitter than death I find the woman who is a hunter's trap, whose heart is a snare and whose hands are prison bonds. He who is pleasing to God will escape her, but the sinner will be entrapped by her."[30] The petition found many parallels in Franciscan thought. Similar to this statement, the demand for a rigorous celibacy was a central point of the petition. The statement also demonized certain women, much like the petition, which demanded that the priests adhere to the standards represented in the brand of Catholic thought to which the Maya had the most exposure.

For the Franciscans the only appropriate union for a messenger of God was a union with God, Christ, and Saint Francis. This union, as a specifically pleasurable act, should have allowed all clergy to focus on their duties. The homoerotic relationship with the male gods was seen as chaste, but still extremely pleasurable. One can certainly wonder what the Maya thought of such a union when they began to understand it. Certainly Maya relationships with their own gods were pleasurable, but far from chaste.[31] Would their sexual desire here have been displaced onto Saint Francis? The text stated that the central symbolic desire was for God, Christ, and Saint Francis. The implicit request was for the choice of Rivas over the other four friars. It was this (displaced) desire for Saint Francis that presented a background motivation for the petition and its strong language.

Of course, the conscious motivation for the petition was to defend a particular friar. In an accompanying note, an Inquisition official in Mérida called the charges against the priests "audacious" and "unfounded."[32] The fact that some Maya people got involved in a power struggle where most likely the results would have few real effects on them highlighted the displacement strategy of colonialism. By getting the Maya involved in these types of disputes, supposedly to curb abuses against them, the Spaniards had successfully displaced much anticolonial fervor. The colonial authorities remained uncriticized as the Maya engaged in a battle that largely was irrelevant to colonial rule and which would have few lasting effects on their lives.[33]

STRATEGIC INVERSIONS

When a petition such as the one cited here exists, it must be recalled that some Maya people (almost always representing a particular town council, the above case being a notable exception) took the time to write a document in their own language complaining of the abuses. In no case can I prove that the acts took place, and it is likely that some of these allegations were false. The charges signified particular strategies in which the Maya attempted to resist some of the worst abuses of Spanish colonial rule.

The Maya developed many strategies to understand their colonization:[34] strategies signifying not overt resistance, but an attempt to achieve adjustments to the colonial order. In many ways the documents resulting from this strategy ironically showed some of the most acculturated arguments.[35] In this context the Maya understood and used Spanish ideas of proper and improper behavior. They used Spanish concepts of morality against particular priests and other Spaniards.

This has been a common strategy used by colonized peoples. They often engaged in strategic inversion of various kinds. Any analysis of colonialism must account for the fact that most colonized peoples used the institutions of the colonizers in order to defend themselves, resist the colonizers, and resolve internal and often long festering disputes.[36] This is what I call strategic inversion, and in this section I have included a series of cases in which the Maya used sexual desire and gender norms to subvert portions of the colonial project. They inverted power relationships by claiming Spanish legal procedures and moral codes for themselves. Indeed, I have found that the Maya, when they could use Spanish rules against Spaniards, did not hesitate to do so. And other scholars have shown that there existed similar strategic inversions in many other indigenous societies both inside and outside of Latin America.[37]

These inversions often were both conscious and unconscious. The Maya nobles (and some commoners) began to understand what the Spaniards wanted to hear, and they told them this in order to gain particular privileges. Then many of those same Maya people came to believe the very stories that they had told. It thus was an unconscious strategy, in the end an acculturative and colonizing device, but a strategic inversion nonetheless.

Importantly, the cases described here linked sexuality directly with power. In the above selection, the petitioner intervened in an Inquisition case in order to defend one particular priest against the onslaught of others, so he was seeking to gain some power over a legal process, and he used sexual desire as the central point to make his case. In these cases indigenous peoples were seeking to empower themselves, often at the expense of others, through the use of a sexualized discourse.

Using Catholicism against Clergy

Maya-language petitions commonly complained about clerical abuse. The genre was a common strategy for removal of a priest. The anonymous text under discussion used strategic inversion to gain power over the four priests. The clergy, as the representatives of Christianity, had much power over the Maya communities, but this power was inverted (even if it was in the context of an internal Church dispute) by a Maya petitioner using the clergy's very prerogatives to complain about them. The Maya thus desired compassion from the officials and an understanding of the abuses against their bodies. These desires played a major role in the strategic inversion of power.

Such a genre of petitions existed almost wherever the Spanish ruled, but it was most entrenched among the Nahuas. In a typical complaint from Jalostotitlan, near Guadalajara, a 1611 petition arguing for the removal of a priest stated, "(The accusation) is not empty, because our father keeps a lady there at the *estancia*."[38] The petition went on to say how the priest had beaten the petitioner. In a fashion similar to the 1774 Maya petition, this Nahuatl document used the priestly violation of celibacy to show the veracity of the statement, which accused the priest of violent abuses. This priest kept a woman at the *estancia*, probably having an affair with her. Such a statement showed the impropriety of the priest and was a strategy designed to get rid of him. The woman was shown only in relation to this priest, and she attained less importance than the women in the Maya narrative. The important point here was the relationship between the petitioner, who testified in the first person,[39] and the priest. The priest abused his power in the community by beating this official. The petition used the woman, constructed as an outsider, as an example which legitimized the narrative.

But this was not the only example of the priest's sexual improprieties: "Once my daughter Catalina Juana went there to the church in the evening to sweep, and there in the church our father seized her and wanted to have her. She would not let him, and there inside the church he beat her. Then she came to complain to me."[40] This time the woman was an insider, representing the community. The priest attempted to rape her much as he abused the town. She denied him what he wanted, thereby maintaining her innocence in the matter. She was represented as a person in need of protection, much as the community needed protection from this priest. She came to complain to her father, who then legitimized the complaint through this narrative. The Nahuatl document was an important example of this genre. The text used the priest's sexual acts in order to make the petition seem more legitimate. It incorporated complaints of both physical and sexual abuse. It demanded the removal of the priest in order to end this violation of the community.

This Nahuatl document had many parallels[41] with Maya texts, including the following petition from several Maya communities. In 1589 another priest, Andrés Mejía, forced Maya women to have sex with him in order for them to receive confession:

> *hahi lae he tilic u ɔaic confesar ti cħuplalobe tilic yalic ua matan a ɔab aba tene matan y ɔab confesar tech lay licil u payic cħuplal ti matan u ɔab confesar ti ua matan u talel cħuplal tamuk u pakic u keban cħuplalob matan u ɔab confesar ti lay u hahil tulacal baix u coilob tu ɔacan cħuplal xan u canan tech . . . tix maxul u kime cech ca yume*
>
> *Apalilon ti Don Ju^u cool gor petu Don fran^co utz tahɔiu g^or alcaldesob tulacal*

This is the truth: While he gives confession to women, he says, "If you do not give yourself to me, I will not give you confession."[42] This is how he abuses the women. He will not give them confession unless

the women go to him. Unless the women fornicate[43] with him, he
will not give them confession. This is the whole truth about why the
women are so upset. We thus appeal to . . . you with your infinite
[wisdom], our lord.

—Filed by don Juan Cool, governor[44] of Petu,
don Francisco Utz, governor of Tahdziu, and all of the alcaldes.[45]

This is only the end of the document, of which, in the fashion of this genre,
the vast majority was used for reverential phrases.[46] The authors strategized
to remove the priest by flooding the Inquisitors with compliments and declaring that the priest attempted to have sex with women in these towns. The
priest here not only violated his own vows, but he also violated the trust of
the communities.[47]

The petition validated its own allegations in the narrative as it claimed to
represent the truth several times. The women were written as insiders, representing the community, at once violated and resistant. They demanded that
the Inquisition address their complaints. The women were provoked and
abused, but they did not succumb. Instead they became angry and asked to
have the priest removed. The male leaders, the protectors of the community,
were the protectors of the women, who demanded that the men act. The
women were shown as part of the community, but as subordinate to the men.

The gendering of the petition was a traditional pattern for the Maya, as
men wrote the documents. But here the act of gendering in the petition extended to the political realm. According to both Maya and Spanish gender
systems, men protected women. In the petition the Maya men played the role
of protectors (the male role). The Maya women were those who were threatened and abused, so they played the victims (the female role). In the broader
context, however, it was the Maya community that was threatened and that
needed defending. It thus was the Maya town that was victimized (playing the
female role). The community asked for the protection of Spanish officials, who
thus played the role of the protector (the male role). The priest played an inappropriate male role: that of the aggressor.[48] At this point the Maya understood many elements of the Spanish gender system. The Maya saw that they
had to play the female role in order to get protection. The Maya then gendered their petitions such that they would be seen as the appropriate recipients: the women to the Spanish men (of course they played the role of women
at least somewhat unconsciously; if someone asked them if they were playing
women to the Spanish men, they most likely would have said no, although
some of them understood their own ritualized feminization).

The women were required to give the priest their bodies. Many of the priests, particularly the secular clergy, were seen as necessarily having sexual desires, which could be contrasted effectively with the good Franciscans, whose desires were played out in their (sexual) relationships with Saint Francis, Christ, and God (and perhaps the Virgin Mary as well). It was this appearance of ritual homoeroticism (bi-eroticism?) which saved many Franciscans in the minds of the Maya. The Maya displaced Franciscan desire (for power over Maya hearts and minds) onto a desire for homoeroticism. This counter-colonial maneuver in fact may have signified one central way in which the Franciscans were able successfully to colonize Maya sexual desire. This, then, was a desire for Saint Francis as opposed to a desire for the traditional Maya gods.

In these petitions, the priests were shown as sexual aggressors. The women in the anonymous petition were presented, as in the Franciscan (and other ecclesiastic) formative training, as sexually alluring outsiders who could corrupt clerics and drive them away from God. In the Nahuatl petition, there was a direct contrast between a woman shown as an outsider who herself was unimportant, and a woman shown as an insider who signified the innocent victim of priestly aggression. The final Maya petition showed women in several Maya communities as victims of the priest. The priestly vows of celibacy were manipulated in this discourse in order to enact a strategic inversion of power relationships. Sexual desire was an element which allowed the petitioners access to political and religious action, but this same notion of sexual desire reiterated Maya colonization by forcing the Maya to become better acquainted with Spanish moral codes. The priests were people who could not bring God properly to the community. This did not change from the sixteenth century to the eighteenth. Yet other priests were implicitly, comparatively, supported in these petitions as it was supposed that they would be better than the current clergy. Desire was displaced onto a different clergy, but one that was Catholic and supported the Catholic configuration of the cosmos: preconquest Maya gods were not present here.

Colonialism and Celibacy

For preconquest Maya priests, celibacy was a temporary constraint. The priests were expected to refrain from sexual activity only during preparation for ritual ceremonies.[49] Even then, in certain ceremonies the priests may have been expected to perform particular sexual acts.[50] It is clear that the Maya did not believe in lifelong celibacy.[51]

The Catholic clergy must have seemed odd indeed. They demanded a rigorous celibacy of themselves and an adherence to strict sexual morality, including virginity before marriage and monogamy after, for all people.[52] One would think that the Maya could hardly have understood these demands any more than they understood the concept of sin. Yet, within several generations, the Maya were found demanding that the clergy adhere to their vows of celibacy. What happened to Maya beliefs and desires in this period?

Two different concepts appeared in the documents. First, the Maya learned Catholic ethics extremely well. After several generations with the Spanish population present in Yucatán, the Maya had learned how to behave like Catholics, at least when Spaniards were around. Second, the Maya had learned that the Franciscans would have been better for them than the secular clergy. The Franciscans at least represented an alternative voice to that of the *encomendero*, while the secular priest was likely to be a member of or a close ally of the *encomendero*'s family.[53] Here the Maya were reduced to arguing for a lesser of two evils.

The Maya learned how to behave like Catholics primarily from two sources: local Spaniards and Hispanized, urbanized Maya. In order to gain political and economic power, the nobles needed to communicate with local Spaniards. They thus learned more about those Spaniards, and they began to replicate some of their actions. Also, as Maya community members were brought into Hispanic cities, these people became disassociated with Maya norms and more closely associated with the norms of their employers. But they did not always disassociate themselves from their family and other members of their community.[54] They brought some knowledge of Spanish/Catholic culture back to their towns.

Imparted in this knowledge were stories about sin and celibacy. The Maya knew that, if the clergy did not adhere to a rigorous celibacy, they could not have access to Christ's body. This certainly was a familiar theme to them, as nobles had always controlled their access to the gods. So celibacy became a central concern of the Maya. Additionally, the Maya knew that they could gain some power over the local priests by appealing to higher authorities. They thought that the violations of celibacy would be treated seriously by those authorities.

The power of the Franciscans partly was in their similarity with Maya traditions. The Maya saw the relationship between the Franciscans and Saint Francis as reminiscent of their own relationships with their gods. This relationship was one of desire: the Maya desired sexual fulfillment with the gods, just as the Franciscans were seen as desiring an intimate and sexual relationship with Saint Francis. This desire thus displaced, the Maya could understand the Franciscans. Moreover, they knew that they could use some Franciscans (as well as Inquisition authorities) as leverage against other friars, the secular clergy, and other local Spaniards. An attempt to maintain celibacy thus was an attempt to gain power over colonialism.

EXCESS SEX: ADULTERY, RAPE, AND THE COMMONERS

The clergy attempted to gain influence over sexual desire, although with limited success, as can be seen through the campaign against Maya concubinage. In this effort, the clergy complained that concubinage was a sign of "moral decay." Yet many of the cases cited by the clergy were perfectly legitimate unions in Maya eyes. Maya officials resisted any attempt at punishing these "concubines." The Maya nobles similarly resisted punishing people declared "adulterers" by the Spanish clergy, only punishing those seen as such based on Maya ideas of marriage and divorce.[55] Spanish and Maya ideas of what concubinage and adultery meant came into conflict. The Spanish gained some influence over bodily and sexual definitions by engaging in a discussion about those definitions.[56] Nonetheless, the Maya defended their traditions, not necessarily by actively resisting Spanish intrusion into this sphere, but simply by attempting to continue to engage in sexual practices based on their own moral codes.[57] This engagement combined with the instructions of the clergy and other Spaniards to form a hybrid sexual tradition.

Terminology of Sex

Translating sexual terminology is always a problematic exercise because of the different boundaries of the sexual terms in the languages. Those who have studied sexual behavior in ancient Greece have found that various terms represented elements of sexual behavior which we in contemporary Western societies do not understand, much less categorize. Moreover, in many cases, elements of sexual behavior which we categorize and posit as identities intrinsic to the individual were not comprehended as such by people in the ancient world.[58] The same difficulties exist for attempts at translating Maya sexual terms.

As noted above, the petition of 1774 described the placement of sexual acts on the human body.[59] These acts were described quite specifically but did not translate easily into English or Spanish. On several occasions the author used the word *chekic*, which I have translated as "intercourse." While I believe this to be an accurate translation of the word in its context, the colonial dictionaries contained several other translations, the relevant one here being "for a male animal to cover a female in order to make them fruitful and reproduce." The phrase *ah chek* was translated as a "stud of any species of animal," *ah* being a masculine agentive, meaning "he who does" something.[60] In a selection from the Ritual of the Bacabs, I translated *chek* as "submerge." Indeed, in that situation the curer used various genitals to "submerge" or "penetrate" a particular male god, perhaps to conquer that god, and certainly to cure a disease. In that context the "submerging" of *chek* involved the curer using the god's lineage to engage in some sort of ritualized sexual act with that god.[61]

In the petition *chek* was a sexualized term relating to intercourse. In this interpretation, intercourse was connected both with ritual sexual behavior with a god and sexual behavior among animals. This could have signified a general word for sexual behavior, but the way this term was used in the petition and the curing ceremony both suggest that this would be too broad an interpretation. The petition only used *chek* in specific circumstances, and it did not use the term when describing most of the sexual activity of the priests. In the curing ceremony the term signified a notion of submersion and penetration which may have incorporated what we might see as both sexual and nonsexual aspects. "What *we* might see" is the key phrase, as sexual boundaries were different among the colonial Maya than those that exist among contemporary Western people.

The last portion of the anonymous petition used the word *pen* to describe the sexual acts of the priests. In each case where the writer used *pen*, I translated it as "fornication" in general. *Pen* may have implied some abstraction of sexual acts, while *chek* and individual descriptions evoked a sense of the immediate situation. The colonial dictionaries translated *pen* as "the sin of lust," "to fornicate," "the sin of sodomy," "the nefarious sin," "for one man to sin with another," and "to prostitute oneself."[62] This author described the priests as *ah penob*, translated as "fornicators."[63] The word for "sodomite," *ix pen*, switched the feminine agentive, *ix*, for the masculine agentive, *ah*.

The colonial dictionaries, as documents written primarily by Franciscan friars, represented an attempt at translation which cannot be idealized. The Franciscans likely searched long and hard for a term which they could interpret as suggesting forms of sexual behavior which Franciscan thought would have decided were sinful. They seem to have found that term in *pen*. The word reflected a negotiated meaning developed during the colonial period. *Pen*, which may or may not have described sexual behavior which society determined "excessive" (see below), came to mean particular acts which were sinful in the Christian world.[64] The important point here is that, as I attempt a genealogy, I do not search directly for the origins of the term, but rather look at its uses before and after the conquest.[65] As the Franciscans attempted to convince the Maya that certain acts were wrong, they searched for terms that provided a negative connotation. They then revised the meanings of those terms; they used the act of translation in order to gain power. The revised meanings penetrated Maya society through the more Christianized Maya, and eventually the meanings actually did change, as did morality. Colonialism and translation thus were linked.[66]

Spanish Narratives

To Diego de Landa, in most cases the Maya deserved praise for their treatment of sexual behavior. He found that the preconquest Maya punished adulterers severely:

> It was their custom to punish adultery in this manner: Once the investigation was completed and a person was convicted of adultery, the leaders gathered at the lord's house and brought the adulterer, tied to a piece of wood, delivering him to the husband of the offending woman. If he pardoned him, the man was freed. If not, he killed him by dropping a large stone on top of his head. . . . For the woman, the infamy, which was great, was sufficient punishment. Commonly [her husband] left her for this.[67]

Landa clearly believed that men controlled the entire connection between sexual desire and the legal sphere. In Landa's narrative, the woman played no role except as victim. The text (together with the fact that Landa did not mention adultery elsewhere) suggests that the wife could not charge the husband with adultery. Moreover, the woman's husband was given a powerful position in this narrative. He was a victim who then ably used the law to empower himself. He received retribution, as the punishment clearly was payment for the husband's loss. Landa interpreted particular meanings from his understanding of Maya adultery, but he did not understand the intricacies of Maya sexual desire or gender relations.

Landa's narrative showed many elements of his own strategy. He gave no sign of moral approval or condemnation of this system, so he remained strategically neutral. Adultery was condemned in the narrative, but he remained a neutral observer of the Maya legal system. Landa's writings evoked a certain

tone in which he condemned only that which directly contradicted Catholic
teaching. Adultery was used in the narrative as an example of how the Maya
people and the Europeans had some things in common, and how both moral
systems could be interpreted in a positive light. While the narrative attempted
to shed light on the process of adultery in the Maya world, it paid little attention to the meaning that the people attributed to these acts.

Landa's commentary stressed a colonial domination which asserted a particular ethnographic view that skewed Maya gender relations. Landa attempted to reinscribe Maya gender and sexual desire through his discourse:
"The Indians are very dissolute in drinking and becoming intoxicated, from
which many evils follow. They kill each other; they violate the [women's]
beds, the poor women thinking they are receiving their husbands; they also
treat their fathers and mothers as if they were in the houses of enemies; they
set fire to their houses, and with this they destroy themselves in their drunk-
enness."[68] From the vantage point of a Catholic system of morality, Landa
determined that the Maya people engaged in excessive behavior during the
festivities. Yet Landa's narrative here differed from both his discussion of
adultery and his condemnation of idolatry. In the adultery discussion Landa
found himself able to praise the Maya for maintaining a system in line with
Catholic morality. He even implicitly found that the situation decayed after
the conquest. Regarding idolatry, Landa swiftly and strongly condemned the
Maya for the evils of this system of worship. To Landa, the ritual festivities signified excess and sin. Yet the Maya officially sanctioned these festivals. Landa
must have been confused, wondering how the Maya could condemn adultery
so strongly and then have these types of rituals. How could the Maya not have
considered these "orgies" excessive and sinful? The conflicts in the systems of
meaning regarding sexual desire were presented as some confusion in which
the Maya were seen as people who could control some elements of their lives
but not others.

For Landa, such excess was a violation of what he understood about the
Maya. In most aspects, Landa described the Maya as a group of people who
maintained moderate and moral lifestyles. For example, he declared Maya
women extremely chaste. They thus earned his respect. "I once received the
complaint of a baptized Indian woman against a baptized man who followed
her, enamored with her because of her beauty. After he waited until her husband was called away, one night he went to her house. When his many pleas
did not work, and his offer of gifts was not accepted, he attempted force. . . .
For the whole night she fought him off." And this woman was no exception:
"The women had this habit of turning their backs toward the men when they

passed them. . . . They taught their daughters this knowledge and raised them excellently in their image. They scolded them, instructed them, and made them work. If they misbehaved, they punished them by pinching their ears or their arms."[69] The narrative here moves from the individual situation to the more general principle. Landa implicitly critiqued male aggression and supported the chaste woman who did not commit adultery. She resisted because she learned from other women who showed her how to act. The women educated each other and made sure that the men could not corrupt their daughters. Here Landa promoted a traditional Catholic morality by stating that the women were very moral, perhaps following Mary. Such morality fit well with Landa's program. At the same time Landa implicitly criticized the morals of Maya men. They got drunk, surprised women in their beds, and attempted to rape them.

In another context, Landa made a similar point, now, however, developing a narrative of decline related to the colonial era:

In old times they married at the age of twenty, but now they marry at that of twelve or thirteen. Therefore, they divorce more easily as they marry without love, and they are ignorant of the married life and the duties of marriage. . . . Men with children also easily left their wives with no fear that others might take them as wives, or that they themselves might later return. Nonetheless, they are very jealous and have no patience with their wives' infidelities. Now that they see that the Spaniards kill their own wives for this reason, they are beginning to mistreat and even kill their wives.[70]

In Landa's story, a gendered norm where one society did not allow men to kill their wives for infidelity lost to a gendered norm of another society which did allow men to do this. This was a strategy in which Landa critiqued Maya men through a criticism of Hispanic norms.[71] This criticism showed that gender was a central marker for his narrative.

Landa here worked to colonize by making gender in the Maya world virtually identical to Catholic conceptions of gender in the Hispanic world. Sex was seen as a weapon, and gender was representative of difference. In this piece of Landa's narrative, Maya women came to symbolize Catholicism just as Maya men came to symbolize idolatry. Sexual desire symbolized the connection between the two and, thus empowered, may either have symbolized that which allowed Catholicism to flourish in Maya society (a combination of abstinence and moderate sexual behavior within marriage) or that which forced Catholicism to submit to idolatrous beliefs (rape, adultery, and other sexual acts which did not reflect moderation in marriage). Here was the use of gender for a particular goal: colonization.

Colonialism was tricky indeed. Landa associated himself with the Maya women, thus perhaps gendering himself and the Franciscans in a particular way. The Maya men were associated with the more corrupt elements of Spanish men. The gendered discourse asserted Landa's colonialism as an alternative to the losses of secular colonialism. But Landa enforced the rule of the Virgin Mary, a rule that forced women to attempt to achieve an impossible ideal.

Another discourse on Maya sexual behavior was evidenced in the early narratives of the Spanish settlers. The *Relaciones Geográficas de Yucatán* were texts written in response to questionnaires sent out from Spain.[72] The local officials often believed that it was in their best interest (probably to get the crown's attention and spur immigration) to say that the Indians had customs hospitable to Spanish ideals. Thus the reliability of the *Relaciones* varied greatly. When discussing Maya sexual behavior, many of the *Relaciones* agreed: "The men did not have more than one wife. They did not eat more than once a day and they were enemies of the vices of the flesh. They took these to be a great sin, even though all of these customs had been lost for sixty years because of the punishment. They punished adulterers and the women with the penalty of death."[73] This statement came from the *Relaciones* of Tabí and Chunhuhub. These officials wanted to make themselves look good and, in doing so, they necessarily attempted to make the "Indians" look good. While the *Relaciones* often admitted that human sacrifice took place,[74] they also went on to state that the Maya were not cannibals.[75] Then they maintained that the Maya followed a moral code seemingly quite similar to Catholicism. The narrative legitimized the conquest by showing that the conquerors saved the Indians from human sacrifice, but then legitimized the settlement of additional Spaniards by saying that the Indians would not scandalize those Spaniards or force them to engage in sinful acts. In this context the discussions of Maya customs were part of a strategy designed to increase prestige and improve the economy.

The goals, of course, were not that simple, as there was some local bureaucrat filling out the forms. The bureaucrat may have obtained testimonies from local Mayas, but often relied on the ideas of Gaspar Antonio Chi, a Maya leader who heavily influenced many of the *Relaciones*.[76] Chi certainly provided much of the testimony on Maya morality.[77] As Chi wanted to be accepted in Spanish society, he strategized in making the Maya look good to Spanish eyes.

The narrative states that the Maya people practiced moderation in both sex and eating. Further, punishment was strong: "These natives did not eat human flesh, nor did they know the nefarious sin as in other parts of the Indies. It is said that in the time of a Xiu lord, they had punished this sin by casting those found guilty in a burning furnace, and that today this furnace exists in the ancient city of Mayapan ... where the said Tutul Xiu lived and commanded the land."[78] Sodomy here was presented as illegal. Those who engaged in this act received stern punishment. The narrative, identical or similar to many other texts in the *Relaciones*,[79] is a text of prohibitions. It constructed a pre-conquest moral system similar to the Spanish system of the time. Sodomy was connected with cannibalism, and the punishment for sodomy was death. This said much about Spanish colonialist goals, as the Spaniards wanted to construct a society that was the equivalent of their (highly skewed) view of themselves. Sexual desire was manipulated in order to gain material power and prestige for particular groups of people.

A similar example exists in the writings of Diego López de Cogolludo, a Franciscan and an early historian of Yucatán. Cogolludo wrote extensively of the conquest and early settlement of Yucatán, but had little to say about Maya sexual behavior. Cogolludo intended to present his narrative as the authoritative word on the Maya people. He thus represented his work as a history, similar to the way in which an empiricist historian might represent his or her work today: as an exploration of the truth of the events which took place in the past.

When Cogolludo discussed sexual behavior, he attempted, as much as possible, to present his word as authoritative. When he mentioned sodomy, he stated that Díaz del Castillo found idols of men engaged in the act, balancing this statement with that of a Spaniard, Gerónimo de Aguilar, who had lived for eight years as a Maya captive, and who claimed that the "nefarious sin" did not exist in Maya society.[80] This strategy, balancing one "expert" testimony with another, was an attempt to convince readers of the objectivity of the account.

For Cogolludo the important element of description came in his understanding of laws and customs. He claimed with authority that the Maya "rigorously punished the vices. . . . The man or woman that committed adultery received the penalty of death, being executed by arrow-shot. According to Doctor Aguilar, they were tied down. It is said that they abhorred this sin very much, having punished notable leaders, as they had no pardon for those found guilty. They thus had much honesty in marriage. Today, . . . being Christians, it is said that they live lasciviously. Due to this situation, they don't

rigorously punish [adultery]."[81] As Cogolludo posited this narrative of decline, he hardly presented the colonial situation in a positive light. Adultery
was used in a strategic text intended to show a golden age past, not an unusual
strategy for a chronicler/historian. Because of the genre's contradictory goals,
such descriptions often were important. Cogolludo claimed to understand
Maya law.[82] He used such an understanding to advance his own claims of ex-
pertise. The existence of such a law against adultery certainly was plausible,
but the important point here is that the existence of various Maya laws and
customs regarding sexual behavior was used in Spanish texts in order to complete particular strategies.

These documents signified Spanish attempts to write history based on
various material desires and constraints which had much more to do with
Spanish society than with the Maya. The texts showed ways in which colonialism was accomplished through the use of a particular sexual paradigm.
Nonetheless, these writings, when combined with Maya narratives, can be
used as evidence of Maya sexual morality.

Maya Narratives

By the time of the late colonial Books of Chilam Balam, the Maya rhetorically
defined excess as that which would destroy society, a rhetoric influenced by
both the colonial Spanish discourse on sexual acts and the Maya discourse on
destruction and rebirth. The colonial Maya hybrid tradition emphasized the
excessive nature of particular activities, such as adultery, rape, and the sexual
activities of commoners.

The word *pen*, as mentioned in several Maya-language documents (including the 1774 petition discussed above), created a whole complex of meanings. The Book of Chilam Balam of Tizimin states that "excessive adultery
was carried and sprouted everywhere."[83] The strategy of this text, which refers to events of the sixteenth century, was to connect excessive sexual acts
with the downfall of society. The historical story found most objectionable
the amount of lustful thought occurring in the period. The phrase here used
for "excessive" was *pen cech*.[84]

In the anonymous petition written in 1774, I have translated *pen cech pen* as
"excessive fornication." A close relationship existed between the concept of
excess and that of sex, as two of four words which meant "excessive" derived
from *pen*.[85] This concept of excess can be connected genealogically with the
colonization process. The text from the Book of Chilam Balam of Tizimin

which began by rejecting the "excessive adultery"[86] continued to show that these excessive sexual acts led to "great craziness." The insanity of this period stemmed directly from the sexual behavior of the people. These people engaged in excessive sexual acts, spoke "crazy words," and committed "crazy actions." The actions were the responsibility of "the holy face of Mérida,"[87] or of Spanish rule.[88]

The text also showed the importance of and desire for the appropriate lineage. It was the problems associated with insanity entering Maya noble lineages that destroyed society. Insanity here was a common textual metaphor signifying the place of illegitimacy in noble lineage. This illegitimacy, stemming from commoner blood, destroyed society because of the reprehensible adulterous sexual acts of the nobles (with the commoners). These nobles failed to maintain the social and political distinctions appropriate to the maintenance of Maya society.

The text states that the matrilineal line was destroyed through adultery. This line, represented in the text by the "children of her, the bluebird, and the children of her, the quetzal,"[89] was an important ritual and social element in the text. In this case the excesses of society destroyed the matrilineage through adultery, thus allowing impostors control over society. The discourse against adultery was a discourse of gender parallelism and social hierarchy. The gendered construct showed that the matrilineage, like the patrilineage, was important to social functioning. The social hierarchy was signified through a series of impostors, commoners attempting to pass as nobles. These impostors never could rule society appropriately. The desire of the text was a displaced desire to understand your own lineage: to be a legitimate noble. This was a desire to understand the sexual activities of your predecessors. One can understand the purpose of the narrative: adultery was connected with the sexual activities of commoners, who then were criticized for engaging in illegitimate and unfit rulership.

In another discussion of sexual desire, excess caused the downfall of society. A passage from the Book of Chilam Balam of Kaua states:

> *24 anos u maya pan u heɔ tun ti uuc ahau chuu ah cuch le la u uich ti*
> *yahaulil necteil u uah katun ti uuc ahau pentacech cal pach lay u tucul tan*
> *mak u hanal ych cansihoo ɏ yuklah ti cab coil than bolon ɔacab uah yal*

For twenty-four years Mayapan was the seat of Seven Ahau. Its burden was the face of the lordship, the spurting flower[90] of the *katun.* . . . Excessive[91] adultery: this was the thought, like eating food. In the holy face of Mérida and all over the earth, there were crazy words. Bolon Dzacab lived as the child of a woman.[92]

The downfall of historical leaders emanated from the sexual excess of the people of that time. Here the creator himself was seen as illegitimate, and the *katun* was an era of spurting flowers (signifying the birth of children through adulterous affairs). The flowers emanated both from a connection with a phallic representation of sexual intercourse and from the idea that the flower was a signifier of Maya duality. As adultery took place, too many children came from the mother's lineage. While matrilineage played an important role in an individual's power before the conquest, patrilineage also was necessary in order to ascertain noble blood. The desire was a desire for lineage, and thus for sexual control and knowledge.

The narrative then states that "there was excessive and gluttonous adultery, and extremely crazy words."[93] Improper sexual desires led to destruction, caused by the insanity of those children coming from adulterous unions: when both nobles and commoners engaged in these acts, mixture, illegitimacy, and a breakdown of social barriers all began.

As Maya nobles during the colonial years attempted to find a socially appropriate and politically powerful identity, they were presented with the various rituals of creation, life, and death. But the masses of commoners likely comprehended these rituals only to a limited extent. This point was emphasized by a narrative related to a war, created by a Maya noble, Can Ul, in which human sacrifice was performed. The war was against his own community, and it was to backfire:

> *ah cootz ac siɔ u cuch katun tu kinil x-ptianoil tu kinil nicte uinicil tu kin u chac tun numya u chom u uuɔ katun tuy oxlahun te ah uaxac ahau uale u lubul u than yokol u halach uinicil y ahau ah ytza ma cetel bin ɔocbal nicte uinicil lai bolon ahau ti paki chimal kal y halal kal lai bin uchuc tu nup katun hun ɔam uale*

The robbers and those with lustful desires[94] are the burden of the *katun* at the time of Christianity, the time of the flower people, the time of the red stones. Suffering occurred on the fold of the *katun.* On the thirteenth, eight Ahau returned, posting his words to the *halach uinicil,* the lords of the Itzá. Otherwise the flower people would be finished. This is Nine Ahau, who plants his shield bundle and his arrow bundle. This will happen on the *katun's* opposite: they return as a pair.[95]

The political role of Catholicism in Yucatán was foreshadowed by this war. The narrative showed that the leader who was in power at the time the Spaniards arrived was at fault for the defeat. Can Ul, because of his sins, his thefts, and the war, could not properly lead Yucatán. This anticipated the fall of Mayapán,[96] and the eventual Spanish rule from Mérida. The narrative constructed a politicized reading of Can Ul's desires. He used his own military might to destroy his people. In destroying their bodies, his political dispute led to an easy Spanish victory. The people who wrote this text identified themselves against Can Ul. They showed him as an incompetent leader, indirectly comparing themselves with him, and thus demanding that the people of their community (Tizimin) follow them, as the alternative would be a leader similar to Can Ul. The alternative to any desire for them as leaders was a desire for Can Ul, a robber and a person with lust. The lustful desires of the text were sexual, but they also signified a desire for destruction.[97] One certainly can suggest that the Maya (both commoners and nobles) would have visualized a connection between Can Ul's desire for sex and his desire to rob the people and destroy their bodies. Lust and sex were used for political purposes, to ensure the survival of the nobility.[98]

Commoners having sex among themselves and commoners engaging in sexual practices with nobles particularly unnerved the writers of the Books of Chilam Balam. A common refrain was that those "without mothers and fathers" would destroy society. The metaphor for commoners was based on the concept of orphanage. They did not have mothers and fathers because commoners could not control their sexual appetites, and therefore they did not know the identities of their parents: more specifically, they could not connect themselves with a noble lineage.

This was, of course, a feat of noble imagination and fantasy. Commoners were concerned about lineage and often could connect themselves to generations of ancestors.[99] Following the disruptions of the conquest, with the deaths of as many as 90 percent of the people,[100] many nobles and commoners alike had difficulty tracing their ancestors. Hence the near obsession with lineage in the Books of Chilam Balam.[101]

Commoner sex was seen as a dirty practice, and the children developing out of such a deed necessarily were deformed:

mehene tub x yanob ah yax oc haobe yanil huntul yx ma na yan yue yan ix u
tzitz moc xan lay peeue ꝑ x ma yume

"Son, where are the first baptized? There is one who has no mother.
There is her necklace. There is also her bell." [To which the son
replied]: "This is small corn. And she has no father." [102]

The commoner, in a double metaphor likened to small corn, was developed
out of the sense of the orphan: the fatherless and the motherless. Those without lineage were seen as a problematic presence in Maya society. They were
necessarily dependent on those with lineage, and, as dependents, they were
commoners. [103] The commoners could not control their sexual appetites, and
thus they could not determine their lineages.

A much earlier document, a petition, shows that these sexual concerns did
not exist just in late colonial times. In a late-sixteenth-century [104] complaint
against a Maya governor from the Tabí area, signed only by the notary, Diego
Pox, the reader was told:

yan u lobil u beel uicnal can muc u kuchul ychil u otoch u cho cho payte in
chuplil u pakic keban yetel u kati ti lolob maixtan u ɔocabal yolah ca tun ua
lae ti u bel don jorge xiu lae

The worst thing that he did was that he came into my house four
times, trying to take my wife by force in order to sow sin [fornicate]
with her. He desired this, but he did not fulfill his desire. [105] This was
what don Jorge Xiu did. [106]

The colonial translation of *pakic keban* was both "to fornicate" and to "sow
with sin." [107] Semen here was viewed as seed, and the sexual act as an attempt
to plant the seed. Sexual behavior was in some way connected with food and
the ability to maintain life. The act of sowing sin was connected with a sexual encounter, seen as illicit by the petitioner, committed by an official (don
Jorge Xiu was the governor). The woman was seen as playing an innocent role,
almost as a bystander protected by her husband. Yet the husband's role in this
affair was far from clear. Diego Pox did not even say if he was present during
the four times this took place. His wife, although not mentioned by name and
thus only attaining an identity through her writer-husband, defended herself.
She played the major role in rejecting the advances of don Jorge, while her

husband only viewed the scene directly or indirectly through her account. His identity, although named and not possessed, was dependent on the identity of his wife.

Sin here was used, in the Spanish legal system, as an attempt to rid the community of the governor. The narrative was a strategic political one (strategic inversion), using the Christian idea of sin in order to impress Spaniards and other Maya nobles about the horrors of the governor. In this case, the governor's actions may have been symbolic of the contradictions in the colonial Maya political sphere. At one end of this sphere there was the governor, who may have believed that sexual access to a variety of people who were seen to be his political and social inferiors was part of the prerogatives of office (or of power generally). At the other end there was Diego Pox's wife, who, in fighting off the advances, could not accept the idea that her body should be something to be used by the governor. In between these two poles there was Diego Pox, who was able to object because he had certain powers in the community and because he knew that his objections would have political importance. The charge of sin here was used to control people but also was part of a paradigm of power which very well may have been shifting.

The charge was one of attempted rape, as Xiu tried to force himself on Pox's wife.[108] The attempted rape was represented as an affront to both Pox and his wife, and thus was a challenge to the family structure. Pox clearly was demanding that the Spanish authorities intervene. Even in this early period, the Maya knew how to use the Spanish legal system. The charges against Pox, of course, may have emanated from Maya traditions.

Commoner sex signified excess. Commoners and nobles having sex together signified both adultery and excess. Rape was viewed as a form of excess in which only a corrupt official would engage. The three concepts, adultery, rape, and commoner sex, were perceived as destruction. Thus the Spanish narratives were in these cases not far off the mark. The Spanish perceived that the Maya knew of disruptive sexual acts. But the Spaniards failed to perceive that this destruction was thought to lead to eventual creation. The sexual acts and desires described here were hybrid colonial concerns.

THINKING OF SEX

During the colonial years the Maya used sexual desire to invert power relationships, regulate society, and explain history. The noble male writers of the texts believed that talking, thinking, and writing about sex could give them power. They used this power both creatively (to engage in strategic inversion) and repressively (to regulate the sexual activities of themselves, other nobles, commoners, and Spaniards).[109]

Colonial Maya discourses on excess, sex, adultery, rape, and illegitimacy presented to the people a moral code of regulation and repression. However, this very discourse also was creative in the sense that sex was used to form new power relationships. Sex also was viewed as creating a new universe. Both political power and sexual desire were changing in a variety of ways. New desires were being formed (sexual connections with Spaniards, symbolic sexual acts with Catholic gods), and old desires were being changed (the desire for interclass sexual relationships was being altered by the new class dynamics inherent in colonialism; the concepts of adultery, concubinage, and fornication were being transformed).

The Maya saw any "illicit" desires of their own nobles or of the Spanish clergy as interfering with their communication with the gods. In many complaints against people with political and religious power, the gods were invoked because the complaint was in fact that the desires of these powerful people were blocking Maya success by impeding access to the gods. Adultery, excess, illegitimacy, lust, and rape displeased the Maya gods, interfered with proper communication between the people and the gods, and led to destruction. Priests violating their vows of celibacy displeased the Christian God and interfered with Maya communication with Jesus.

In the eighteenth century, Maya nobles wrote about this lack of communication, showing that the preconquest gods still existed in the Maya mind, but that all had been changed. Those gods were infused with competitors from Catholicism, and they claimed many Catholic morals. The changes that had taken place had formed a new moral code, one which developed in the spaces in between Catholic and traditional Maya ideas. By the late colonial period, Maya ideas of proper and improper behavior had changed, and these ideas were used in a different manner. The Maya before the conquest had used sexual activity as a method of gaining and maintaining power, and after the conquest they would continue to do so. But by the eighteenth century, the rules of power had changed: Maya nobles had to challenge the colonizers as well as their local competitors.

For the commoners, power and sexual desire were connected partly in order to displace other desires. So commoners were told that, if inappropriate leaders (commoners) came to rule, the society would be destroyed. Commoners' desires were displaced onto a desire for appropriate rulership by either legitimate nobles or Franciscans. This type of displacement appears universal in any state system, as the state has existed based on inequities, "torture, blood, [and] sacrifice."[110] The colonized Maya system needed ways of maintaining these inequities, particularly when the central rituals of bloodletting and human sacrifice no longer could have the same public meaning.[111] They found new ways in which they could displace desire, through homoerotic and bi-erotic desires for the appropriate gods and nobles.

A hybrid sexual discourse was created during the colonial years. Possibilities for bodily pleasures and definitions of those pleasures changed as bodily views changed. These views were altered as a result of a series of desires, some sublimated and others expressed. Colonialism and other factors modified these desires—not, for the most part, by repressing them, but rather by reinscribing them with new meaning.[112] Colonialism altered Maya minds through this process of reinscription and hybridization. Saint Francis and Jesus were two among many Catholic "gods" who were sexually desirable. These gods, re-presentations of preconquest Maya gods, attained their power through the process of hybridization. The sexual code that these gods signified was not a continuation of undisrupted preconquest Maya tradition; nor was it a traditional Spanish sexual ideology: it was something new and different.

FIVE

The Unvirgin Virgin

In Chapter 2's overview of Maya religion, I presented the idea that the Maya gods were repositioned in the colonial years in order to merge with the Catholic saints. Chapter 3 showed that in using the metaphors related to warfare and sin, the colonial Maya were concerned with meeting the needs and desires of the gods. Chapter 4 concluded that Maya concerns with sexual behavior related to their wish to have appropriate communication with the gods. In this chapter I return to the powerful sexual deity, the Moon Goddess. By late colonial times the Virgin Mary was more prominent in the documents, but she still was invested with many of the powers of the Moon Goddess.

I argue here and throughout the remainder of this book that the Maya notion of the power of the gods was more than theocratic superstition. Maya society, like perhaps almost any other state system, required a repositioning of desire into the personification of the leader. This Maya leader ruled because of supposed divine intervention, whether of the Christian God or of the Maya supreme deities. Desire was placed upon these gods. People were told that in order to reach the gods they were required to maintain society with its social, economic, and political inequalities. The Maya had a developed class structure which was maintained partly through interest in the gods. However, on a social level, the Maya certainly did not act and react simply according to the supposed wishes of the gods. Instead, they placed high values on self and collective interest and on the preservation of a particular, highly ritualized notion of order.[1] The Virgin Mary Moon Goddess hybrid, a colonialist and anticolonialist god, showed the people both the power of the cosmos and the limits of that power.

Given the nature of the extant Maya documents, it is impossible to say when the Maya first adopted the Virgin Mary or even exactly when and how the Moon Goddess and Virgin came to be two parts of a single figure. Nonetheless, the documents present a hybrid notion of the Virgin Mary Moon Goddess, and they show change through time. This chapter is based on a progression of texts that discuss the two figures. The Dresden Codex is a preconquest hieroglyphic text that shows the Moon Goddess as having powers parallel to those of the other gods. It presents her as being sexual with various deities. In the Ritual of the Bacabs, a text probably written in the seventeenth century, the Moon Goddess continued to have parallel power to the other gods. Here she remained sexual, spreading her sexual desires through the population. The Books of Chilam Balam were written primarily in the eighteenth century. The Moon Goddess had little presence independent of the Virgin Mary, and the Virgin for the most part was not associated with sexual desire in the same manner. The Songs of Dzitbalché were written in the late eighteenth and early nineteenth centuries. The Moon Goddess had a somewhat hidden presence while the Virgin Mary was worshipped openly. Both were associated with sexual desires. The changes which took place moved the Virgin Mary to the forefront of the rhetoric of Maya desire.

The Maya adopted the Virgin Mary and the Christian God because Christianity was the conquering religion, and, according to Mayan (and Mesoamerican) tradition, the conquerors' gods were added to the pantheon of those conquered. The Maya certainly did not believe that they were giving up their preconquest deities. The Maya people desired to have the most powerful gods protecting them. The desire for the Virgin Mary herself was an important one: she was desired in order to replicate some preconquest Maya beliefs. She was to be a central signifier in the act of colonization as she became the powerful Unvirgin Virgin or the Virgin Mary Moon Goddess.

THE MOON GODDESS

The preconquest Maya gendered gods in order to signify various concerns, including a division of the world into masculine and feminine. However, instead of representing the gods and goddesses as opposites, the texts present them as a duality: two to four parts of what often was considered the same deity, and which clearly constituted the whole.[2] In the constitution of ritual circuits (ceremonies which moved in a set pattern in the various directions), there often existed a male god representing one part of a ritual circuit and a female goddess another.[3] In essence, as these were two parts of the same god on a larger level, the god was engaging in a gender transformation. The male god could become female and the female goddess could become male.

Andrea Stone has shown that the Moon Goddess represented a variety of explicit sexual behaviors, and that those behaviors may have included homosexual acts. In a Classic period Maya cave painting (see Chap. 8, Fig. 8.2), the Moon Goddess herself was engaged in a clearly erotic embrace with a god.

The Dresden Codex

One can hardly pick up the Dresden Codex without noticing the Moon Goddess and her sexual activities.[4] The Moon Goddess was associated with weaving, childbirth, creation, sexual "promiscuity," and disease.[5] She was described as both "our mother" and "lady,"[6] descriptions also used for "virginal maidens" and the Virgin Mary.[7] She was favored by the Itzá, and her representative appeared among the pictures of warriors in Chichén Itzá.[8] The Moon Goddess signified many elements of Maya duality, and, as one would expect by now, she symbolized both destruction and creation. Importantly, the Moon Goddess attained a large amount of power, becoming a key leader of the cosmos.

The Moon Goddess's picture was not very different from the images of the various male gods in the codices. In Classic period documents she was pictured in the Moon sign holding a rabbit (see Chap. 1, Fig. 1.1). In these documents her head was a glyph for both the number one and the phonetic *na*, a translation of "motherhood," which also represented "noblewomen" and the importance of the matrilineage.[9] This distinction related back to the Moon Goddess and showed a matrilineal line of descent which worked together with patrilineal descent groups. The kinship represented here was a narrative technique which gave both women and the Moon Goddess some social status. This technique also showed the importance of desire for lineage and nobility. Gender was an element with boundaries which differentiated and allowed for women to have certain social status in Maya society.

There existed some strong distinctions between the idea represented by the *na* and European concepts of gender. The *na* preceded both male and female names but represented the name derived from the matriline. The Moon Goddess was a linguistic and textual representative of this matriline before the conquest. No single male god was represented as the universal head of the patriline.[10] Rather, many male gods were shown as the heads of individual patrilineage groups. Since lineage symbolically separated nobles from commoners, the Moon Goddess's position, as a representative of matrilineage throughout the Maya world, showed that she was given great symbolic power. It was through a connection with her that Maya men and women were able to prove themselves members of the nobility. Such a powerful image for a goddess contrasted sharply with Catholic imagery.

Her power was that of a colonial goddess: she probably came from the Itzá region, and she colonized much of Yucatán.[11] Her power derived from the desire for completion, a need felt by the Maya to understand the ritual nature of sexual intercourse and the role of sexual activity in the process of creation. She was portrayed as the head of matrilineage because she was considered separate from and above the rest of the goddesses. This stemmed from her considerable power to colonize.

Charles Hofling, seeking to understand Maya discourse structure in the Dresden Codex, provides a transliteration and translation of the Moon Goddess pages. While Hofling has many questions left regarding the translations, his work makes several important points. (In the following passage, the Moon Goddess is Chel—more commonly, Ix Chel.)

Muluk Chak u-kuch Chel-?, ahaw-lel Ok (Death God A) u-kuch Chel-? ah-kim-il. Kimi Itsamna u-kuch Chel-?, ahaw-lil? Kimi (God Q) u-kuch Chel-?, ?-men. . . . Uuk Ahaw, Chan Chel? y-atan-e (God L) ahaw poop Hun Manik', Chan Chel y-atan-e Tsul, u-muk. Waxak Ix, Chan Chel y-atan-e Ibach, ? Ka Imix, Chan Chel y-atan-e ?, ah-kim-il. . . . Kaban, y-atan ? Chel, Ahaw Poop. Ik', y-atan Yax-? Chel, loob-il. Ak'bal, y-atan Bakab, ?, ahaw-lil?. Kawak, y-atan ? Chel, ah-kimi.

On Muluc, Chac is the burden of Chel, rule. On Oc, Death God A is the burden of Chel, Lord Death. On Cimi, Itzamna is the burden of Chel, rule. On Cimi, God Q is the burden of Chel, Augury. . . . On Seven Ahau, Little Chel is the wife of God L, Lord of the mat. On One Manik, Little Chel is the wife of Dog, its omen. On Eight Ix, Little Chel is the wife of Armadillo, Augury. On Two Imix, Little Chel is the wife of ?, Lord Death. . . . On Caban, the wife of Bacab is Chel, Lord of the Mat. On Ik, the wife of Green God Ch is Chel, evil. On Akbal, (she is) the wife of the Bacab, Augury, rule. On Cauac, the wife of God Q is Chel, Lord Death.[12]

In the first selection, it is possible to detect that the Moon Goddess signified many things. Here she was the signifier of rulership and death. The second selection showed the Moon Goddess married to (and the pictures showed her having sex with) various gods. The marriages signified rulership, death, and an omen. The third selection presented her as married to (and having sex with) more gods, where the marriages represented rulership, evil, and death. The story was that the Moon Goddess married various gods, showing the ritual importance of marriage and sexual acts. This signified the power of the Moon Goddess, who could enforce good and evil, and in traditional Maya fashion, she could reproduce society and destroy it. She was the head of many lineages in these texts (in other sections, the Moon Goddess was pictured with children, probably from these marriages), which represented the founding of Maya society.

The duality of the Moon Goddess and the portrayal of good and evil were not dependent on the Moon Goddess's lifelong monogamous commitment to a single partner. She was able to have many sexual partners so that she could produce the appropriate lineages. This certainly promoted the concept of gender parallelism in Maya religion. Both the Moon Goddess and the various gods with whom she was associated were necessary for the production of Maya society. They played complementary roles which developed into a complementarity apparent in Maya lineage arrangements.[13]

In one of the first series of pictures of the Moon Goddess in the Dresden Codex (see Fig. 5.1), she is seated with various birds perched on her shoulders.[14] Here her attributes are associated with the birds that she sports. Eric Thompson identifies the first as the *muan* bird, apparently connected with evil. The second picture shows the quetzal bird, representing "very good tidings." Children would emanate from this Moon Goddess.[15] The sexual desires of the Moon Goddess were positive, giving this piece of text its good tidings. The third bird is the macaw,[16] which is associated with the "macaw seizure" both in this text and in the colonial era medical documents.[17] The Moon Goddess here is associated with disease and death related to a particularly serious form of seizures. The Moon Goddess herself was not associated with either good or evil; rather, she retained dualistic associations with both good events and bad. She signified more than one element, but in all she retained her power as an important mother goddess. Similarly, the male gods represented both good and bad events.[18] The dualism here was not a belief in binary oppositions, but rather a belief in eschatology, cyclical repetition, and complementarity.

FIGURE 5.1   The Moon Goddess with a series of birds on her shoulders. From the
Dresden Codex. Reprinted by permission of Akademische Druck-u.

In the duality of the Mesoamerican religious structure, the Moon Goddess could signify both childbirth and sexual excess. In the Dresden Codex the authors pictured the Moon Goddess having sexual intercourse with several other gods.[19] She signified a certain ritual acceptance of excess, as her power remained strong throughout the codex. Yet she also signified a condemnation of excess, as her behavior was associated with death and destruction. Such was the dual nature of Mesoamerican religion.

In Figure 5.2, the first picture shows the Moon Goddess engaged in some type of sexual activity with a *bacab*, a powerful god. The positioning of the two figures engaged in intercourse is typical of the Dresden Codex. In no case is the penis displayed. The Moon Goddess is recognized both in the glyphs and in the picture by her hair, while the god is recognized by his headdress. Neither figure is naked, and the distinguishing characteristics of this scene when compared with noncoital amorous scenes (as in the next two pictures) are the proximity of the two bodies and the location of the Moon Goddess's hand. In

FIGURE 5.2   The Moon Goddess engaging in sexual acts with gods, having children as a result. From the Dresden Codex. Reprinted by permission of Akademische Druck-u.

every picture of the Moon Goddess engaged in sexual activity, she places her hand on her partner's body.[20] The rituals maintained both the importance of sexual intercourse in the Maya pantheon and the importance of the Moon Goddess as a highly sexual goddess.

The Moon Goddess symbolically regulated all sexual behavior in the Maya world. She was a powerful religious figure who engaged in "promiscuity." She signified the Maya concept of women's symbolic power, shown as virginity during the colonial period. She thus was a representative of both virginity and promiscuity. As the Moon Goddess was pictured engaged in intercourse with many gods, she was the mother of many lineages. In a Maya world so concerned with lineage, the Moon Goddess would be an extremely powerful, perhaps *the* most powerful, deity.

Figures 5.3 and 5.4 show the progression of the Moon Goddess from a picture where she carries a death figure to a picture where she carries a bundle of food, representing life, to another picture where she carries a death figure,

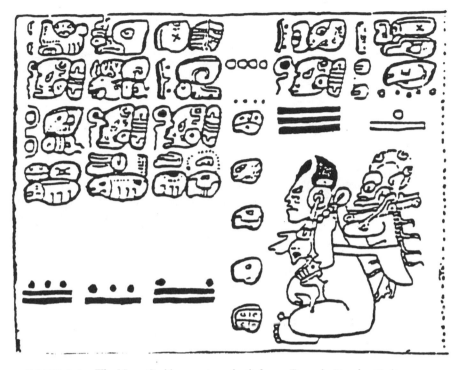

FIGURE 5.3   The Moon Goddess carries a death figure. From the Dresden Codex. Reprinted by permission of Akademische Druck-u.

and finally to one where she carries a skull.[21] The rituals in the pictures served as warnings to people: they must respect the Moon Goddess, for she had great power over them. She delivered both life and death, engaging in childbirth, curing, disease, and rituals of death.[22]

The Moon Goddess's life demonstrated the implicit power of sexual desire in Maya religion. She first had an "affair" with the sun's brother, the planet Venus. She later eloped with a vulture and then was rescued by the sun. She and the sun apparently still argue about these incidents.[23] Or so the story goes. Although J. Eric Thompson's description elicits comparisons with Eve, the comparisons were not so clear. While Eve lost much of her power through her transgressions in the Garden of Eden, the Moon Goddess actually gained power through her "violations." The Moon Goddess had intercourse with powerful figures and used those figures to raise the various lineages. Her power stemmed from her sexual behavior.[24]

In one instance she was shown engaging in a type of sexual behavior hardly

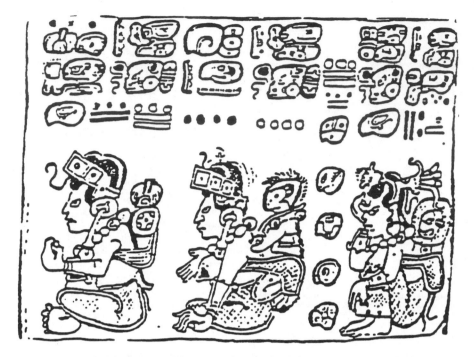

FIGURE 5.4   The Moon Goddess carries life and death figures, representing the duality of Maya religion. From the Dresden Codex. Reprinted by permission of Akademische Druck-u.

distinguished from the others. In Figure 5.5 the Moon Goddess is engaging in some type of sexual behavior with a death figure who is gendered female.[25] The representation suggests a symbolic importance to lesbian sex not easily confirmed by other documents. The action here could have signified the results of a gender transformation to be shown in Chapter 8. The text states that the Moon Goddess could engage in sexual acts with those whom she desired, regardless of gender. The figure is a powerful death figure, allowing the Moon Goddess access not only to live deities, but to the dead as well. The Moon Goddess could engage in a variety of sexual acts with a variety of gods, all the while enhancing her ritual status. As she had intercourse with a female death figure, the Moon Goddess and this death figure were able to "reproduce" a matrilineage. If the phallus existed in such a scene, it was disconnected from the male body and allowed the Moon Goddess and her partner, of either gen-

FIGURE 5.5   The Moon Goddess engaging in sexual acts with a female death figure. From the Dresden Codex. Reprinted by permission of Akademische Druck-u.

der, to engage in reproduction. As the phallus was removed, perhaps the Moon Goddess penetrated others and was herself penetrated. Her body was a central metaphor for the reproduction of Maya society. While the metaphors may have required penetration of some sort, they did not require the anatomically "correct" male body with its penis.[26]

Still, as the Moon Goddess was sexualized in general terms, the sexual identity of lesbianism played no role here. The text does not declare her a lesbian or bisexual goddess any more than it declares her a heterosexual. None of the documents mentions such a sexual identity. Instead, she remained at the center of the universe, a goddess for all people, a goddess whose desires were seen as important. And the desire for her was explicitly sexual. She was desired by both men and women, for she signified something to both. It is here that the texts present a bi-erotic desire.

Power and the Postconquest Goddess

After the conquest the Maya certainly desired their traditional gods. After all, it was these gods who had allowed them to survive that long. In fact, there were many Maya attempts at maintaining preconquest rituals and deities.[27] The texts of the Ritual of the Bacabs exhibit much Catholic influence. Still, in the seventeenth century, stories of the Moon Goddess and the other preconquest Maya gods had been preserved in oral traditions, and they were written down by the Maya scribes in order to help future shamans. These texts signify an attempt by some Maya both to preserve remnants of preconquest culture and to appeal to preconquest religion in one area—curing—where Catholicism did not attempt to intervene.

All the gods, including the important Bacabs, were presented in many ways: as sexual beings, as curers, as diseases. Itzamna and the Moon Goddess often were constructed in complementary and parallel fashion as those who helped in the creations of both the disease and the cure. The following is a selection from a cure for asthma in which the author was very concerned with the lineage of the disease and the possible lineage of a cure. Both the cure and the disease thus were personified and were seen as having parents. In this way the text was able to develop ritualized ideas for cures.

> *can kin cu lothic chacal tente can kinix bin cu lothic chacal kabala can kinix*
> *cu lothic u uich chacal ix chel sacal ix chel kanal ix chel can kinnix bin cu*
> *lothic uich chacal itzam na max tah chabi max tah akabi ti sihie u ciil sihil*
> *bin u chabaccen bin ah coocbal tun ca ti sihi*

Four days have passed without the crushing of the large object. Four days have passed without the crushing of the large substance. For four days the face of the red Moon Goddess, the white Moon Goddess, the yellow Moon Goddess has spasmed. For four days the face of the red Itzamna has spasmed. Who created you? Who hid you? Its birth, the respectable birth, was created by me. It is he, the asthma, that was born.[28]

The Moon Goddess and Itzamna are given a parallel construction in this text. Both are associated with the face of the ill person, both are related to colors, and both are portrayed as oppositional figures to the personified disease. The two together signified a potential for a cure and thus remained associated with power over disease. The Moon Goddess and Itzamna both were needed in order to give birth to the disease and the cure. The two gods were structured in similar manners to stress their sexual complementarity.

Both the Moon Goddess and Itzamna have much power on their own in these texts, as they create, maintain, and destroy disease. The Moon Goddess is shown as a curer and a mother figure:

> *balx bacin u chichil balx bacin u mutil chac tan bac hol bacen chulub u chichil*
> *balx u che bax yaban ɔacal bac bax u che bacel ac u chel bacal che bax u che*
> *bal in uayasba ca tin ɔe kaxtah ca tin nohkaxtah chacal kax ix chel sacal kax*
> *ix chel chacal kax ix ku sacal kax ix ku oxlahun ytzen yn chacal ɔonot tin*
> *peɔ kaxtici u kinam*

Which are their birds? Which are their pheasants?[29] The birds are the *Chac Tan Bac*, the *Hol Bacen*, and the *Chulub*.[30] Which is their tree? Which is their grass?[31] The *Dzacal Bac*.[32] Which is their tree? The *Bacel Ac*.[33] Their tree is the *Bacalche*.[34] Which is their tree? Which is my sign?[35] I tied it up gently, I bound it tightly in the red Moon Goddess forest, the white Moon Goddess forest, the red goddess forest, the white goddess forest.[36] I am the holy shaman.[37] In my red cenote I tightly bound the pain, Him of the Pain, Him of the Heat, Him of the Pain.[38]

The Moon Goddess here, following the conquest, was related to a forest and associated with both curing and disease. The narrative strategized to gain power for the shaman by associating him or her with the Moon Goddess. The shaman then attacked the disease by tying it up in the sacred forests, thus killing it.

The narrative also strategized to maintain the power of the Moon Goddess by using the term *ix ku*, "goddess." This repeated the idea signified by *ix chel*, recognized by the Maya of the period as a term for the Moon Goddess. The term *ku* by the seventeenth century had come to be used in many texts, followed by the Spanish term *Dios*, to describe the Christian God.[39] The term *ix ku* connected the feminine agentive to the term for a god. This particular narrative put the Moon Goddess on an equal footing with the Christian God, who never was mentioned. While this does not necessarily suggest that the Maya actually believed the Moon Goddess to be as powerful as the Christian God, the strategy showed a powerful Moon Goddess.

The forest was the sign of the Moon Goddess and became the position of a cure. This strategy allowed the Moon Goddess to show her sign, permitting the shaman to attain access to strategic power. The Moon Goddess's ability to maintain her sign well after the conquest, at least in certain rituals, showed that she was considered very important by some postconquest Maya. These rituals necessarily were hidden from most Spaniards, yet they survived. The Moon Goddess was a representative for more than just a small group of elite curers. Rather, many of the people, including commoners, must have believed in her, fantasized about her, in order for the rituals and cures to have had a plausible effect on the population.

The need for the Moon Goddess was shown as a desire for a cure. She also was desired as the goddess of lineage, although this meaning often was hidden in the ostensible goal of the cure. After the conquest, despite Catholicism's attempt to eradicate traditional Maya religious practices, the people continued to apply Maya religion where Catholicism had no parallel. They had a desire for the Moon Goddess because she was seen as the central curing deity. As such, she retained much of her preconquest power. Yet she was limited in her power by the presence of the Christian "gods." But the Moon Goddess was tricky, as her power was transformed and reinscribed through a hybrid Christian framework.

THE APPEARANCE OF THE VIRGIN MARY

For the Maya people, the preconquest gods became a part of Catholic ritual.[40] The movement of Catholicism to Latin America threatened to displace the ritualized gender and sexual systems encouraged by indigenous religions, especially on the periphery of the Iberian colonies.[41] In the central areas, Christianity was more likely to mix in some way with the indigenous religions,[42] thus bridging the gap between two different systems of meaning.

The Virgin Mary was presented to the Maya as an important figure in Catholicism. The Maya saw her picture, and they saw the reverence given to her by the Spaniards. They thus interpreted her as the central goddess in the Catholic pantheon. The Virgin Mary's existence among the Maya was far from tenuous, and they clearly did not just accept her in an effort to subvert Christianity by placing on her all the aspects of the Moon Goddess. Changes in the structure of the Moon Goddess, and in the existence of the Virgin Mary, were evident throughout the colonial period. As the Virgin took over from the Moon Goddess, who had a more tenuous existence in many of the later colonial documents, gender status and ritual hierarchies changed.

The Ritual of the Bacabs

The Ritual of the Bacabs, as a collection of archaic texts, did not emphasize Christianity. The central roles in the rituals were reserved for traditional Maya gods and ceremonies. But these texts were written down well after the conquest, and they betrayed some significant mixture of the two religious traditions. In a world dominated by Christianity, colonialism, and the development of a more Hispanized culture, it could hardly have been otherwise.

Each incantation in the Ritual of the Bacabs ends with the shaman saying "amen." Eight (out of sixty-eight) incantations include invocations to the Christian God, Jesus, the Holy Spirit, and/or the Virgin Mary. Six of these eight cases occur in the texts toward the end of the manuscript (which were written later than the others, in the late eighteenth century. I have not used these texts). In all cases but one,[43] the statements are either just the names, "Jesus, Mary,"[44] or versions of a simple formula, also common in Maya testaments: "In the name of God the father, God the son, God the holy spirit . . ."[45] The small number of citations in such a large text (237 folios) shows the power of the Maya traditions in this document. Many indigenous gods are mentioned throughout the text.

In the one case where the Virgin Mary is cited as a part of the cure, she comes into the text in an obscure manner suggestive of her connection with the Moon Goddess. The text is a cure for an obstructed airway:

> *jesus maria a uik cu lukul che a muc cu lubul che ti lakin maci a uikal xx*
> *xx* [46] *jesus maria a uik cu lukul che a muk cu lubul ti xan maci a uikal che*
> *xx xx jesus maria a uik cu lukul che a muk cu lubul che ti nohol maci a*
> *uikal u kasul chabe u kasul sihile canchelic tun bacin mayn pecbes macmac ti*
> *chuuen macmac ti munyal macmac ti luum macmac ti yikal macmac tii kin*
> *macmac ti akab macmac tin tan macmac tin pach macmac tij hun suyi u*
> *macul che u ɔoc amen*

Jesus, Mary, Oh! Your breathing is taken away. Oh! Your strength falls. It was in the east where your breathing was captured. Jesus, Mary, Oh! Your breathing is taken away. Your strength falls. Oh! Your breathing was captured. Jesus, Mary, Oh! Your breathing is taken away. Oh! Your strength falls. It was in the south where your breathing was captured. How has the semen of creation; the semen of birth been spread forcefully? I have not moved it. It is captured in the *Chuen*;[47] it is captured in the clouds; it is captured in the land; it is

captured in the wind; it is captured in the day; it is captured in the
night; it is captured in front of me; it is captured behind me; it is
captured in the virgin.[48] Oh! its capture. The end. Amen.[49]

Mary and Jesus are invoked here just with their names. There are no grammatical connections between their names and the rest of the text. Nonetheless, the position of their invocation is suggestive. They are placed at the end
of a lengthy cure, showing that they were part of the solution. In this part
of the cure, they were related to the ritual circuit and other Maya traditions.
They were given a role in the "capture" or curing of the disease, which was
accomplished through the ritualistic hiding of semen. While this was likely a
symbolic positioning of semen, it is clear that the semen, captured in the skies,
in the heavens, was intended to be the powerful force of creation.

This phallic notion gave tremendous power to semen and sexual desire itself. The semen was intended to show the positioning of life as an act dependent on the male role in the creation of a child. In a way similar to the example
discussed earlier in this chapter, where Bolon Dzacab's semen created the universe,[50] here a deified notion of semen created the cure. Many traditional Maya
deities were present in the ritual, so it was perhaps the semen of one or more
of them that was placed in the text.[51]

Jesus and Mary were part of the sexual desires/acts/fantasies which led to a
cure, and they may in fact have been part of the phallic notion of desire signified here. Their presence could have been a "sacrilegious" curse, but since
the other gods were treated in a similar manner in this text, it seems likely that
their significance was more complex. Mary, while powerful (as a part of the
cure), was present only with her son. In fact, in this case, she was not identified with her virginity, perhaps because she was not seen as so powerful (see
below).[52]

The Books of Chilam Balam

The Books of Chilam Balam gave more power to Mary, describing her as a
virgin and placing her in stories in which she had the power associated with
her in Catholic ritual. This power, however, was different from that of the
Moon Goddess. Mary in Catholicism was associated with purity and social
control over women's sexual activities.[53] She was subordinated to representations of the Christian God and of her son. The Moon Goddess, as has been
shown, was a powerful goddess who was a parallel deity to the most powerful male gods. In the repetition of Catholic rituals related to the Virgin Mary

and other figures, the Books of Chilam Balam, although they appear at first glance to be replicas of preconquest Maya culture, show late colonial aspects of women's status related to religion.

Still, the Books of Chilam Balam are not centered on the Virgin Mary as a figure, even though the ideology related to her permeates much of the texts. A narrative which mentions the arrival of the Virgin Mary in Mérida is purported to have emanated from the sixteenth century:

> *tijx eɔlahi u chun santa yglesia mayori u kakal na Diosi u xiuil xitel na Dios citbil tix eɔlahi u ch[un] uucpel sacramento y çatebal . . . tix hopi ban meyah chumuc cah u . . . numya balcahi tix u uatal ca u I. . . . lic u than kui xanomistali tu chi Dios [cit]bil ti yulel çac tun lah pal tal ti caan çuhuy chuplal u kaba u na uucpel chachak ek*

[The *katun*] established the foundation of the great holy cathedral, the fire house of God, erecting and decorating[54] the house of God the father. It established the foundations of the seven sacraments and the forgiveness [of sins]. The great work began in the middle of the community . . . the world's misery. Then there was erected our . . . according to God's word, which was delivered by the face of God the father. Then the white stone child[55] arrives from the heavens. The Virgin Lady, as she is called, is the mother of the seven great stars.[56]

The Virgin Mary was implicated here in a method of looking at history in which Catholicism was used as a marker for understanding the aftermath of the conquest. Whether the results simply were seen as the building of a church or the creation of misery, history was understood by showing the presence of the Catholic symbols. The Virgin Mary was, however, only a secondary player in this particular narrative, the focus being on "God the father."

The Virgin still controlled people: she was seen as the leader of the people, the one who gave birth to the people from heaven. She thus maintained a powerful role. But the role of the Moon Goddess as a god who had parallel powers with other gods was not present in this narrative. The timeline was not very suggestive of historical change. If this text was written in the sixteenth century and the texts from the Ritual of the Bacabs were written in the seventeenth, the changes are unclear. Perhaps the different purpose of the Ritual of the Bacabs was to present itself as a text which more accurately portrayed feelings and fantasies. The Books of Chilam Balam were significantly more focused on political history and prophecy than fantasy. One could suggest that the outward structures of Maya politics and Catholic religion had fused in such a way as to present the Virgin Mary as the traditional mother. Maya minds, fantasies, and ritual performances may have developed a more hybrid notion of gender and desire.

However, this hybrid was also found in the historical texts. The Book of Chilam Balam of Chumayel contained a text which purported to have been written in the seventeenth century. This text, introducing a series of riddles, began with a description of the ritual circuit and moved to a hybrid notion of ritual ceremony:

> *he maniie chun peten campech u ni xik peten calkini u chun u xik peten*
> *ytzmal u chumuc u xik peten çaci u ni xik peten conkal u pol peten chumuc*
> *cah ti hoo yglesia mayor u kakal na u uitzil na akab na u uil u Dios yumbil*
> *Dios mehenbil Dios espiritu santo mac x oc tu nail Diose yume lay ix kalem*
> *u kabae bax u kinil takci tu nak suhui chuplale yume canil oc takci tu nak*

This is Mani, the base of the country. Campeche is the wingtip of the country. Calkini is the base of the wing of the country. Izamal is the center of the wing of the country. Valladolid is the wingtip of the country. Conkal is the head of the country.[57] The center community of Mérida [has] the great church, the fire house, the mountain house, the night house of the moon,[58] of God the father, God the son, God the holy spirit. Who entered the house of God? Father, her name is she the radiant. What was the time of the conception in the womb of the virgin woman? Father, Four Oc was the time of conception in her womb.[59]

The structure of the text shows that it was both ritual performance and geopolitical marker. The ritual performance was the outlining of a circuit moving through the various communities. This ritual circuit certainly related to similar preconquest events.[60] The geopolitical marking was the assertion of Christian power in the central community of Mérida. This community controlled the rest of the land based on its assertion of Church power. The Virgin Mary played a role in this as the mother, but the Moon Goddess also played a somewhat more hidden role. As the church was the house of the moon, the moon was associated with the trinity. While the Moon Goddess herself was not mentioned, the presence of the moon in this text was evocative of Maya preconquest ritual lore. The text signified a hybrid notion, but one which connected the moon more closely with the trinity than with the

Virgin Mary. Mary attained power in this text through her womb and through the conception of Jesus. While this certainly related to the Moon Goddess's power through lineage, it did not assert gender parallelism.

The text shows that Maya minds and fantasies had developed a hybrid contextualization of ritual performance. The preconquest circuit and the power of the moon combined with the Christian symbols to develop a colonial ritual. This ritual asserted a changing relationship of the moon and the ritual circuit with the people.

The Songs of Dzitbalché

The Songs of Dzitbalché, written in the late eighteenth and early nineteenth centuries, evoke much about religion, beauty, and love. The Virgin Mary is a central figure in several songs, and in some she is associated with the moon. By this late colonial period, the Virgin had changed into a hybrid who attempted to control women by promoting chastity and virginity.

In a flower-related song, the people of the community of Dzitbalché assert virginity based on the direct presence of the Virgin Mary:

COOX H C KAM NIICTE	We are going
CIMAAC OLAILIL	To receive the flower:
TAN C KAYIIC	We are singing
TUMEN BINCAH	happily
C'KAM C'NIICTE	because we are going
TVLACAILIL X CHVVP	to receive the flower.
XLOOB BAYEN	All of these women together
CHEN CHEHLAH	only laugh,
CHEH LAMEEC	only laughter is seen
V YIICH TVT ZIIT	in their faces,
V PVVCZIIK[AL]IL	in the beats of their hearts,
TVTOVV VTZEM	in their bosoms.[61]
BAILX TVMEN	Why is this done?
TVMEN YO[H]EEL	Because, you understand,
T'YOLAL V OIIC	it is for the surrender
V ZVHVY[LIL] COLELIL	of your female virginity
TI V YAA[CVNAH]	to the one who loves you.[62]
KAYEEX NICTEIL	Sing of the flower,
C'YANT CEEX	accompany
NAACON YETEL	the war leader

NOH YVM AH'KVLEL	and the great lord Ah Kulel,[63]
AH TAN CAAN CHE	present at the tree.[64]
AH CVLEL HKA[Y]	Ah Kulel sings:
CONEEX CONEEX	"Let's go, let's go
C'ƆA C'OLAALIL	let's give our hearts
TV TAAN X ZVHVZ	before the Virgin,
X'CIICHPAN ZVHVY	the beautiful Virgin,
COLEL BIL V	the lady
LOLIL LOOB AYEN	of the blossom,[65] of the maidens,[66]
TVT CAN CAAN CHE	there on her high throne,
[V]COLEBIL XM . . .	the lady . . .[67]
ZVHVY KAAK V	the virgin fire of the moon,[68]
BEYX[A]N X[C]ICH[P]AN	and the beautiful
X'KAM LE OOCH	lady of the maize,[69]
X CIICHPAN X AH ZOOT	the beautiful rattle,
YETE[L]X CIICHPAM	and the beautiful
COLEL X ZVHVY X	lady Virgin,
TTOOT MVCH	the rain frog.[70]
LAITIE ƆIIC VTZIL	It is she who gives goodness
CVXTALIL VAY YO[K]	to life
PEET [N]E VAY YO[K]	here in the country,[71]
CHAK ME TV ZVVT	here in the fields and the lands,[72]
LVMIL VAY VITZIL	here in the mountains.
COOX COOX CONEEX	Come, come, let's go,
PALALEEX BEEY	children.
C ƆAIC CICI CIMAC	Let's give great happiness
OLIL VAY ƆITIL	here in Dzitil Pich,[73]
PIICH ƆITIL BALCHE	in Dzitbalché."[74]

The text presents a specifically female virginity. This related to the Catholic tradition, as one finds little evidence of a preconquest Maya morality that prioritized virginity specifically for women. However, in a postconquest text, the Maya author prioritized female virginity and related this virginity to the flower. As a woman could only give her virginity to a person who loved her (this concept was like much of the romantic poetry of Baroque Spain[75]), the romantically inclined woman had to save her body for her "true" life mate. Indeed, much as in Spain, writers in late colonial Mexico believed that their society was in the midst of great upheaval and disorder.[76] This perception of disorder led writers and political leaders to attempt to curtail these changes by asserting a particular order through regulations related to marriage and sexuality.[77] Nonetheless, the "disorder" reigned, and various social, economic, and ethnic groups continued to mix.

The songwriter made a similar attempt at control. As the late colonial period saw an expansion and globalization of the Yucatecan economy, Maya women had more opportunities of various kinds, some of which they took. The Maya writer attempted to curtail some of these opportunities by using his narrative to assert a moral code that demanded female virginity. At the same time, the ceremony and the song were dedicated to women surrendering their virginity: it was a ritualized sexualization of women.

This text could be interpreted as an attempt at a particular brand of seduction. Women were required to maintain virginity for their true loves, those with whom they would at the time of the ceremony engage in sexual activity. In this sense, one might maintain a Hispanic origin for the song, suggesting particular types of courtly love. The song would then have come to the Maya, who simply translated and repeated many stock phrases. However, the song in many senses has traditional Maya content and can be seen as having developed a hybrid force.

The flower metaphorically signified the happiness of the young women: it signified their virginity. The young women had saved the flower, and the women (and perhaps the men) were required to sing of the flower. This maintenance of virginity may in fact have enhanced women's empowerment. They, after all, had a gift that they could give or withhold. However, this sense of empowerment clearly was limited.

If the men were to receive the flower, the text asserted a connection between masculinity and control. This song was designed to support the community (through the war leader and Ah Kulel, the community's representatives) and connect the community with Catholicism (through the Virgin Mary). The people demanded the flower, symbolizing virginity, in order for the community to survive. Virginity here was a component of the colonial context. The community, under a perceived attack from outsiders, needed to struggle in order to survive. This struggle metaphorically took place on the bodies of Dzitbalché women. The bodies of the women threatened to cross boundaries, moving beyond the community, and thus threatening the existence of the group. Virginity was asserted as a strategy in order to maintain community boundaries and affirm a local identity and nation. Desire thus controlled, the women were disempowered. The maintenance of ethnic boundaries and fears controlled local concepts of gender and sexual desire.

And the town official, supposedly attempting to maintain community distinction, presented a seemingly Christian reflection on life. The narrative moved from a discourse about virginity to a statement related to the Virgin Mary.[78] Ah Kulel began a strategy which invoked both himself, an icon of preconquest Maya politics, and Mary, a central icon of Catholicism, in order to control the sexual behavior of women in his community. Mary here was seen as a figure who could lead, in preconquest fashion, a kinship line of women, and who thus could control the discourse around the behavior of those women. She was seen as a radically revised Moon Goddess.

Mary was the "lady of the blossom, of the maidens." She represented and protected the flower. The flower here may have suggested not just virginity but the entire array of women's sexual desire. Mary, both directly and metaphorically signifying virginity, demanded control over sexual behavior through her control over the blossom and the maiden. But the narrative took this control further. Here Mary, called upon by a male preconquest political official, asserted the importance of virginity. The woman had to be a virginal maiden until she found the one she loved. After that point she could give this one her body and her virginity. Her desires thus were defined based on the search for love. Unlike in European Catholicism, however, here the women were to become sexual following a public mass ceremony. Marriage nowhere was mentioned.

The ideas presented in this reading of the song showed the hybrid mixture of pre- and postconquest elements. As if she were a preconquest goddess, Mary represented and controlled a line of women. She remained a central Catholic icon and emphasized a virginity not mandated by preconquest religious doctrine. The narrative showed such a blending of attributes in its extended description of Mary. She sat on a throne and represented maize, a sacred or virginal fire, a rattle, and a rain frog. All of these aspects signified preconquest notions of the religious and political hierarchy. Many of the pre- and postconquest Maya worshipped these elements. The maize, fire, and rain particularly represented preconquest Maya conceptions of the appropriate role for a goddess. The Moon Goddess had some control over all of these aspects (although each had its own assigned deity), as they were seen as controlling life and health. The Moon Goddess also had some control over the throne and the rattle (both signifying political power) through her authority over the matrilineal line.

Mary's presence signified a blending of religious discourse, allowing access to an understanding of historical change. By the late colonial period of these texts, Maya ritual discourse had changed radically, emphasizing virginity and chastity. But this discourse also maintained many elements of preconquest lore, showing the power of rain, fire, maize, and politics. The narrative implicitly claimed that the survival of the community depended on how the women listened to Mary. Without the flowers, the community would become decentered and disorder would reign. The narrative was a statement defending monogamy and perhaps endogamy, asserting the symbolic centrality of the flower as the maintainer of the life of the community. In this picture, gender parallelism was left behind as the hybrid Virgin no longer had the power of the Moon Goddess. She no longer had equivalent powers with the male gods. Maya women's sexual desire, continuing to be situated in the Virgin Mary Moon Goddess hybrid, was more restricted.

By the late colonial period Maya desires for gods were placed primarily upon Jesus, the Virgin Mary, and the Catholic saints. But the Maya were able to keep many of the preconquest gods in some hidden texts. They also were able to inscribe some of the aspects of the preconquest gods into the frameworks of these Christian "gods." Some sense of preconquest Maya religion remained throughout the colonial period, and some remains today. However, many of the central aspects of the Virgin Mary were contradictory to the Moon Goddess's powers. The Virgin Mary Moon Goddess, even after the fusion of the two, was significantly different from the preconquest Moon Goddess, just as she was different from the precontact Virgin Mary.

THE MOON GODDESS AND THE VIRGIN

On several occasions in the texts, the Moon Goddess and the Virgin Mary met in various ways. Their meeting was not so violent or contradictory as one might think. The Moon Goddess asserted her traditional powers and privileges just as the Virgin Mary asserted hers. But the two deities most often did not maintain separate and distinct identities. The two became fused into one through the power of reinscription and colonial domination.

Two Become One

The Virgin Mary herself was elevated in her position, and the Moon Goddess continued to move past the conquest. These figures signified a desire that went beyond a strategic maintenance of the male gods. Like the desire for the saints, the concept of the Virgin Mary Moon Goddess perhaps pushed Catholicism to its limits.

The Virgin met the Moon Goddess in a variety of textual spaces, and both figures were reinscribed. Here I show the Virgin Mary Moon Goddess in another Maya song, one that inscribed the hybrid with a different identity. The following song was dedicated to the flower, discussing it as a multifaceted metaphor and particularly emphasizing its relationship with sexual behavior. At the same time, this song, like the above one, emphasized notions of gender, desire, and virginity. The song was based on both the flower and the moon, two items of importance in traditional Maya religion. Note the position of the people in the community as they responded to the course of the moon. This song allowed the people to act based on the actions of the moon:

KAY NICTE	*Flower Song*
X CIIH XCIICHPAN V	The very beautiful moon
ƆV LIKIL YOOK KAAX	has risen over the forest.
TV BIN V HOPBAL	It will light up[79]
TV CHVMVC C[A]N CAAN	the center of the sky,
TVX CV CH'VVYTAL	where it will be suspended
V ZAZICVNZ YOOKOL	in order to illuminate
CAB TV LACAL KAAX	the earth and all of the forest.
CHEN CI CI V TAL IIK	Only sweetness comes as the air
V VƆBEN BOOC	is fragrant.
V ƆV KVCHVL CHVMVC	It has arrived at the center
CAAN CHEN ZACTTIN	of the sky, shining alone over
CAB V ZAZILIL YOOK	the earth, illuminating
TVLACAL BAAL YAN	everything. There is
CIMAC OLIL [TI V TVLACAL]	happiness in all
MALOB VINIC	good men.
ƆOOC COHOL TV ICHIL	[We][80] have arrived inside
V NAAK KAAX TVVX	the abdomen of the forest, where
MAIXIMAC MEN MAX	no one
HEL V YILCONEIL LEIL	will be able to see [us],
BAAX [C] TAAL C'BEET	whatever we may come to do.
T TAZAH V LOL NIC TE	[We] have brought the flower
V LOL CHVCVM V LOL V	blossom, the *chukum*[81]
T TAZAH POM H'ZIIT	blossom, the dog jasmine
Ɔ VL VLOL X . . . MILAH	blossom,[82] the . . . blossom.[83]
BEYXAN XCOC BOX	[We] have brought the copal, the cane vine,
BEYXAN TVMBEN HIIB	also black tortoise shell,
TOOK YETE TVMBEN	also new hard, crystallized
KVCH TVMBEN LVCH	stone[84] and new spun cotton,
BOLOM YAAX TOOK	a new vase,[85] magnificent flint,

TVMBEN PEEƆILIL	new weights,[86]
TVMBEN XOOT BEY	new spun cotton,[87]
XAN V CAN X VLVM	also a number of turkeys,
TVMBEN XANAB	new shoes,
TVLACAL TVMBEN	all new,
LAIL XAM V KAXIL	including the bands tied around
C'HOOL V TIAL C	our heads, so that we
POOC NIICTE HA	can gather the nectar.[88]
BEYXAN C HOOPZA	Likewise, we scatter [the flowers]
[H]VB BEY V X KI	and the old times end.[89]
LIIZ ƆOCI ƆOCI T	They end.
YANON TV ƆV KAA[X]	We are in the heart of the forest,
TV CHI NOH HALTVN	at the edge of the stone pool,
V TIAL C'PAAT V	in order to await
HOKOL X CIICHPAN	the appearance of the beautiful
BVVƆ EK YOOKOL	smoking star[90] over
KAAX PITAH	the forest. Remove
NOOKEEX LVVZV	your clothes.
KAXIL A HOLEX	Untie your hair.
BATENEEX HEE	You are as
COHICEEX VAY	you arrived here
YOKOL CABILE	on earth,
X ZVHVYEX X CHV	you virgins,
PALELEX HEL V	you maidens from the moon.[91]

The flower song began by presenting a picture of the moon rising. The song combined symbols, showing that the flower ceremony depicted by the song was dedicated to the moon, or specifically to the Moon Goddess and her sexual acts. The Moon Goddess, never mentioned directly in the narrative, had a strong interest in women's sexual behaviors, and she showed her ability both to participate in and to control those behaviors. She in fact controlled the acts of all the community members. Here the moon metaphorically portrayed the presence of the lineage of the Moon Goddess, representing a sexual "promiscuity" that gained the Moon Goddess powers through her desire.

As the moon rose, it began to show the presence of the earth and the forest. The moonrise metaphorically symbolized the young women, rising and moving into their sexual maturity. Before the moon rose, these women were girls, but then they became maidens, eligible for sexual relationships. This created a sense of happiness in the community, which considered the sexual blossoming of the young women an important event. As the moon rose and the maidens reached an age of maturity, the people celebrated. Here, sexual desire was ensconced in a community ceremony.

The narrative appears to state that as the moon set, seemingly before sunrise, no light existed at all. The moon could not return the sight of the people. However, reading the metaphor, I find that the moon, representing women's sexual behavior, arrived in the middle of the forest where no one (perhaps meaning no outsiders) could return its sight. In this reading, the people participated in some sort of community orgy in the presence of the moon. The relationship to desire here implied that the maidens, coming of age, had sex secretly in the forest. The maidens engaged in sexual activity as part of a flower ritual, a ceremony designed to enhance their connections to the community, their matrilineage, and the gods.[92]

This metaphorical interpretation is confirmed through reference to the language of the flower. Singing of the flower according to the *Motul Dictionary* was to sing of "dishonorable love."[93] The flower here was a metaphor for sex itself. While the flower in different contexts could mean many things, and it could not always be interpreted as meaning sexual desire,[94] in this case the context of the document, combined with the interpretation of the metaphor by colonial sources, confirms that this is the correct interpretation.[95] The Flower Song thus was a song about sexual desire; it was a ceremonial group celebration of sexuality. Desire was strategically located in the community, and the moon asserted control over the sexual desires of the flower.

The location of the sexual behavior, in the "abdomen" of the forest, was an important narrative focus which took the sexual behavior out of the center of the community, and put it instead in the forest. The text thus posited a strategic outside, a place where such behavior might be more acceptable. Nonetheless, this strategic outside remained centered, by placing the sexual behavior in the metaphorical human body through the use of the abdomen, by allowing the behavior to take place in the economically important *kax*,[96] and by permitting it to exist in a ceremony of some importance. The sexual behavior thus, although unseen, was not ignored. It was an important ritual event designed to enhance life and happiness.

The young women then became sexual, and the old times ended. This process led them into adulthood, where, with the implements given to them in the flower ceremony, they could continue to live their lives, now dramatically changed. And here the group sexual activity began. As the people awaited the comet,[97] they began to tell the maidens to undress. The narrative prioritized the group, demanding that the women show their bodies. While the women had some control over their sexual behavior, they also were required to connect with the community and the gods, particularly the Moon Goddess.

The narrative strategically placed the desire for the Moon Goddess and for the flower in a place to assert the maintenance of community through an internal ceremony ending virginity. The document asserted male authority and took control over women's bodies. The women made a connection, as they undressed, with both the moon and the people. They had to return to their naked bodies in order to proceed with their lives. The ceremony allowed them to move on as the narrative strategically controlled their desires. Here, despite the presence of the Moon Goddess and the flower, the women were given little apparent control over their sexual acts. These were controlled by the town and the gods. Their own desires were displaced onto desires for the deities. Virginity and the Virgin Mary played important strategic roles in this process.

The Virgin Mary entered the song, this time as part of the Moon Goddess. She controlled the maidens by controlling their virginity. They had to remain virgins in order to please the Catholic Church, in order to assert chastity. The text then turned this concept around by ending the virginity in a community ceremony.

Both of the songs discussed above presented the importance of a strategic virginity. Rather than simply repressing sexual behavior, the two narratives showed the proper and improper places for sexual desire. The first song stated that women had to allow the Virgin Mary to control their sexual behavior by keeping their desires inside the community and preserving virginity for their "true" loves. The second narrative demanded that women allow the Moon Goddess and the flower ceremony to control their sexual behavior, maintaining their desires inside the town and in a specific ritual structure. Both songs were signifiers of a hybrid colonial culture. Both of the narratives together asserted control over sexual desire, and both showed that the colonial context scared the author and forced him to reassert control over a society seen as disordered. It was asserted that women should have positive sexual values which would allow the community to survive. And the Virgin Mary Moon Goddess was the hybrid figure who controlled these desires.

The Power of Reinscription

The Moon Goddess and the Virgin Mary, playing the same role, being seen as mother goddesses, and doing the same things in the texts, were in fact the same goddess. While Spanish popular culture may have blurred the line between the holiest woman in Catholicism and the possibility of asserting her as a goddess, certainly Spanish nobles and educated commoners would have known that Mary was not in any sense a goddess. Yet many of the Maya nobles who wrote the Books of Chilam Balam and the other texts and the Nahua nobles and commoners who participated in the production of the Nahuatl documents considered her just that. One must ask why, and the answer is that the Maya hybridized and reinscribed both the Moon Goddess and Mary. The "promiscuous" Moon Goddess had become the "Virgin" Mary.

The apparent disjunction between promiscuity and virginity was resolved by the power of reinscription. In the colonial context, the colonized peoples metaphorically reinscribed their own traditional concepts, placing those concepts within a package designed by the colonizers.[98] In this case the package was the Virgin Mary; the reinscribed concepts were parts of the Moon Goddess.

The hybrid figure has been present in many places in Yucatán. The Classic period Moon Goddess was shown as patroness of a series of diseases signified by the term *kak*. Today in Yucatán those diseases are termed "*kak* of the Virgin."[99] In the Book of Chilam Balam of Chumayel, the hybrid was presented in connection with the Maya universe:

paxi cah emal chac etzemal ti emi yix mehen hahal kui u yumil caan yx ahau yx suhun yx mactzil ca yalah ahau emem chim kin ich kak mo ma paat ti ahaulil uaye uay ti pati yx mactzil yx ɔayatzil emom sum emem tab tal ti caan emem u than tal ti caan lay cicuntabi yahaulil tumen u chucan cahob ca yalahob ma pati yahaulilob emmal

The great community of Emal was destroyed. Izamal was where the daughter of the true God, Lord of heaven; the Queen, the Virgin, the miraculous one descended. Then the lord said, "The shield of the glorious Kak Mo shall descend. [But] his rulership will not be declared[100] here. She the miraculous one, she the compassionate will be declared here. The rope shall descend, the cord shall descend from heaven. The word shall descend from heaven." There was happiness[101] as the lordship of all the towns was told not to declare the lordship of Emal.[102]

In this text the Virgin Mary was associated with the destruction of the lord (or god) Kak Mo. Her association with Catholicism, however, was problematized through her connection with the cord descending from heaven. Such a cord had no origin in Christian thought, but rather came from the cord which connected preconquest Maya shamans and others to the heavens. This cord was invoked through sacrificial rituals, and it was a symbolic representative of the umbilical cord: it was a way in which the gods gave life to humanity, a way in which humanity gave birth to the gods, and a way in which communication with the gods was maintained.[103] This cord was the way in which the Moon Goddess descended to engage in her curing rituals. Here the two became one.

But the hybrid was not a simple combination of the two figures, as the Virgin Mary had to incorporate aspects of other goddesses, and as there necessarily were powers which were gained, lost, or altered.

haxom kaak tu chicul maya suhuye hunab ku tu suhuyil hunab yglesia ti yauati la u yub u than u yumil caan u yumil yokol cab

Fire was ignited as a sign of the Maya Virgin. The one God of the one virginal Church cried out.[104] Thus what was heard was the word of the Lord of heaven, the Lord upon the earth.[105]

The fire in the text was evocative of the Maya preconquest fire goddess.[106] Here the Maya Virgin, intended to refer to the Virgin of Izamal, was endowed with this quality. This Virgin was supported by a shrine in Izamal where cures were performed. The Virgin Mary's qualities incorporated both those of the fire goddess and those of the Moon Goddess. Yet in many respects, both goddesses' powers were limited by the advent of Christianity: the Virgin still attained most of her status from her son.

The Virgin Mary Moon Goddess was a metaphor for the ideals of womanhood. The concept thus was gendered through the relationship of women and men to religion. Men, following the male gods, in preconquest Maya religion asserted their religious powers. They demanded control over the political sphere but understood that this control was dependent on them being able to maintain their patrilineal *and* matrilineal lines. After the conquest, following the same concepts, the men were able to follow the new male gods and assert religious and political power through only the patrilineal line, and only through the colonial gods and their representatives, the Catholic clergy.

Through the Moon Goddess herself the Maya understood the role and power of femininity. But as the hybrid desire for the Virgin Mary Moon Goddess developed, feminine power changed:

. . . *CAH IN YACVMAECH*	. . . I love you,
X CICHPAN COLEL BIIL	beautiful lady.
LAIBEILTIC	That is why
IN KAAT CA I[LABE]ECH H'AACH	I want you to look truly
ZEMPEECH CII[CHPAM]ECH TVMEN CV	very beautiful, so that you appear
YAN CA CHIICPAACEECH TI X BVVƆ	like the smoking star,
EK TV MEN CAV ƆIBOOL-TEECH TAC	as you will be desired[107]
LAIL V YETEL V X LOL NICTE KAAX	as the moon and the flowers of the forest.[108]
CHEN ZACAN ZACAN A NOK H'X ZVHVY	Your clothes are only white,[109] very white, maiden.[110]
XEN A ƆA V CIMAC OLIL A CHEE	Go, give out the happiness of your laugh,
ƆA VTZ TA PV CZIKAL TVMEN HELAE	Give out the goodness of your heart, because today
V ZVTVCIL CIMAC OLIL TV LACAL VINIC	is the moment of happiness for all men
LAIL CV ƆAILC V YVTZIL TI TEECH	who are giving their goodness to you.[111]

Femininity here was linked to the woman's body, as her beauty was desired by the men of the community. The desire for the woman's body was equaled by a desire for the moon and the flowers. Desire here, as a translation of *dzibol*, was meant to present a specifically sexual desire.[112] The moon and the Moon Goddess signified a gendered notion of power, but here they simply represented feminine beauty, applied to the virginal maidens. As the maidens clearly were intended to evoke values supported by the Spanish world and the Virgin Mary, this sense of appropriate femininity was another example of hybridity.

After the conquest women's status was asserted through the Virgin Mary. As she was reinscribed as a goddess, albeit a less powerful goddess than the Moon Goddess, her powers advanced. Women were able to assert matrilineal status, evidenced in the near obsession of the Books of Chilam Balam with both matrilineal and patrilineal legitimacy and noble status. Gender thus maintained some sense of parallelism through the power of reinscription.

The matrilineal line and women's gendered statuses were asserted through the Virgin Mary, and specifically through the reinscribed notion of *suhuy*.

THE LANGUAGE OF VIRGINITY

How could a goddess who had and continued to have sex be classified a virgin? In early modern European Catholic thought, Mary's very identity was based on the "Virgin" label. How could she become the same goddess as somebody who gained power by having sex? The answer related to the concept of virginity.

In certain ways virginity was one of the most complex sexual terms used in the colonial Maya language.[113] The language problems related directly to discussions of virginity and of the Virgin Mary herself. In several documents the Moon Goddess was declared a virgin through the use of the term *suhuy*. This word was used for the Moon Goddess in order to associate her with the Virgin Mary, who also was described as *suhuy*. The Moon Goddess attained great ritual power through her sexual activities with other gods. Yet she was called a virgin after the conquest.

To the clergy, the ultimate aim for women was to attain the virgin motherhood of Mary. Such a concept allowed women access to the ritual sphere in Catholicism. When the clergy came to Yucatán (and the rest of Latin America), they attempted to understand the moral systems of the indigenous people in order more successfully to impart knowledge about the Catholic moral system. In developing dictionaries and ethnographic studies, the clergy revised particular terminology, establishing different boundaries of meaning for many terms, including *suhuy*, "virgin."

Many of the narratives related to virginity have been discussed above, and I refer the reader back to them now. In one song I noted the high value placed on virginity, and specifically on female virginity. The language was very specific: the dictionaries translated *suhuy* as "virginity," and *colel* as both "lady" and a "woman's condition."[114] Here the condition of existing as a woman (or specifically a noble lady) implied an effort at virginity. The Catholic conceptualization was transferred onto a Maya framework. The song specifically discussed a festival to the Virgin Mary. She was the essential element in *the* woman's condition.[115]

In the text from the Ritual of the Bacabs discussed above in relation to the Virgin Mary, "virginity" was an important element early in the text, showing the power of various female ritualistic items in opposition to the woman who produced the disease:

> *in heɔcunt yokol ueyul al. . . . oxlahun than tix heɔeb tun ca tin hom*
> *kaxhhech ti suhuy tzotz ti suhuy cibix tij suhuy ɔoy suhuy tab can ix chac*
> *anicab ix kaxab yuc tin kaxciech bla bax chuylic cech u suhuy hohol*

My seating is through the child of a mistress. . . .[116] The thirteen statements were established. I tied you down with the virgin hair, the virgin *cibix* plant, the virgin *dzoy*,[117] the virgin serpent vine, she the great one of the world, she the bound deer. I bind you. So with what are you suspended? With the virgin bark.[118]

The virginal aspects were considered powerful elements in the text: elements that would allow the curing ritual to take place. These elements were feared and desired: feared for they could kill; desired for they could cure. In each case these were virginal female impressions of what was to save the patient. Tying up the disease, in these texts, was a common metaphor for the curing ritual itself. The disease here was tied to the virgins, using the cord of perhaps the Moon Goddess. These metaphorical representations were signifiers of the Moon Goddess which presented the power of the term *suhuy* and the power of the female line in the cure. The female line was represented as a central aspect through reproductive power. The women who produced the "illegitimate" child thus could reproduce disease, destroying society. The goddesses, with their virginal items, could engage in further reproduction to accomplish the cure.

The cure itself, however, as has been shown, ended up being a phallic cure. It became phallic upon the invocation of Jesus and Mary. The power of the women through the term *suhuy* and their relationships to curing were lost as the semen was invoked. Mary did not represent a powerful figure in these texts, where she never was called a virgin, never represented as *suhuy*.

In another incantation from the Ritual of the Bacabs, the word for virgin was written several times to describe both the Moon Goddess and a stingray spine. If the term *suhuy* was translated as "virgin," the Moon Goddess, described with several adjectives in the incantation, became *suhuy ix chel*, "the virgin Moon Goddess."[119] But in this incantation, the Moon Goddess was presented in a sexual manner, apparently arousing a spider's "penis." The text used sexual metaphors to engage in the cure. The stingray spine itself was an entity possessed by the Moon Goddess. The spine also was virginal (*suhuy pudz*) as it was associated with the Moon Goddess as a sexualized entity. This spine was an instrument which enabled the Moon Goddess and the curer to engage in the cure. In this context, *suhuy* signified the idea of ritual power through the Moon Goddess's sexual desire. She had *suhuy* as she engaged in a curing ceremony. She developed her power through her desire, participating in sexual acts in order to cure the patient.

This ritual power, while having little to do with the Catholic concept of virginity, related to a gendered notion of sexual desire in a similar manner to that of the "Virgin" label for Mary. In Mary's case, virginity allowed certain symbolic status in the Catholic world. It allowed her access to a ritual world otherwise inaccessible to women. In this sense the Maya could interpret the virgin label as a direct and correct translation of *suhuy*, a term which allowed noble women and goddesses access to the cosmos. Nonetheless, as the case of the Moon Goddess shows, the term *suhuy* could not have implied a lack of sexual experience.

Before the conquest, Maya attitudes toward virginity were quite complex. Thompson asserted the importance of virginity for human sacrifice. He said that children were chosen because they were *suhuy*, or virginal. Thompson believed that *suhuy* signified a positive portrayal of the "uncontaminated virgin," thus allowing the term to be used for natural elements as well as people.[120] Indeed it appears that the Maya placed some importance on sacrificing people who were not contaminated. However, human sacrifice often was reserved for war captives. These captives usually would not have been considered *suhuy*. Moreover, the concept of *suhuy* appeared in the documents relating either to Catholicism or to powerful goddesses in Maya religion.

The term was related to ritual power in most texts. It was a common expression only when discussing Mary and in the Ritual of the Bacabs. There *suhuy* clearly signified the ritual power of femininity through sexual desire.

> *cech fel u na ta uach u suhuy puɔ bin a chich a chah oc ta uach u suhuy kak bin a chich*

> You! The vagina's mother with your penis. You will enter grasping your grandmother's virginal needle with your penis and your grandmother's virginal fire.[121]

Here the term *suhuy* modified both the needle and the fire.[122] These elements, as possessed by the grandmother (who probably was intended to be the

Moon Goddess),[123] related to the importance of the matrilineal line. The penis, so powerful in the Western phallocentric universe, needed the grandmother's power in order to engage in the cure. This ritual power was indicated only by *suhuy*. *Suhuy* in this situation did not represent the "uncontaminated." Nor did it signify the maintenance of a sexually "untouched" body. The idea of virginity was a representation of sacred power related to a goddess's sexual desires.

The connection between the Virgin Mary and the Moon Goddess allowed for a gendering of religion different from that promoted in either European Catholicism or preconquest Maya religion. The idea of *suhuy* became associated directly with virginity only through the act of translation, an act which placed different boundaries on the term. The Virgin Mary and the Moon Goddess were signs for these different boundaries.

THE RESILIENCE OF THE MOON GODDESS

The relationship between the desires of the Moon Goddess and the "real" desires of the colonial Maya people is a relationship that will remain unknown. The colonial Maya people continued to see the Moon Goddess as a god worthy of great respect, both with her traditional name and with the name and identity of the Virgin Mary. This respect, stemming from a belief regarding a debt of obligation,[124] suggested that the Maya were intended to learn lessons from the Moon Goddess: lessons about desire, creation, excess, and destruction.

As Catholicism colonized women through the use of a new understanding of gender, it also presented the Moon Goddess with the possibility of survival. She survived, vastly altered, in the figure of the Virgin Mary. She also maintained a powerful existence of her own in those parts of the Maya universe where Mary dared not tread. But neither the Catholic clergy nor the Maya traditionalists could find their traditions here. The hybrid had formed, and this hybrid was not going to resemble either of its two predecessors. For the Virgin Mary Moon Goddess was to have power precisely through her new qualities; precisely by filling the empty spaces in between Catholicism and Maya traditional religion. The Moon Goddess no longer could command public rituals of support, at least not without subterfuge. The Virgin Mary no longer could be a Virgin, at least not in the fantasies of many Maya. In this in-between space, where the Moon Goddess could be a virgin, where the Virgin Mary could be connected to the heavens with an umbilical cord, a hybrid colonial culture was to be defined.

Gender in the Maya world certainly changed through the introduction of the Virgin. Both Mary and the Moon Goddess were used in strategic maneuvers to disempower women. And both were used to preserve some status for women through matrilineage. Both charged the Maya ritual universe with gendered notions of power. Without them (and the other Maya goddesses) and the position of *suhuy* in the power structure, the entire ritual sphere would have been dominated by a male conceptualization of the world.

The desire for the Virgin Mary worked well for the Franciscan friars, the Spanish leaders, and the Maya noblemen, as this desire was reinscribed to cope with the new situations of colonialism. This reinscription allowed desire to be repositioned in a way that would allow the people to desire their rulers. From the viewpoint of the friars, this desire allowed them to instruct the Maya in Catholic rituals. The Spanish leaders saw this as an opportunity which gave them greater access to Maya individuals. For the Maya noblemen, the desire for the Virgin Mary stemmed from a desire for protection. Many commoners and nobles wanted their traditions to remain the same, and these traditions included powerful goddesses and a symbolism of gender parallelism. The nobles thus maintained some perceived status quo in a rapidly changing society. The gendered notion, from their perspective, allowed for a certain parallelism which maintained the traditional structures of power. If this parallelism had suddenly ceased to exist, there would have been a massive change in the ritual hierarchy. The nobles rightfully would have feared that commoners would have started to believe that their nobles had attempted to trick them, for society would have continued to survive without the appropriate rituals.[125] Thus commoners would have begun to question the social, economic, and political hierarchies.

The gendered structure of colonialism maintained the social hierarchy and stood for the interests and desires of the nobles. So why did the commoners desire the Virgin Mary Moon Goddess? Why did they believe in this sexualized virgin? First, the commoners desired protection. They had come to believe that they could only get this protection from their ritual hierarchy, and so they desired to maintain that hierarchy. Second, the gendered notion of the hierarchy made sense to them. It did not just take men to engage in creation and maintenance of the world.[126] Third, the highly sexualized notion of the Moon Goddess also made sense in such a framework. A goddess necessarily must have engaged in sexual acts in order to create children. And while there was more than one goddess, it also made sense that the supreme goddess would have engaged in sexual acts with a variety of gods. She herself would have signified protection and unity. No doubt the origins of these concepts of creation existed in some (pre-Spanish) colonial maneuver where other peoples came to desire the Moon Goddess because her people engaged in conquest of others in Yucatán. The conquerors then associated their lineages with the others in order to gain power over those communities. Eventually the Moon Goddess reigned supreme. Whatever the origins of this desire, the commoners would have understood one element of power: if you had a powerful god conquering your community, then you began to worship that god.

And the same would have applied to the Virgin Mary, as the commoners understood her as a powerful goddess. They saw her as a leader of the Spaniards, perhaps even more so than Jesus or the Christian God. She was seen as a goddess because that made the most sense based on the traditions of the commoners (and the nobles). She was seen as sexual because any other understanding of her would have meant that she could not have been the mother goddess.[127] And for commoners who knew little, if any, Spanish, this perception of tradition was far more important than anything that a Franciscan friar told them.

The nobles presented the commoners with a metaphorical view of history, religion, philosophy, and the world. The metaphors allowed for conquest and control.[128] I have shown how this hierarchical and metaphorical culture was maintained through the colonization of desire. The displaced desire to stay away from sin and the desire for Saint Francis and the Virgin Mary were acts of colonialism which made sense to the Maya. The Virgin Mary Moon Goddess was a central entity in this paradigm of displaced desire. Through Spanish culture, the Virgin Mary was asserted as an equivalent of the Moon Goddess. She thus fit into the Maya religious hierarchy. Slowly and subtly that hierarchy changed with the insertion of the Virgin. The hybrid figure became more like the Spanish figure than the Maya goddess. And the Moon Goddess's reinscription became an act of colonial domination and hegemony, an act reinforced by hybridity.

SIX

Gender, Lineage, and the Blood of the Rulers

Maya ritual discourse made it clear that lineage was a central concern of many of the nobles, and probably of the commoners as well. The kinship lines of the leader of society were vital markers which determined whether he would be a successful ruler. Before and after the conquest, a leader ruled by developing alliances through kin groups.[1] I metaphorically center the concerns related to lineage on the body of the ruler. In essence the Maya were asking about the relationship of their rulers' bodies to other bodies in the Maya universe. The body and blood of the ruler symbolized the prosperity or lack thereof of the people.

The preconquest notion of political power related to the protections the rulers and nobles provided for the people, symbolized by the shedding of noble blood and the corresponding obligations that the commoners felt toward the rulers. This was the same in colonial times, but the protections that the Maya rulers could provide were altered radically and in many cases circumscribed. Rulership was determined in preconquest times by struggles for political power among those who could determine nobility through patrilineage and matrilineage. Lineage was determined differently in colonial times, with matrilineal descent taking on significantly less importance. So the desire for the rulers changed during colonial times, as this desire, marked by the bodies of the nobles, would have to alter according to the appropriate context.

BODIES OF KINGS

A Maya king's body was marked by accoutrements which established hierarchy. The king was always an impressive figure because of some combination of his physical stature, his clothing and jewelry, or the people and objects that surrounded him. His body was marked in various ways so that his followers understood his high status.

The human body was used as an element of memory, an element which maintained hierarchy. The bodies of the Maya nobles were purported to represent the body of the community. The leaders placed their bodies in central positions designed to make them the recipients of desire. The people desired a connection with, even a dependence on, the body of the leader.[2]

The human body was important as it signified blood and lineage. Nobles could rule; commoners could not. This was related to an understanding of blood as that which the gods wanted and that which would make the community survive. Under normal conditions, a noble was the preferred person to be sacrificed because his blood was not tainted and therefore that blood was able to maintain the community. Implicit in this idea was a critique of the sexual desires of the commoners: they did not know what to do in order to reproduce effectively. Sacrificing them did not symbolically enhance the community's chance for survival as much as sacrificing a noble. The blood and body of the noble were important in order to trace lineage and prevent any commoners from gaining access to the religious and political spheres.

The body of one type of ruler was signified directly as the *halach uinic*, "the true man/body." This body signified truth because of its lineage, ensured that the person in power was the appropriate person, and made it so that the Maya community did not court disaster. The political system centered around truth, signified in the body of the *halach uinic*, and proven through his blood.

The Meaning of Sacrifice: A Late Colonial Example

Human sacrifice was an accepted practice among Mayan peoples since at least the late Preclassic times.[3] The iconography of warfare made it clear that many captives were sacrificed. Additionally, children, slaves, and losing members of the team in a Maya ball game also could be killed in this way.[4] The rationale behind these sacrifices was not always clear. Household heads sometimes attempted to please the gods and ensure a strong harvest by sacrificing a slave.[5] A noble's illegitimate child was vulnerable, likely because of the perceived need to sacrifice nobles and the questionable position of the illegitimate child in noble society.[6] The losing warrior was sacrificed by the community of the winning side in order to thank the gods for the victory and in order to appease those gods.[7] When an important leader died, his or her burial was accompanied by sacrifices of people (probably some of the leader's noble aides, servants, and slaves) to help him or her in the afterlife.[8] The practice of human sacrifice among the Maya, however, has been overestimated, and until Postclassic times animals were much more likely to be sacrificed than humans.[9]

Only a handful of extant postconquest texts mention sacrifice. Moreover, such acts appear to have ended to a great degree after the Spanish conquest, Diego de Landa notwithstanding.[10] The meaning of sacrifice necessarily changed dramatically after the conquest. In postconquest times human sacrifice certainly could not have been performed as a public event. Sacrifice as a strategy of rulership could not hold, as the strategy mandated a public forum.[11] The ruler felt the need to sacrifice people so that he could show his community that he coordinated sacrifices to the gods. It was a method of placating the people as much as the gods. By late colonial times, the Maya had found an unsatisfactory replacement for human sacrifice: adherence to the terms of Catholicism. This was unsatisfactory because it was difficult to instill the power of Catholicism in Maya leaders since those leaders could not be the intermediaries between the community and the gods.[12]

The late colonial Songs of Dzitbalché present two examples related to the ritual of human sacrifice. In one case, the Maya text alleges that a particular song and ceremony was written and performed in 1440.[13] Nonetheless, the version that we have was written some time after 1740.[14] In this example the position and identity of the person in the center of the plaza are the central elements of the ceremony, and thus of the spectacle.

X' KOLOM CHÉ	*The Broken Tree/Clefted Stick*[15]
AH' PAPAL H'MVVKAN	The strong youth,
VINIC PPIZAN CHIMALIL	men of the order of the shield,[16]
C YOOC LOOB T CHVMVC	should come forward to the
C'KI VIC VT TIAL V	center[17] of the plaza so that
H'PPIZV V MVVKOOB	their strength will be tested
TX KOLOM CHE OKOOT	in the dance of *Kolomche*.[18]
TV CHVMVC C'KI VIC	In the center of the plaza,
YAM VN PPEL XIIB	there is a man
KAXAN TV CHVM OCOM	tied to the bottom

TVNIICH CI CI BONAN	of the stone column
YETEL X CIIHCHPAM	well painted
H' CH'OO ƆAN EN	with beautiful indigo,
YAABLOL BALCHÉ V BOCINTÉ	and a scattering of many *balche* flowers,
BAYTAN TV KAB TVT	which should perfume his hands
YOC TVT VINCLIL XAN	and his feet as well as his body.
CIH A VOL CIICHELEN	Raise your spirits,
XIIB TECHÉ A CAA	beautiful[19] man.
A VILAH V YIICH A YVM	You shall see the face
CAAN MAA TV YANTAAL	of your Father in heaven.
. . . N ZVVTCEECH VAY YOOK	It will not be necessary for you
[CAB] IL YANAL V	to return here to the earth,
KVKMEELLIL CHAN ƆVNVN VA	with the feathers of the small hummingbird[20]
YANAL V KEV LEL V	or in the skin of . . . ,[21]
. . . EL CIICH CELEM CEEH	the beautiful deer,[22]
H'CHAC MOOL CHAN	the great jaguar,[23]
X KOOK VA CHAN KAMBVVL	the small nightingale, or the small yellow bird.[24]
ƆA A VOL TVCVLNEN	Give all of your spirit, place your thoughts,
CHEN TI A YVMIL MAA	only in your Father.
A CH['A] ZA[HAC]IL MAA	Do not be afraid.
LOOB CVN [BET]BIL TECHIL	You will be treated well.[25]
CIICHPAN X CHVPALAL	Beautiful maidens
LAKINT CEECH TAA	will accompany you
ZVTVCIL A TAL A VAL	on your journey as you go.[26]
TAM BIN MAA CHIIC	Do not be afraid.
ZAHCIL ƆA A VOL TII	Place your spirit into your task,
BAALX CVN MANTECH	for you will succeed.[27]
H'E CV TAAL NOHYVM	Oh, the great lord is coming,
H'OL POP TV N TAAL	The head of the community[28] will be coming,
YETEL V H'ACVLEEL	with his lieutenant.
BEYXAN AH' AHAV	Also the lord Can Pech,[29]
CAN PEECH H'EE CV	he will come.
TAALO TV XAX CV	By his side will come

TAAL NOHOCH	the great
NACON AKÉ HÉ	Nacon Ake.[30]
CVTAL BATAB H . . .	And the governor is coming.
CHEE NEN	Laugh
CIMCIMACAC A VOL	and rejoice in your spirit
TV MEN TECHEÉ	as you are the one,
LAIL ALAN TEECH	as is being told to you,
CA A BIIZ V	to take
THAN VET CAHALOOB	the words of the people[31]
TV TAN C'CIICH CELEN YVM	before our blessed Father,
LAITI ƆAMNIL	as it has been decreed
VAY T YOOKOOL CA[B]	here on earth;
ƆOCILIL V MAN	a custom which began
YAACAACH . . .	a long time
TITVN ZALAM . . .	ago. . . .[32]

The ritual of human sacrifice was played out on the body of the man in the center of the plaza. The narrative attempted to convince him to accept his fate. I discuss human sacrifice here because the Maya developed an intricate connection between sacrifice, blood, war, and sexual desire.

Warrior Status

In this particular late colonial text, many preconquest rituals and offices had survived, at least in the memories of those writing the songs. This ritualized song and the related dance had a history in Yucatán from at least the sixteenth century, and it must have been copied from the earlier versions. Landa described the dance without commenting on its meaning.

[It] is a game of reeds which they call *colomché*, the word having that meaning ["defense of wood"].[33] To perform it, they make a large circle of dancers, whom the music accompanies. In time, two come into the circle. One of these dances upright, holding a bundle of reeds, while the other dances squatting, both keeping time around the circle. The one with the reeds throws them with all his force at the other, who, with great skill, catches them with a small rod. When all are thrown, they return, keeping time, into the circle, and others come out and do the same.[34]

The dance, which was intended to signify warfare and human sacrifice by arrow, expressed concern for the warrior, helping him develop his martial skills.

Here the sense of the warrior as the central person inside the circle was related to the person to be sacrificed. Those on the outside were tossing reeds at the central warrior, who dangerously caught those reeds. In the sacrificial ceremony, the reeds had been arrows, and the warrior did not catch them; they pierced his skin. After the conquest, with sacrifice no longer feasible in such a public format, the dance had become a ritual which signified some of the elements of sacrifice but did not go through with the actual event. In both cases, however, the people called upon the warrior's bravery to face all obstacles.

How did the person to be sacrificed relate to the warrior catching the reeds? They were the same person: the person to be sacrificed often was a noble warrior captive, and his blood signified the blood of rulers. The warrior in the center of the ritual certainly was a skilled practitioner, and hence a leader of society. This text created a particular understanding of connections, through blood, between warfare and sacrifice. Metaphorically, both signified penetrations of the human body.

After the conquest the warrior's status must have been questioned. For without more wars to fight, what position would the warrior have in society? This text shows that the warrior, or at least his memory, had not ceased to exist in late colonial times. While his status certainly was not the same, he could participate in ritual dances and other ceremonies. But he could not fight a war, an act central to his preconquest identity. The warrior necessarily harked back to the past, when his body would have been worshipped. The warrior's meaning changed dramatically: he became a noble or a commoner, most likely by late colonial times a rural laborer. His body no longer was the center of attention.

This text related a time when the warrior's body was the center of the universe, the center of the spectacle. And the dance allowed this warrior's body to emerge again at the center of the community. While his body once again became a unifying force, the dance ended quickly and the people went back to work, never fooled by the concept that the warrior's body remained important.

Nobles and Youth

To many people, including the Catholic clergy of the early period, human sacrifice was the most objectionable element of Maya life. Sacrifice to them was the ultimate in cruelty: a person apparently was killed for no reason at all.

Sacrifice thus was the ultimate in irrational vengeance, where a person was killed simply because that person existed: the vengeance of the gods demanded this. Particularly objectionable to the clergy was the sacrifice of children.[35] But why would the Maya have engaged in such a cruel act? How can one understand the desire for human sacrifice?

The European concepts of cruelty and vengeance were constructed in a context which the preconquest Maya did not accept. Let us imagine the previous text as a description of a preconquest event. In the document there existed various elements of desire not too different from European historical notions. The central character here was the person tied up in the middle of the plaza. The narrative presented his body as a spectacle, since the people of the community came to see the dance, and he was the center of attention. The people of the town arrived, in a sense, to see the body of this man tied up in the center of their plaza. His body was covered with many flowers, which gave him a wonderful fragrance, drawing more attention to the spectacle. This technique also elevated the body that was about to be destroyed. The narrative explained human sacrifice as a beautiful event, one in which bodies had a wonderful odor. The spectacle was a desired piece of entertainment. It was desired because the person in the center of the plaza was embarking on a wondrous journey to the gods. The people wanted to wish him well and send their requests with him, so they participated in the spectacle. But it was not only the commoners of the community who came to watch this spectacle. The presence of the lords and governors signified the importance of the ritual and placed them in the position of communicating with the gods. The narrative legitimized the entire content of the text by placing on it the approval of the dignitaries. Their very bodily presence (for they said nothing) recalled a legitimizing strategy. Human sacrifice was represented as a unifying element for all of the community. The people came to see the spectacle, and this event encouraged the support of the gods. The desire here thus maintained community and hierarchy as the people saw the spectacle of the man in the plaza. This man was to give his life for the gods and the lords and dignitaries. The commoners viewed this, and they saw how serious the leaders of society were about the maintenance of the community. This showed both the legitimacy of the leaders and the presence of the gods. So the desire for human sacrifice here signified continuity for the state.

The commoners and many of the nobles were the intended audience of the text/dance. The man to be sacrificed also was represented as an audience member as he supposedly was convinced by the narrative to go through with his sacrifice (one would guess that, in real life, there would be many exceptions to this), thus impressing the people watching the dance. They were convinced of the necessity of human sacrifice and of the commitment of the nobles. The text wanted to raise the spirits of this man. In doing so, the spiritual world was connected with and in some senses became a part of his body. This body had to smell beautiful, and he could not be afraid, because, if he was afraid, he would not have a successful journey. His spirit and body became central narrative techniques: they both were required to be in excellent shape in order for the sacrifice to be successful.

The beautiful women were going with him on the journey, suggesting that these women were to give him pleasure, thus stimulating him to connect his sexual desire with human sacrifice. From the perspective of the audience, while they may not have seen these women,[36] they could begin to understand the noble's desire to be sacrificed. He would go through this journey with women whom he desired. These women were to make the gods and the noble happy, so there was no reason to feel sorry for the person being sacrificed, nor was there any reason to stop these practices. The person being sacrificed was to be engaging in (sexual) acts which would ensure the maintenance of the community.

But this song did not explicitly state that the Maya were going to complete the sacrificial act. Another song detailed some of these procedures:

. . . A CI CHOIMAA V BA V	. . . Anoint yourself well
TZATZEL XIBIL CEH TV	with the fat of a deer
MVVK A KAB TV MVVK A	on the muscles of your arms,
VOC TA PIIX TA TTOON	on the muscles of your legs, on
	your knees, on your genitals,
TAA CH'ALATEL TAA TZEM	on your ribs, on your chest.
ƆAA OXPPEL ALCA ZVVT TVT	Make three running turns in front of
PACH LEIL OCOM TVM BONAN	and behind the painted stone
	column,
LAIL TVVX KAXAAN LEIL XIBIL	where that man, the youthful, pure,
PAL H'ZAC ZVHVY VINIC	and virgin man is tied.
ƆAA V YAAX TI CA ZVTIL	Make the first, and on the second
	turn,
CHH'A A PPVM ƆA V HVL	take your bow and point your arrow
CH[EI]L	straight
TOH TANT V TZEM MA KABEILT	at his chest. It is not necessary to
A ƆIIC TV LACAL A MVVK TIYAL	use all of your strength so that

A HVVL LOMTCI TIOLAL MAV	your arrow will be jabbed right into the heart.
KILIC TV TAMIL V BAKEL V	Do not wound him to the depths of his flesh,
TIAL CA PAATAC V MVK YAATIC	for he should suffer[37]
HV HVM PPIITIL LEY V YOTA	little by little. That is the wish
CILIICHCELEM YVM KV	of the beautiful[38] Lord God.
TV CAA ZVVT CA ƆAA TI LEIL	On the second turn that you make
OCOM TVM CHO CA ZVVT	around the stone indigo column, on the second turn
CA ƆAE CA HVLIC TV CAATEN	that you make, shoot, then shoot a second time.
LAILO YAN A BEILTIC XMA MA	This is what you have to do without
A PAATIC A VOKOOT TV MEN	leaving the dance, because
BAIL V MENTIC MALO CHI	this is what is done by the good
MA[L] H'BATEL VINIC TVT	shield bearers, the warrior men,
TEETAL V TIAL V ƆA VTZ	as they choose to delight
T YIICH YVM KV. . . .	the eyes of the Lord God. . . .[39]

[The beginning of the text referred to the training and the early approach of the warriors, as well as to the preparation of the arrows.]

The practice of sacrifice not only gave ritual importance to the body of the one to be sacrificed but also made a spectacle of the bodies of the sacrificing warriors. Their bodies had to be anointed with the fat of the deer, and their skills were tested.

As in the last example, the person to be sacrificed was central to the text, although this text clearly was intended to be sung or told to the sacrificers. The man to be sacrificed was described as both a full-grown man (*xib*) and a virgin (*suhuy*). While this is the only case I have found of a man being described as *suhuy*, it again points to the fact that this term did not refer to virginity as such. The man's position as a good person to be sacrificed (a noble and a captive) and his servile situation were signified by *suhuy*. And this man was to suffer; here, in contrast to the previous text, the man's pain was emphasized. If he lived long after being wounded, then the warriors would be considered more valorous. And, of course, the people would have seen more of a spectacle. Here the spectacle of human sacrifice was used again as an element to stratify relationships and to show the power of noble warriors.

Another notable aspect of this text is its reference to the "Lord God."

While the text did not refer to *Dios,* the use of the singular to apply to God meant that the Christian God probably was intended. The hybridity of the text thus showed that this Christian God was ordering human sacrifice. The Maya certainly at some point believed that the sacrifice of Jesus related to their traditional rituals, and they unconsciously and consciously applied this concept to these ceremonies. The songs allowed the nobles to be connected to the blood of Jesus. At the same time, the blood of the sacrificed and the bodies of the sacrificers signified a noble adherence to community and connection with the gods. Noble blood thus was able to stratify relationships within a hybrid colonial tradition. These texts have shown some of the important relationships of Catholicism to preconquest Maya religious practices.[40] The narrative strategy combined (probably unconsciously) the two religions. The texts do not tell us if the Maya actually practiced human sacrifice to the Christian God.

A late colonial text describing a dance related to sacrifice was a text seemingly without power, as human sacrifice could not be performed. But the text still had meaning, and this meaning gave the text power. Referring back to a time when the preconquest leaders could protect the community was reminiscent of narratives showing a "golden age" past. In this narrative technique, the Maya leaders provided the people with a reason to reestablish the past. At the same time, the text supported the late colonial Maya leadership by giving them a chance to appear at a community festival. The dance was intended to show the leadership's commitment to the maintenance of community and traditional Maya culture.

Blood, Sex, and Sacrifice

Blood symbolized many things in the colonial Maya universe: sexual acts; childbirth; warfare; sacrifice; and differentiation based on gender, aristocratic status, class, and ethnicity. It stratified not only politics but also ritual life and the social and economic spheres. It often signified displaced sexual desire, or a desire for knowledge of the sexual acts of the lineage. And these sexual desires were represented in many ways.

The terms used, as shown above, for some sexual acts, as well as warfare, sacrifice, and piercing, related to excess. Additional linguistic analysis led to an understanding of a direct relationship with blood. *Top* was another Maya term related to sex, which several dictionaries defined as "sexual acts" or "carnal acts." The word *top* also meant "promptness" and "to pierce or penetrate part way."[41] Piercing of the body was one of many potential bodily desires which the Maya connected with sex. The modern Maya use the term *top* as a direct translation of the Spanish word *joder*, "to fuck."[42] The construct makes sense on some level: to have anal or vaginal intercourse suggests a penetration of the body. Penile oral sex also can be viewed as a penetration. Using another object to make a hole through the skin further involves penetration. The use of an arrow, spear, sword, or gun represents yet another penetration of the body. Bloodletting and human sacrifice also signify penetrations by a knife. A strong metaphorical connection existed in Maya thought between the body, sexual desire, human sacrifice, and war. The flower was a metaphor related to this concept of penetration. This metaphor signified blood itself; the desire thus was a desire for blood.

This can be seen more effectively by returning to an analysis of Maya rituals of death.[43] A historical text, mentioned above, describing the end of the era in which Mayapán controlled much of Yucatán, showed the relationship between human sacrifice, blood, and warfare:

lei tah mehen hapai can lae ca natabi tumen kukul cane ca xoti u cal u yiob u yubob tu lacal yal u mehen cu pactic u luk hapai caan lei ah cuchteob u cuchah u keban y ahau ob ca tun hopi u tumtic itzam caan ca tal yocol u keban y ahau can ul ca hoki ahau caan tu chichenob vai max can ul tu chicane ti hoki ahaui oxlahun te u cuch ca sihsabi tumen u yum lai hunpel cuyuhil sinic balamil calam koh che y ah ca cap chan tokil oc na kuchil ma ya cimlal kintunyabil

This was the division of the son[s] of Hapay Can, as was understood by Kukul Can.[44] Then the throats, eyes, and ears of all the children of women and men[45] were cut. Then he [Kukul Can] viewed[46] the removal of Hapay Can, who [with his kin] were made the bearers and thus carried the sin of their lord. Then began the testing[47] of Itzam Can. Then came theft, the sin of the lord Can Ul. Then Ahau Can and those of Chichén Itzá appeared here. Who was Can Ul? He was manifested, and he appeared as lord, his thirteenth burden, for which he was created by his father. This was one mantle[48] of ants, jaguars, coral snakes, wood masks, stabbers, and little blood makers[49] as death without pain[50] arrived and appeared at the houses during the calendar round.[51]

This text reacted to an early colonialism of a central Mexican–influenced group over Yucatán. This was another strategic narrative designed to show the problematic behavior of prior leaders as compared with their contemporaries and the current leadership.

A series of destructive acts took place as Kukul Can became a powerful figure in Yucatecan politics. The throats, eyes, and ears marked the places where Kukul Can engaged in great destruction. The parts of the body stood as markers for maiming and death. They also stood as political symbols, since the acts stressed both the political power of Kukul Can and the protest against that power. The narrative politicized these acts, using body parts to stress that politicization. The acts of Kukul Can and Can Ul created blood through the prioritization of the human body. This blood, represented as nobility (they were the children of men and women, so they knew their lineages), was spilled in a manner that was intended to signify destruction. The sacrifice, for whatever reason, did not please the gods, as the people still were to be destroyed. Blood marked the death and destruction caused by Can Ul's alliance with the military orders.

These warriors promoted "death without pain," a reference to human sacrifice. Maya ideology considered human sacrifice a privileged way to die as it allowed the body to traverse the skies.[52] The ethnographic knowledge of this act as well as the linguistic construction of the terminology privileged ritual sacrifice as a preferred method of death. The idea of a "painless death" showed an attempt in the language to recommend this type of death as a good thing. Sacrifice was a central strategy of the text, an account of preconquest destruction. Perhaps the sacrifice was performed improperly. Or perhaps this postconquest text sought to condemn this preconquest practice. Or perhaps "Toltec" methods of sacrifice were seen as insufficient to please the gods.

Linguistically, the concept of human sacrifice pointed to the nobles. The sacrifice was termed not just "painless death" but also "Maya death." The word *Maya* in the Books of Chilam Balam most often signified the nobles. They were the ones who would face this painless death because their blood clearly was connected with the gods. They thus were distinguished from the commoners, who, according to these texts, did not understand the importance of the desire for blood.[53]

Both war and human sacrifice served as cultural unifying factors put in place to resolve internal disputes of the community as well as disputes between communities. Internally, stratification remained ordered as desire was displaced onto warfare and a desire to win. This warfare structured ideas of ethnicity, allowing the people of one community to understand that they were a different nation than the other community.[54] Yet it also allowed for a cross-Yucatecan cultural unifying scheme for nobles: they knew the relationship of blood to warfare, sex, and human sacrifice. War permitted the ritual shedding of blood for the gods, and it created a textual space for the maintenance of a hierarchy through the displacement of desire.

Human sacrifice was related to a particular strategy of rulership as important to the West as to the Maya, and the sacrifice here was intended to create a memory for the community. Friedrich Nietzsche was correct in this sense: "Whenever man has thought it necessary to create a memory for himself, his effort has been attended with torture, blood, sacrifice."[55] Here the blood and sacrifice were not punishment or vengeance. There was no representation of the vengeance of the gods in this or any other Maya texts related to sacrifice. The people sacrificed often were nobles, and they had done nothing considered wrong (It is here that I disagree with Nietzsche, who claimed that punishment was an important element in this).[56] Instead the sacrifice was directed toward the community in order to show commoners the fairness of the system and the commitment of the nobles. Memory here, unlike in Nietzsche, was about remembering the importance of community and society: it was about displacing desire onto the maintenance of the life of the state.[57]

The rituals of death were strategic maneuvers which told partial, sometimes contradictory, truths.[58] Whether or not the ideas contradicted, historians must provide a context for them that does not attempt to place them under a system limiting the contradictions.[59] These narratives begin to allow for an understanding of the power of blood. The political notion here was that the leaders, the rulers, would be allowed to rule through the ritual shedding of blood attained in warfare and sacrifice, which established the legitimacy of the leader.[60] After the conquest, different forums were required for the establishment of this legitimacy. These forums were dependent on the Spanish colonial structure. However, memory of sacrifice remained important through the colonial years.

The two songs presented a particular show of masculinity through blood and sacrifice. The central figures were gendered male, and they proved their masculinity through their relationship with blood. The sacrificers were to prove their masculinity by providing a slow, painful death; the sacrificed man was to prove his masculinity by being stoic in the face of great torture; all proved their masculinity by providing a good spectacle. The women showed the proper feminine role in that they accompanied the sacrificed man. Their power was limited, but the feminine sphere was still present, even in the rituals of the warriors.

THE BLOOD OF THE NAME

Lineage and the naming process often develop into a hierarchical relation. Naming is an event related to any genealogical analysis of desire, as people in many societies obtain names and connections through their understanding of the sexual desires and acts of their predecessors. Thus, in the modern West children are named by their parents, and the children establish a position at birth through this name. The name gives the child an initial place in society, and it is very suggestive of gender and often of race and ethnicity.[61] The power to name is a power to place a person in society, and the desire to name is a desire for power.

In the preconquest and colonial Maya world, blood marked this desire for power. In the above story, Kukul Can and Can Ul clearly were nobles, but they were not the nobles of the community. Bloodlines came into conflict because several lineages coveted political power, and, because of this, blood was spilled. The leaders themselves, as noted above, were termed *halach uinicil* or "true people." This term, which also could be translated as "true body," showed the historical construction of the terms of political power. The leaders were presented in this narrative as the "true people" or the people who should represent truth to the community. This truth related to their understanding of lineage, as these people supposedly inherited high political office through ritual tests of kinship. They understood the "truth" of the sexual acts of their predecessors, so the true people were connected back to their bodies through their bloodlines. Kinship related to this anatomical entity through the object of blood, which allowed the leaders to maintain themselves as the "true people."[62]

Lineage and blood were central themes throughout that text as we were introduced to Can Ul with a question: "Who was Can Ul?" The Cans had led Mayapán, through Hapay Can. Now the Uls would lead, although the Cans still had some power as the maternal lineage of Can Ul. This presented some consternation, resolved by a determination of Can Ul's legitimacy through the matrilineal line. But Can Ul still was a sinner, a legitimate leader who was to destroy society. The text strategized to displace desire once again: the people had to support the current leaders because history showed that there was too great a chance of having sinful leaders come into power anytime a change was made. Appropriate lineage lessened the chance that this would happen, but this lineage could be obtained only through an understanding of noble blood.

Noble Blood

Maya nobles were categorized as *almehen*, which derived from *al*, "child of a woman," and *mehen*, "child of a man." [63] The concept maintained that nobles were those who had noble lineage on both sides, and nobility was determined through a leader's mother and father. But this was not taken too literally, as the leader had to know more than his mother and father in order to be considered a noble. He was required to have knowledge of his lineage from time immemorial, going back to the gods themselves. He knew about the sexual acts and desires of those who came before him. These were the people who controlled their own sexual desires as well as having economic, social, and political control over society.

In reality it certainly was more complex than this since entrance into noble status had much to do with wealth, prestige, and political influence in addition to lineage. This situation paralleled Spanish and Nahua societies, which gave similar linguistic evidence linking the concept of nobility to one's parents. [64] The virtually constant concern of the Books of Chilam Balam with determining the legitimate nobility reflected political struggles between and within various noble groups. The ritual tests and other ploys in these historical documents certainly showed that the nobles were fearful of discovery as they could not always calculate noble lineage. So they displaced this fear through the representation of the desires of others: if you talk about lineage enough, the people will begin to accept the concept that you really can trace your bloodlines.

Michel Foucault, in a series of unpublished lectures, recognized the importance of the symbol of blood in the construction of race. To him, the blood of the name was an early element in the development of a specifically racist discourse in Europe. [65] The aristocracy engaged in torture, in the taking of the blood of its own members as well as others, in order to maintain power. [66] The construction of difference in the Maya universe may have stemmed from a similar type of system. The Maya used blood to distinguish one noble lineage from another. And they engaged various noble lineages in warfare (shown ritually as war conducted by the gods themselves), embracing the shedding of noble blood. This distinguished them from commoners, but this distinction was displaced onto an ethnic and national, and later a racial, distinction. [67] The nobles said that warfare was a defensive mechanism designed to maintain the life of the community through the ritual shedding of blood. As the community thought of war, the desire for war was mandated by a desire for the protection of the ethnic name against the advances of another ethnic group. That ethnic group then was portrayed as a separate nation, and revolutionary desires were displaced onto the desire for war to protect the name.[68] The name was represented as blood which was maintained through sexual acts, war, piercing rituals, and human sacrifice.

The nobles claimed a certain birthright due to their existence as *almehenob*. In many texts they asserted that birthright by saying that they did not get sufficient tribute; nor did they live in proper noble houses.[69] But this birthright could be asserted only through blood from both the matrilineage and the patrilineage. The social hierarchy thus required a gendering of kinship, so, even if women in Maya society had little political power, they gained social access through their participation in the Maya kinship system.

Archaeologist Patricia McAnany has shown that the preconquest Maya developed a cognitive system whereby ancestors were worshipped. In this system, which went beyond a lineage structure, ancestors incorporated people and land into a larger system of exchange. The people in the kinship group were connected with their ancestors, and they needed to worship those ancestors in order to gain a variety of privileges from them. If those ancestors were unhappy, disaster might befall the lineage, but if the ancestors were happy, the lineage would prosper. And the worship of ancestors took the form of an extensive array of burial and reburial techniques.[70]

Matthew Restall found that the lineage groups retained their power after the conquest in the form of the patrilineal descent group, the *chibal*. The *chibal* allowed various powerful groups to attain dominance in particular regions throughout Yucatán. Moreover, the groups protected their own members by working to provide for their needs.[71] The major noble groups ruled the communities in Yucatán at the time of the conquest, and they continued to rule throughout the colonial period.[72]

For the Maya, social status in the Books of Chilam Balam was signified by contrasting the accomplishments of the nobles with those of people without mothers and fathers, the commoners. But the commoners also placed some importance on the concept of kinship, and before the conquest commoners paid much attention to their ancestors.[73] They developed a system of ancestor worship which was similar to but not necessarily based on the noble lineage structure. The commoners continued to give importance to lineage after the conquest. The testaments show that commoners were concerned with establishing linear connections with other kin and that they bequeathed items to various people in the patrilineal kinship group.[74] But the lineage groups were colonized at the time of the conquest, and by the late colonial period many changes had occurred.

Colonizing Blood

The naming patterns in Maya society told many stories about both gender and social stratification. The naming patterns changed through time, partly as a result of colonialism. Before the conquest the Maya developed an elaborate naming system that incorporated patronyms, matronyms, "boy names," joke names (nicknames), and names related to official titles.[75] The most important were the patronym and the matronym, called a *naal*. Roys stated that the patronym was always the most important of all the names.[76] While I agree that the patronym developed as a more important name following the conquest, I argue that the preconquest naming system had a certain sense of parallelism, allowing two gendered lineages to survive as important, traceable elements. Landa clarified the importance of lineage to the Maya:

> They have much knowledge of the origin of their lineages, especially if they come from one of the houses of *Mayapán*. They get this knowledge from their priests, that being one of the priests' jobs, and they brag a lot about a notable man whom they have in their lineage. The father's name always endures with his sons, but not with his daughters. Both sons and daughters always received the name of their father and their mother, the father's as the proper name, and the mother's as the surname. So, the son of [the father] Chel and [the mother] Chan was called *Nachanchel*, meaning the son of so and so. Thus the Indians say that all of one name are relatives, and they treat them accordingly. Therefore, when they go to an area where they are unknown, and they are in need, they have recourse to those of that name. If there are any that carry the same name, they receive [the travelers] and treat them with kindness. Thus no woman or man married another of the same name because they believed this to be a great infamy.[77]

Landa stressed both the functional and the structural reasons for the lineage markers. The people could use their lineages to get favors from others of the same lineage. These people could help them in their travels since they could provide them with food and shelter as well as connections for when they desired to migrate.[78] The lineage marker also provided individuals with an important regulation that told them who they could and could not marry.

Landa also showed a connection between the desire to track lineage and the existence of a noble class. The nobles, those of the houses of Mayapán, were most obsessed with tracking lineage. They were most likely the ones who found many ancestors about whom they wanted to brag. The lineage marker thus was an important element in social stratification. The marker allowed many people of both the noble and commoner classes to brag about particular members of their lineages who they could suggest did important things. This bragging apparatus could serve as a relief valve which helped to hold the community together, allowing commoners both to believe in a glorious past and to connect themselves to the noble lines.[79] The lineage markers could help to maintain both social stratification and community connections.

This social stratification contrasted notably with the parallel descent patterns of men and women. Here women and men were able to maintain their lineages on both sides. A man's *naal* was not derived from his mother's patronym but rather was derived from the mother's matronym, which allowed the child to trace a "female line of maternal ancestors."[80] The people thus would mark both a female and a male line.[81]

The texts which discussed preconquest names used patronymics far more often than the *naal* names.[82] Part of the reason for this certainly was the fact that these documents were written after the conquest, when the *naal* had virtually disappeared and the patronymic had gained importance.[83] The postconquest authors would have had great difficulty tracing themselves to a preconquest *naal* lineage.

The preconquest matronymics often alternated with boy names, nicknames, and title names. As the documents which discussed preconquest names all primarily talked about the names of nobles and their dependents, the names consistently employed the important titles. There were names such as Batab Canul, signifying the appellative *batab*, "governor," and the patronym Canul.[84] The appellative here was an important element in the social and political hierarchy as it replaced the *naal* in order to stress the high level of the person involved. This does not mean that the *naal* disappeared, as it signified another important element which proved Batab Canul's lineage. The Maya chronicles, late colonial documents which were used in land disputes, often discussed both the title name and the *naal* name, in an attempt to prove both lineages of the person as well as the individual's political power. The lineages presented parallel descent lines, not necessarily of equal importance, but rather lines which asserted the importance of the name, and of blood, to maintaining one's social position. The political and social hierarchy stressed in the chronicles showed much about the uses of these various names, as well as the relationship between blood, gender, ethnicity, and desire.

After the conquest, the Maya naming system, coming into contact with the Spanish system, changed dramatically. However, unlike the Nahua, who adopted Spanish-influenced second names within several decades of the conquest,[85] the Maya retained their traditional patronymics. The other names appear to have been lost quickly after the conquest, as the Maya people were baptized and took on Catholic first names.[86] This renaming allowed for the appearance of an image of a purely patrilineal system.

But the Maya authors of the chronicles knew about the tradition of the *naal*, as well as the other names, although these documents were written in the eighteenth century, two hundred years after the last known contemporary written uses of the *naal*. It seems most likely that the authors remembered the *naal* because they had some experiences with the vestiges of this naming system. In the same manner they likely gave people nicknames, despite their disappearance from the documents. They also kept track of people's offices through the use of titles, a usage clearly present in the colonial documents.

So what happened to the *naal?* It appears to have gone underground, perhaps residing with the blood line of the Moon Goddess herself. For there was not a naming pattern based on the Virgin Mary Moon Goddess that was legible in the documents. However, there remained some vestiges, showing the importance of lineage.

The postconquest name was based on baptism in the name of Jesus Christ. For the Maya people as a whole, the blood of Christ became an important symbol. Christ's death clearly signified a particular, powerful form of human sacrifice. His blood perhaps replaced the blood shed during sacrifice. The blood related to Christ's name may have helped to establish appropriate lineage ties during the colonial and postcolonial years. Christ was the hybrid Maya form, allowing for the tracing of two parallel lineages. And the name continued to be powerful, although it was to be the name of colonialism.

BLOOD, NAMING, AND MASCULINITY

The blood and body of the ruler was desired by the society because the state needed the ruler's blood: it needed proof of his lineage; it needed him to go to war and risk the shedding of his blood; it needed him capable of shedding the blood of others through human sacrifice. Through the protection of the blood of the ruler, nobles and commoners could survive. Lineage arrangements, memory, and knowledge were structured through sexual desire: the desires of the nobles were known; those of the commoners were not. The sexual desires of the ancestors had to be recalled, both by reading histories (to prevent moral lapses) and by understanding blood. This was the only way society could survive.

Colonialism presented a challenge to Maya readings of blood, as sacrifice was outlawed and the matronym forced into hiding. Although sacrificial rituals may have continued for a while in secret, the public nature of the events necessarily was curtailed. And lineage was altered, both because many members of the noble lineages died and because lineage no longer could be read in the same way as before the conquest. So the challenge for the Maya was in how they were to maintain the memory of the ruler's blood and thus maintain the social and political hierarchy.

Masculinity was constructed with an eye toward blood and lineage. Much shedding of blood itself was portrayed as a particular symbol of masculinity. The proper masculine role was the role of the political leader,[87] the warrior, and the one who engaged in human sacrifice. He was the one who risked the shedding of his blood. In contrast, the feminine sphere was more likely to be invoked in discussions of lineage and nobility. But, as will be shown, colonial Maya femininity was more complex than this, regularly invoking symbols of the shedding of blood.

Sexual acts were related closely to rituals of blood. The sacrifices which took place were intended to evoke a sense of the spectacle and a desire for nobles, rulers, and gods. This desire was marked by the blood which was shed. Noble lineage was regarded as such because nobles knew their parents, their grandparents, and their lines all the way back to the gods. They knew their lineages, or so we are told, because nobles controlled their sexual desires and only had children in the confines of marriage. Commoners could not control those desires.

The colonization of gender was to play a central role in the new colonial readings of blood. For, before the conquest, the Maya could read blood through the maintenance of a gender parallel structure, since lineage was read through both male and female lines. But after the conquest, this parallelism was displaced and blood had to be read in a different manner, and gendered accordingly. The Maya were required to begin to read blood through a ritual kinship with Jesus, the Virgin Mary Moon Goddess, the Christian God, and the saints. Some limited gender parallelism remained in this reading of blood (the *naal* was remembered; the Virgin Mary Moon Goddess still was partnered with various gods), but most of the parallel lines of descent disappeared. The blood became the blood of the hybrid gods, and this blood led to new forms of lineage, ritual, and sacrifice.

SEVEN   # Blood, Semen, and Ritual

Let us imagine a preconquest scenario related to phallic blood:

AS THE YOUNG NOBLEMAN walked through the community, he knew that the people wanted something from him. They would not be satisfied until they had blood from his penis. This was, after all, his sacred obligation. It would allow the gods and the people to see that he was willing to commit to his responsibilities. It would mark him as a potentially successful warrior, and perhaps a future king. He could maintain the community only by giving his blood. Yet the noble youth felt some anxious anticipation as he knew somehow that the stingray spine must hurt. He hadn't pierced his penis before, but he had seen it done many times, every time wondering what it would be like. Part of him certainly was intrigued, but he also was scared.

He looked down at his penis in order to avoid the glares of all the people around him. He knew that the blood from his penis was his most prized possession, something that he would only provide for the gods on such a special occasion. And he knew that through births and marriages and deaths, through feasts and famines, he would be required to cut into this penis many more times.

Walking into the temple, he saw the stingray spine in front of him. He was resolved; this would be his time to cut into his penis. He would do so for his father and his gods and his people.[1]

●   ●   ●

This phallic scene presents a scenario that may place far too much weight on the psychology of the severed penis. Certainly the preconquest Maya placed different emphasis on the phallus than do modern Western peoples. But the ritualized taking of blood from the penis was an important event which served to solidify community support for a leader. His shedding of blood, like his participation in warfare and human sacrifice, signified the commitment of the nobleman to the maintenance of the life of society.[2] And no doubt, the ritual shedding of his blood, combined with the knowledge that at some point in the future his entire life might have to be sacrificed for the gods, must have had a profound psychological effect on the noble youth.

Blood signified much to the Maya, both before and after the conquest. Blood was part of the Maya world of ritual, fantasy, and fear. The next two chapters analyze the ways in which Maya fantasies and desires played a part in the rituals related to curing and the shedding of blood. These rituals placed Maya fantasy in an appropriate context, allowing people to see themselves as communing with the gods by engaging in a variety of sexual acts. The rituals presented what was shown in preconquest Maya art: that there were only "vague boundaries that separate[d] themes of fertility/sexuality and sacrifice in Maya thought" and that "the act of blood sacrifice from the penis . . . [had] inherent sexual overtones related to fertility."[3] The fantasies were such that many Maya men and women were able to believe that these acts would promote the continuation of society through ritualized ceremonies.

BLOOD OF THE VAGINA

While the ritual shedding of male blood through the penis was recorded more strongly than that of female blood in the documents, there existed several aspects of these rituals that showed that the prioritization of the phallus partly was an artifact of the extant documentation. First, Maya women ritually shed blood through their tongues and ears. Second, menstruation was given great ritual and physiological importance. Third, women's blood was associated closely with creation and birth. Finally, the rituals showed that goddesses and objects deemed "feminine" controlled much of the penis-piercing events. These four elements showed that the prioritization of penis piercing in the

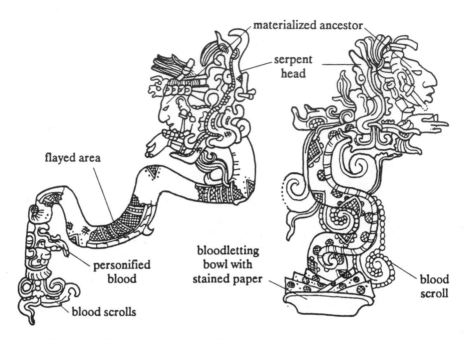

materialized ancestor

serpent
head

flayed area

personified
blood

bloodletting
bowl with
stained paper

blood
scroll

blood scrolls

FIGURE 7.1   The Vision Serpent, signifying the connections between the gods and the people which were opened by the piercing ceremony. From Linda Schele and David Freidel, *A Forest of Kings: The Untold Story of the Ancient Maya*, copyright © 1990 by William Morrow and Company. Reprinted by permission of William Morrow and Company.

documents did not necessarily signify a strong emphasis on the phallus as the most important physiological organ in the Maya fantasy world.

Preconquest Bloodletting

Linda Schele and David Freidel describe the bloodletting ritual as one in which the blood symbolically showed the path of communication between this world and the "Otherworld" of the deities and the dead. The ritual opened a door of communication to the Otherworld, which allowed the people to converse with the gods. The people who let blood saw the "World Tree" by using the "Vision Serpent" (see Fig. 7.1).[4] Patricia McAnany confirmed that bloodletting connected people with deceased ancestors. Some depictions of bloodletting ceremonies showed images of ancestors "emerging from the body of a serpent."[5]

Royal women were depicted in the iconography of the preconquest blood-

FIGURE 7.2   Lady Xoc pulls a rope, perhaps barbed
with thorns, through her pierced tongue. From Linda
Schele and David Freidel, *A Forest of Kings: The Untold
Story of the Ancient Maya*, copyright © 1990 by William
Morrow and Company. Reprinted by permission of
William Morrow and Company.

letting rituals, and they may have played an important public role.[6] They
primarily were pictured pulling "barbed rope" through their tongues (see
Fig. 7.2).[7] A section of the Madrid Codex (Fig. 7.3) showed male and female
gods letting blood from their ears. The implication of these images is that
women were in a high enough position in Maya society that the vision of
them letting blood would have meant something to the community and the
gods: the blood of women attained some importance in these rituals. The desires and fantasies behind this letting of blood are clear from the hieroglyphs

FIGURE 7.3 Women and men let blood from their ears. From the Madrid Codex. Reprinted by permission of Akademische Druck-u.

and the ethnohistorical documents. The Maya fantasized about the gods and ancestors thriving off the blood. The gods would get the blood and ingest it, making them well fed and content.[8] The conscious desires of the ritual were connected with both communication and fertility.[9] The Maya were concerned about survival, and the blood sacrificed would ensure the future.

One case of a large and important bloodletting ceremony was depicted in Yaxchilan. Schele and Freidel imaginatively re-create the event, which took place on July 1, 741.[10] Schele and Freidel present the following bloodletting of Lady Eveningstar (see Fig. 7.4), mother of the ascendant to the throne of Yaxchilan, Bird-Jaguar:

> Dressed in a brilliant white gauze huipil, high-backed sandals, and a flower headdress, she stepped forward to stand before her son. . . . Holding a shallow plate within the circle of her folded arms, Lady Eveningstar knelt before Bird-Jaguar. The bowl was filled with strips of beaten-bark paper, a rope the thickness of her first finger, and a huge stingray spine. Her eyes glazed as she shifted her mind into the deep trance that would prepare her for what was to come. Closing her eyes, she extended her tongue as far out of her mouth as she could. Bird-Jaguar took the stingray spine and, with a practiced twist of the wrist, drove it through the center of his mother's tongue. She did not flinch, nor did a sound pass her lips as he took the rope and threaded it through the wound. She stood near the edge of the platform so that all the assembled witnesses could see her pull the rope through her tongue. Her blood saturated the paper in the bowl at her chest and dribbled redly down her chin in a brilliant contrast to the deep green jade of her shoulder cape. . . . Lady Eveningstar pulled the last of the rope through her tongue, dropped it into the bowl, and stood swaying as the trance state took possession of her consciousness. In that moment Bird-Jaguar saw what he had been seeking in her eyes—the great Serpent Path to the Otherworld was opening within his mother.[11]

After the ceremony the community responded with trumpets blaring and smoke billowing.[12] The queen's blood was central to the entire ritual process, as this blood allowed the future leader to communicate with the gods and the ancestors. The ceremony signified a birth process, whereby the mother gave birth to the path of communication. The utensils used signified the ceremony's power as spectacle. The large stingray spine impressed the audience, and the rope was used both to stress the importance of the rope connecting people to

**Lady Eveningstar pulling the rope
through her perforated tongue**

FIGURE 7.4   In a ceremony represent-
ing a leader's ascension to power, Lady
Eveningstar pulls a rope through her
pierced tongue. From Linda Schele and
David Freidel, *A Forest of Kings: The
Untold Story of the Ancient Maya*, copy-
right © 1990 by William Morrow and
Company. Reprinted by permission of
William Morrow and Company.

their ancestors[13] and to show the community that the bloodletting really did
take place, that there really was a hole in the queen's tongue.

The gendered implication of these rituals showed that it was necessary
to have both male and female blood in order to perform the most important
bloodletting ceremonies. The queen here had power: she was the one who
would access the ancestors. She also showed the community that its leaders
were willing to engage in acts of ritual sacrifice; they were willing to shed
blood for the people. And her blood was a powerful gendered marker of this
sacrifice.

The Politics of Menstruation

The phallic images constructed by the bloodletting ritual (the World Tree and the Vision Serpent) allowed a specifically gendered access to the cosmological world. Gender manifested certain male powers through the creation of the phallus, and even through its maintenance in the penis-piercing rituals. In many societies the importance of the phallus in maintaining a hierarchically gendered social structure is based on its position as a symbol, particularly a symbol of fantasy.[14] The concept of bloodletting, in creating and developing the phallus, was a central fantasy of preconquest Maya religious ritual, but that fantasy, it should be recalled, was initiated in the above example by a queen. Indeed, as men had their blood let, they copied women who bled through menstruation.[15] This may have been why goddesses and feminine objects were seen as having some control over the penis-piercing rituals. As women maintained ritualized status through their blood,[16] the men copied this ritual status. Here the constructions of masculinity and femininity could be taken in many different directions.[17]

The menstruation of Maya women was connected with both the moon and the image of the Moon Goddess. The context and symbolism of blood was presented in many of the incantations:

> *bin Inca ix hun puɔub kik ix hun puɔub olom u colba cḃab u coolba akab tit*
> *kax u kinam icnal ix hun puɔub kik ix hun puɔub olom*

> In the company of her, the one needle of blood and her, the one
> needle of the lineage,[18] creation[19] and the night are untied. His/her
> strength is tied up in the company of her, the one needle of blood
> and her, the one needle of the lineage.[20]

In this text, the needle (probably the stingray spine), clearly gendered, signified blood. The blood here was both the blood of the penis-piercing ritual and the blood of menstruation. The female needle was going to pierce the penis and thus assert control over the ritual of masculinity.

The first mention of blood, a translation of the term *kik*, also translated as menstrual blood.[21] This connected with the suggestion of feminine ritual power with regard to women's access to blood. The term that signified lineage here, *olom*, translated as blood or coagulated blood.[22] Both terms signified the ritual effects of blood and lineage. They were central symbols which had power both to make one sick and to engage in a cure. The blood and the needle connected to sexual desire as they untied this desire through the act of piercing the penis. This act, connected with sexual intercourse,[23] took place because the objects, constructed as feminine, took action and untied creation and the night. The masculine (blood from the penis) and "phallic" (the needle) images thus were resignified and reinscribed in this framework: they signified a notion of desire gendered female.

Blood was represented as an important element of femininity in many different ways. In both of the two texts Ralph Roys discovered which discussed cures for problems with menstruation, the word used, *yilic*, derived from *ilah* or *ilmah*, which translated as both "to menstruate" and "to see":[24]

> *u man yilic u nok xcbup caxan t le ah chicam kuch bay zac seboya cici huche catun a puk y haa a ɔa yuke cu hauzic*

For a woman not menstruating:[25] Find some jicama,[26] [which is] like a white onion. Grind it well and dissolve it. Give it to her to drink and that will end it.[27]

Here menstruation doubled as a particular form of sight. The gaze was fixed as emanating not from the eyes, but from the blood and the womb. When that gaze needed to be fixed, however, jicama was required, here gendered male (by the *ah*). The gaze showed that power and desire had parallel notions of gender. Men gained political and ritual power through their penile blood and semen. Perhaps women gained ritual power through their menstrual blood. Sexual desire and fantasy played major roles in the structuring of power.

Menstrual blood here was a signifier of gendered power. Women gained power through their blood, which connected them with the gods, much as male blood connected men with the gods. Yet, for women, this power clearly was limited. The rituals were intended to promote a masculine sense of valor and power through the shedding of penile blood, and through acts of warfare and human sacrifice. Further, menstruation, connected with life, obviously was a "natural" event over which women had little control. After the conquest, there did not appear to be significant change in the writing of this ritual: menstruation still was represented as sight. However, as shall be shown, this gendered notion of blood changed dramatically in other ways.

Blood and Childbirth

At the time of the conquest, the concept of birth was used to understand the relationships between people and the gods, at least through the symbol of the umbilical cord.[28] The Nahuas symbolized birth with the acknowledgment of the power of women's blood and men's semen in developing the child.[29] The child was born into his or her matrilineal and patrilineal lines.[30] And there was a series of Nahua ceremonies related to the birth of the child, including ritual bathing, the burial of the umbilical cord, and naming according to an astrological account.[31] The Maya codices told of astrological readings related to the births, marriages, and deaths of kings.[32] Maya childbirth clearly was connected with the relationship between the gods and the earth. The birth of children symbolized life and continuity, and it was related closely to blood.

Menstrual blood and sexual desire were acknowledgments of women's role in the act of creation:

> *ti yilah sihil ti yilah c̣hab ci bin yalabal can chah kik can chah*[33] *olom tu pach*
> *kabbal te kabal tun tu leɔah tu kam cu chi chacal kuxub tu kam cu chi tu*
> *yilah sihil tu yilah c̣hab*

S/he saw the birth, s/he saw the creation. That is what will be said. Four drops of blood, four drops of coagulated blood,[34] were on the back of the hand of wood, the hand of stone. S/he licked it for breakfast; s/he breakfasted on the red *achiote*.[35] Then s/he saw the birth, s/he saw the creation.[36]

Birth and creation related directly to blood. The Maya, seeing a relationship between sexual desire and reproduction, related that desire to blood and sight. The birth and creation, fixed by the gaze, occurred when the four drops of blood emanated from the wooden and stone hands, representatives of the body, to the mouth. The blood was a grain which then recreated life. Blood was fixed and implicitly gendered through the gaze, written as *yilah*. Menstruation, also signified as *yilah*, was connected with the central gaze, that which caused birth and creation.

Creation itself was centered on the position of sexual desire. The Maya term *c̣hab* signified "carnality" and creation.[37] The creator, *Ah C̣hab*, was related to the Chorti hermaphroditic deity, *Ih Pen*, "He, the fornicator." Moreover, statements about creation in the Ritual of the Bacabs often were paired with statements about lust and regularly were associated with women's blood:[38]

> *bolon ti ku oxlahun ti kue yanac xu uilal yanac xu pak u col c̣hab u col akab*
> *sam u kasah uinicil te uinicil tun fel u na ti yach kak bacin xotom bacin che*

*yal x hun tah kik x hun tah olom la bin u na la bin u col cḥab ca yum kin
colop u uich kin u uich akab bacin*

The nine gods, the thirteen gods: for that they have the vagina,[39] they
have the vagina to fornicate for the lust of creation, the lust of the
night. The body of wood, the body of stone has been destroyed. The
vagina's mother[40] with your penis: how is the fire; how is the cutting?[41]
The child of wood is she, the great one of blood, she, the great one of
lineage. Here is his/her mother; here is the lust of creation of the Lord
Sun, the flayed face of day, the flayed face of night.[42]

The vagina controlled creation, signified as lust. This lust also related to night,
which Roys describes as the feminine principle to the masculine, *cḥab*.[43] If
these signified the two principles of creation, then this demonstrated yet another gender parallel structure.

Here the vagina existed specifically for creation. It created the universe
through the redevelopment of humanity (the body of wood and stone), which
had been destroyed. It created humanity by making an offer to the sun: the
sun was to receive the blood from the leaders of this ritual, and the blood
was to be the blood of the penis. So the gendered structure here was that
the vagina engaged in the act of creation, but it needed the penis in order to
complete the process. The vagina represented blood, as did the penis, but
one needed the two types of blood in order to engage in any act of creation
or birth.

The symbolism was decidedly phallic, but the fantasies were not necessarily so. The Maya fantasy here was that the engagement of creation was similar to the birth of a child. In either act one needed both the penis and the
vagina. The piercing of the penis, as will be shown, was a gendered phenomenon, with goddesses and objects designated "feminine" taking control over the
process. In this case the vagina was ritualized as the central actor in creation,
utilizing the penis when necessary.

The feminine here was associated with blood in the menstrual process. The
blood itself had a powerful ritual connection which was related to the gaze.
The menstruation of women was similar to the penis piercing of men, who
obtained ritual sight through their blood. This asserted a certain masculine
power, similar to the feminine power seen through the relationship between
menstruation and the gaze.

The parallels here attained from the sense of a parallel structure in the creation of lineage. These related back to the blood, which was derived from

penis piercing and menstruation. This was a desire to produce and create a world through the symbolism of sexual reproduction, so sexual acts necessarily played a central role in bloodletting rituals. These desires signified a certain displacement: the political power of men was assured through their blood, and this blood had to be maintained by controlling sexual desire. The blood also had to be enhanced through a knowledge (a sight) of the menstruation of women and the penis piercing of men in the lineage. The political and religious power of men (specifically, noblemen) was maintained through a structured fantasy of gender parallelism.

All of these texts were an attempt at archaism: a reconstruction of preconquest ritual. The fact that these were written well after the conquest shows that knowledge of these preconquest rituals survived the conquerors. It is unknown whether these rituals continued to be performed out of the sight of Spaniards, although the existence of such performances, at least on a small scale, was likely. Much of the gender parallelism in these rituals survived, although its meaning within the broader context of colonial rule certainly changed. The meaning of vaginal blood changed following the conquest, but the clear import of these rituals showed that some of the changes were slow in coming.

BLOOD OF THE PENIS

The blood of the penis, particularly in penis-piercing rituals, was marked more clearly in the documents, showing both the importance of the phallus to Maya society and the documentation of a highly ritualized event. Both blood and semen emanating from the penis were aspects of creation which were seen as central to Maya community survival. But, even though the phallus clearly was important to these rituals, one should not overestimate the way in which this importance gendered ritual and political power. For Maya fantasy demanded that the penis could not act in these rituals without the prior presence of the vagina. In fact, the rituals presented a damaged penis and a vagina that controlled much of the ceremony. Moreover, the penis often was a free-floating object which did not connect with any particular body or gender. This, of course, did not suggest that the Maya did not connect the penis directly to the male aspect of creation, but as the phallus disconnected from one body and connected to another or was left in limbo, the power of the man in this act of creation clearly was limited, even though the presence of the male principle continued to represent him.[44]

The historicity of these rituals is once again somewhat vague as the texts clearly were archaic. As postconquest representations of preconquest rituals, they contained information primarily about what postconquest (seventeenth-century) Maya shamans thought. But they were particularly partial thoughts, as I do not know if the shamans continued to practice these rituals or if they simply knew of them from oral histories or preconquest texts.

Preconquest Bloodletting

Bloodletting was an important element in preconquest constructions of masculinity,[45] and it had many phallic implications in the penis-piercing ritual. Schele and Freidel say that the men with pierced genitals performed a dance that drew the blood out of the perforations onto "long paper and cloth streamers tied to their wounded members." This allowed them to engage in a vision quest where they saw into the "Otherworld." It also was related directly to birth, and it was viewed as ritually giving birth to the gods.[46] In terms similar to the gendered gaze and menstruation, masculinity was constructed as entrance into the ritual world through warfare, bloodletting, and sacrifice. This concatenation stemmed from a femininity determined through menstruation, childbirth, and the gaze. The narratives strategized in such a way as to allow masculine bloodletting and feminine menstruation similar access to ritual power.

The ritual shedding of blood from the penis was a central community event which asserted the power of the king, the lineage leader, the community official, and/or the household head. The shaman in charge of the ritual was an honored noble official.[47] No doubt this was an effort to connect the particular person with powerful and popular and/or feared ancestors.[48] The ritual also asserted a sense of masculine valor. It signified the male principle in warfare and in the shedding of blood. It was in this sense that the penis-piercing ritual fit into the parallel gendered structure of society. The male bleeding was equivalent to female bleeding through menstruation and through the female aspect of the ritual: the piercing of the tongue.

In continuing their re-creation of the bloodletting ceremony marking Bird-Jaguar's ascension, Schele and Freidel described more:

> Face impassive, Bird-Jaguar squatted on his heels, spreading his muscular thighs above the basket. He pulled his loincloth aside, took the huge stingray spine, and pushed it through the loose skin along the top of his penis. He pierced himself three times before reaching down into the bowl for the thin bark paper strips it contained. Threading a

FIGURE 7.5   A god pictured piercing his penis. From the Paris Codex.
Reprinted with permission of the American Philosophical Society.

paper strip through each of his wounds, he slowly pulled it through
until the three strips hung from his member. His blood gradually
soaked into the light tan paper, turning it to deepest red. From the
saturated paper, his blood dripped into the bowl between his legs.
When he was done, his wife reached down for the bowl and placed the
blood-stained paper of his sacrifice in the nearby censer along with
offerings of maize kernels, rubber, and the tree resin called *pom*.[49]

While Schele and Freidel certainly could not prove that this was the format
of the ritual, their creativity was not without some basis. Pictures of penis-
piercing rituals do exist (see Fig. 7.5), and the case that they discuss was amply
documented in the hieroglyphic and pictorial record at Yaxchilan.[50] The interpretation here shows that it was an important public rite in which Bird-
Jaguar proved his worth as a warrior by communing with great ancestor
warriors and the gods. He then was able to engage in a vision quest with
those gods. No doubt the sheer hype of this very public festival asserted Bird-
Jaguar's power and inspired awe in the populace.

Blood and Semen

As seen above, the postconquest texts in the Ritual of the Bacabs described
the penis-piercing ceremonies. These texts asserted a sense of the rituals not
as promotions of an unbending male dominance but rather as rituals of masculinity that showed gender parallelism by presenting the power of the vagina and the penis. As will be shown, this was based on a metaphorical and
symbolic association of creation with sexual intercourse between a man and a
woman. But this symbolic association broke down as gendered bodies became
degendered, and as body parts became separated from bodies in fantasies of
the ritual sphere.

The Ritual of the Bacabs was not the only postconquest text to discuss penis piercing. Diego de Landa's commentary reserved a special place for this
ritual. While on most occasions he provided little moral analysis, instead
choosing to discuss elements such as modes of government and particular
clothing,[51] Landa did reserve much judgment for actions such as human sacrifice, bloodletting, and (as noted above) rape and murder. Landa equated (as
would have the Maya) bloodletting with human sacrifice: "[T]hey had a *dirty
and grievous sacrifice*, gathering together in a line in the temple, where each
person pierced a hole all the way through the virile member. They passed
through as great a quantity of cord as they could stand. And thus fastened and
strung together, they anointed the statue of the *demon* of those parts with all
of the blood. He who was able to endure the most was considered the most
valiant" (emphasis added).[52] Landa's moral condemnation of these acts is clear
in the highlighted language. He demanded that the act itself signified a sacrifice, something he strongly condemned both in this text and elsewhere.[53]
Landa's objections centered on the ritual nature of the violation. He represented the event as based on the "demon of those parts," the deity or ancestor
to whom the sacrifice was directed. The positioning of this god as an oppositional figure to Landa (and thus to the Christian God) was the center of
Landa's objections. The narrative here used the figure of the Maya male and
his penis, strung together with other men and their penises, to show the utter
disdain that a good Catholic would have for this idolatrous worship. The blood
which emanated from the pierced penis came to represent the idol, the demon,
the deity. The narrative further denigrated Maya masculinity, picturing this
ritual as an event designed to evoke the masculine through valor. The masculine figure, the one who could endure the most, represented, to Landa, the
dire figure of him who was most important to the demon, and thus most hor-
rific to a good Catholic.

Landa certainly did not recognize the desire and fantasy implicit in the piercing rituals. These desires related to connections between the penis, (menstrual) blood, and semen. It was here that one found Maya conceptualizations of appropriate sexual desires. The discourse on masculinity allowed men particular access to realms of curing and religious ritual. But even these penis-piercing rituals were controlled by concepts of the relationship between femininity and blood.

In one text, "tarantula seizures" were associated with penis piercing and the ritual shedding of blood and semen. They also were associated with menstruation and the vagina in general. This text presented a cure for these seizures:

> *thanex to oxtescun tancase ci bin yalabal uoh ci bin nuc than yal bacin uoh ti*
> *caan uoh tij munyal ti ul bacin chac tan chiuoh chiuoh kik chiuoh kak chiuoh*
> *tancas ti oc ti chiuoh haail u chi kaknab elbin oƥol elbin yaxun can kin cu*
> *tuhal cay ti u leɔah yom haa la oc tu sac tub chiuoh tancase*
>
> *u lubul tan kakal chakan tij chook chacal cus tu cali u lubul bin ycnal som*
> *chi som pul tij tu chaah u ɔul u cali u kasic chacal boken haa la oc tu sac tub*
> *chiuoh tancase hutlic chacal kab bal*
>
> *ti tu kas uincil te uinicil tun uet u lac yn chacal toon yn sacal toon uchic*
> *yn can max cunic yokol uinicil te uinicil tun oxlahun in chacal batil ha uchic*
> *in tupic a kinam hunac ah siscuna hen cen ti ual hen in tup a kinam cen a*
> *nue cen a yum hunuc can ahau amen*

You declare, "Three greetings, seizure." It will be written and declared. How will it be written? [It will be] written in the sky and the clouds. How will it arrive? As the red tarantula, the bloody tarantula, the fire tarantula, the tarantula seizure. Then enters the water tarantula from the seashore. The *oppol* [tree] burns; the *yaxum* [tree] burns. For four days the fish rotted,[54] as s/he licked the foam of the water. From that came the white saliva of the tarantula seizure.

It falls on the dry flatland as the red-colored item is crammed into his/her neck. It falls at the place of Som Chi and Som Pul.[55] S/he takes the obstruction from his/her throat and spoils the red, beaten water. Thus enters the white saliva of the tarantula seizure, to be cast into the red liquid.

Thus the body of wood, the body of stone is destroyed. Together with [the body], my red penis, my white penis arrives and I forcefully beat it over the body of wood, the body of stone. Thirteen times my red hail-water extinguishes your pain. I am the great soothing one; I

am the child who extinguishes your pain. I am your mother, I am your
father: Hunuc Can Ahau.[56] Amen.[57]

This incantation emphasized the importance of ritual for curing the sick
person. The gods took the disease (signified as blood) and coaxed it out of
the throat. They pictured the disease in the form of a tarantula invading
the body.

The tarantula unambiguously signified a disease, some sort of seizure. The
tarantula in modern Maya is a double entendre for the vagina,[58] here suggesting the vagina as an infectious agent. Moreover, the Moon Goddess was very
closely associated with spiders. Just as the vagina could carry disease, it also
could carry a cure. Both the vagina and the penis contained a certain amount
of ritual power. The tarantula showed access to more than the cure itself as
it presented access to the gods through the sky and the clouds. These gods
helped the tarantula ravish the body parts much as they helped the shaman
engage in the cure.

Hunuc Can Ahau was the "real" curer in this ceremony since he extin-
guished the fire created by the seizure. He was both the mother and the father of the ill person and the disease. He thus maintained kinship ties with the
community, enabling him to enter that community as a healer. His body was
represented as that which was desired and needed. His blood had to be found,
both through his bloodline and through his penis. Perhaps the blood from
the penis signified the bloodline itself. The vagina/tarantula here was a challenge to that bloodline.

The desire for the body of the god was sexual and ritualistic at the same
time. His important attribute was his penis, which he pierced in order to engage in this cure. The penis rained the red hail water onto the ill person,
showing that the cure was a phallic representation, curing the disease created
by the vagina. Hunuc Can Ahau also experienced orgasm in order to engage
in the cure: this was his white penis. He pierced his penis to allow the blood
to help the semen: this was his red penis and the red hail water. In both cases,
masturbation ("forcefully beat") may have allowed the god to engage in the
cure. While the text implied that Hunuc Can Ahau may have had two penises,
one red and one white, this simply was a fantasized way of understanding two
of the uses of the penis.

The curing ceremony itself rested on a phallic signification, allowing
Hunuc Can Ahau to engage in the cure only through his possession of a penis. He remained the soothing one, a mother, a father, and a child. He thus
maintained control over the curing ceremony through his multiple posses-

sions and identities. His representation as mother, father, and child showed his ability to engage in the cure: he had all the necessary body parts, all the necessary connections. The text itself was phallocentric, signifying a cure by the phallus of a disease perhaps created by the vagina. Such a scenario is a common element in any phallic signifying economy.[59] However, the power represented in this text stemmed from the erotics of blood and semen more than from the penis itself. After all, if the text simply wanted to mention the penis, there would have been no reason to discuss the colors coming out of it. This symbolized the curing power which emanated from the heavens. Such power showed the importance of sexual desire, blood, and semen in the Maya symbolic structure. The connection between blood and semen was maintained as a desire for life itself.

And that life was maintained through Hunuc Can Ahau's ability to transport across genders. This figure was mother and father. It was only through the Maya fantasy of deified transsexuality that the cure could take place: it was necessary to have all of the body parts of both genders/sexes in order to be the ritual curer. This deified transsexuality signified masculine power for the great lord, Hunuc Can Ahau.

The Maya knew that semen was required in order for reproduction to take place. They also understood a relationship between male sexual desire and semen. In the curing rituals semen was treated with great respect as an element which cured various diseases. In virtually every case, however, the semen needed to be associated with blood for it to engage in the relevant cure.

In this text, the red from both the throat and the penis signified the centrality of blood as the bodily element which represented disease and cure. Blood apparently went up and down the throat during the disease. As his penis bled, Hunuc Can Ahau could cure the seizure. As Maya men proved their masculinity through the penis-piercing ritual, the importance of this ritual to the cure would have made sense. This showed a relationship between masculinity and curing. The penis-piercing ritual itself was a central element in Maya religious life. It allowed for tests of masculinity for warriors about to engage in battle. The relationship with semen stressed the sexual desire seen as inherent in the blood rituals.

The rituals also mentioned semen directly. As was shown in the last chapter, semen was constructed ritually as an element of both creation and birth. Semen was seen as at least a portion of the masculine element in creation:

can kin cu tuhal cay uchic u sihil u kasil chaboc bin tij xux tan sil u chi
kaknab lubcie u kasul chabe

For four days, the fish have rotted because of the birth. The semen of creation was to be introduced. The wasp seizure[60] fell at the seashore to the semen of creation.[61]

Semen here signified the important masculine element in creation.[62] This ritual allowed the male principle to have a role in the larger framework of the universe. Yet the role of the semen and the male principle was suggested to be somehow bad, as an alternative translation of *kasil* ("semen") was "evil."[63] The masculine role was questioned throughout the Ritual of the Bacabs, which determined that both the male and female principles were required to play parts in any conceptualization of creation.

In Maya fantasies, creation was visualized as needing semen and blood. The blood would come from menstruation and from bloodletting. Perhaps the penis-piercing ritual signified some concern about the male role in creation. It was an attempt to assert male power and privilege by the suggestion of a fantasy that men, if they produced both blood and semen, could engage in creation and birth by themselves. But the fantasies clearly showed that the Maya world demanded both blood and semen, both male and female, in order to create and maintain the world.

Real Bodies, Real Organs

The penis-piercing ritual demanded a highly gendered world where male and female principles were kept separate. Women bled from different organs than men, and male blood was a different concept than female blood. But the gendering process was not at all so clear, and gendered boundaries were blurred in the ritual ceremony.

The gendering and degendering of Maya bodies, largely an unconscious enterprise, showed the importance of transgressing sexual and gender boundaries in Maya ritual discourse. The body and its parts may have been disconnected.

> *u thanil sinan tu chibal lae chib chib chib bul moc a ne ɔacal mo ca tun*
> *tulix mo a pol pichin tech bin tu chi kaknab ti bin lubech . . . ti bin a cḅah a*
> *yuxil kabi pichin tech bin yicnal saba yol tij chuuen ti bin lubech ti sinan*
> *kabil ti a cḅah a kaba ti sinanili cech fel u na ta uach u suhuy puɔ bin a*
> *chich a cḅah oc ta uach u suhuy kak bin a chich la bin oc t kinam ta uach ti*
> *lah han u nek sisbic ta uach picchin tech tan ku la ti bin a cḅah u yamulil a*
> *pachi pichin tech bin tan yol che ti bin ta cḅah u yax chelil a pachi a yax cheil*

naki cech fel u na ta uach chib chib bul moc a ne cech ix yal actun cech ix yal
poxche ce[ch fel u n]a ta uach la bacam a uach la bacam a sian tu men a na
tu men a yum

The scorpion's statement is for its stinger: sting, sting, sting. Your tail
is well curved. The macaw cure and then the dragonfly-macaw are in
your head. You are to lance [the scorpion] by the seashore, where you
fell. . . . You level it in your hands, lancing it at the place of *Saba Yol.*[64]
You fall into the hands of the scorpion. There you take your name,
scorpion.[65] You! The vagina's[66] mother with your penis.[67] You take
your grandmother's virginal needle and introduce it into your penis
with your grandmother's virginal fire. This will introduce pain into
your penis. Its point is thus cleaned and your penis is frozen. You
lance it in front of the god. Thus numbness enters your back. You
lance it in the middle of, at the heart of, the tree. Thus it enters the
first wood of your back, your first wood belly. You! The vagina's
mother with your penis: sting, sting! Your tail is well curved. You are
she, the daughter of the cave; you are she, the daughter of the crater.[68]
You! The vagina's mother with your penis. This is your penis; this is
the genealogy of your mother and your father.[69]

This document was a direct textualization of the penis-piercing ritual. As
such, the text should have signified masculinity. After all, as has been noted,
it was through the ritual shedding of blood that Maya men proved their masculine worth. The cure was ostensibly about a scorpion sting. A close analysis of this narrative finds the significance of the relationship between Maya
desire and the transsexualizing of the human body.

Gendered boundaries may be crossed when they are viewed cross-
culturally. By using the word "crossed" here, I emphasize that the boundaries
of the Maya gender system differed from the boundaries of the European
gender system. I do not, therefore, suggest that the ritual texts simply allowed
people to cross genders. Rather, I interpret the texts in a cross-cultural analysis as documents which used the metaphorical constructions of gender/sex.
This document was about the relationship of fantasy to ritual.

The beginning of the text hardly seems to suggest anything sexual. The
stinger may have referred to the pain coming from the sting, while the sting
itself may have referred to the eating of meat,[70] but neither signified any sexual acts. As the curer moved on to lance the stinger, destroying it, the stinger
was not allowed to exist, and the curer had to destroy its lineage.

Lineage was a central concern throughout the text as the patient was named in the document in an obscure manner, allowing him or her to have some connection with a lineage. This naming process only occurred as the curer destroyed the stinger. Naming was important, as this patient was named not only through his or her lineages, but also through the actions taking place during the curing ceremony. This showed some connection between particular lineages and particular cures or aspects of the ritual world. Lineage and blood thus were central, but the centrality of lineage would appear to have heavily regulated sexual desire. Why, then, was desire such a free-floating entity?

The vagina's mother entered the text to relate the matrilineal line. The idea of the matrilineage was expressed by the mother being represented as the mother of vaginas. Here, though, the anatomically correct human body may not have played an essential role. The text was not referring specifically to women as the vagina. And the penis appeared along with the mother, signifying the importance of the phallus for the cure. The penis and the vagina's mother together signified sexual desire, marked as central to the ritual.

As the penis encountered the scorpion and the mother, it used the grandmother's virginal needle (stingray spine) and then began to move to the grandmother's virginal fire. The penis needed the grandmother's objects in order to engage in this ritual. The needle and the fire were used to pierce the penis. The penis-piercing ritual, a sign of masculinity in the Maya world, was controlled by these objects possessed by the grandmother, who represented the Moon Goddess and the matrilineage. The phallus here hardly seemed powerful. The actual ritual took place in two symbolic representations of the sign of women's lineage. The needle and the fire both came from the grandmother. Both were signified as sacred through *suhuy*, the concept of a specifically feminine sanctity. The women's lineage was empowered to engage in the ritual, simply using the phallic image of the penis as a mechanism to control what would seem at first glance to have been a male-dominated ritual. Desire here signified a desire for the ritual, and thus for some connection with the deities. The penis and vagina both entered the picture in order to stress the importance of sexual desire to creation and the gods.

The penis was shown as somewhat weak and certainly damaged. This image signified the concept of male fear, showing the penis to be a frail part of the anatomy, but also showing that the penis could engage in some type of sexual activity with the mother. The penis was both damaged and sexualized in what may be seen as a heteroerotic construct. But was heterosexuality really signified here?

The penis apparently helped to clean the needle. In doing so, the penis was damaged in some way, once again pointing to its symbolic weakness in this ceremony. The penis was pierced and thus damaged. Yet the piercing of the penis was considered a central part in the development of the man. So the symbolism represented a stronger man with a more beautiful penis, but the reality of the event also showed that the penis itself was hurt. While the ritual symbolically signified masculinity, it also maintained the frail nature of the penis and asserted the control of the matrilineage. The remainder of this text presented some confusion between the penis, the needle, and the stinger, all signifying phallic images. Nonetheless, the context made clear that the text intended for the curer to lance the stinger while at the same time it signified a double entendre for the penis-piercing ritual.[71] The stinger/penis was lanced in a central location, and it dripped down the back (perhaps of the scorpion). The narrative strategically centered the cure by showing the blood dripping down both the belly and the back. The bodily metaphor combined with the tree to show that the ritual was intended to be manifested as important but also positioned in the tree or the forest, on the strategic outside. This strategic outside allowed for sexual acts to take place in a ritual context.[72]

As the vagina's mother connected with the penis, creating the child, the passage referred to reproduction, particularly the act of vaginal intercourse leading to reproduction. It also may have referred to some sort of castration. The selection crossed genders in the sense that the author addressed the child as a person with a penis, while stating that the child was the *daughter* of the vagina. This child, marked as a daughter, was to be the transsexual child. She could attain particular body parts, thus moving her into a perception of the female-to-male transsexual. But this is not precisely what was intended here.

The body parts connected with the earth and the underworld in that the vagina was the cave and the crater, and the child (who may have been marked as "androgynous" or "hermaphroditic" as well as "transsexual") emanated from the earth.[73] The narrative prioritized the role of the vagina and never referred to the father's penis. Rather, the mother had intercourse with the penis of the "transsexual" child. Both mother and child were defined through genital organs.

The vagina's mother, damaged by the scorpion sting, needed a cure. The person who we find out is the daughter engaged in that cure through the use of her penis and her grandmother's needle. The needle may have been a phallic signifier, a mirage of some sort, that pointed to the need for the phallus to engage in the cure. The phallic signification also could have represented the need for a body part which later would disappear as it became unnecessary.

This could have been any body part vaguely resembling a needle. The three women together (grandmother, mother, and daughter) attempted to cure the mother. While the daughter needed the penis to engage in her part of the cure (as she had to engage in intercourse with the mother), she remained a daughter, and thus was transsexual, but perhaps did not cross genders.

The final section of the text strategically used the second person in order to command the daughter to engage in intercourse. The text demanded that the daughter understand and respect her lineage. Yet here she used her penis to enter and penetrate the mother. If this act signaled disrespect to the lineage, it strategically reversed the usual narrative pattern, empowering the daughter and disempowering the elders. As the daughter obtained the penis, that penis also disappeared.

The sexual act was connected with the mother eating the penis. The vagina was connected with eating, and the penis with providing food. It was quite common in these documents, as well as in Mayan preconquest religion in general, that the female body was connected with eating and the male body with food.[74] The act of eating the penis here was based on the double entendre of *chib*, which may have translated as "sting" or "to eat meat."[75] Just as the mother ate, the scorpion stung. The act of eating, here gendered female, was connected with the disease, just as the act of curing also was connected with the eating of the penis and the participation of the lineage of these women.

As it was the mother of the vagina who ate the penis, one might begin to suggest that this text referred to some sort of castration complex, and thus to Oedipal triangulation.[76] Yet, whatever the validity of such a statement in contemporary Western societies, it had little applicability here. Throughout the narrative there were references to feminine control over various "phallic objects." The grandmother controlled and harmed the penis in an earlier episode. She also possessed the needle. In other texts both the needle and the penis were controlled by feminine objects. The mother of the vagina only ate the penis in this case. The metaphor here referred to women's access to the ritual ceremony of penis piercing. The women necessarily played a central role in the curing ceremony. They used the penis when it was necessary, and then they discarded it. The penis was "eaten" only in a metaphorical sense. It was a free-floating object which vanished just as it no longer was needed. As the mother noticed the daughter's "tail," which could have referred to either the penis or the anus,[77] this cross-referenced the concept of eating. This did not signify a castration complex; rather, desire was encoded in a particular strategy to cure people while signifying the importance of lineage and thus maintaining the social hierarchy.

Just as the mother completed this act, the daughter was named as a daughter. She was declared a daughter with no known father, thus perhaps representing her as a commoner.[78] She was the daughter of the cave and the crater, references to both the vagina and the earth. The vagina was constructed as earthly, signifying a perceived connection between women and the earth. The sexual act which created the daughter may have been connected with a lack of knowledge of her father. Given the importance the Maya placed upon lineage, such a reference would have been a negative comment. The terms, however, did not refer to illegitimacy. They did not state, as the texts did with commoners, that "she had no mother or father."[79] Rather, the term *ix yal* referred to the mother. This daughter was the daughter of a woman, or of a line of women. The mother played a central role. The cave and the crater also referred to an acknowledged role for women in the ritual sphere. This role allowed them significant access to that sphere.

The final statement, that the vagina's mother and the penis were related to the genealogy of the mother and father, reconnected this passage with the Maya kinship system. The father suddenly was named at the end, connected with kinship. Unlike the mother and grandmother, the father played no role in the cure and played only an indefinite role in the creation of the daughter. The kinship system gave the mother and the child permission to engage in their ritual intercourse. While this statement does seem to violate many of the psychoanalytic views about a transhistorical incest taboo,[80] one should not assume that the passage gave Maya people permission to engage in incest.[81] The ritual, rather, presented a discourse developed around the creation of humanity that prioritized the woman's role in this creation and allowed the woman's partner to create a gender boundary significantly different from the boundaries which exist in contemporary Western thought. The Maya boundary separated the symbolic language of gender from the language of genital organs.

One must remember that the ritual was performed on a man, whose shedding of penile blood gave him access to the gods. The feminine role here was designed to assert what the Maya people believed to be obvious: the fact that the cosmos required male *and* female principles in order to create and maintain the community. This assertion did not take away from the fact of masculine power. Maya fantasies must have allowed for a gendering of some of the ritual world that was separated from the gendering of both people and the gods. This gendering metaphorically signified the transsexuality of the fantasy and allowed for the cure to take place with organs displaced from human bodies.

PHALLIC MOTIONS AND TRANSSEXUAL BODIES

Transsexual and transgender bodies[82] here were represented not as sexual or gender identities, but rather as narrative techniques designed to allow for an understanding of sexual desire in the ritual of penis piercing. Transsexuality was placed in several narratives in order to signify Maya fantasies related to completion of sexual acts and the need for these sexual acts to take place in order to cure a patient. The power of transsexuality through the movable phallus thus was immense.

The Power of Transsexual Desire

The text discussed above problematized the notion of a binary gender system. The ritualized child first appeared hermaphroditic or transsexual, but this appearance failed to acknowledge the value of the symbol in the ritualized phenomenon. The cross-cultural appearance of the figure of the daughter with the penis did not signify that the Maya supported transgender or transsexual people. Nor did it show that this figure became transsexual, in the sense of transforming her body. Nor did it show her as transgendered: there existed no information to show that this figure ever was gendered male. The narrative showed that a daughter had certain body parts which Western thought prioritizes as determinative of sex (and usually gender as well). But the anatomical body did things in a wide variety of texts that we in the contemporary West would consider impossible. In the Western world prior to the Enlightenment, there were accounts of men who supposedly lactated and "pictures of the boy Jesus with breasts." Girls were said to turn into boys and boys into girls simply because they associated too much with the other gender.[83] The anatomical bodies were secondary to factors contemporary Western societies would consider cultural. Still, gender differentiation was central to society.

As the research moves cross-culturally, anatomy moves further from "destiny." In contemporary Native North American societies, anatomical sexual markers are not the same in different societies. Not only are the meanings different, but the actual body parts which define those sexual markers are different.[84] The variations in anatomical markers represent a variety of possibilities, including the development of a multiple gender system[85] (although this is unlikely to have been the case among indigenous peoples of the Americas).[86]

The Maya case did not present the existence of such a multiple gender system but rather showed different strategies in texts related to the ritual world. These texts were central discourses about ritualized access, and they allowed anatomical body parts to disconnect from their owners. In this case we have no knowledge of the child's actual appearance. Did the child have both a vagina and a penis? Was the child's penis removed? Did the sexual act between mother and daughter refer to lesbianism, even though, at the time of the sexual act, the daughter had a penis? The text here engaged the mother and the daughter in a sexual act which was ostensibly both heterosexual and lesbian. One can suggest that this symbolized Maya understandings of the multiplicity of desire and a societal strategy that formulated all desire into a mode of understanding lineage (and thus of maintaining social distance between nobles and commoners).

In order to discuss the meaning of the seemingly outlandish idea that this sexual act was both heterosexual and lesbian, I must briefly discuss the position of "hermaphroditic" desire in Mesoamerican thought. Alfredo López Austin, writing about the Nahuas, points out that the word used by Bernardino de Sahagún's aides as a translation for "hermaphrodite" literally meant "she who has something broad." He says that the word in correct Nahuatl usage meant "lesbian." He thus discerns some confusion on the part of the Nahuas as to the difference between lesbians and hermaphrodites. The passage he cites accentuates this "confusion":

> THE HERMAPHRODITE. The hermaphrodite is a loathsome woman, a woman with a penis, mistress of a penis, owner of a penis, mistress of a penis, owner of testicles. She seeks another woman as a companion, she makes herself a friend of a woman, she provides herself with a young woman, she is mistress of a young woman. She has a man's body, the top part of her body is that of a man, she talks like a man, walks like a man, has a beard, has down, has hair. She practices lesbian love, she makes a woman her friend. She never wants to marry. She detests men, and can't see them. She creates scandal.[87]

The attitude presented in this source does not appear to have any duplicate in the Mesoamerican corpus. While both the Nahuas and the Maya may have treated "hermaphrodites" and "lesbians" with extreme disgust, the documents were very unclear on these points. I argue that, rather than deciding that the Nahuas and the Maya were confused, one instead must consider that these documents showed differently sexed and gendered boundaries for the human body in Mesoamerican thought.

Here the hermaphrodite and "lesbian"[88] both were associated with bodies which had anatomical markers attributed to grown men. Much as in the example of pre-Enlightenment Western societies, it seems plausible that these anatomical markers represented textual spaces different from what modern Westerners understand. Anatomy in this case would not signify a determination of "sex," but rather would be associated with the "improper" gender role assigned to both hermaphrodites and lesbians in the text. This "improper" gender role allowed both the hermaphrodite and the lesbian strategic "in-between" positions. These positions were dangerous, as society labeled them "illegitimate." The Nahuatl text, however, was a text intended for Spanish eyes, and thus was mediated by great Spanish influence.[89] The desire signified in the Nahuatl text was influenced heavily by colonialism such that this may have been a strategic text where Sahagún's aides were trying to win his favor. It may have signified intentional or unintentional lies, or it may have been a distortion of truth.

Through an analysis of symbolic language, the Maya case becomes more clear. The narrative may have defined bodies as containing two genders. In the text, gender may have been disassociated from genital organs. In the ritual sphere the text portrayed, anatomical "sex" may have been secondary to a gendered notion of access to the cure and to the ritual itself. In such a text, the differentiation between a "natural" zone of anatomy and a "cultural" zone of social roles made little sense. Genital organs themselves may have existed in the symbolic realm. The daughter could have a penis and still have been considered female. The narrative thus prioritized a (hetero)sexual intercourse which led to the birth of a child: the penis and the vagina engaged in this sexual act. Yet the narrative also prioritized the same act as a (lesbian) sexual act: the two people who engaged in this act both were women. The textualized and sexualized body could prioritize women's (lesbian) sexual behavior. The notion of identity based on sexual behavior was problematic here, as this sexual behavior was at once (lesbian) and (hetero)sexual. The text asserted a desire which could be read in many ways. No doubt the Maya themselves understood these texts in a variety of different manners. The transsexualization of the text thus was a strategy which attempted to place desire in the context of appropriate lineage leading to a cure.

Here this strategy was phallocentric, where the body may have been defined as necessitating the penis for sexual contact, even between two females. The metaphor showed the necessity of both the penis and the vagina in the act of creation. At the same time, this metaphor stressed the importance of matrilineage in accessing the ritual world. The phallocentric image was one of the maintenance of masculine power through a specifically gendered notion of sexual desire.

This desire is implicated in in the work of Jacques Lacan, where he develops his psychoanalytic study of infantile gender and sexual identity, stating that in Western society people engage in the act of masquerading as the phallus.[90] The notion of masquerade represents the miming of the signifier. The woman presents the notion of "being" the phallus while the man presents the notion of "having" the phallus. Neither can be the case because the phallus, as a signifier, is not a body part.

The Maya selection questioned whether the symbolic order of the phallus played a role in Maya society at all. The textual child uncovered the masquerade. To Western eyes the child seems non- or multigendered and therefore almost entirely incomprehensible to our linguistic system. The "female" child had no desire for the phallus since she already had the phallus. This phallus, as a linguistic symbol in the act of masquerade, related incomprehensibly to Western gender and more incomprehensibly to the penis itself. The essential part of this child's femininity, which Lacan sees as lost, may never have existed, since the feminine and masculine both played roles in Maya society which perhaps cannot be understood in the psychoanalytic framework. How could the daughter have had the phallus? How could she have gone beyond the reach of the rule of the father?[91]

And notions of active and passive roles were switched. The daughter here engaged in the "aggressive" act of penetrating the mother. She was the "active" partner in the sexual intercourse. The active partner signified power, but in certain instances the Maya allowed the passive partner to be a very powerful, although degraded, figure. So while the daughter attained her "masculinity" by penetrating the mother, this did not necessarily signify disrespect to the lineage. Instead it was a way for the daughter to harness power when she needed it. At the time of the sexual play, the daughter was not even born, for the act itself was to create her. This act took place on the textual space of her body, but before her anatomical body could have existed.

Then she attained her "femininity" with the creation of her vagina. But again she was not presented as attaining a specific identity through her vagina. She did not use her vagina to engage in any textual action. Instead she used her penis. Sexual acts were understood in an environment where gender and the body had significantly different boundaries than in Western thought. And the phallicism of desire here was not present in the way Lacan suggests. Instead, it signified access to power for the daughter.

It is clear that the daughter harnessed power when it was needed. She used her power to make the mother a passive partner. She thus inverted power alignments. Yet the text signified masculinity and masculine power: the transsexuality of the daughter was used as a narrative strategy designed to make it clear that the masculine figure could create and control the cosmos through the piercing of the penis. Transsexuality and gender parallelism were used to assert male power.

The Phallic Movement

Of course this does not mean that a phallic symbolic order played no role in Maya society. If Lacanian analysis is reconfigured in the form of the masquerade, one may gain a greater understanding of the ritual presented here. Lacan's theories can be used in order to understand the phallus as signifying any body part, and, in this case, prioritizing the vagina over the father's penis. Judith Butler, in a chapter entitled "The Lesbian Phallus," shows that the phallus can signify "a number of body parts, discursive performatives, alternative fetishes" and other things. The phallus may prioritize any body part, whether it "really" exists or not. If the phallus signifies all of these things rather than an actual particular body part, the masquerade has little to do with sexual anatomical divisions. For Butler, if the phallus is lesbian, it then displaces anatomy and "(re)produces the spectre of the penis only to enact its vanishing."[92] The phallus itself becomes, in a sense, transsexual as it shows a penis which continually is shown, yet continually vanishes.

One can then see the heterosexual-hermaphroditic-transsexual-transgender-lesbian-castrating sex scene shown above in a different light. It could have both prioritized the vagina as the important sexual organ and engaged in ritual play with the vanishing penis. The signifying chain at work here showed that the phallus may have made the ritualized play understandable in the context of creation. The penis was necessary at a particular point, after which it vanished. The existence of the penis showed the necessity of both the penis and the vagina in order to engage in an act which eventually created a child. The penis was used only for the ritual play, after which the symbolic order (temporarily) resignified the vagina as the important genital organ.[93] In this text the penis and vagina signified strategic maneuvers to control the cosmos. The penis then was not a referent to the male body at all, but rather referred to creation.

So the penis's power in the text was immense, but not in the way Lacan would understand it. The penis's textual role was that it was shown, damaged, and then discarded. The damage to the penis was not a cause for concern (after all, the ritual intended to cut the penis), and the lack of a penis after it disappeared was meaningless. The penis had power to engage in the cure only when it was the daughter's possession.

In crossing anatomical sex, the daughter accounted for the presence of the penis, where later she enacted the penis's vanishing. Here her imagination was constructed through the text as allowing her to obtain the penis. The body as a singular entity did not exist in this symbolic world, which could invest a bodily image with a variety of parts which never were visible.[94] The symbolism created a unified being, but it also reconstructed that being to obtain other parts. The imagination allowed for an anatomy with different sexual anatomical divisions. The (male) author of this passage reconstructed a curing scene to allow "male body parts" some power in a scene symbolically dominated exclusively by femininity. The discordant unconscious could not create a tremendous amount of power for the penis, as the penis here felt pain coming from sacred objects (both the needle and the fire) controlled by a goddess, and the penis later vanished. The power invested in transsexuality here was assumed metaphorically by women, leaving men little power in the text. This was a discursive maneuver allowing men to have some role (and thus significant power) in the narrative of masculinity. The perception of female power in the text was thus a mirage, a way of asserting a fantasy of gender parallelism in a world dominated by the masculine. Maya culture and traditions represented themselves through metaphorical writing. Ritual discourse, often based on bodily foundations,[95] could "play" with gender in such a manner as to move the conversation beyond traditional gendered divisions. These ritual traditions presented themselves in the texts under discussion. And the traditions demanded transsexuality.

Similar expressions connecting the penis with the vagina, in an apparent effort to recall intercourse, occurred throughout the Ritual of the Bacabs.[96] In many cases, the statement was a derogatory expression. A text which partially paralleled the scorpion text discussed a cure for "worms in the teeth." The text ended with an expression of pain:

can techlic yn chacal xamach [yn sacal xamach] yn ekel kanal xamach can tech [lic] yn chacal x kan kilis che la tah kakil tin kelci a uich ca tin kelhe che co fel u na ta uach coe co co co

My red griddle, my white griddle, my black griddle, and my yellow griddle are in the four directions. My red *kan kilis* plant goes in the four directions. In the fierce fire, I roast your face. I roast the tooth.

The vagina's mother with your penis![97] Oh! tooth, tooth, tooth, tooth![98]

The curing ceremony elicited pain, sympathy, and humor. The ritualization of the plant/flower and the four directions stressed the importance of the cure. Yet the patient's face was roasted in the fire and she or he then yelled about the pain of his or her tooth. The dental procedure apparently was very painful. This pain was expressed through the relationship of the penis with the vagina. This derogatory marking showed the use of the term as an expression of pain. Arzápalo Marín states that a similar expression is used in contemporary Yucatán as an insult directed toward the mother.[99] He shows that the derogatory expression has survived in some form. The intent here seems a relevant ground for exploration. Why was a derogatory expression in the middle of a serious ritual and medical incantation? Were the texts attempting to insult women?

One may recall the importance of ritual humor, which may have been derogatory in daily life, but took on a ritual meaning which may or may not have altered its derogatory nature.[100] Looking at the above texts, it appears that they clearly referred to the act of creation as well as to a derogatory epithet for the vagina. The vagina, as a powerful cultural symbol that created (and ate, thus destroying), also was an object of ridicule. The texts strategically used the cultural signifier of the vagina in order to allow gender parallelism in fantasies related to the ritual world but then limited the power of femininity by using a derogatory term. The narratives permitted a hierarchical organization (women in the nobility had access to the ritual world) while also allowing for a humorous escape from that ritual power (men and commoner women could insult the vaginas of the noblewomen, thus insulting and perhaps challenging their ritual power). The narratives allowed for a system of gendered parallelism while also supporting a strong social hierarchy. The transsexuality of the text may have been intended to insult the ritual power of the women, saying that they needed penises in order to be powerful. Thus masculine power was asserted even while femininity was viewed as in control of much of the ritual.

Another example which paralleled the above text about the needle put forth ideas about creation:

max u na max u col yal yx hun acay kik yal ix hun acay olom tan yol can fel u na ti yach u canil chab u canil akab hun yah nal uinic hun yah ual anom

Who is his/her mother? Who is his/her lust? It is said that she is "she, the great bloodletter." It is said that she is "she, the great lineage finder"[101] at the heart of the sky. The vagina's mother with the penis of the four[102] creations, of the four nights, is the great pain of the man coming from the mother's line, the great pain of the first man.[103]

Creation again was gendered as the mother made the penis and the first man. Yet the first man came from the mother's lineage and his father was represented as unknown. The importance of his position as *first* man certainly maintained noble origins. The penis apparently involved in the creation was the metaphorical free-floating penis. If the first man had a mother and the creation of that first man involved both the penis and the mother's vagina, who could have had the penis? The penis either could have belonged to the mother (who thus impregnated herself) or to an unnamed entity. The free-floating penis retained great importance, but not as a male appendage, at least not at the time of the act. Rather, the penis was an appendage to some other entity.

The phallus signified the transsexuality of the text. For if it was not a man who had the penis, it must have been something or someone else. The text was using a sexual marker to allow for a creation ritual which did not engage men. Instead the ritual needed to involve some other creature in its act. It did so by creating the free-floating transsexual phallus.

Importantly, the vagina once again was denigrated, even in the act of creating the first man. The mother's power seemed to cause pain to the sons, who reacted by writing this tract and this insult. The mother was represented as the mother of lust. She thus created the lineage and the community, and she was the central creator of the nation. Yet she also was the one upon whom all the nation's problems got blamed.

The concept of the mother of the vagina using her own vagina to combine with a free-floating penis in order to create children was a very common notion in the Ritual of the Bacabs. The ritual invested the vagina with much power and allowed women (goddesses?) symbolically to cross Western concepts of sex and gender in order to gain access to the penis. The phallus, if signified at all, was a symbol either of the vagina or of some detachable body part, thus decentering the psychoanalytic notion.

The Maya ritualized their fantasy world in such a way as to connect masculinity and femininity to the powerful signifier of transsexuality. It was through this discourse on transsexuality that blood was taken from the penis. The penis became an object possessed not by its supposed owner, but rather by the women and men, goddesses and gods involved in the ritual ceremony.

GENDERED BLOOD AND TRANSSEXUAL BODIES

The reader might ask about the historical importance of these texts. Indeed, the bulk of documents here were representations of preconquest rituals. Yet the documents were written during postconquest times, at least a few generations after the conquest. So what could these rituals have meant to postconquest peoples who could no longer publicly participate in such extensive rites? While certainly some of these ceremonies continued to take place in hiding, the primary point here was that these texts were still known to postconquest peoples. They thus continued to have some influence over conceptualizations of fantasy, desire, masculinity, and femininity. By the seventeenth century, however, these texts would have competed with other notions of these elements. The documents, hidden as they were, certainly could not compete with the public and private rituals of Catholicism and the Spanish legal system. Systems of masculinity and femininity changed dramatically. But the changes were not total, and these narratives were markers of hybridity. Not only were these texts remembered, but Catholicism would not gain complete dominance over the Maya people. This, after all, was not the center of the Spanish Empire. So these texts did show some remnants of a preconquest sexual and gender system that survived, however much it was altered, into the mid-colonial period. These narratives, when combined with Catholic rituals which the people attended, showed ways in which Maya minds and fantasies were hybridized through the colonial years.

The gendering of blood signified the transsexuality of fantasy and desire. The blood allowed for a Maya femininity which had a great presence in the ritual sphere. Yet the presence of this femininity never challenged but instead supported the immense power of the masculine in the Maya universe. The Maya fantasy world showed that the people would allow the phallus to play a central role in creation. But this role was mitigated by the importance of the vagina, and of menstruation in particular. Women did bleed, and their blood held great ritual importance. Men's blood may have signified many different things, but most importantly it signified the recognition of gender parallelism in creation. Blood and semen were symbols of the desire to understand creation. While the Maya world was a world with extreme gender hierarchies, the sexual desires were implicated in a system of ritual parallelism and phallic exchange. The phallus certainly was vital, showing a male dominance, but its vitality was most important when it was attached to nobody.

EIGHT

Transsexuality and
the Floating Phallus

The textual placement of the phallus was vital to the success of the Maya texts. These documents were intended to evoke an understanding of the preconquest bloodletting rituals, but this understanding had to come, for the most part, without the public display of the ceremony. The mid-colonial importance of these texts centered on the figure of the phallus and the fantasy of transsexuality. If the phallus was placed appropriately in the text, the reading of this document could serve both to entertain an audience and to convince the people that preconquest kings, lords, and nobles sought to protect society by doing everything to commune with the ancestors and the gods. The fantasy of transsexuality signified the gender and sexual crossing that was done in order to protect the community. The texts themselves contained a strategy of memory: they worked to make the people remember the preconquest rituals even when those rituals no longer were performed. The rituals in this sense were a strategy of resistance, an attempt by traditional Maya nobles to regain control over the Yucatecan population.

One should recall here that the strategy of transsexuality did not signify any sense of gender "equality."[1] From the perspective of the Maya writers at the time of the conquest, transsexuality in these texts was used to assert the power of the warrior in a society that considered warfare to be a key event in the life of the community. The warriors, almost all male, used their own blood to create, maintain, and recreate life. In essence, they copied the feminine sphere in order for them to gain more power and control. So the blood rituals and the strategy of transsexuality were used to assert an ever more dominant masculinity.

This chapter seeks to uncover such a strategy by focusing on theoretical material related to the phallus and transsexuality. This material is used to see the ways in which the texts maintained a floating phallus and a symbolic transsexuality.

THE PHALLUS WITHOUT A BODY

The centrality of semen and blood to the political system, as the ritual markers of lineage, connected directly with the phallus. The leader derived power from his knowledge of semen and blood, both ritually shed from the penis. He imparted this knowledge to other nobles in an obscure language which could not be understood by most people. It was this connection with the phallus, then, that stratified gender in Maya society.

Jacques Lacan argues that the phallus is central only in an androcentric universe. If this phallus is hidden, if it does not fit into a male-centered perspective, then it is meaningless. And the desire for the phallus itself is symbolic, not some natural drive for the penis.[2] Yet this is not what was seen in the Maya case. This was not a space where a triangulation of Maya desire could be observed. The phallus was not always desired, not always the central signifier.[3] To suggest that it always was the central element of desire is to support an Oedipal colonialism.[4]

In political documents that stressed "Zuyua" speech,[5] the narratives themselves were based on a particular concept of (unintelligible) speech and language. The phallus which was desired was located on the body of the central leader of the Maya community, but this phallus was always hidden and never mentioned. Unintelligible speech necessarily was a language of stratification. As a game that the nobles played when they attempted to prove their nobility, it was presumed that the commoners could not understand this language. The language itself was based on the blood and semen located in the phallus. As such, that phallus itself was a political weapon, used to stress differences in social status. This phallus was related directly to political and social stratification, and it must be understood as such. In Maya society it was not to be viewed as a castration complex.

The hidden phallus in the Zuyua texts was extraordinarily powerful. It

stratified society based on age, class, and gender, and it controlled the political rituals. It never was shown; on the contrary, the texts focused on the desires related to the ruler, and thus presented the body parts of those he desired.
This notion of the hidden phallus, attached to the male body, contrasts directly with Lacan's perception of Western society, where the (male) phallus
is always visible and the female relationship with the phallus is confined to a
masking exercise.[6] Instead this (male) hidden phallus exercised power over
society in a method that was not reducible to the psychoanalytic model. This
went beyond both Oedipus and the family.[7]

The Maya certainly placed some importance on phallic power, but this
power is not framed easily by psychoanalysis and other Western theoretical
approaches. The political texts themselves coded and hid the phallus with
"unintelligible" language, deriving even more power from it than they might
have if the phallus were visible.[8]

Oedipus as Colonizer

Psychoanalysis is the major theoretical movement that has led to a discussion
of desire and the relationship between this desire and the phallus, but psychoanalysis has certain limits.[9] Those scholars who have studied sexual desire in
non-Western societies have noted these limits, and they have moved beyond
traditional psychoanalysis in order to study the various levels at which desire
and power have been formulated in both biological processes and psychosexual development.[10]

In the Maya ritual world the phallus was used in a strategic anticolonial
maneuver. This maneuver, from the perspective of psychoanalytic theory,
might have stemmed from a desire for the phallus. Psychoanalysts have attempted to tackle questions of desire right from its theoretical origins.[11] Following Freud's lead, they found that many people had difficulty fitting into
preassigned gender categories.[12] They also believed gender was rooted not in
nature but rather in a kinship system based on the primary taboo of incest.[13]
These conclusions often led psychoanalysts to state that gender, although not
based in nature, was a fixed entity based in the most fundamental prohibition
of all societies.

Psychoanalysis delineated two central related concepts of desire: Oedipus
and the phallus. The Oedipal complex is based on a theory of triangulation.
People develop their psyches out of incest taboos related to their mothers and
fathers (hence the mother-father-me triangle). These incest taboos are universal and are related to the deepest needs of society. In order for society to

exist, it must have an incest taboo which allows for the creation and maintenance of the kinship group. This group then allows us to separate ourselves
from others (thus leading to the creation of ethnicity, race, and nation).[14] From
the perspective of traditional psychoanalysis, this would be an unchangeable
manifestation of society's drive to reproduce itself.

The phallus relates directly to the Oedipal complex, for it is in the vision
of the mother that the male child begins to develop a castration complex and
in the vision of the father that the female child begins to develop penis envy.[15]
From the initial shock of seeing the parents with different genitalia than themselves, there develop certain fears about a perceived "lack." The daughter fears
that she needs a penis and the son fears that his penis will be removed. This
immediately is transferred into an incestuous desire which must be repressed.[16]
For psychoanalysis the theory of sexual desire is one in which society represses
basic desires in order for that society to survive.

The "lack" represented in psychoanalysis is problematic here. Do all people
necessarily desire what they lack? Do we naturally give so much symbolic importance to these particular organs? Or is libidinal desire stressed throughout
the body, and perhaps throughout society?[17] Is it incest that is repressed, or
is this a displacement of desire based on law?[18] Is repression itself really the
primary operation of society when sexual desire is discussed?[19]

Some psychoanalysts and anthropologists influenced by these theories, including Lacan, have moved beyond the traditional Freudian framework, arguing that the construction of gender is more complex and multilayered than
the traditional psychoanalytic discourse allows. Rather, Lacan argues, gender
and sexuality have a linguistic and symbolic base.[20] Lacan appears to show
that the Oedipus complex is historical, based on the creation of the "I," the
individual subject.[21] This subject is distinguished from the Other based on
the maintenance of the symbolic order, and particularly on the phallus as
privileged signifier.

For Lacan the phallus is not the penis, and gender therefore is not nature.
The phallus is a privileged signifier, *not* "the organ, penis or clitoris, which it
symbolizes."[22] In Lacanian theory the phallus is not a representative of anatomy. Anatomies can change in the symbolic world, and the phallus may be situated on a site where one would not normally assert the presence of a penis
or something representing a penis.[23] Instead of being reducible either to anatomy or to fantasy, the phallus is a signifier which serves to guard the unconscious. The image of the phallus can be used to analyze the psychoanalytic
patient and to assert the problematic nature of the relationship between sex-

uality and the life of the individual.[24] Psychoanalysis is supposed to uncover what the phallus signifies in any particular instance. In Western societies the phallus regulates access to the symbolic world. Only by accessing and understanding the phallus may one enter this world. Nobody can have a phallus.

Such a theoretical advance from Freud allows more space to understand historical change. But for Lacan the phallus still appears to be a universally applicable signifier, and the Oedipus complex in many ways is the logical result of that signification. The end result of Oedipalization is a concern with "lack." The centrality of the phallus makes sense in such a theory, but scholars must question whether the phallus has cross-cultural and transhistorical importance. Lacan's methods have been used both to suggest transhistorical notions of universal patriarchies and to show the ways in which our imaginations are historically constructed.[25] Here I reject the transhistorical narrative and instead argue that scholars need to understand all ideas in the relevant historical context.

Yet one must not underestimate the importance of Freud and Lacan. I have included them here because, as I study Maya conceptions of desire, and the penis/phallus is represented in a wide variety of ways, many of my readers will think of Freud and psychoanalysis. Some may consider the Maya a phallocentric society on this basis alone. But psychoanalysis needs to be applied very carefully to non-Western societies. For the Maya at the time of the conquest this sense of "lack" could not be shown to exist. There were few cases of sexual dysfunction posited in the documents. Although triangulation was represented, this was symbolic of a wider concern about lineage. And the phallus itself was not divided easily into the symbolic phallus and the real penis.

Poststructuralist work perhaps brings one a bit closer to understanding Maya concepts of phallic desire, as the poststructuralists connect desire to political power.[26] The Maya discourse certainly did this, showing a connection between religion, politics, desire, and the phallus. It is in poststructuralist and postcolonial theory that desire is seen as discursive (Foucault), performative (Butler), or political (Spivak). And it is here that desire is linked specifically to a history which changes. But poststructuralist analysis often does not see the relationship between its own academic enterprise and colonialism, therefore failing to comprehend the very real situations of people in non-Western societies.[27]

It is in the performative analysis of the human body that I find further clues to understanding the movable/floating phallus. Many scholars have come to critique the idea of an essentialist notion of the body. Essentialists claim that

the body exists as a physical, biological entity, on top of which people develop
their own identities and lives. The constructionist critique of this position
states that the body is constructed only through a series of repetitive acts
which allow the material, natural entity to enter into imaginations and fields
of vision.[28] This approach says that traditions form the body. Judith Butler
states that "reiterative and citational practice" produces the body as a "performative effect" of its naming.[29] The body exists in contemporary Western
society as a performance of the traditions which delineate the body's meanings. The body itself, of course, has a natural, physical presence. Yet there is no
way of delineating the differences between the natural and the constructed,
because that which is natural and that which is constructed through tradition
and the imagination are not different parts of the body, but are rather the very
same parts.[30]

Butler's analysis of the body's performativity fails to take into account the
importance of colonialism and power in the development of the body in non-
Western, colonized societies. For here the body could not have engaged in a
performative reiteration of the individual subject as that body in many ways
was controlled by the colonizer. The colonizing apparatus allowed for a repression of both bodily performance and the discursive creation of gender
and sexual desire. As such, the performance of desire in colonized societies has
been limited by the apparatus of the colonial state. Gayatri Spivak has shown
that such limitations on the performance of desire effectively have displaced
the desires of the colonized in such a way that they cannot be understood as
performances: their desires must be analyzed as ways of responding to and
coping with colonialism.[31] I argue that these desires must be understood as
part of the forces which have created hybridity.

It is here that both Spivak and Luce Irigaray are helpful. Spivak argues that
the historian may seek to understand colonized desires by decoding the multiple levels of power involved in the production of various colonized actions.
Irigaray argues that scholars may analyze the important roles of gender and
sexual desire by reading documents as enterprises used to assert phallic dominance. Irigaray states that the documents may be comprehended only if this
phallic dominance is reread with an appreciation of the way that women's
consciousness is placed and displaced in the shadows/margins of the texts.[32]
Both Irigaray and Spivak maintain that in the documents there exist expressions of subaltern consciousness (in Spivak's terms) that necessarily always
will be clouded by the power of representation used by the colonizers.

The changing performance of the human body and its colonization may
tell more about Maya notions of the phallus. Perhaps this floating phallus

simply signified a different discursive construction of the human body. But perhaps it also signified a political maneuver where ideas of colonialism and domination interceded into the descriptions of desire. The Maya floating phallus thus was used by particular sectors of Maya and Spanish societies in order to promote certain interests. If this phallus really existed, it would have represented debt and exchange in the ritual sphere. The curer owed a debt to the patient; the patient owed a debt to the gods. The gods gave something to the curer: this something was the phallus.

Colonialism was vital in this phallic production. Spanish concepts of the roles of bodies influenced Maya thoughts. The citational practices that produced those bodies changed at the time of the conquest,[33] and the bodies produced different genders and sexual desires and phalluses than ever before. When the Spanish colonized the Maya, they inserted a particular structure of desire into the process. The elements of desire have been shown above: in a particular reading of history, the Maya stressed a desire to survive; in an apparent reaction to colonialism, the Maya desired Saint Francis; in a hybridizing maneuver, the Maya desired the Virgin Mary Moon Goddess; in viewing blood and semen, the Maya desired to maintain the social hierarchy. For the Spaniards all of these signified positive results of the conquest. The Maya were able to give the Spanish what they desired.

This colonization was part of the Oedipalization process and the movement toward a colonial society. Here the desire for the king was a displaced desire for the father. Through the religious hierarchy there existed the establishment of fictive kin. The clergy told the people, "take on a new father, that of God/Jesus/Saint Francis." This not only created a new family structure, but it also created an obligation of debt. The Maya "children" owed these figures their allegiance, as the child owed the father. And the eroticization of the mother figure, the Virgin Mary Moon Goddess, not only allowed for the desire for the mother but also allowed the Maya to continue to desire the traditional mother while they moved on to desiring the Catholic mother. The consecration of debt and libido was nothing new to the Maya, but after the conquest it would take on new forms: the debt and desire were hybridized.

This was the colonization of Oedipus, who asserted that the Maya would not engage in incest as they supposedly had been desiring. They instead had to respect the father and the mother. They were indebted to them.[34] As the symbolic mother and father asserted this power over the various communities, the Maya resisted, but they also began to accept the false premise: they once desired incest, and now it was to be regulated.

Who Lacks the Phallus? Gender and the Symbolic

But these regulations would not have directly regulated anything if the Maya did not have a desire for incest and the phallus. Lacan claims that, in our desire for love as structured through the drive to incest, we search for the phallus because we in fact lack that phallus.[35] So I must ask if the Maya phallus was structured in the form of a "lack," or if it was a mask for power relations to displace desire. The phallus may have been used to signify lineage and to cure people or to make them ill. Slaves and flowers also were phallicized in the Maya texts, and the symbolic connection revealed that the phallus did have power.

Maya society sexualized its slaves linguistically, socially, and ritually. The narratives discussed below allow for a reconstruction of the ritualized sexualization of slaves, both in the form of the constructed and enslaved disease and in the form of the sexualized male slave. The idea of slavery presented here shows that the Maya used the term symbolically to understand disease, sacrifice, and warfare. The "slaves" ritually and linguistically were connected to both excess and sex. The ritualized sex of slaves provided a narrative which legitimized the Maya social hierarchy.

The fight against disease was described as an effort to enslave it. Disease was the child of slavery.

> *hek u xotol bin u cal tu men u na tu men u cool hek uiɔil bin u kikkel yocol bin tiix uixunili kikkel oc bin x buhumil ix cuyum sucil yx cuyum chakanil yx ho ti tzab yal pentac yal ix munach ix catil ahau yx maɔil ahau yx pokol pic yx hun puɔub kik*

His[36] head will be cut by his mother, by her lust.[37] His blood will be splashed; the blood will be penetrated and it will have left. It penetrates the woman's sterility, she the serpent of docility and she the serpent of the field, she the rattlesnake,[38] child[39] of the male slave, child of the female slave, queen of the jar, queen of the grain,[40] she the forceful wound, she the one needle of blood.[41]

The disease was pictured as the daughter of slaves. The woman's body, presented as a dangerous element to be feared for its ability to kill, but an element which nonetheless was to be desired for its ability to maintain society, needed protection from this disease. The woman's sterility could cause only the end of society. The woman's lust was presented as a dangerous element of society, one that courted the disease, the offspring of the slaves. The woman was penetrated and infected by a disease gendered as female (and perhaps transsexual, as the disease appeared at first to be male), despite the fact that the medical text never implied a sexual relationship between the two "women." One "woman," of course, only existed in the realm of metaphor, as she actually was the disease.

The symbolic representations of the serpent and the needle allowed the feminine disease to penetrate the woman. The snake, gendered male and phallic in Western thought, here was associated with female (and perhaps transsexual) attributes. The needle also developed a connection with disease and curing, particularly being related to the penis-piercing ritual. Here was perhaps a (male) phallus (the needle) and a (female) phallus (the snake). If one posits that a phallic order existed at all in Maya culture, then the association of the phallic with the female here shows that the phallus, divided in any society, may have been deployed partly as a feminine entity.

In contemporary Quiché Mayan society, snakes represent fertility and can connect with gender crossing in the rituals. Eric Thompson presents one such ritual in which the men who have snakes dance around female impersonators. The male dancers make obscene gestures and then place the snakes under their shirts.[42] While the snake clearly has erotic meaning in this context, it is related to the penis. Nonetheless, the connection of the snake to gender crossing and sexual desire still exists.[43]

The bleeding needle also related to similar events. In another context, the Ritual of the Bacabs mentioned this needle as a female entity:

cech nicte tancase max tan[case] cech co tancase bin ycnal yx hun puɔub kik
yx hun puɔub olom u colba cħab u coolba akab

You are the erotic/flower seizure.[44] What seizure? You are the lustful seizure.[45] Go with her the one needle of blood, her the one needle of lineage,[46] the mitigation of creation, the mitigation of the night.[47]

The needle here crossed genders and became feminine. The blood that was on the needle signified menstruation, penis piercing, and creation. The blood and the lineage showed that the curer was looking back to the period of creation, the assurance of a female line, and the insecurities of the male line. The naming of the lineage and the bloodline as female presents a strong contradiction with Western practices of patrilineage, which assert the psychoanalytic law of the father, perhaps maintained through the symbolic order of the phallus.[48] The imaginary in Maya symbolism gendered blood and lineage at least partly female, while in social practice lineage before the conquest was gendered *both* male and female.

In the previous text the child of the male and female slaves entered the woman's body, attempting to destroy society. This child herself may have been the phallus of the text. She signified ritual fears of inversion (slaves rebelling against their masters; slaves engaging in sexual acts with noblewomen), and thus became the phallus of the phallic male slave, entering the woman's body in order to gain power for the slaves. Thus the fear of the text was related to the desires of the slaves: here fundamentally sexual, in social terms fundamentally political.

The gendering of the disease connected directly with the sexualization of the slaves, who themselves were the parents of the disease. They engaged in sexual acts which led to the generation of this disease. This text produced a concern with the sexual behavior of the captives. The relationship to slavery maintained a connection between the development of a social hierarchy and the creation of disease. The disease, shown as the product both of a sexual alliance between captives and a sexual alliance between captive men and free noblewomen, penetrated society through the connection between the slaves and the woman's immune system. In a feared strategic reversal of the social hierarchy, the woman was dominated and overtaken by slaves.

Such a reversal resonated with European-generated concerns about witchcraft. Witchcraft, as imported to Latin America, primarily was a concern of various middle- and upper-level social groups with the more marginalized peoples. As the fear developed, the marginalized people were able to create some sense of agency through the use of magic and witchcraft. Ruth Behar, commenting on the complaint of witchcraft of a Mexican friar against his female slave, showed that this slave's background as both a slave and a mulatta allowed the master to be scared of her specifically because she was both marginalized and powerful. She, after all, prepared her master's meals and took care of him in a variety of ways.[49] Her slavery and her status as a person of mixed race left her with access to little power and social status. The slaves were a threat to the nobles precisely because they lacked power in most arenas. They gained power through their ability to instill fear.

The Maya notion of slavery also allowed slaves little access to social status. The slaves had little power outside their ability to instill fear. The Maya case suggested, moreover, the penetration of European ideas about witchcraft into Maya society.[50] It showed a comprehension of a connection between slaves and the ability to create disease, a connection firmly embedded in European ideas. The above narrative presented a hybrid notion which connected Maya traditions of slavery and disease with European ideas of witchcraft. The Maya imagination was colonized and altered, but it remained concerned with similar things.

This hybridity emanated from the phallus. The disease itself, which had been captured, now escaped and penetrated the woman. This penetration may have signified a cultural anxiety manifested in the sexualization of the body of the male slave, viewed as defeated and therefore perhaps penetrated. The penetrated male body may have been a symbol of Maya preconquest slavery. Such a relationship between penetration and defeat showed that the Maya gendered warfare in such a way as to assert male dominance (as penetrator) over women and slaves (as the penetrated).[51] As the woman "involved" in warfare penetrated society, she allowed society to penetrate her. The phallus penetrated her just as she was able to use the phallus to penetrate others.

The woman in this text was connected with and penetrated by a disease gendered female. This symbolic connection of two "women" presented some anxiety about sexual desire. Of course, one could hardly consider this sexuality, and the women did not engage in any sexual activity. Once again, no sexual identity was formed in any manner. Any woman could get sick in this manner, and any disease could be gendered female to present a penetration of one woman by another.

In this case the anxiety presented related more closely to the possible relationship between the male slave and the noblewoman. The male slave linguistically was connected to excess and sexual desire: *pentac* translated as "male slave." The construction of the word *pentac* shows that the notion of sexual behavior deemed as excessive, my gloss on *pen*, connected closely with the construction of Maya slavery. *Pentac* derived from *pen*, *-t*, representing agency, and *-ac*, representing the future form of the verb. If I connect *pen* with some form of penetration, then the notion of *pentac* signified something that will penetrate something else. Perhaps fear of the slave was a fear of the male slaves penetrating society. More likely, the language showed the symbolic penetration and effeminization of the slave and the war captive.[52]

In an attempt to legitimate land titles in the eighteenth century, the Canul lineage of Calkiní put together an extensive land document attempting to prove their noble status and large land holdings at the time of the conquest.[53]

They tried to convince the Spanish that this document was written in the 1540s. In this attempt, they described their relationships with Spaniards of various levels, which was the purpose of the following selection.

huntul ppen tac kub ti nahua tzel u kaba u pentac naun canul mulmanbil

A (male) slave named Nahua Tzel was delivered. He was the (male) slave purchased by Naun Canul.[54]

Slavery in this passage was both gendered and sexualized. The term for female slave, *munach*, had no known relationship with any sexual function. The term for male slave was the above-mentioned *pentac*, related in some manner to *pen*. The sexualized body here was constructed in a very different manner from that of the European tradition, where women's bodies were sexualized and female slaves were subjected to rape.[55] It is clear that Maya slaveowners had the right to engage in sexual activity with at least their female slaves (and almost certainly with their male slaves). The linguistic construct here showed a cultural association between male slaves and the sexualized body, but it did not give us any more information. The male slave was connected with the concept of penetration. He was a Nahua, and he penetrated or was penetrated by Maya society.

The Maya male slave may have played a similarly complex role in the discourse around warfare. When Maya captives were pictured, they did not appear penetrated. Rather, as in Figure 8.1, the captives were bound, often naked, and had erections. Andrea Stone notes that the painter did not intend for the erection to show that the prisoner was about to penetrate the mouth of his captor, but rather he simply intended to show that the captive was nude.[56] The image did, however, show that the phallic symbol could be reversed. In this case the phallicized (however functional the reason for his erection) captive was dominated by his captors. The phallus did not give the captive power, except perhaps through the power of fear. His position thus recalled the Maya slaves, who were sexualized through a linguistic relation. This linguistic construct showed that the male slaves were phallicized and feminized.[57] The phallus, however, was itself a floating object, positioned as an element of disease or warfare; as a penetrated or penetrating slave. The phallus here may have signified a form of transethnicity and transsexuality, a way of incorporating a slave from another ethnic group into his or her new state as a feminized and inferior being.

As I return to the symbol of the flower and another text of the flower seizure, it is apparent that the narrative phallicized this element as well.

FIGURE 8.1 A bound prisoner pictured with an erection. From Andrea J. Stone, *Images from the Underworld: Naj Tunich and the Tradition of Maya Cave Painting*, copyright © 1995 by the University of Texas Press. Reprinted by permission of the University of Texas Press.

u thanil nicte tancas
coconac u than uinic tu menel chacuile tacitac yalcab uinic tu men u coilxan
hunuc can ahau kin lic u chabtabal hunac ah kinam can u hol u yax ɔulbal
uchcu sihil u cool al u cool chabcan eɔlic u chacal kabalil u sacal kabalil uchci
u sihil ix on ix nicte uchci u sihil ɔunun nicte tij tun bacin tu chah u hol
acan puɔ bal yokol bax tun bacin u uayasba tin chucci chacal pat ix uinic
sacal pat ix uinic oxlahun sutlic u sut tan yol caan tilic u kamchictic chac ix
chichibe chacal kutz sacal kutz tan bacin tin chucci he bacin u uayasba chacal
bacalche sacal bacalche u uayasba tin ɔamah u ciynte sac nicte u tas u uay
sabac nicte u u tas u uay x kan mukayche u tas u uay u tial bacin ɣ u kab
chichibe yetel u kab sac nicte tin ɔamah yuke chee ten c lib a chu yum ac
uinic yk yetel nicte tancas pakte bin alabal yokol uinic hach co u than alcab u
cah haɔaan tu men yk lay bin alabac yokol caaten bin alabal ca tu hopoc u
tokol yak ti ye ci ɣ chumuc u pach caa tun chinhatabac tij cho haa Amen

The statement of the erotic/flower seizure:
The words of the man are incoherent because of the fever. The man has the impulse to run because of his craziness. Hunuc Can Ahau is the day for the creation[58] of the great pain.[59] Thus began the first

branch[60] of the birth, the lust of the children of women, the lust of
creation. The red substance and the white substance were firmly set at
the time of birth of the avocado and the flower,[61] the time of birth of
the happy flower.[62] Thus it was that they copulated. Thus began the
groaning and the sliding. What is the sign that I have identified of the
red human form, the white human form? It has returned thirteen times
at the heart of the sky, to receive the red *chichibe*,[63] the red tobacco,
and the white tobacco. This is what I identified; these are its signs: the
red bone tree and the white bone tree. These are the signs of my steep-
ing of the sweetness of the white flower mattress, the black flower
mattress, and the yellow seed mattress. These are for the *chichibe* juice
and the white flower juice as I steep them for him to drink. All are
of my throne. Hey! I will be the one to destroy your spell, Lord Ac
Uinic Ik[64] and erotic/flower seizure. Together, this will be said to
cure the person of his very crazy words, his desire to run, and his being
attacked by the wind. This is what is said to cure him. It will be said
twice. Then will begin the bleeding of the tongue with a maguey
point. The center of the back then is bathed in hot water. Amen.[65]

Erotics here was based on the phallicization of the symbolic flower as it interacted with the avocado. As noted, the sixteenth-century Motul Dictionary
translated *nicte* as both "flower" and as "the vice of the flesh and the naughtiness of women."[66] This interpretation, almost certainly by Franciscan friars,[67]
showed a direct correlation between sexual desire, particularly that of women,
and the symbolism of the flower.

The flower was a metaphor for female sexual behavior just as the avocado
linguistically and metaphorically was connected with male sexual behavior.
As the avocado and the flower signified sexual acts, one should be careful not
to assume a direct correlation with anatomy. The avocado (*on*) had a close linguistic relationship with male genitalia (*ton*), but this relationship may have
existed only in the various dictionaries. In Maya thought the avocado related
to a general notion of male participation in sexual behavior. It may have related to the genitals, but it also may have had no direct correlation.[68] The
flower, moreover, related, as a metaphor, to female sexual acts. No direct relationship to genitalia exists in any of the sources.

The notions in this text showed that the flower and the avocado, as signifiers of sexual desire, were central to any acts of creation. The happy flower,
evoking a positive notion of sex, was part of the allusion of erotics as we found
that this flower "copulated" with the avocado. The phallic flower was pene-

trated as sexual acts began and creation occurred. The groaning and sliding, evocative of various sexual acts, were markers for those acts. Penetration took place in order to create both the disease and the cure.

The narrative connected the lust of creation with the children of women. This connection, related to the Spanish Catholic concept of original sin, was a Maya translation of that notion. The children of women, who may at first have seemed to signify illegitimacy, rather became children whose mothers strategically were emphasized in the narrative. The lust of the mother passed to the children through the colonial phallus: here the phallus penetrated mother, children, and society.

The act of penetration certainly may have prioritized the phallic notion of power in the penis. However, the phallus was not central to the text, and really only entered the document as the important maguey point, a type of Maya "needle." As noted above, the needle often was gendered feminine. As this phallus disconnected from the anatomical body, it signified a reconfiguring of that body and showed that anatomy did not guard access to the ritual world. Rather, the body was remade as the ritual sphere became a type of mirror, a type of vision into a Maya unconscious. Lacan notes that the mirror does not represent the body "before" it. The mirror itself produces the body and re-creates it.[69] The ritual world, as the Maya mirror, was a world full of delirium, but it also was the only possible world in which people could live. Much like us, the Maya understood their bodies through various processes of recognition. The penetration here was part of a world of symbolism which allowed the phallus to exist, but in a position that did not always directly connect it with the male penis. So the discordant male unconscious was deployed, as Irigaray would have suggested, in a strategic maneuver to assert the power of the phallus, even as the male subject could have only limited power in the text.[70] This discordant unconscious asserted a transsexuality of desire.

The phallus promoted a ritual designed to use sexual desire in order to engage in a cure. This situation allowed the ritual circuit and political power to be maintained (through the colors and the mattresses). The flower itself was represented as sexual, both creating and destroying the disease. The wind and the bloodletting destroyed disease and maintained social hierarchy. In an act showing Maya dualism, the disease, presented as male, was cured through sexual desires and acts designed to integrate masculine and feminine aspects.

The phallus in the symbolic texts had little correlation to the psychoanalytic notion of "lack." Instead, political power and social hierarchy were cemented by particular views of the relationship between the phallus and sexual desire.

Who Lacks the Phallus? Gender and the Real

If the symbolism did not signify the phallus in the way that psychoanalysis says it should, the phallus reappeared in its more traditional form in the "real" world where the Maya faced readily apparent colonialism. For it was here that the greatest combination of Maya and Spanish norms existed.

The petition against the four priests narrated these priests as penetrators.[71] The writer demanded that he was the "informer of the truth" and that the four priests about whom he complained had disgraced the community. Homosexual acts were mentioned just once, and the Maya prioritized the act of penetrating a particular body part as opposed to prioritizing the person as an object choice. The acts of the priests, however, were going to be denigrated. Their penetration of others, their use of the phallus, prevented God from penetrating the community, as he could not descend in the host.

One might be tempted to present the priests as heterosexual aggressors, but the petition never suggested such a clear identity. The petition focused on body parts as objects of penetration. There was only one mention of "men's anuses," while the author mentioned the vagina several times. The vagina[72] was presented as the object which the priests penetrated with particular devices which Lacanians would believe resembled images of the phallus: hands and penises. The vagina and the anus were objects of concern for the petitioner. The writer wanted the priests to refocus their energies on the community instead of on these body parts. The penetration of the anus and the vagina signified violations of trust. Both the community and the Catholic rituals demanded that the priests remain celibate. Instead, they acted on desires of penetration. Their "stiff penises" were the objects which they used to engage in a violation by penetrating their mistresses. It was the priestly penis that was the most objectionable.

For Lacan, this discourse would have emphasized that the writer represented his desires through the Other.[73] The desires of the petitioner could not be shown through his own libido but rather had to be emphasized only through the libido's connections with other people, and particularly with other body parts.[74] Here the desire (signified as a split desire, for the priests and for the women) was connected with those people whom the writer wanted to "become." Indeed, the petitioner may have wanted to become the women in order to engage the attention of the priests. However, the writer primarily wanted the priests to adhere to their vows of celibacy. And, of course, his real desire, to help another priest, was hidden. The desire here was presented as a desire for that unknown quantity: the priestly penis. This penis indeed was imagined to be the phallus, a super-penis with great powers. It was in this text that the Maya connected a desire for power with the phallus.

Lacan's discussion allows me to emphasize the role that penetration played in a discussion of colonial Maya desire. If this desire, represented through the body parts of the Other, manifested itself primarily in a discussion of the parts to be penetrated, what role did the act of penetration play in the colonized Maya sexual universe? How did the role of penetration distinguish the sexual object as Other?

The act of penetration showed a subject who had body parts (hands, penises) which pursued other body parts (vaginas, anuses). The subjects (the priests) in this case moved into the realm of excess sexual behavior by violating the trust of both the community and the religious authorities. They breached this trust by violating their vows of celibacy and giving improper sacraments. This violation became excess through the priests' penetration of women's vaginas and through the unfulfilled penetration of men's anuses. As the body was penetrated with sexual behavior determined as excess, society itself was penetrated and damaged.[75] The narrative showed that the priestly penetration of the women allowed the priests to experience their own personal pleasures as it empowered them. Yet it prevented the community from being penetrated by Catholicism and by Jesus. While the text clearly distinguished between genders and prioritized the damage done by the various acts, the concepts provided an equivalent notion that the act of penetration in excess would damage society, whatever the gender of the sexual object.

The phallic signification here showed that the people were looking to the priests because they found their lives lacking. The priests, through their penises, signified access to the phallus. Christ himself became this access, and Christ may have replaced the father and allowed the Maya people to be colonized by Oedipus. Yet much of the Maya world remained outside of the realm of Oedipus, and the desire for incest was not relevant. Oedipus was a colonialist displacement of desire. Of course here I am using a broad conceptualization of Oedipus. I am not suggesting that the Maya understood psychoanalysis. Rather, this analysis demonstrates that the Oedipal signification of psychoanalysis was not present in every society. It was a sociohistorical, colonialist phenomenon.

TRANSSEXUALITY

Transsexuality highlighted both Maya tradition and Oedipal colonization. The texts were transsexualized by their authors in an effort to understand the place of the phallus. This allowed the postconquest people to whom the text was directed to understand the context of the preconquest rituals. Even though they could not see those rituals, their imaginations and fantasies allowed them to understand the transsexualization of the phallus.[76]

As the phallus floated in the open, the transsexual as a singular figure presented some problems. The phallus needed to be able to transsexualize the text by allowing all of the gods, ancestors, and shamans to move into a ritualized transsexuality. It also is likely that cross-gender status can play a role in any society, and there is some anthropological, archaeological, and historical evidence of men wearing women's clothes in the Mayan universe.[77] So what role did transsexuality play in the Maya ritual world?

Transsexual Identities

The Spaniards themselves had severe penalties for transgender individuals. The Spanish regulations, however, were normative parameters, violated in special circumstances. Catalina de Erauso dressed as a man to fight wars of conquest in the seventeenth century, and Erauso may have considered him/herself to be a man. S/he was not discovered until s/he confessed, having sought refuge in a bishop's residence. Then, after finding Erauso a virgin, both Pope and King eventually granted him/her a dispensation to continue wearing men's clothes. Erauso was a sensation in Baroque Spain, and s/he produced a sensationalistic autobiography which recounted him/her murdering men and blaspheming the church and titillated readers by suggesting a sexual preference for women.[78] Erauso fit into a tradition of transgender behavior, where some anatomical females dressed as men and engaged in pursuits reserved for men. Such ritualized gender crossing, however, told little about normative Spanish views. Rather, these cases were exceptions for those who strongly desired to engage in the "superior" male sphere.[79] The Spaniards connected transsexuality with desire. In this case, the desires represented were specifically political and had little connection with the ritual world. But, from this perspective, the Spanish would have understood some of the connections that the Maya texts made between transsexuality and desire.

As the Maya texts asserted transsexuality as a strategy, one may ask about the possibility of a transgender or transsexual identity. In transgender communities in contemporary Western societies, people move across gender boundaries through both surgical and nonsurgical techniques.[80] More than occasionally, people in these communities question the boundaries of gender, and they engage in ritualized play with those boundaries.[81] Such a destabilization of gender may have radical potential.[82] But how may such a destabilization relate to the colonial Maya understanding of transsexuality?

Despite the great ritual power of the feminine appropriation of the phallus and the use of transsexuality presented, these texts did not assert any transgender or transsexual identity. The notion of transporting across sex and gender appears to have had universal applicability in the Maya ritual world. The gods themselves and perhaps the curers and patients could be transported across the sex/gender divide. It was plausible that anybody could do this, so it did not just pertain to one group of people. However, transgender and/or transsexual people may have existed. There may have been people who actively sought to transgress gender boundaries. Or this feeling may have been repressed.

A Third Sex? A Third Gender? A *Berdache?*

When many anthropologists and gay studies scholars think of transgender identity in indigenous societies, they think of the *berdache*, a figure found in anthropological literature on North American cultures. The modern *berdache* exists in many Native American societies. Historically this figure was apparently an anatomical male who took the dress and performed the work of women in the society. The *berdache* sometimes married another man, and s/he often was forced to play the "passive" role in sexual activity with men.[83] There also existed anatomical females who dressed and performed the work (particularly related to hunting and warfare) of men.[84] The evidence still is far from clear, and one scholar has said that the *berdache* role in North American societies was a role reserved for despised people.[85] Still, in Latin America the Spanish chroniclers observed figures similar to the *berdache*.[86]

Richard Trexler has revised views of the *berdache* by looking at the significance of this figure to indigenous societies throughout the Americas. Trexler finds much evidence that the role now termed *berdache* was used to degrade various people by stressing gendered relationships of dependency. The *berdache* role in most of the Latin American cases (Trexler focuses on the societies about whom there is the most documentation: the Andeans and the Nahuas) was given to people who were kept as slaves. Most were kept for sexual purposes as they were to be the "passive" sexual partners to lords, nobles, and warriors who wished to make use of them. Trexler maintains that most Latin American indigenous societies despised the concept of a male playing the passive role during intercourse. The gendered structure of Native and Spanish discourses showed that the *berdache* may have been a war captive or another community member forced to degrade him/herself.[87] There was evidence that the Nahuas forced some defeated or "cowardly" male warriors to dress in women's clothes.[88]

There is only scattered evidence of a Maya equivalent to the *berdache*. While the *ix pen* (sodomite, constructed with the feminine agentive, *ix*)[89] conceivably could have been a *berdache*-type figure, this term did not appear in the documents. One letter, discussing the conquest of the Itzá, said that Itzá leaders kept some men dressed in women's clothes, and those men were used for sodomy.[90] It seems unlikely that the Maya had developed a notion of sexual identity in line with the observations some have made regarding the North American *berdache*. As has been shown, the Maya notions of sexual desire would not have suggested the existence of a figure dedicated to one particular set of sexual acts. And the Maya conception of the importance of transsexuality made it unlikely that they would have allowed one group of people to claim such an identity and to formulate it in a way that would have suggested that it was an expression of the internal psychological desire of the individual.[91] Based on Maya concepts of sexual desire, such a formulation would have been unimaginable.

There did exist, however, two types of Maya male figures who "impersonated" women. The first, unlike the *berdaches* cited by Trexler, had great power. Maya iconography from the Classic period presented several images of rulers dressed in the traditional clothing of noblewomen. These images probably were related to the bloodletting rituals. William Fash has shown that one of the best preserved images in Copán probably pictured 18 Rabbit, a celebrated male ruler. In this picture, the king was wearing a woman's skirt. Linda Schele has argued that in the bloodletting rituals Maya men were considered nurturers and were providing mother's milk. Some Palenque rulers were called "mothers" of particular gods. Since they were playing the roles of women, they thus were dressed as women.[92] This signified to the Maya an understanding of the duality of the ritual structure. However, one must understand the significance of this role: the symbolic power of rulership was sustained by the ruler accessing masculine and feminine realms of ritual power. In doing so, he may have dressed as a woman on certain ritual occasions: he did not wear such clothes on a regular basis. This was not in any sense an approval of a biological male playing a feminine role. The bloodletting ritual was part of a warrior ethic that maintained staunch masculinity.

The second figure who engaged in cross-gender activity was a priest and/or an entertainer who performed ritualized cross-dressing. This person was

FIGURE 8.2 A cave painting picturing a god and the Moon Goddess in an erotic embrace. From Andrea J. Stone, *Images from the Underworld: Naj Tunich and the Tradition of Maya Cave Painting*, copyright © 1995 by the University of Texas Press. Reprinted by permission of the University of Texas Press.

intended to be the penetrated, feminized, and in certain ways degraded figure. Andrea Stone has found a cave painting that depicted explicit sexuality, ostensibly between an ugly god and the beautiful young Moon Goddess (see Fig. 8.2). The Moon Goddess here was likely a priest wearing a hairpiece. Stone notes that the Moon Goddess figure appeared to be wearing a male loincloth and that this person had no visible breasts. Further, such an impersonation was common in Maya ritual activity.[93]

Victoria Bricker notes that among the modern Mayan peoples of Chiapas, men dress as women in order to engage in what are considered vulgar displays of sexuality. The cross-dressing figures are intended to provide entertainment and laughter, their identities are ritualized jokes, and they certainly are not considered positive role models in any way.[94] Stone notes that this likely was the case in the cave painting, as Maya vase paintings with similarly explicit themes clearly were intended to entertain.

Yet, as Stone states, the ceremony depicted in the cave clearly had ritual importance. The Maya, who considered caves to be places for important ritual ceremonies, including bloodletting and human sacrifice, found this picture to be of some importance in the worship of the goddess. Stone argues that these pictures showed a Moon Goddess in the important ritual space of the cave, supporting intercourse and autosacrifice. One might speculate, as does Stone, that the embrace was intended to represent fecundity and thus evoke a response from the gods, who would provide the Maya with a strong yield of crops. This goddess endorsed a wide variety of sexual acts, and she gave them the intensity of ritual performance.[95] This cross-gender figure appears not to have lived life as a *berdache* or a woman but rather as a man who performed a feminine role and perhaps played the "passive" role in sexual acts.

The Transsexual Phallus

There was, as has been shown, a highly visible phallus in some of the ritualized medical texts. Diseases were personified in the Ritual of the Bacabs, leading to a symbolic gendering of the curing rituals. Above, the tarantula, signifying the vagina, was the disease. The penis engaged in the cure. The phallus was signified in the cure and, as Lacan maintained, this may have allowed for an entrance into the realms of symbolism and the unconscious.[96]

> *u thanil u siyan am lae*
> *hunil am cabil am oxil am canil am yax am te yax am tun ox kin bayanech*
> *tu chemil u cab ah uuc ti cab tij tun bacin a chah u cabil a pach can kin*
> *yanech yalan u yamtunil u mukay a chich ti suhuy ix chacal ix chel sacal ix*
> *chel u uayasba u pach yax am te yax am tun he tun bacin u suhuy puɔ tun*
> *bacin suhuy ix chel sacal ix chel chacal ix chel la bacin u uayasba a uachoxla-*
> *hun uol u bon kuch suhuy ix chel chacal yx chel sacal yx chel la tun bacin u*
> *uayasba a ka sam tun bacin yn colob sam tun bacin yn lukes sam tun bacin*
> *yn chochob fel u na ta uach cech yax am te yax am tuncan heb tun bacin yn*
> *ekel nok la tun bacin tin ɔuɔci he tun bacin canlahhun pul tun bacin yn*
> *battil ha oxlahun pul yn sissala la tun bacin tin siscunci u kinam yax am te*
> *yax am tun am am am am Amen*

Words for the enchantment of spiders: [97]
First spider, second spider, third spider, fourth spider: first spider of wood, first spider of stone. For three days you were away with the bag of poison, Ah Uuc Ti Cab (He of the Seven Poisons). How did you acquire the poison on your back? For four days you existed beneath the garden. [98] The grain of your grandmother, the virgin Moon Goddess, the red Moon Goddess, the white Moon Goddess, is the sign on the back of the first spider of wood, the first spider of stone. How is the virgin needle? How is the virgin Moon Goddess, the white Moon Goddess, the red Moon Goddess? This is her sign, your penis. [99] Thirteen balls of dyed thread of the virgin Moon Goddess, the red Moon Goddess, the white Moon Goddess. What are the signs of your ugliness? [100] How am I to take them away? How am I to free them? How am I to untie them? [101] The vagina's mother with your penis: you are the first spider of wood, the first spider of stone. The four parts: how is my black cape? Is now when I am to kiss? How are the fourteen jars? How is my hail, the thirteen jars of my cold water? How am I to cool the pain of the first spider of wood, the first spider of stone? Spider! Spider! Spider! Spider! Amen. [102]

Recall that among the modern Maya the tarantula is a common and derogatory metaphor for the vagina. [103] Here the spider was gendered female in her close association with the Moon Goddess, so femininity here was associated with a disease that was to be cured by the phallus.

The spider was the first spider of wood and stone, showing a relationship between the spider and the human body, as wood and stone related directly to the treatment of the body in the Ritual of the Bacabs. The human body was enchanted along with the spiders, probably as the individual moved into a trance. The poison itself was gendered male, while the spider was gendered female. The gendering implicit in the early part of the text was a symbol for creation gone wrong.

The spider was connected to a matrilineal line. It lived beneath the garden of the household (the garden itself gendered female in both colonial and modern times). [104] The grandmother's grain further gendered the spider, who hailed back to her grandmother, the Moon Goddess. The Moon Goddess signified the ritual matrilineal line of disease. She, through her own reproduction, placed her mark on the disease. She still had significant control over the ritual, possessing the needle used to kill the spider and pierce the penis. The gendering of the disease signified some ritual fears. These stemmed perhaps from a fear of the power of women through their sexual desire and their ability to reproduce. For if women could reproduce humans, they could destroy humanity by reproducing disease.

As the virgin needle entered the scene, it resembled the phallus. But the needle was possessed by the Moon Goddess. The needle was sacred and virginal, much like the Moon Goddess. And through this specifically gendered notion of the sacred, the Moon Goddess controlled so much. But the phallus then showed up as a disguised but still marked penis, first present and then disappearing. Now the sign became none other than the penis. But either the spider or the Moon Goddess, both gendered female, possessed the penis. The transsexuality of such a text was an assertion of its ritual power through the use of the floating phallus.

Perhaps the penis was invoked here only to show a male role in this cure. Perhaps the penis scared off the spider. Perhaps, but it seems more likely that we are entering an arena of ritualized humor that the narrative controlled. The text, in a move intended both to promote the Moon Goddess and to show the problematic ideas presented by her presence, invoked many elements to enchant the spiders and get rid of the poison. The shaman again referred to the sign (perhaps the penis?), this time in the plural, stating that they were ugly. The shaman insulted the Moon Goddess just as the curer would have insulted any other god in these rituals. Here the shaman wanted to take away these signs and destroy them.

As the text entered the central curing ritual, the vagina's mother (using a derogatory word for vagina) mixed with "your" penis ("you" this time clearly marked as the spider). The spider, gendered female, obtained a penis. The two together created the disease and perhaps the cure. The vagina's mother, the Moon Goddess, portrayed the matrilineal line through a gendered notion of desire that allowed for parallel lines of descent.

And how did the shaman kill the spider? Apparently by raining some sort of hail on it. This signified "hail" coming from the phallus itself.[105] The blood and semen engaged in a phallic cure.

The needle, feminine and possessed by the Moon Goddess, engaged in the penis-piercing ritual. The Moon Goddess had control over this ritual through her control over the needle and the colors red and white. As the penis was pierced, the curing began, and the phallus was given great power connected with lineage arrangements, nobility, and the political structure. The pierced penis was in pain, but still placed the hail water/blood on the spider, enchanting it to leave.

Did the phallus rule the connections between gender, ritual, and disease? Gender in this ritual text seems to have been quite malleable, allowing women great powers related to reproduction. Women, however, much like men, used the phallus in order to engage in the cure. And still, outside the sphere of symbolism, the Maya had strictly defined gender roles. The religious hierarchy responsible for maintaining these rituals was dominated by men. But the phallus disappeared into the double entendre, as, perhaps, did the Western conception of gender.

The strategy of transsexuality, however, here was not used to assert the power of women. Gilbert Herdt, engaging in an extensive ethnographic study of the Sambia of New Guinea, shows that this group has a series of transsexual fantasies within ritual discourse. These fantasies are based on the fear that, since masculinity is not created by nature but needs to be deployed by men, boys who do not receive sufficient masculine training (partly through ritualized homosexual fellatio) might become women. This fear is portrayed in many parts of male ritual discourse, and it is most prominent in the retelling of a creation myth. So the fantasy of transsexuality is deployed among men, but the society promotes a rigid masculinity, a warrior mystique, in which women are denigrated severely and are seen as polluting influences.[106] While the colonial Maya did not engage in the same type of denigration of women, the position of the warrior clearly was very important to Maya discourse, and women were excluded from this warrior status. The gendered implications of the Maya transsexual discourse did not empower women, but they did show a Maya belief in the power of femininity and gender parallelism.

This power was evident in the humor portrayed here. When discussing ritual humor in contemporary Chiapas, Bricker separates it from everyday jokes and insults. Ritualized humor occurs in a specific context of great importance.[107] The humor makes significant social points and maintains community standards.[108] It tends to poke fun at outsiders and those seen as exercising power over the community. It often rests on double entendres and tricks of various kinds. In one case, Bricker points to a "curing" ceremony in which sexual organs are presented in double entendres. A broken leg or back signifies the genitalia. The cure signifies sexual intercourse.[109] The double entendres in a festive setting allow the people (of Zinacantan) to laugh at the sexualized discourse. The "curer" is an entertainer. Rituals related to sexual behavior are central to the narrative. The rituals point to the genitalia but also describe more than just the body parts. The host of the ceremony chants:

> Find your place, bones!
> Find your place, muscles!
> Don't leave your hole, muscle!
> Don't leave your hole, bone![110]

Bricker points out that the narrative here invokes a certain spatial imagery which allows the "curer" to coax the bones and muscles into their appropriate places. But the bones and muscles mentioned are intended to refer to the penis, while the hole refers to the vagina.[111] Sexual intercourse is the "real" aim of the "curer," who thus allows sexual desire certain power in the narrative. In contemporary Chiapas the text is used as an effort both to entertain and to assert the importance of (hetero)sexual intercourse.

The rituals of these ceremonies in contemporary Chiapas have a vastly different context than the ritual ceremonies of colonial Yucatán. But the importance of understanding ritualized humor was relevant to several of the colonial documents. The texts in the Ritual of the Bacabs often contained extensive metaphorical language, probably used both for entertainment and to get across particular, often sexual, messages which related to the power of the curers.[112]

The Moon Goddess engaged in some type of act with the spider, apparently penetrating the spider in an effort to get rid of it. The Moon Goddess also may have penetrated the person to be cured and/or the curer. So the Moon Goddess necessarily was the active partner in the narrative. She must have had the phallus in order to engage in these acts. Yet she clearly was pictured as female and never was pictured with a penis. The passive partners were put in an asymmetrical relationship with the Moon Goddess. At the same time, the Moon Goddess was denigrated by the curer, suggesting that perhaps she was the passive partner to the active curer. She may in fact have switched roles within the goddess-shaman-patient triangle.

The spider, gendered female, had a penis. Yet the spider certainly did not attain a male identity. Rather, the text required the genitalia of both sexes, and the genitals moved around onto different bodies. The penis itself, as presented in the above text, was a device to allow the phallus some ritual power, thus creating a male privileged access into this ritual world. Yet, if the phallus was not associated with any body, did this floating phallus really give men any privileged access or power?

The penis was mentioned again when the vagina's mother engaged it in an act of creation. The vagina's mother used the penis to engage in the cure. The penis, if still associated with the spider, signified a sexual act which might be termed "lesbian." But no lesbian identity was shown in the text. The penis attained ritual power through its use as the phallus in (hetero)sexual intercourse. The sex was both heterosexual and lesbian. The rituals destabilized these categories of sexual desire. The penis, even here, had an uncertain possessor. Could the penis have belonged to the patient? The curer? The Moon Goddess? The spider? A god? The phallus remained a free-floating symbol in this narrative. Moreover, the text showed that the Moon Goddess penetrated the spider/curer/patient. Would she then have had the phallus?

As a free-floating symbol, it would seem at first glance that the Maya text understood the importance of the phallus in much more depth than people in contemporary Western societies, where the phallus is said to be represented in the demand for love. According to Lacan, the child in its desire for the love of the mother actually wants to *be* the phallus.[113] As the Western child has the desire to be the phallus, and it is impossible to be this signifier, the child engages in grand delusions. The free-floating signifier in the Maya text, however, was attached to no person. No person was the phallus and no person had the phallus. Nonetheless, the signifier became more complex as the body parts in the Maya text disconnected from their hidden "origins" and placed themselves on other bodies in order to engage in the cure.

Butler reworks much Lacanian theory in order to visualize the phallus as free floating. In doing so, she has removed the phallus from the signified penis, and she demands a broadening of the body parts upon which the phallus bases itself. And the phallus may base itself on no body part at all.[114] The Maya phallus may have moved around onto various bodies. It became a free-floating phallus, questioning any original basis on the male body (what was the original? what was the copy?) and showing instead that it here signified the relationship between sexual desire and ritual discourse.

This and other rituals were based on a Maya notion of fantasy, desire, and imagination. The ritual discourse demanded that the people imagine a situation in which the shaman let the blood of himself and/or others in order to commune with the ancestors and the gods. As the people imagined this communication, they were told to desire this connection with the gods and to desire the rule of the shamans, monarchs, lords, and nobles. In order to make the people understand the desire for this rulership, the text invoked sexual and gender fantasies. First, the people were required to fantasize about sexual intercourse with and/or between the leaders, ancestors, and gods. Second, these fantasies could only achieve completion as the people fantasized about the leaders, ancestors, and gods changing sexes/genders through the free-floating phallus.[115]

COLONIALISM, OEDIPUS, AND THE FLOATING PHALLUS

All of the texts mentioned in this book only signified partial truths. There often were discursive maneuvers designed to limit the impact of colonialism. There were other maneuvers designed to increase or maintain the power of indigenous nobles. The discourse on transsexuality was no exception to this rule. As the documents themselves produced particular strategies, the relationship between transsexuality and power was clear. Transsexuality was used as way of signifying completion and wholeness. In a Maya world marked by at least some gender parallelism, the ritual and symbolic spheres could not be complete without combining male and female principles. If these principles were combined in the powerful shamans and rulers participating in the ceremonies, then the people could rest assured that the rulers could and would protect them. The textual use of transsexuality was to maintain a hierarchical and male-dominated power structure.

Lacan and Butler both helped us understand the role of the transsexual phallus in regulating access to the symbolic world of the colonial Maya. However, neither of these theorists understood the colonial context or the place of colonialist displacement in the texts. Irigaray's theories presented us with a methodology for reading gender in the texts, which were narratives designed to gender the unconscious. Spivak provided an analysis of the ways in which non-Western rituals were used to perform anticolonial agency. These theories have helped me to analyze the phallic colonialism apparent in the narratives.

Colonialism altered much of the context of these narratives, and the mid-colonial texts could not rely on public rituals to assure the power of the rulers. The public displays of Maya ritual necessarily were replaced by public displays of the power of Catholicism. The Maya leaders understood this display, and they used it to assert their authority. But there remained some part of the populace that was unconvinced, and the colonial texts served them, and allowed the leaders to beckon back to the preconquest past in order to convince more of the people. These texts combined an assertion of sexual desire with an assertion of transsexuality in order to maintain some of the power of the colonized noblemen.

Many of the documents mentioned Christian gods, but those gods did not change genders. The archaic texts in the Ritual of the Bacabs attempted to maintain in many ways a preconquest ritual structure which was disappearing into the hybridity of colonial rule. Transsexuality was a strategy to maintain that structure. It also was a move of colonial stratification, demanding the appearance of nobility and power in an increasingly hybrid discourse. And, despite the ostensible transsexuality, the texts continued specifically to gender notions of power and ritual in ways that asserted masculine domination.

Texts here were presented as having reasons and contexts for existing. They also had more obscure contexts, related to their role in the development and displacement of desire. The texts in each case demanded certain things from various authorities, whether they were gods, Spaniards, Maya rulers and nobles, or even Maya commoners. These demands were represented through the displaced desires of the text.

The phallus was a central entity in the colonial Maya world. It structured a symbolism of blood, semen, and lineage. It regulated many aspects of sexual desire. It caused diseases and then cured them. Cutting the penis actually maintained the social hierarchy. So the Maya would be an excellent example of a non-Western people on whom to test psychoanalysis. Yet Oedipal triangulation was not important in the documents. And "lack," as imagined through castration and penis envy, could only account for a small segment of the documents which mentioned the phallus.

It seems, from the Maya documentation, that the poststructuralist emphasis on Lacan[116] is somewhat overstated and fails to account for the critiques of earlier works.[117] But Lacanian analysis does bring the phallus and the unconscious to the forefront, while rejecting many of the transhistorical notions of the Oedipal complex. Lacan's emphasis on language and textuality allows scholars to discuss phallic symbolism without relying on an essentialist notion of desire. In other words, Lacan allows historians to remain historians. One can use this form of analysis and engage in historical deconstruction. While this history is hardly the traditional focus on people and events, it emphasizes cultural change, disruption, and the historical placement of metaphor, symbol, rhetoric, and text.[118]

The Maya phallus gives us a chance to see that the penis was not always the central entity upon which the phallus was based. The symbolism of the phallus may have been a creative symbolism as opposed to a signifier of "lack." The historical content of the Maya transsexual phallus was one of the disruption, colonization, and reinscription of a symbol placed in the texts.

Transsexualization and transportation across gendered binaries was assumed to be textually appropriate in much Maya ritual discourse.[119] The transsexual texts coded the Maya ritual world with a theory of desire: the stated desire in the texts was a desire for transformation, inclusion, and completion. The texts were an attempt at maintaining power for a colonized group of nobles, ancestors, and gods. Transsexuality was a historical symbol for this attempt at revitalization: an attempt to reestablish a colonized cultural structure that was under attack. Transsexuality signified the symbols, metaphors, and rhetoric of power.

NINE

Ritualized Bisexuality

In Western fables about Mayans, we are told that sodomy was discovered in the founding myths of several of the Mayan peoples and that the acts always were shown as belonging to "outsiders" or to the realm of ritual. According to some highly speculative sources, the story went something like this: long before the Spanish conquest, the Olmecs, in conquering the Quiché Maya of Guatemala, demanded that the people give them two young men for the purpose of sodomy. While the people resisted, they had no choice but eventually to give in to the demands. In Yucatán during the same time period (or so we are told), there was a strong association between ritual and homosexual behavior. Some shamans engaged in homosexual acts with their patients. And priests engaged in ritualized homosexual acts with the gods. When the Toltecs arrived to conquer the region, they brought more sodomy and public sex of all kinds.[1] Then when the Itzá conquered the area, they brought more sodomy, more eroticism, and extensive sexual ceremonies.[2] Bernal Díaz del Castillo found remnants of this past when he discovered idols of men committing sodomy with each other.[3] But by the time of the conquest, Antonio Gaspar Chi, a Maya informant, assured us that sodomy no longer existed because a former leader of Mayapán, Tutul Xiu, had destroyed it.[4] After the conquest, however, sodomy reappeared in the figures of the *ix pen* and the *cobol.*[5]

These were rather fanciful stories which cannot be substantiated. In this chapter the challenge is to understand the roles presented as homo-, hetero-, and bi-eroticism. I discuss elements of ritualized and nonritualized bisexual and homosexual acts in order to analyze more about Maya erotic desire. This desire continued to be linked with power, and notions of identity based on sexual behavior did not emerge in any real way until the late colonial period.

SODOMITES, HOMOSEXUALS, BISEXUALS

Given the fact that the Maya before the conquest were a non-Western people with no contact with Europe and no understanding of European sexual norms, the reader may legitimately ask how it is possible to understand "homosexuality" and "bisexuality" among a people seemingly so far removed from the current Western notions of homosexual and bisexual identities. The concept of a homosexual or heterosexual identity was invented during the modern era. This identity, with the advent of modernity, became something that was seen to be ingrained in the psychological or biological makeup of the individual. So homosexuality and heterosexuality as ingrained identities only have existed for a relatively short period of time.[6] However, such a definition can be used to limit the study of sexual desire among societies outside of this modern Western paradigm. While other societies have developed psychosexual processes in different manners than they have been understood in the modern West, all of the societies of which I have knowledge have understood some forms of sexual differentiation, and they have categorized people based partly on the society's conceptualization of gender and/or sexual desire. I follow other historians and anthropologists in discussing the frameworks of sexual desire, rather than allowing the concept of identity to be the core of the analysis.[7] The acts cited here did not and could not correspond to modern Western notions of homosexuality, as the colonial Maya did not have any similar way of conceptualizing and categorizing sexual desire.

Did the Maya Persecute Sodomites?

The stories with which I began this chapter very well may have been flights of fancy by a conqueror, a tourist, and a Maya leader trying to tell the Spaniards whatever would benefit him and his community. While it is believable that the Maya presented themselves in such a light to the Spaniards, this said more about the use of power during warfare: friends and enemies who lost wars were said to be the passive recipients of sodomy; friends and enemies who won wars were said to be the active partners. This the Spanish would have understood. Was there a Maya abhorrence of sodomy? Or were these statements essentially power games that the Maya informants were playing with their Spanish listeners?

Mythology about sodomy structured some discourse in the Maya sources, but significantly more in the European narratives. All of the stories discussed above were told through European sources. Although many of them claimed legitimacy through an understanding of Maya culture, there were European reasons for stressing these factors.

Sodomy in the West was a complex term which could refer to the practice of anal intercourse, whether between a man and a woman, a man and a man, a man and a boy, a man and an animal, or a woman and a woman. Yet often bestiality and pederasty were considered different categories in early modern European images. Still, in the sixteenth century a new discourse on sodomy had begun to emerge. Prior to this, sodomy had been seen as a sinful act which anyone could commit but which one also could avoid. The new paradigm altered that perception and began to connect sodomy with infection: it was to become an element in which all people of a particular society might have engaged. A later discourse gradually emerged in the eighteenth century which began to structure the sodomite as a self-contained individual unit. While these changes certainly were gradual, and not necessarily contradictory, they meant substantially different things to the colonial enterprise.[8]

In the paradigm of infection, the Europeans distinguished between societies where they believed that sodomy was endemic and those where it was not. They thus created a "geography of perversion" based on developmental theories. For many, this meant that the more technologically advanced societies in Latin America (Nahuas, Andeans, Mayans) did not have much sodomy present. The less technologically advanced, nomadic societies had endemic sodomy. Thus the discourse on the Maya indicated that at previous levels of development the Maya and their conquerors had engaged in significant sodomy. At the state of development in which the Maya existed at the time of the conquest, however, sodomy was not present. However, this developmental discourse still combined with a discourse that used sodomy as a justification for conquest. Thus the European sources were inconsistent.

In addition to this European-centered discourse, one must also see that the discussion of sodomy was based on particular goals and perceptions. For the colonizers who wanted more Europeans to settle in the area, it was in their interest to deny the existence of sodomy. For Gaspar Antonio Chi, who wanted to present himself as a sophisticated, cultured person who still could understand the Maya people, it served his interests to deny the existence of sodomy. For others, either those who engaged in a polemical discourse in favor of the conquest or many of the conquerors themselves, it served their interests to show the presence of sodomy. And all stories of sodomy and sex between women were bound by various assertions of power and privilege. So when Diego de Landa told us that because of their preference for female brothels, there was little homosexual sodomy among the Maya,[9] he was no more or less accurate than Díaz del Castillo.

As shown below, there existed at the time of the conquest a bi-eroticism related to the gods which did not apply to the documents mentioning homosexual sodomy and the people. At the same time, the documents related to curing and warfare made it clear that, at least in a ritualized context, playing the "active" role in homosexual sodomy was perceived as a way for a man to harness the power of, and feminize, another man. For the late colonial Maya, the documents, clearly and directly influenced by Spanish discourse, presented sodomy as the "nefarious sin."

Spanish sexual views affected the reproduction of sexual norms in colonial Maya documents. During early modern times the Spanish produced an extensive array of sexual regulations. Spanish laws of the sixteenth century strictly forbade sodomy, although the effectiveness of such prohibitions may be questioned.[10] The behavioral codes were based on a gender system which punished women for taking the place of men (through dressing like men or using sexual appendages that were copies of men's penises).[11] While sodomy was considered to be an act that could involve men and/or women, almost all of the cases prosecuted in Seville in the late sixteenth century involved male homosexual sodomy. This certainly suggests, as Mary Elizabeth Perry has shown, that the real crime was not the act of anal penetration, but rather was "in requiring a male to play the passive 'female' role and in violating the physical integrity of a male recipient's body."[12] Perry's emphasis on the force of the active partner was supported by the legal documents of the time period, where the active partner clearly was considered the one to blame for the commission of the act. The passive could be punished only if he was over 14, and only if it could be proven that he voluntarily engaged in the act.[13] Sodomy was defined based on the gender and role of the participants, but the passive partner, according to Richard Trexler, was the one who was, in popular culture, considered the one to be abhorred, as it was the passive who was playing the "wrong" gender role in the sexual act.[14] The active partner was the one to be punished because he was seen as the person who must have lured the other into the act: in the Spanish mind the act of sodomy was being constructed as a forced encounter. Spanish social (as opposed to legal) condemnation of the passive partner engaged in homosexual sodomy often was severe, and the passive who voluntarily engaged in such behavior was roundly condemned. Despite this atmosphere (or perhaps because of it), some Spaniards participated in an extensive male sexual subculture which also was present in seventeenth-century Mexico.[15] This subculture involved an array of people from all class backgrounds, and members of the subculture generally accepted intergenerational sexual relationships between men and boys.[16]

The Maya, as a people with a hybrid culture, had many influences on their views of homosexual sodomy. The Books of Chilam Balam regularly contained sexual insults, most often directed toward the Itzá, which were connected with sodomy and pederasty. As has been shown, the legitimacy of the social hierarchy was a central concern of the sexual insults in these texts. In a passage related to the destruction of Maya society, the authors of the Book of Chilam Balam of Tizimin related some ideas about the death of angry gods. Various gods harmed each other and brought the society to the point of destruction. Kukul Kan (Quetzalcoatl) himself was damaged seriously, perhaps destroyed during this time. The time period was described as related to various problems with the "anus." In fact, this anus itself was representative of the *katun:*

ix tan yol haa u chab u matan coil chab coil u coil mehen yal u mehen tzintzin coc xul

She who was in the heart of the water created the reign of madness, creating madness, the madness of the children of men and women and the children of the anus,[17] the anus buggers.[18]

These "anus buggers," the sodomites, destroyed the order of society by producing children through their anuses. The two types of children, those created through homosexual sodomy and those created by a man and a woman, were both seen as illegitimate, showing a disturbance in the social hierarchy. The children were no longer proper nobles: they became mad and they did not know how to run society. This disorder stemmed from both homosexual sodomy and the madness of the metaphorical mother.

The relevant phrase here, *u coil mehen yal u mehen tzintzin,* showed that the authors meant to imply that these two types of children came from sodomy.

The anus itself was gendered as both the mother and the father of the children, who were described as *al* and *mehen*. The anus, as both mother and father, signified the lineage. The two pieces of the text were connected grammatically, with one mention of madness (*coil*) referring to both. The second mention of *mehen* confirmed the implication that some of the sodomy mentioned took place between two males. The word *tzintzin* derived from the Nahuatl *tzintli*, "anus."[19]

The passage went on to state that the leaders struggled with each other, eventually destroying the society. The message from this passage showed a strong association between sex and destruction. Sex, particularly that related to the anus, had the ritual power to destroy. As the reader already knows, the Maya historical texts were related to the concept of destruction and rebirth. The authors wrote such a passage after the fact in an effort to explain the conclusion of an era and the fall of particular leaders of Maya society. The text was written in the mid to late colonial period and thus signified a strategy designed to make people remember this preconquest era. Looking back at the causes of the destruction, the Maya found that various leaders insulted each other. This led to the creation of an era of madness characterized by the actions of the children. Lineage here was the central concern of the text. The inappropriate desires and actions did not keep the lineage together, and thus nobility was destroyed.[20]

The ritual connection showed the importance of penetration to any understanding of Maya sexual desire. The society and the social hierarchy were penetrated much as the anus was penetrated. The penetration led to madness and destruction. But there was no sexual identity furnished in the text. Quite the opposite: the text presumed that essentially all of the people (at least all of the nobles) were engaging in the various acts of sodomy. Society had been degraded and the people no longer understood that they had to reproduce. Instead, they engaged in anal intercourse, which reproduced only madness. Catholicism certainly supported the notion of connecting destruction to sodomy. But this idea came in the form of a colonial Maya text and thus signified a hybrid Maya idea.

The hybridity of this text was related to its critique of the sexual norms of the Itzá. The text was able to use Catholic ideas of correct and incorrect behavior, and in doing so the text critiqued the active partner in sodomy: the anus bugger. But the narrative also was part of the Maya tradition of asserting destruction as the result of excessive penetration. The Maya here believed sodomy to be one of many causes of madness and destruction. But could homosexual desire also lead to life and rebirth?

Bi-eroticism and the Moon Goddess

The Moon Goddess's sexual desires connected directly with Maya religion, as the Moon Goddess penetrated Maya society. But the Moon Goddess herself was penetrated in her sexual acts with the gods. Her body was the desired body, the ultimate body for the Maya people. Their desires were represented through her, and she continued to be desired by them for the remainder of the colonial period. This desire signified a desire for penetration. Her penetration signified the bi-eroticism of Maya desire.

As noted above, the Moon Goddess engaged in sexual acts with both male and female figures. In no case was she associated specifically with bisexuality as an identity. She had an association with various sexual acts and many acts which were not considered sexual.

The Moon Goddess was to be both penetrator and penetrated, both active and passive, no matter who her partner was. She penetrated society by colonizing the various peoples. She was penetrated by those peoples as they desired her body. She was penetrated by both male and female gods and people; she penetrated both male and female gods and people. This was the nature of the Moon Goddess as the most powerful goddess in the pantheon. This level of penetration signified an active/passive dichotomy that was complicated by the fact that most of this was occurring in ritual. Nonetheless, it was clear that the Moon Goddess, to be worshipped so vigorously by both men and women, must have been desired by both.

Bi-eroticism was presented in many of the ritualized texts. Note that in the text from the Ritual of the Bacabs designed to scare away spiders, the Moon Goddess was presented in sexual acts with the female spider. Yet the spider had a phallus. The Moon Goddess thus was presented in acts that might be considered bestial, lesbian, and heterosexual all at the same time. This presentation of her sexual acts undermined the very notion of an identity based on sexual behavior. In the other cases of bi-eroticism that have been mentioned in the Books of Chilam Balam and the Ritual of the Bacabs, no bisexual identity ever was shown. None of the texts mentioned here asserted any identity based on sexual behavior, but rather they all had a broader interpretation of sexual desire. The texts further demanded that this desire was used to understand many aspects of life. And the desire continued to stratify society.

The Moon Goddess's bisexual desires were categorized as the desires of a goddess. Her representation in the documents did assert that she was a goddess who promoted and participated in a variety of sexual acts which ostensibly were bisexual. In the picture of the Moon Goddess standing with a naked male god who has an erection (see Chap. 8, Fig. 8.2), she appears at first glance to represent heterosexual intercourse. Yet Andrea Stone has shown that in fact these very likely were two men, one disguised as the goddess.[21] The "goddess" did not engage in her characteristic display of breasts, and her naked body did not display any apparent genitalia. While a penis could have been hidden behind the penis of the other figure, the breasts could not have been hidden so easily. This intriguing suggestion signified a gender-crossing homosexuality which related to the element of ritual discourse that I have called the floating phallus. The Moon Goddess in that situation represented a homosexual eroticism that was disguised. Yet, that eroticism was signified by a male god with a pseudo-hermaphroditic figure who did not have any apparent genitalia: this was hardly what we in the modern West consider homosexuality. The Moon Goddess herself signified a ritualized and accepted bi-eroticism of desire.

Sexual Identities

Jacques Lacan has noted that sexual desire was defined and fixed through language. Desire could not be placed at all without language,[22] so terminology was vital. Here I explore the relationship between Maya ideas regarding penetration and the concept of a specifically colonial Maya (bi)sexual desire. The notion of a Maya discourse related to penetration emanated from the metaphorical connection of sexual acts with war, bloodletting, and human sacrifice.[23] The definitions of sexual terminology in the colonial dictionaries and the positions of penetration in the various documents showed that the Maya gave this notion some importance. This was the place where an identity based on sexual behavior began to emerge and become fixed.

The late colonial petition accusing the four priests of engaging in sexual acts with the various women showed a more Europeanized discourse leading to the formation of a sexual identity.[24] The priests themselves were presented as having voracious sexual appetites, and while they were not portrayed as heterosexuals, the petition came much closer to doing so than other documents. Indeed, they were being represented in a case against a friar who was being charged with "heretical activity." Among the charges against this friar was sodomy. Although this charge does not appear to have been given much validity, this petition very well may have been written in response to the sodomy charge.[25] So there was a distinction in the petition between the four priests (who did everything but sodomy) and the other priest (who was a sodomite).

A Maya-language confessional manual from 1803 presented male homosexual sodomy in a way intended to make the reference very clear: "Have you sinned with a man thinking that you were with a woman?"[26] The priests presented here a conceptualization of homosexual sodomy clearly in line with European thinking of the time.[27] No fixed sexual identity was presented, but sodomy was configured as sin. In order for this confessional to have been effective, the Maya must have understood the terminology and the concepts presented. Sodomy as sin had entered Maya society.

Maya terminology related to homosexual activity emphasized this point. The phrase *top it* was used in the petition: where the priests only lacked "carnal acts with men's anuses," the Maya stated *topob u yit uinicobe*. The colonial dictionaries translated *top* as "carnal acts" and *it* as "bottom, behind," or "anus."[28] *Uinicob* translated as "men." Thus the ecclesiastical authors of the dictionaries believed *top it* to be a very literal translation for "sodomy." Note the connection with other sexual behavior. As the Maya could use *top* to describe any of a number of sexual acts with various parts of the body and people of either gender, this phrase did not signify a clear separation between homosexuality and heterosexuality. The Maya here had a general word for sexual acts, not unlike the word "sex" in English.[29] The emphasis on *it* as the body part showed that Maya sexual acts were defined by the part of the body which the "active" partner aimed to penetrate. Maya discussions of sexual acts were inclined to focus on specific descriptions of the acts and the body parts used, as opposed to referencing sexual identities. Still, the penetrative aim was "men's anuses," so this may have represented the beginnings of a conceptualization of identity based on sexual behavior.

The petition described the priests as *ah penob*, which I have translated as "fornicators." One word which the dictionaries translated as sodomite, *ix pen*, simply put the feminine agentive *ix* in the place of the masculine agentive *ah*.[30] If the Maya interpreted *pen* as some form of sexual behavior deemed excessive, *ah pen* should have meant something like "he who has excess sex," and *ix pen* perhaps should have meant something like "she who has excess sex." But *ix pen* did not refer to women; it was referenced specifically to men. *Ix pen* could have referred to a man who cross-dressed. The idea behind *ix pen* may have referred to a sexual partner who was penetrated.

The term *pen*, which was used to describe various excessive acts, was used by the translators and writers of the dictionaries as an effective synonym for "sinful sexual acts." It thus retained its original meaning, but in a new context. Now the acts were deemed sinful, and the term was used to describe sexual behavior which Catholicism would have understood as sin. Thus the colonization of sin could be accomplished partly through language related to penetration.[31] Maya attitudes toward the *ix pen* remain unclear, but one can certainly see this figure as a penetrated person, perhaps desired by the community, but also likely defeated, as suggested by his or her relationship with passivity.

The colonial dictionaries translated *ah top chun* as "sodomite" or "pederast," *chun* coming from "cause, origin, base."[32] *Chun* may have referred either to the anus itself or to the origination of the act. I translate the whole phrase as "he who originates or causes carnal acts." It also appears that, while society did not always require further specification of the actor, the Maya could specify the sexual object by instead calling the active partner *ah top it*, "he who has carnal acts with the anus."[33] The Maya may have defined the *ah top it* or the *ah top chun* as the active partner to the passive *ix pen*.[34] The sexual practices of these people were defined in relation to a Maya discourse on penetration.

There is little context, however, for dictionary definitions. In the petition and the confessional manual, the Maya and the Catholic clergy were on their way to developing a colonized notion of desire, complete with an identity based on sexual behavior. But there is no evidence that such an identity was formed before the end of the colonial period.

ACTIVITY AND PASSIVITY

When the position of the phallus was asserted in the texts of the Ritual of the Bacabs, that position was signified by a hidden discourse on activity and passivity. The phallus was needed in the texts to signify a place in the symbolic world for the parallel positions of the male and the female principles. Those positions, however, far from being equal in the Maya world, were representative of hierarchy and power. The male principle signified the active role in sexual acts; the female principle signified the passive. Both were ratified in discourses related to warfare and gods. In the discourse on war, a hierarchical relation privileged the active role over the passive, thus gendering a central structure in preconquest Maya society. The discourse on gods, however, was more contradictory.

Warfare

Maya concepts of war were structured by an intricate belief system whereby the gods were seen as warring with each other. As noted above, Maya beliefs structured ethnicity based on a porous division between Self and Other. The Maya Self could have been the local community, the lineage group, an alliance of several communities, or, on occasion, all of the Maya people. After the conquest some of this changed and the Maya Self was limited to the local community and the lineage group. The Other was represented as the enemy, structured this way based on ethnic and political markers. The Maya structured the Self/Other dichotomy through a discourse on war marked by a division between the winner, shown as the active sexual partner, and the loser, shown as the passive.

Yet there were exceptions to this rule when one considers the broader discourse on Self/Other divisions. The Books of Chilam Balam supported the active/passive divide when they used sexual terminology in the form of direct insults. The Book of Chilam Balam of Chumayel stated that a certain preconquest era ended because of the misdeeds of two lords, Kak U Pacal and Tecuilu.[35] *Kak u pacal* translated as "fiery glance." *Tecuilu* came from the Nahuatl *tecuilonti*, meaning "the active partner in the act of sodomy."[36] The insults treated these lords as leaders who destroyed the society. The authors used the word "sodomite" to insult the memory of the lords. Perhaps the two were being represented as sexual partners who destroyed society. The use of the Nahuatl either could have been unconscious or it could have stood as a further insult, suggesting that the lords went beyond the linguistic construction of Maya sodomy into a different linguistic construct (one which the Maya could denigrate further), Nahua sodomy. The word used for the active partner was based on *cuiloni*, "the passive partner in sodomy." This construct showed a prioritization of the role of the passive, at least in the Nahua world.

Sexual insults did not limit themselves to sodomy. The Books of Chilam Balam used prostitution, adultery, fornication, pederasty, and more obscure elements of sexual desire as insults. The Tizimin, insulting the Itzá, said that under Itzá leadership, "in that time there were anus buggers; in that time there were anus pederasts."[37] Note again the use of Nahuatl to refer to the anus. The authors so often used Nahuatl (*tzintli*) to describe the anus that the Maya during some time may have understood a connection between Nahuatl speakers and this body part. In this text a group of outsiders was seen as taking the children's anuses, properly the possessions of the community. If the parents and the community were seen as owning the anuses of the children, then this implied a normative potential for pederasty. Below I show that this assertion of pederastic ownership was not an anomaly. The community and the kinship group had rights over children's bodies. These rights were maintained through pedagogic and pederastic rituals. The anus buggers and anus pederasts, however, were those Itzá who attacked and defeated the traditional Maya: they were the ones therefore who "buggered" the Maya. Often the meanings of the sexual insults themselves are elusive. As noted above, in one case in the Book of Chilam Balam of Tizimin, the authors insulted a ruler because he did not know his mother or his father and because he was born "through the nose and the tongue."[38] While this can be understood as an insult, I cannot know to what, if any, sexual act the "nose and tongue" referred.[39]

When the discourse was related specifically to warfare, the evidence of a hierarchical active/passive dichotomy was very strong. This was confirmed by the naming of towns, as a Chontal Maya town is named Cuylonemiquia, "the killing of the passive partner in sodomy."[40] Here space was used as a marker of sodomy, as well as a marker of war.[41] The connection with Nahuatl showed the use of the sodomitic insult as a weapon against enemies. Moreover, it placed sodomy as an element used specifically for warfare. Sodomy denigrated enemies and stratified societies.

Passivity was used here as a marker of space and power. The active partner was seen as the victor, while the passive was seen as the loser. This also suggested itself in the place-name located in the anonymous 1774 petition. Pencuyut, "the fornicating coyote," is a Yucatecan town. This place-name may have presented the coyote as an active partner. While the coyote represented the Nahuas, the town name (which has no grammatical markers) might in fact have been extended to say "where we fornicated with the coyotes." Such an interpretation again presented the members of the community as the active partners and the Nahuas as passives.

The connection with Nahuatl is intriguing, though hardly conclusive. One colonial Nahuatl document suggests that the Nahuas abhorred sodomy:

PASSIVE PARTNER IN SODOMY[42] . . . He fills people's noses
with the smell of excrement. Effeminate. He passes himself off as a
woman. He deserves to be burned, he deserves the flames, he deserves
to be cast in the fire.[43]

This text was based on testimony given by a group of Nahua nobles from Tlatelolco to a Franciscan friar, so it hardly was conclusive evidence of a Nahua hatred of sodomy. However, there certainly is significant evidence of Nahua denigration of passivity and effeminacy in men. The use of Nahuatl in the Maya texts could lead to one or more of the following three conclusions. First, an analysis of the Maya language shows that there were a significant number of Nahuatl loan words in Maya. These words were borrowed before the Spanish conquest, when a Nahuatl-speaking group conquered much of

Yucatán.[44] The terms *cuiloni* and *tzintli* could have been two loan words, borrowed because the earlier Maya terminology was less precise (*pen*, "sodomy," could refer to many sexual acts; *it*, "anus," may have referred to the "back side" of anything[45]). Second, the Maya could have used the Nahuatl terminology as a conscious insult against people perceived as "outsiders." This would in many ways have replicated a similar Nahua tradition.[46] In this interpretation the Nahuas were seen as "passive," and their masculinity was insulted. Finally, the use of Nahuatl could suggest a particular conceptualization of difference. The meanings represented by *cuiloni* and *pen* could have been recognizably different to colonial Maya (and perhaps Nahua) peoples, but the translations into Spanish and English eliminated recognition of the differences.

The themes of social death and destruction were prevalent in the Books of Chilam Balam, and sexual insults, often related to sodomy, presented these concepts. The power mandated in these texts showed that control over one's sexual desires allowed one to be victorious. Those desires had to be used in an active (and thus masculine) way rather than a passive (and thus feminine) way. The active partner was going to be the winner. Personal identity based on sexual behaviors played no role, as anybody could be active or passive. If you controlled your desires and won in warfare, you would be considered the active partner. If you lost, you would be considered passive. Nobody had a static sexual identity during times of war. Everybody faced the possibility of their sexual activity becoming excessive and then destroying their own society. As you became excessive you also became passive. Here sexual desire linked directly with warfare, as it had in Europe at the time (and in many other Latin American societies).[47] War related to sexual desire, not just because of some mythological connection through penetration, but also because of the use of a discourse of desire to engage in warfare and a discourse of warfare used to engage in sexual acts. Warfare itself in the early modern period was often about the protection of the integrity of the community against perceived invasions from outsiders. This protection was based on the notion of ethnicity constructed through sexual desire.

The Book of Chilam Balam of Chumayel presented the following prophecy from Chilam Balam.[48] This prophecy used the idea of an age-stratified active/passive dichotomy:

ox al a mukil x cuch lum yɔinil ɔaman yol cimen ix u pucçikal tu nicteob
xan ah uaua tulupoob ah ua tan çinoob nacxit xuchit tu nicte u lakob ca ca
kin y ahaulilob coylac te tu ɔamoob coylac te tu nicteob ca ca kin uinicil u

thannob ca ca kin u xecob u luchob u ᵽoocob u co kinnob u co akab u maxilob
yokol cab

The three children of your strength[49] are the bearers of the land of
the younger brothers. They have surrendered their spirit, and the
hearts of their flowers are dead; those who are often back turners,
those who are spreaders:[50] Nacxit Xuchit, with the flowers of his
companions, the two-two day lordships, the crooked in their thrones,
the crooked in their flowers. Two-two day men are there words, two-
two day are their seats, their gourds, their headdresses. They are the
lust of the day, the lust of the night, the monkey of the world. Their
necks are twisted, their faces are wrinkled, their mouths are slobber-
ing in the lordship of the lands, oh, lord.[51]

The destruction here predicted by Chilam Balam was the Spanish conquest
itself. This conquest caused the death of many people and gods. Nacxit Xuchit,[52] an Itzá leader, was associated with eroticism and particularly with
sodomy. Erotic figures found representing the final statements here clearly
showed that the Itzá were being portrayed as sodomites, effeminates, and lu-
natics.[53] Nacxit Xuchit was central to this phenomenon as he signified the
flower, itself a vital metaphor for eroticism and destruction in the Maya world.
The two-two day people were those who sat on the thrones, the illegitimate
rulers who allowed Chilam Balam to foresee the disasters.
    The sexual stratification and hierarchy was signified based on an interpre-
tation of the metaphor. The back-turners were the younger brothers, representatives of the Itzá people.[54] They lost the war, and thus, because of perceived cowardice, they were degraded in Maya eyes. They then turned their
backs to the Spaniards, who defeated them in war, ritually sodomizing them.
This interpretation was based on an understanding of the flower as signifier
of both warfare and sexual desire. The flower here signified the sexual acts
that were performed ritually between the Spaniards and the backsides of the
Maya. So the flowers were presented as an important ritual element in Nacxit
Xuchit's name and in the Maya text. The younger brothers lost their hearts
and their spirits to their older brothers (the Spaniards),[55] who then killed their
flowers by symbolically engaging in anal intercourse with them. The Maya
fighters thus were defeated and sodomized: they were feminized effectively in
a discourse that masculinized the winning warriors, the Spaniards.
    The picture we received of the Itzá was that of a group of people who slob-
bered with their necks twisted, a picture intended to evoke intense eroticism

and insanity. Figures have been discovered that show people from Itzá areas in similar poses, in some cases with erect penises, in other cases linked to figures of men committing sodomy with each other. One friar, who lived among the Itzá in the southern part of Yucatán, accused the people of widespread homosexual sodomy.[56] Another, as noted in the last chapter, accused Itzá leaders of keeping a house of boys for the purpose of sodomy.[57] Clearly, the Itzá, portrayed as defeated outsiders (after the Spanish conquest), were linked with homosexual sodomy and effeminacy.

The jaguar priest, Chilam Balam, a very powerful prophet in these texts, signified the older brothers (who symbolically became the Spaniards *and* the non-Itzá Maya, both struggling against the Itzá) through his prophecy. The older brothers were shown as the bearers of good tidings. The younger brothers lost their spirits and thus spiritually and militarily were defeated. The stratification was apparent in a particular context: that of the Spanish conquest. The older brothers, the Spaniards, had the power over the younger. The Itzá were represented as the younger brothers in another part of this text, and they were denigrated because of their position outside of Chumayel. The politics of this text was clear: the Itzá had to submit.

The stratification between Chilam Balam and Nacxit Xuchit showed that Chilam Balam was the active partner to the other, as the "true" Maya were to be the active partners to the Itzá. In the metaphor of war, Chilam Balam sought to defeat Nacxit Xuchit through the latter's anus. And the Spanish did the same.

The narratives used sexual desire in order to discuss and stratify various elements of society, particularly using this desire as a metaphor for warfare and disease. They could do this through an active/passive dichotomy, but the dichotomy remained significantly different from that of early modern Europe. The stratification of power supported the active partner as the masculine one. The passive was the back-turner and the younger brother, the one who was to be penetrated and defeated.

Deities and Disease

Warfare was not the only place where a discourse on the relationship between homosexual sodomy and desire entered the Maya system. Constructions of ritual in the form of disease and cure also gave sodomy a major role. Here again the discussion was organized around the notion of clearly differentiating between activity and passivity.

In the metaphors of war, the passive partner, at least when gendered male,

was denigrated and destroyed. These notions of activity and passivity signified particular ways of seeing the universe. For Europeans, the structures were
in many ways similar, but the European victors represented sexual desire often in strictly ethnic terms, dividing themselves as victors (and therefore
active partners) from the people defeated (who were therefore treated as passives). A counter-discourse running through all of this was that of the European active defeating another active, and thus proving the European as the
most masculine of men. But for the Maya, this counter-discourse did not appear to exist.

The sodomitical relationship and the notion of difference between active
and passive roles was a central strategic maneuver in these texts. This allowed
for the shamans to engage in cures by invoking the gods and committing ritual sexual acts with them. These ceremonies destroyed disease by emphasizing sexual acts which placed the shaman in the role of the active partner. The
person being cured was, of course, conceived as passive, but so were, in some
cases, the gods:

> *tin can xot cuntah tin can max cuntah u col chab u cool akab ma uen ci*
> *ma coy la ci uinicil tun uinicil te tumenel tin chim tex tah lah tex tu cal ual*
> *tu cal xol cex can tul ti ku cex can tul ti bacabe ɔam tun yn uayasba ca tin*
> *ɔam chektahech tu ca cobol a na tu ca cobol a yum cech u cool ale u cool*
> *mehene Amen*

> I cast a spell to forcibly cut and pound the lust of creation and the lust
> of the night. The body of wood and stone does not sleep, does not
> curl up. As I hurl stones at you, as I slap you with a log and a staff, you
> four gods, you four *bacabs*, my sign is submerged. I am submerging/
> penetrating you[58] with the genitals of your mother and the genitals of
> your father.[59] You are the lust of the women's children, the lust of the
> men's children. Amen.[60]

Here the body was presented as a creation of wood and stone which was affected by the lust of creation and the night. The text sought to convince the
listener that the body could not be lustful or else he/she/it would need a cure.
The person to be cured was required to desire the shaman to be the active
partner. As the shaman became this active partner, it was only then that the
ill person would be cured.

The narrative (unconsciously?) connected Catholic and traditional Maya
feelings about sexual desire. The body itself was renarrativized and colonized

as the social body with feelings which fit into both the Catholic and Maya frameworks. It was the sexual desire for this body that was the central displacement strategy of the text. To end the illnesses of society, the shaman had to engage the hybrid notion of desire, placing emphasis on both original sin and on the restoration of lineage.

The narrative did not allow the initial sexual acts to be isolated on the body. Rather, these acts were located in "lust" and "creation." The text here showed the sexual behavior necessary for procreation in a manner clearly compatible with Catholic thought. These acts did not enter the body, nor were they shown as pleasurable. Sexual desire was cast out by both the Maya shamans and the strategically invisible Catholic priests.

The text then placed the shaman in the position of the physical aggressor: he punished the gods by hurling stones at them and hitting them. Here the active partner was presented as a violent partner, and the whole scene marked violence. The active partner in all of these texts signified an aggressive, violent figure, but one who also engaged in much self control.

The shaman then moved on to become the sexually active partner by engaging in intercourse with a god. This ritualized intercourse was necessary in order to cure the ill person. The shaman's sign was submerged in a sexual act. The word *chek*, which related directly to sexual intercourse, was used to describe how the shaman submerged the god. The shaman then specified that he submerged/penetrated the god with the genitals of the parents of the god.

The structure of the gods was an important element of this text. They were represented in two sets of four. Where the text discussed the parents, it treated them as if they existed as one god. As has been noted, in Maya cosmology gods often had many identities, and those identities usually had quadripartite divisions.[61] These four deities were shown as two sets of four, but the narrative switched strategies to show the set of gods as one god with one body. The god had parents and thus existed as part of the Maya kinship system. This deity had a humanlike body which could engage in sexual acts. The deified body was a central actor in this ritual, and the desire for the body of the god was vital because it was his body that allowed the shaman, as the active partner, access to the cure. The sexual acts were used to denigrate the deity, as well as to engage in the cure. The shaman used his own sign (his penis?) to enter the symbolic world and to engage in sexual acts with the god. This sign thus signified a power by which the shaman could move across boundaries separating humanity from the gods. These boundaries necessarily were crossed in an attempt to engage in the cure.

The cure itself required the sexual act signified by *chek*. The context here demanded a broad interpretation of the meaning of this term. The shaman used the genitals of the mother and the father of the god in order to engage in sexual acts. Such acts signified the possibility of an "incestuous" homosexual assault, legitimized in the ritual sphere. The "incest" here was somewhat problematic, as the parents of the god were not pictured as engaging in these sexual acts. Their genitals did engage in sexual acts with their child, but their bodies and "selves" did not. The free-floating genitalia, detached from the bodies of the gods, and attached to the body of the shaman, may make one think of the Lacanian notion of the phallus as a linguistic sign rather than a body part.[62] The legitimization of such a potentially incestuous relationship presented a strategy which again empowered the shaman. This shaman could do away with the disease only by using the presumably powerful genitals of the parents of the god. Incest itself was maintained as an important strategy. The desire for the gods was a central desire which would maintain societal stratification. This desire, represented as incest, thus had an important role to play in societal structures. It was through this desire that the shaman would convince the person to be cured that he had done his job.

And the empowerment of the shaman did not end here. He had to engage in a sexual assault on the god. The god was a passive participant in this whole affair, being given no choice as to the sexual act. The god was denigrated through this ritual activity, again showing a disempowering aspect to the passive position in sexual behavior. The narrative empowered the shaman by allowing him to engage in the active role in a sexual act, while disempowering the god by forcing him to engage in the passive role.

The notion of empowerment of the active was a common one which was seen in many European and non-European societies. Most often, the male sexual role was viewed as active and the female as passive. Here there was no specific declaration of a gendered notion of sexual positions. The passive partner being denigrated also was a *bacab*, an extremely powerful god in the Maya pantheon.[63] He certainly would have been worshipped by the shaman. Yet the shaman was willing to denigrate the *bacab* by throwing stones at him and forcing him to play the passive sexual role. This sense of disempowering your own god was something foreign to the European notion of passivity. Here, while passivity certainly was denigrated, it also was considered a necessary part of life.[64] Society needed the passive partner, and shamans needed to desire the passive partner's body in order to engage in the cure.

To commit these sexual acts, the shaman needed the genitals of both the mother and the father. These signified the importance of both matrilineal and patrilineal kinship as well as the duality of the gods themselves. It certainly appears that the ritual sexual act signified here is rather difficult to conceptualize in Western minds. The acts did not divide into heterosexual and homosexual. While the narrative strategized carefully to determine a difference between active and passive sexual activity, it did not determine a clear binary difference between genders. Why were the genitals of both the mother and the father needed? After all, the shaman only should have needed one set of genitals to engage in sex.

This signified to the Maya a particular concept of the bi-eroticism of desire. It was only through the lust of the children of these mothers and fathers that disease was created. Society needed the mothers and fathers to return in order to control and defeat the disease. The shaman had to force the "child" to engage in sexual activity, and the only way he could do so was with the genitalia of the mother and the father. These genitals signified the kinship line itself, and they represented a conceptualization of the desires of the *bacab*. He was bisexual in many senses, but he did not have any choice in this matter. The sexual act was represented as a conquest, and indeed it must have appeared to be one. This conquest over the *bacab* was a conquest of desire. And such a conquest could be accomplished only through the genitals of both lineages and both genders.

That phallus here was not specifically a sign of the masculine. The detached genitalia included the mother's genitals as well as the father's. In this sense the phallus was reconfigured as a sign of libidinal power which was not necessarily attached to one gender.[65] Perhaps the mother's genitals were attached in some way to the son, the raped god. This would confirm the idea, stated by Trexler, that the passive male was feminized. But the narrative suggested that the active partner, the shaman, used the genitals of both the mother and the father. If both sets of genitals were attached to his body, this text would signify sexual acts that are not necessarily comprehensible to people living in modern Western society.[66] If these genitals were not attached to the shaman's body, but rather simply were used by him in some manner, then he may have symbolized the metaphorical power of both the male and the female aspects of the cosmos to engage in acts of incestuous rape (signifying the unpredictability of the cosmos). In either case the text used the "concept" of genitalia to alter the bodily metaphors related to the shaman. Either he took on the genitalia of the god's father, the god taking on the genitalia of his own mother, or he took on the genitalia of both father and mother. In the first instance, the shaman's sign would have been changed into the sign of the male father god: his phallus would have been deified, and the son god's phallus would have been "transsexualized" into the genitals of his own mother.

In the second instance, the shaman's phallus would have been "transsexualized" into the mixed gender phallus, combining both the sign of the mother and the sign of the father. In either case, symbolic transsexuality played an important role in the text, signifying much about Maya desires, fantasies, and fears as they related to the cosmos and the world of curing rituals.

The deity, as a passive participant in this whole affair, the raped god, appeared to have little power. But the rape actually showed the Maya people the intense power of the sacred and the small amount of power reserved for humans. The sacred world developed all of the genitals used in these sexual acts. And it was only through the sacred that the shaman was able to engage in the various acts mentioned. The shaman was helpless until the gods were willing to help him. And they were willing: the gods (parents) were willing to assist the shaman in raping another god (son). The god was one of the most powerful: a *bacab* divided into his four parts. The sacred power was perceived as overwhelming. If the gods could and would rape another god, then humans would stand little chance if they placed themselves in the disfavor of these gods.[67] The power of the sacred certainly was an important element in Maya society, and the rape of a god would have pointed to the unpredictability and harshness of that sacred world. Sodomy here was used to point to the fear of rape and to the fear people had of the sacred world.

Penetration itself was a central discursive maneuver for the Maya. Penetration was associated closely with rituals related to warfare, disease, human sacrifice, and penis piercing. Each of these signified elements of Maya desire. The sexual aspects of this desire, organized around a matrix of activity and passivity, allowed for it to be conceptualized as something which affected the people. Their desires for life had to be maintained through the nobility, who had to remain the metaphorical active partners. They engaged in ritual sexual activity with the gods, forcing those gods into passive positions. Symbolically, they engaged in sexual activity with enemy warriors during warfare and human sacrifice, signifying themselves as the active partners, and the enemies as the passives. They used their pierced penises to represent the duality of the entire structure. That which penetrated was itself penetrated: such was the duality of this Maya discourse. And the gendering of power was both parallel and hierarchical.

PEDAGOGY, PEDERASTY, AND POLITICAL POWER

The relationship between homoeroticism and Maya ritual discourse extended to the political realm.[68] In a set of texts from the Books of Chilam Balam of

Chumayel and Tusik, the Maya placed a hierarchical relation upon noble youth as those youth were required to learn from their elders. The learning that took place existed in the context of riddles which were from the "language of Zuyua"[69] and related texts. They signified a normative pederastic desire, implicated in the spread of knowledge, symbolically represented as blood and semen.

The Rituals of Zuyua

Here the Maya political rituals were shown as rituals of desire, but they also discussed the relationship between pedagogy and the sexual politics of the nobility. The Books of Chilam Balam gave great importance to the *halach uinic* ("true man"), often simply translated as "governor". The *halach uinic* was represented as the "true man" through his knowledge of lineage and community. Both the *halach uinic* and the *batab* ("governor/chief") were extremely powerful before the conquest. The *batab* remained powerful following the conquest. The *batab* and the *halach uinic* both were present in the pederastic political rituals. These were ceremonies which discussed the relationship between pedagogy and the sexual politics of nobility. The Books of Chilam Balam contained a set of these rituals which delineated political roles and discussed events in which political power was questioned. The Maya called these rituals *suiua than*, "Zuyua speech" or the "Zuyua word." This literally translated as "unintelligible speech," textually represented as a test in which the nobles made unintelligible speech intelligible.[70] The tests were about knowledge: those who had knowledge of society could rule over that society. This knowledge was both libidinal and kinship oriented. Those who knew these things would have great political futures. Zuyua was representative of a set of standards designed to determine nobility and truth. The rituals showed the power of the *halach uinic*, "the true man," over the rest of the nobility. The power relationship presented by the riddles showed the *halach uinic* as a trainer and teacher of noble youth.

These ceremonies often used the human body and its actions to discuss other elements of society, implying much about correct and incorrect uses of the body. The following introduction came from the Book of Chilam Balam of Chumayel:[71]

> *kat naat cu talel ychil u katunil licil [u ɔ]ocol hele lae ti kuchi tu kinil u*
> *katabal u naatob u batabil cahob u yohelob uchic u talelob u uinicilob*
> *yahaulilob ua tzolan u talel u batabilob u halach uinicilob ua u chibalob*
> *ahauuob ua batab u chibalob ti u hahcunticob*

The questions and answers come into the *katun* as it is ending.[72] Thus arrives the day of questions and answers of the *batabob* of the communities: Whether they know how the people and the lords came;[73] whether they explain the coming of the *batabob* and the *halach uinicob*; whether they can prove that they are of the lineages of the lords and the *batab* lineages.[74]

The *halach uinic*, the "true man," asked questions of those aspiring to take his place. The engagement centered around his bodily space without ever mentioning his body.[75] The narrative treated all of the aspiring nobles as inferior to the *halach uinic*, calling them both "sons" and *batabob*. These sons appealed to the *halach uinic* by answering his questions, which later were discovered to be riddles. They thereby proved themselves capable of governing. The pedagogical relationship was clear: these *batabob* were those who would learn from the superior *halach uinic*. The learning which would take place was designed to ascertain the lineage of the nobles. In these rituals the *halach uinic* placed the *batabob* in an asymmetrical relationship to himself.[76] He used his bodily space to represent his own power and authority. This space signified an acceptable and desirable social hierarchy, but one which could be questioned through rituals. Perhaps those who gained knowledge would replace the *halach uinic*.

My interpretation of these rituals has shown that they involved adolescent boys aspiring to become nobles.[77] The many discontinuities in Maya life at the time of the conquest and throughout the colonial years made it very difficult to establish the proper kinship ties for a noble. The nobles wanted to have a way of separating out the true nobles from the others. This theoretically could be accomplished by a test given to adolescent noble aspirants. Those who passed the test could go on to take political office, or they simply could live their lives as nobles, but at least their nobility was "proven." The kinship ties to the *halach uinic*, who, by his very name, had proven the truth of his nobility, showed a connection to a very "real" noble lineage. The adolescent boys were called *batabob* in an effort to imply both their unity with and their dependence on the *halach uinic*. This relationship was both pederastic and pedagogical: the leader taught the adolescent boys how to rule, and, in doing so, he required the services of these adolescents. The "true man" demanded that they prove their "truth" to him. This ritual was a lesson to the adolescents: they were required to respect their traditions and their elders.[78]

These tests determined the identity of the "true man": "This is what the first jaguar is, seated over the sun, drinking its blood/semen. Zuyua is its meaning."[79] The powerful jaguar drank blood and/or semen, two interrelated elements.[80] The jaguar, represented in these books as the sign of the prophet, stratified his relationship with the adolescent nobles. The symbolic knowledge which the nobles sought was placed within the semen and the blood. The sexual connotations signified political desires: in order to gain the political power of the *halach uinic*, the youth had to gain his semen and blood. This ritual in all likelihood did not involve actual sexual activity. However, the symbolic relationship was a homoerotic one, with the leader imparting his knowledge to the younger male nobles through blood and semen. The blood, either signifying menstruation (and thus presenting the semen/blood connection as one which maintained the *halach uinic* as the guardian of men and women) or penis piercing, located the desires of the adolescent nobles.

The "phallic signifying economy"[81] presented here stratified the political system based on gender and age. The adolescents desired the blood of the various rituals, the blood of the lineage. The ceremonies, designed to test knowledge of blood and semen, both gendered and phallic, showed that these adolescents were required to understand lineage, directly related to political power. The rituals of blood may have been seen as replacements for secure lineage alignments. The stratification of the lineage, apparent in both warfare and politics, allowed for a homoerotic desire to emanate from both of these fields.

The meaning of Zuyua was located in this understanding of lineage. The rituals located another meaning for Zuyua in the answers to the riddles themselves. In this case the sun that was requested actually was a fried egg. The often quite humorous questions and answers led the aspiring nobles into the possibility of political power. This text constructed asymmetrical relationships, however humorously, in an effort to gain (perhaps fictive) political office. The blood and semen were central symbols in this construction. While other documents described narratives of universality in which all people were created, this ritual discussed a narrative to which all aspired: to be declared the "true man." The text, although signifying universal aspirations, was a highly particularized story in which few people actually were represented. The people shown all were male nobles. They desired to represent the "truth" through the phallus, constructed as political power.

Zuyua speech made a humorous attempt to require those aspiring to be nobles to have knowledge of rituals of politics, religion, and creation, relating these to particular notions of desire, symbolized as semen and blood. While the text never said how the adolescents would gain the knowledge of semen and blood that the leader possessed, these elements signified sexual acts, creation, childbirth, warfare, penis piercing, and human sacrifice. The *halach uinic* may or may not have literally pierced the youthful penises (or had them pierce his: the active/passive dichotomy is unclear in this act). His semen may or may not have literally penetrated their bodies. He was to test them on their knowledge of semen and blood. He was to show them that he had this knowledge because it signified his knowledge of all aspects of society.

Riddles, Entertainment, and Sexual Politics

The stories themselves showed the bi-eroticism of desire as they primarily discussed sexual acts between men and women while they presented the male body in an erotic manner, attaining the pederastic relationship. Some showed an erotic connection between the older noble and the adolescents. For example, the elder noble stated:

mehene xen cħa ten a uex yn uui u booc uaye y nach u booc ce u booc yn uexe u booc yn noke u booc yn yubake pay num u boc tu ɔu caane tu ɔu muyalle y yn yax pakab chee yan ti çac hothe ua halach uinice chi be
    yume bin yn tales cij u tħan hex u boc yex lic u katice u pay num u booc tu ɔu caane lay pome tħabbil elil u cah hex yax pakab chi lic u katice lay muxbil cacau cho u uae

"Son, bring me your trousers[82] so I may smell their odor here, and get rid of their odor, the odor of my trousers, the odor of my cloth, the odor of my incense, and the great odor of the center of the sky and the center of the clouds, and my green garden plant which has white seeds. If you are the *halach uinic*, let it be done."
    "Father, I will bring it," are his words. Here is the odor of the trousers for which he asks, the great odor of the center of the sky: it is incense burning in the fire. This is the green garden plant for which he asks. This is ground cacao seeds.[83]

The joking language allowed the older man to contemplate his desire to sniff or eat the pants of the younger. The young male body was associated with creating pleasure for an older, superior man. This pleasure was associated with great ritual power as the youth's body was equated with the smell of the center of the sky.
    As the older noble searched for something in the pants of the younger, he enjoyed the adolescents' odors. The search, likely for the anus, situated the

homoerotic tenor of the ritual. It also gendered political power through the phallic connotations. It was the desire for the phallus that allowed access to political power. But this text was structured through the desires of the leader, who was looking for the anus.

The discourse showed that nobles were permitted to engage in intergenerational erotic games that stressed the power of the elder noble over the younger. Unlike in classical Greece,[84] there were no textual discussions among the Maya about the nature of intergenerational sexual relationships. The pedagogical relationship was eroticized through the provision of service by the younger male for the elder. The elder male had power over the younger in an erotic, political, and educational sense. The event thus maintained the hierarchical social order.

The younger noble, of course, played a joke on the elder, legitimizing both of their positions. The position of the younger noble signified a position of access to political office. The older noble represented the old leadership, a group which maintained its dominance of rituals, but which was both pompous and ridiculous. The elder noble was powerful, and he would maintain that power through his discourse and his actions. However, he would not always be powerful, and it served his strategic interests to allow others to laugh at him.

In another example, the leader maintained his stance as a protector of his people by the instructions he gave to the youth:

mehene ca a tales ten hun tul noh xib lay ma kalan u botonil u ha bone hom tochac u kabae
  cay bacac be yume hex lic u katice lay ybache yx ueche

"Son, go bring me an old man, but don't confine his testicles, his water balls. Hom Tochac (Submerged Impotent) is his name."
"That is how it shall be, father." Here is what he asks for: armadillo.[85]

The younger noble needed to take care of the impotent man's testicles. The male body, constructed as somewhat broken down, needed care to reenergize the impotent and to prevent further damage of the goods. The elder noble taught the younger how to care for the bodies of other men and, in doing so, expressed concern over the loss of the phallus. While the unconscious representation may have suggested a concern related to a castration complex, it more clearly showed the relationship between sexual desire among men and the power relationships developed in such desire.[86] The connection to a community of elder nobles was apparent.[87] The older noble could instruct the youth in the care of the male body. The younger noble could take care of another elderly man. Both the older noble and the younger had certain political responsibilities. The phallic symbolism signified a concern for the future of society which was unveiled in a concern for the place of the male body in the reproductive act. Here the authors had some anxiety about the fact that the male body could become incapable of engaging in intercourse and reproduction. The potential impotence of the man required the care of the youth in order for the male body to be rejuvenated. While the text did not specify the actual acts performed, the youth may have had to engage in a variety of sexual and nonsexual activities to get the elderly man potent. It was the youthful body that was placed at the center of the discourse. The homoerotic desire represented (in the idea that the older man would desire these youth so greatly) was an element constructing particular power relationships such that the youth were required sexually to service older nobles. Of course, in the end the *halach uinic* received an armadillo, which, submerged in its shell, had some metaphorical relationship with impotence.

As the riddles of "Zuyua speech" became more clear, they asserted the patrilineage, allowing the actors access to speech and power only if they were male. The riddles structured a hierarchical masculine sphere where the leaders were concerned with their lineages and their futures. The relationship between desire and bi- or homoeroticism was not only age and gender structured. The Books of Chilam Balam also contained related riddles that stratified society based on class, gender, and sexual desire. The *halach uinic* said to the youth:

> *mehene tales ten ah canan colob noh xibob hun tuch u tal u choone y y atane t ix mumil chac tale cex uaye: y ix ah canan col chuplalobe bin çaclah chuplalobe ten ix bin lukçic u picob y okole ca tun in hante lay chicame*

> Son, bring me the field guards, the grown men who have pubic hair that comes as far as the navel, and their wives who are cheery and big. Bring them here with the women guards of the fields.[88] The women will be white-[faced][89] when I remove their skirts that they are wearing. Then I will eat them. This is jicama.[90]

The senior noble desired both men and women to be brought to him. Both would please him, and perhaps he would eat both. Here sex and the human body related to food. The riddle's implicit statement was that peeling the jicama was similar to a man taking off a woman's clothes. The riddles included several cases where the noble removed the clothes of a commoner woman and then ate her, connecting sex and the commoner female body with food. The text showed that the *halach uinic* assumed a right to have at least fictive sex with particular commoner women by using the male youth to attract these women. It showed that sex in such a ritual context was acceptable, and even promoted by the nobility, as it was seen as an act which ensured the continuation of the society and the social hierarchy.

Nobles made fun of commoner men and women, particularly emphasizing the relationship of their bodies to food. Commoner women had to make their bodies available to noble men. The riddles also made fun of nobles, including the actors in the texts. They often discussed their anatomy, looking at their bodies as food. Commoners and other nobles were at the disposal of the leader, showing some of the ways in which stratification was marked on the human body.

In the Books of Chilam Balam of Chumayel and Tusik, there were a variety of related texts that showed the ritual importance of bi-erotic desire marking the body. This sexual contact, both in the documents and in the ethnographic context, did not disavow age- or gender-structured homosexual desire. The various desires presented in the texts signified the "truth" that the "true man" sought to impart to the noble youth. This "truth," symbolized as blood and semen, was linked explicitly to the libido. The Maya structured the political power of pedagogical pederasty by placing a variety of bodies at the hands of the leader of society. The eroticization of these texts does not correspond to modern notions of homosexuality, bisexuality, or pederasty. We might see these as more along the lines of "sexual banter." Yet the eroticization of male and female bodies in a text of some ritual importance signified the desires, if not the acts, of the nobility. Their bodies represented and maintained a social and political hierarchy.

SEXUAL CONTROL

The control over sexual desire has been linked to various forms of political power. Here it has been shown that the Maya were no exception to this general rule. But the control was about a bi-erotic stratification of desire, rather than being linked to any identity based on sexual behaviors. These desires were linked particularly well with struggles: war and disease. As Michel Foucault pointed out, the creation of warfare was a way of understanding and maintaining sexual and ethnic boundaries.[91] The sexual aspects of warfare for the Maya clearly were portrayed in the dichotomy between active and passive sexual roles.

The conqueror who was being supported by the text most often was signified as the active participant in sexual acts. The conquered always was seen as the passive, disempowered partner. Unlike texts related to early modern Europe, it was the established person in the hierarchy who could switch roles. The defeated warrior always was seen as passive, but the powerful god also could be viewed in this role. The passivity and ritualized rape of the god signified the immense power of the cosmological sphere. It is clear that the active/passive dichotomy was important to both the Europeans and the Maya. This dichotomy allowed for a gendered structuring of the Maya universe which positioned the active partner (read as male) on top of the passive partner (read as female). Yet the gendering of the Maya texts was hardly so clear as this. Gender often was unmarked, and the specifics of the sexual acts were unclear. The Moon Goddess, herself representative of the bi-eroticism of desire, was both penetrator and penetrated. She was both active and passive.

Age and class stratification were marked more clearly through the textual desire. Zuyua speech made it clear that it was the desire of the elder leader of society that would mark the space in which all of these games were to be played. His body was the central entity as he desired the bodies of the male youth as well as those of the commoners. And the noble youth were able to take the desires of the elders and subvert them through trickery. Political power here was signified specifically through sexual desire. The marked desires were the desires of the leaders for the bodies of those who could service them. The unmarked desires, those of the youth, women, and commoners, were placed in the texts only in relation to the desires of their superiors.

Colonialism altered the Maya sense of sexual desire and identity. Homosexual and bisexual desire, once linked with a wide variety of elements in the Maya cosmos, was now to be placed in the category of sin. Yet the Maya developed a hybrid discourse in which some political and religious rituals remained places which used homosexual desires to signify power relationships related to curing and warfare. At the same time, other political and religious rituals (e.g., petitions and confessions, respectively) emphasized the sexual identity of the sodomite as sinner. The hybrid discourse had been born.

TEN Finding the Virgin Mary

The Virgin Mary Moon Goddess of the colonial Maya people was a virgin, a bisexually active woman, and perhaps a bisexually active man. I look at this sentence and believe that something has gone awry, and indeed something has. The categorizations and boundaries that modern Western peoples prescribe for sexual acts cannot be applied to the colonial Maya. They were not "freer" with sexuality than we are in the modern West, nor is the issue that they did not have sexualized identities at all. Rather, the colonial Maya used a sexual discourse to understand many of the things around them, to contemplate life and death. And the Virgin Mary Moon Goddess, rather than embodying a single sexual identity, signified this search for understanding: she symbolized the hybrid sexual discourse of the colonial Maya.

SEXUAL ACTS, SYMBOLS, AND DESIRES

Searching for the Moon Goddess and finding the Virgin Mary is a historical irony. The conceptualization of the Virgin from the perspective of the friars certainly was not that of a sexual being nor that of a goddess. However, the friars themselves taught the people about parallels between Maya traditions and Catholicism. The Maya nobles at the time of the conquest did not plan to hide the identity of the Moon Goddess within the Virgin Mary, but here too they soon strategized to understand parallels between Catholicism and Maya tradition. The Moon Goddess and the Virgin Mary for both the friars and the Maya nobles were more than personified figures who had particular identities. The two were important signifiers: for the friars the Moon Goddess signified the sexual decadence of the devil, while the Virgin Mary signified the most desirable and chaste state of being for humans, and particularly for women. For Maya noblemen the Moon Goddess signified the vitality and sexuality of creation, while the Virgin Mary signified the colonizing goddess, the Spanish parallel of the Moon Goddess. By the end of the colonial period, both views were hybridized into the figure of the Virgin Mary Moon Goddess.

In completing this book, I have used a method of historical writing that is most prevalent in what have been called the new cultural and political histories.[1] This method has shown that the meanings of documents require significant interpretation, that the texts themselves express and hide meaning in a particular cultural context. I have found it necessary to attempt to understand the cultural and psychological premises in the act of Maya writing. As an ethnohistorian analyzing a particular group of people long dead, I am aware of the dangers involved in such an interpretative framework. The people may seem frozen in time, the culture may seem static,[2] the cultural and psychological tools which we use may be inappropriate. However, I believe that it is necessary to use these tools with great care in order to find some connections between culture and history. To me the most important aspect of historical writing is in the search for metaphorical connections between the subjects and issues.[3] I have attempted to bring those metaphorical connections, and the tools that I have used to make the connections, to the foreground. I have analyzed the Maya in order to understand the historical connections between colonialism, gender, and sexual desire.[4]

In most of the texts that I have used, Maya writing ostensibly was about politics, religion, ritual, and warfare but subtextually was about gender and sexual desire, important themes related metaphorically to the other issues. In the Books of Chilam Balam, sex was used to understand past events and leaders and to signify warfare. In the Ritual of the Bacabs, sex symbolized diseases, cures, and the ritualistic involvement of the gods. In the Songs of Dzitbalché, sex was connected directly with a variety of ritualistic and religious ceremonies. In the petitions, sex was a form of complaint that signified a strategic inversion of power relationships. These differences were results of the different purposes of the documents, but it is important to note that *none* of the documents in isolation can be permitted to stand for the true views of the colonial Maya. I have shown throughout this book that these documents were written for particular purposes. They were produced to emphasize some points and deemphasize others. They promoted strategies to gain some form of power. Nobles wrote about the sexual behaviors of other nobles in order to discredit the others and make themselves look good in comparison. They asserted gender parallelism in order to make it easier for the commoners to understand the importance of maintaining a social hierarchy. When I compared the documents and contextualized them, I discovered more about Maya views, but even this did not present me with the Truth.[5] Instead, I found several truths which signified a variety of views of the Maya people; the different truths signified the fact that the Maya had a structured hierarchy that rigidly empowered male over female and noble over commoner.[6]

There was no single Maya "way of being" or "way of knowing the world." Maya views structured social stratification in such a way that nobles and commoners, men and women could hardly have experienced the same reality. The Spanish reinforced and expanded this system both by supporting the nobles as their intermediaries and by separating the Spanish world from the Maya. All of my findings are representative of the views and struggles *within* the Maya male nobility. There were certainly many cultural disputes which were not marked directly by these documents. Women resisted the gender hierarchy and commoners resisted the social hierarchy. There are clues to this resistance even in these documents. Women were shown resisting adultery and rape as well as using their ritual and social status to control men. Commoners rebelled and demanded that nobles owed them debts of obligation. The documents overall, however, present a sexual culture as it was viewed by male nobles. Hence my conclusions relate to the ways in which these nobles used and manipulated gender and sexual desire.

The Maya and Spanish documents show that the Maya at the time of the Spanish conquest knew of and certainly engaged in vaginal intercourse; anal intercourse between men and other men, men and women, and men and animals; sexual acts between women; pederasty (men with boys and/or girls); group sexual activities; oral sex; and masturbation. The Maya appear to have preferred serial monogamy for commoner men and all women, and polygyny for noblemen. It was accepted widely that men and women often would not remain with one partner for life. After the conquest polygyny and divorce were outlawed. The Maya texts used all of these sexual acts to denigrate leaders and enemies, invert power relationships, and worship and harness the power of gods.

Desire, fantasy, and fear all were mental processes that the Maya used to understand their world. The symbolic signifiers of blood, semen, and the phallus marked many Maya desires. Blood was perhaps the most powerful signifier in the Maya world as it signified gender parallelism, masculine power, birth, death, war, and sacrifice. It was blood that gave birth to the gods. Male and female blood and male semen combined to create the world. Maya noble masculinity was based on leadership in warfare, politics, and ritual. The Maya noble's blood and semen symbolically signified this masculinity, for it was these elements which allowed him to create and protect the community. Noble femininity was based on childbirth, creation, and leadership in ritual. The noblewoman's femininity was marked by her menstrual blood and blood from her own piercings.

The phallus, the pierced penis, often controlled the community's access to the gods. Yet the penis-piercing rituals were envisioned as being controlled by goddesses and objects perceived to be feminine. So the phallic signification was hardly so clear as to be a simplistic assertion of male power. Instead, masculinity had to be asserted through a discourse that symbolized gender parallelism. Importantly, the relationship between blood, semen, and the phallus signified Maya desire for a connection with the gods, a desire supported by the fantasy that Maya nobles (and, to a lesser extent, commoners) could commune with and give birth to the gods through the use of these sexualized markers.

Both fantasy and fear also were symbolized by the flower, penetration, and transsexuality. The flower was a metaphor for both the Maya and the Nahuas which signified the connections between creation, destruction, and rebirth. For the Maya this flower had a symbolic connection with penetration. The actions of the flower and the penetrator were to be feared in warfare and religious ritual, but they also were to be desired on the same occasions. The Maya desired to be the symbolic penetrators in warfare, and they symbolically wanted to penetrate the bodies of the gods in order to harness their power.

Fantasies and fears worked together to mark bodies in the ritual sphere, and transsexuality was used in this marking. The Maya documents showed that transsexuality was used to understand the duality of the sacred world. Transsexuality also related to the way in which the penis both was penetrated and bled, thus making it similar to the vagina. These symbolic connections signified both a desire for the Maya male to be able to engage in creation by himself and a fear of the penetration of the male body. In a Western sign system, the bodies pictured would be marked as transsexual, but here they signified not a normative acceptance of transsexuality but rather a symbolic desire to understand the duality of creation.

These fantasies of transsexuality existed alongside a colonial structure that demanded adherence to relatively rigid categories separating masculinity and femininity. As the colonial period progressed, concepts of gender changed: blood no longer was a central marker of femininity; now virginity and chastity were central markers. Masculinity no longer was marked by rituals of semen, blood, and warfare, but now was marked by strategies for gaining wealth and protecting communities. Gender parallelism certainly has been over-utilized to suggest great equality between men and women.[7] The Maya had some elements of ritual structure that asserted this very gender parallelism. The concepts of creation and deified sexual desire demanded a certain parallelism. Lineage arrangements were seen at least partly in parallel lines of descent. This existed, though, in conjunction with some strongly hierarchical elements. Politics was a domain for men. During the colonial years, patrilineage was asserted as the dominant kinship structure. Maya men held more property than Maya women. Men were the ones who worked the fields, and they were seen as the heads of households. Masculinity was prized and asserted in almost every context. And the very gender parallelism marked in the documents was used to assert the power of the noble male to commune with the gods.

The Mayan approach to a symbolic understanding of gender and sexual desire was similar to that of the Nahuas. Like the Maya, the Nahuas formulated petitions which used sex as a strategy to engage in strategic inversions of power relations.[8] The Nahuas had a similar understanding of the metaphorical meaning of the flower. Further, the Nahuas used sex symbolically to feminize enemy warriors, to degrade leaders, and to understand historical events.[9] Moreover, the symbolic relationship of sexual desire with harnessing the power of the gods appears to have been understood in a similar manner by the Nahuas.[10]

Ramón Gutiérrez has shown that the Pueblos also used sexual desire as a symbolic element in their relationships with the gods. They believed that sexuality related to harnessing the power of the enemy warrior and the hunted prey. Women would engage in simulated intercourse with a dead deer or enemy warrior. Unlike the Maya, however, the Pueblos appear to have had a symbolic system of gift exchange which served to structure their social hierarchy. This gift exchange incorporated normative understandings of sexual desire.[11]

THEORIZING HYBRIDITY AND SEXUALITY

The colonialist impulses of the conquerors and of the Maya themselves were signified through the sign/symbol of the Virgin Mary Moon Goddess. She signified hybridity through the challenge of desire based on colonial power. The Maya commoners desired a stable community in order for their political, structural, and economic goals to be met. This was a displaced desire, one which both allowed Maya nobles to maintain a colonial social hierarchy and allowed Spaniards to develop a stratified economic structure. These displacements were based partly on a series of sexual symbols used as codes designed to provide a structure for cultural norms.

The Maya texts presented a hybrid mixture of ideas, such that it was clear that the discourse presented was not an unchanging preconquest analysis of sexuality, but nor was it a set of Spanish or Catholic concepts. To cultural theorist Homi Bhabha, studying English colonialism, resistance was maintained through a nonreading of colonial texts and images. As the colonized people attempted to understand colonial power, they often tried to live their lives as if nothing had changed. Finding this to be impossible, they consciously and unconsciously reinscribed the ideas of the colonizers with their own conceptions of the way things should work.[12] The Maya adapted to various outward changes, but they attempted to ignore the intended readings of those changes. When the Spaniards presented them with the Virgin Mary, the colonial Maya were able, at least at first, to see the Moon Goddess. This was not what we usually term resistance: it was not rebellion or revolution. Yet Bhabha appropriately reinscribes "resistance" to say that the acts which produced it were much more complex. The recoding of the Virgin Mary as the Moon Goddess supplied the Maya with a symbol that they could understand and respect. This was an element of resistance and hybridization.

Bhabha did not state that no changes took place in the views of the colonized. Hybridization related to the power differentials between colonizer and colonized: the colonized could not ignore the colonizer. So the Maya sign system did not remain the same. The systems of meaning came into conflict, and the Maya attempted to fill the Virgin Mary's outer shell with the guts of the Moon Goddess. But the Virgin Mary came to Yucatán with her own innards intact, and while colonialism would change her internal structure, it would not destroy her either. Serge Gruzinski has shown that Nahua culture was changed dramatically by the colonizers, for, while the Nahuas were able to place some preconquest traditions in the new framework of Catholicism, that framework was to change the meaning of the traditions that were placed within it.[13] Susan Kellogg similarly has shown that while Nahua participation in the colonial legal system in the form of petitions and criminal complaints allowed the petitioners to engage in short-term strategic inversion, these same legal maneuvers served as acculturative devices.[14] And James Lockhart has shown that the acculturation had a strong effect on Nahua society in the late colonial period.[15] The Maya cultural norms, placed in the new framework, had all of their meanings altered, and the Maya petitions too served as acculturative devices.[16] As the Moon Goddess became more like the Virgin Mary, this led to greater acceptance of the Virgin, and even if this acceptance was due only to political logic, the Virgin Mary gradually became more ingrained in Maya imaginations. As time went on the Moon Goddess faded from view. Hybridity, while a strategy of resistance, was for the Maya a strategy which led to the colonization of the mind. The Virgin Mary Moon Goddess became a sign of colonialism and a sign of colonial sexual desire.

Theories of colonialism must move toward an understanding of hybridity. There are many cultural implications to this type of analysis of the hybrid. The Virgin Mary Moon Goddess was neither Spanish nor Maya. She specifically was colonial: a combination derived from the discourse of Catholicism, incorporating virginity and chastity, and the discourse of Maya tradition, incorporating a gendered notion of blood, semen, the phallus, and creation.

For the Maya, the sexual categories of "homosexuality," "heterosexuality," and "bisexuality" would have made little sense as sexual desires were constructed somewhat differently. However, the Maya, at least during the colonial period, did find reason to identify people based on their sexual behaviors. While the sexual identities may have changed through a person's lifetime, they were coherent identities that placed individuals in history. So Nacxit Xuchit was identified with the passive role in homosexual sodomy and with sexual excess. His political actions and his ethnic identity served as an excuse for Maya historical writers to give him an identity based on their perceptions of his sexual behavior. Thus, unlike Michel Foucault, I argue that sexuality was constructed, even during the early colonial period, and even in a non-Western society, as an element which stratified power relationships. This was no *ars erotica*. Further, it is unlikely, despite Foucault's attempt to assert some sort of almost universal erotic art which preceded the modern Western era of sexuality, that there were many profound global similarities in the ways that premodern peoples organized sexual desire.[17] However, all societies appear to have related sex to political and economic structures.[18] All societies, whether labeled "pre-" or "post-" or just "modern," invested sexual desire with power.

Foucault's understanding of the relationship between sexuality and power also was problematic for me as I was writing this book. For Foucault, the confessional, as it was a method of creating discourse related to sex, signified a central method of state control.[19] For the Maya the sexual system changed not because of confession, but rather primarily because of daily contact with a variety of lower-level Hispanic peoples. It changed as the Maya understood more about Christianity, and as both the religious and secular people intermingled. Power thus was more complex in the colonial situation, and it was transmitted through the reinscription of cultural norms, a reinscription which took place on a daily basis.[20]

The power of the colonial state had many different levels to it which related closely to an understanding of sexual desire. Gilles Deleuze and Félix Guattari state that "it is indeed the story of desire and its sexual history (there is no other). But here all the parts figure as cogs and wheels in the State machine. Desire is by no means an interplay between a son, a mother, and a father. Desire institutes a libidinal investment of a State machine."[21] In the case of the colonial Maya, the desire to understand the sexual activities of the kin group was displaced onto a desire for the nobles. Commoners were told to have some desire to understand noble sex. This was a theme repeated again and again in the historical documents. After all, it was the illicit sexual activities of the nobles that most often led to the downfall of society. The nobles wrote such controls over their own sexual behavior because they knew that the way they could displace the desire to rule was by appropriating this desire onto something else. The powerful specter of the libido entered the picture, and the nobles used this to create (not repress) new sexual desires. In a state system the libido always is invested with power as it is used to distinguish castes, classes, ethnicities, races, genders, nations. Sexual desire in colonial Yucatán was not posited simply as a social construction or an essential fact, but rather as something which was developed through the power of the state in coordination with the social hierarchy and the individual psyche. In colonialism sexual desire was a central element of struggle and disruption. Desire was used to stratify but also to challenge stratification.

Jacques Lacan's notion of the importance of the phallus and the unconscious is relevant to historical studies of sexual desire, as to understand sexuality one must delve into the individual psyche and the relationship between that psyche and the larger cultural and social structures. For the colonial Maya, the individual's psyche was in a state of flux as his or her understanding of the world necessarily had to change. In the Maya ritual texts, the unconscious world of fantasy, fear, and desire was based at least partly on notions of the phallus that were different from the modern Western concept. In some of these documents, the phallus was decentered and then vanished. In many of the texts the phallus was penetrated and transsexualized. And the Maya system of phallic signification related to the floating phallus, something almost incomprehensible to a Western imagination. For the Maya sexual desire and fantasy went beyond the field delineated by Freud and the sexologists. Sexual behavior did not exist as a discernible category of sexuality but rather as an element of ritual.

A Maya ethnohistory of sexual desire teaches us about theories of sexuality and gender. Both are implicated in the construction of the state, nobility, and economy. If colonialism is seen as a series of relationships between people and institutions that renegotiate their power with each other, rather than as people acting independently of the codes and norms created by their society,[22] then one can begin to process the relationship between sexual desire and the formation of the colonial state. The connection between sexuality and the state was suggested by the attachment of the population to the ruler and the gods. Of course, this was not the only story nor the only truth. It is clear from the documents that Maya commoners did resist some stratification, that they too developed strategies to curb abuses perpetrated upon their bodies by Maya nobles and Hispanic peoples. The Maya case certainly suggests that state formation rests on, among other things, both implicit and explicit uses of sexual desire. The implicit manifestations tend to separate Self from Other in order to create ethnicity and gender and to stratify society in order to create class. But the notion of a universal system of sexual morality also stresses sameness. And class, gender, and ethnicity create sexual desire in order explicitly to maintain and/or challenge the order of the state.

Sexual desire for the Maya existed inside a colonial system of power relations. Sex was used to reify these power relations but also to challenge them. Sexual desire never was inert but rather was in a constant state of flux, and it always was used to create a discourse which related to power.

PREFACE

1. Díaz 1989: 3–24.

2. See Farriss 1984: 12–25; Means 1917; Chamberlain 1948. The conquest also was an ongoing, never completed process. See Restall 1997.

3. Roys 1943: 33–37; Farriss 1984: 125–131; Coe 1987: 155–160; Quezada 1993: 32–58; Restall 1997: 178–182.

4. Ricard (1966) rightfully asserted that the Spaniards, and in particular the mendicant friars, attempted to engage in a spiritual conquest of the indigenous peoples. However (see Lockhart 1992: 203–260), this spiritual conquest never was completed and never entirely repressed indigenous spirituality. On this point, see Farriss 1984: 286–351; Restall 1997: 148–165.

5. On the development of Maya culture through the colonial years, see Farriss 1984: 286–351; Restall 1997: 121–165. Note that Farriss sees radical change in Maya culture, while Restall emphasizes continuity. On the notion of hybridity, see Bhabha 1994: 112–122; García Canclini 1995: 206–263.

NOTES ON TRANSCRIPTION AND TRANSLATION

1. Hanks 1988.

2. See Tozzer 1977: 39–40.

3. See Tozzer 1977: 66–80.

4. Edmonson 1986: 2–7.

5. See Hanks 1988.

CHAPTER ONE

1. The Moon Goddess and the Virgin Mary do speak in an altered form. Here I am arguing that it is their engagement in speech, within the text, that presents us with lessons about the ways in which sexual desire and power related to the colonial Maya people. These figures worked with others to control the cultural matrix and thus to empower and/or disempower particular actors. See Spivak 1988 for some explication on the speech acts of "subalterns" and the relationship of those speech acts to the broader cultural codes.

2. The Maya population was reduced by 70–80 percent in two major epidemics of the sixteenth century. For an extensive demographic analysis, see Farriss 1984: 57–67. Also see Restall 1997: 3. Despite such a massive upheaval, the Maya were able to maintain many of their communities. Matthew Restall's monumental book (1997) is testament to such a survival.

3. See Patch 1993: 94–133 and passim. The Yucatec economy expanded from the middle of the seventeenth century to the early eighteenth. Despite the economic decline following this period, the economy continued to place great stress on land and labor in large parts of Yucatán.

4. See Hunt 1974; Farriss 1984: 355–388; Restall 1997: 281–292, 305–312.

5. On the Maya-language texts, see Restall 1997: 229–292. On the Spanish texts, see Farriss 1984: 399–406.

6. *Mayathan* (literally, "Maya word") referred to speeches and texts of some importance, either political or religious.

7. See Thompson 1970: 363–373.

8. The Moon Goddess is called *ix ku* in several of the pre- and postconquest texts. See CD: 16C; RB: 210–211; Roys 1965: 70; Arzápalo Marín 1987: 418. See Notes on Transcription and Translation for more information on my citational practice for Maya-language documents.

9. Thompson 1970: 363–366.

10. This tale has been extant from at least Classic times to the present. Thompson 1970: 366–373; Hammond 1982: 275–277.

11. The Dresden Codex called the sexual scenes between the Moon Goddess and the various gods marriages. This term, of course, is culturally laden. On Maya marriage and the theoretical implications of this description, see Chapter 2.

12. *Ix Chel* (lit., "She of the Rainbow") was the term most commonly used for the Moon Goddess. It was used as a parallel term to *ix ku*. This overview of the story of the Moon Goddess is a compilation of many myths derived from pre- and postconquest Mayan peoples. For more detailed Moon Goddess stories, see Chapter 5.

13. On the performativity of gender, see Butler 1990; 1993. This story used the gender of the Moon Goddess in order to assert a particular social order. It performed gender for particular purposes.

14. The Itzá was an ethnic group that conquered much of Yucatán in the Postclassic period. They were influenced culturally by central Mexico, and the Maya Books of Chilam Balam professed great hatred for the Itzá, whom they perceived as a group of outsiders.

15. Hammond 1982: 146; Schele and Freidel 1990: 377–378.

16. See particularly Quezada 1993: 19–58; McAnany 1995; Restall 1997: 87–97.

17. However, relative power is always difficult to measure. She was clearly venerated as one of the central gods in the Maya pantheon. And, despite Thompson (1970: 248–249), the Moon Goddess remained a powerful goddess throughout the colonial period. Itzamná, one of the Moon Goddess's consorts (Hofling 1989: 67; Schele and Freidel 1990: 502 n44), may have surpassed her in veneration. Hammond 1982: 277.

18. Throughout this book, I engage in what some scholars have called "deconstruction," an analysis of texts that takes particular care in understanding the ways in which the texts, and the language of the texts, are used to assert particular power relationships. Michel Foucault uses this type of analysis to discuss what he calls "discursive formations," or the creation of a set of concepts designed to place the world in a certain order (Foucault 1972: 31–39). Jacques Derrida suggests that a key to the analysis of texts is understanding how those documents form their own signs of their origins and the origin of language. He argues that the origins were placed onto paper in a particular strategic maneuver designed to connect the individual subject to a deity. The only way to understand this maneuver is to deconstruct the texts, paying close attention to the production of power and the creation of a logocentric system at the behest of metaphysical and theological senses of truth (Derrida 1974: 157–164). Hayden White describes such an analysis as finding the "context in the text" (White 1987: 185–213). While each of these scholars has an approach which is somewhat contradictory with the other two, my point here is that they represent three types of "deconstruction."

19. On Oedipal triangulation, see Lacan 1977: 141–142. The fact that the Maya before the conquest asserted some elements which related to an Oedipal complex does not mean that one can suggest that they can by analyzed with tools of traditional psychoanalysis. See Chapter 7.

20. The term "discourse" will be used throughout this book to describe a set of expressions "in which meaning constantly is negotiated and constructed." Discourse here, based on definitions by Derrida and Ernesto Laclau, emanates from any attempt within a society to signify a set of meanings. The rationale behind using such a laden (some would say jargonistic) term is that it is the simplest way of denoting a structure that includes speech and writing as well as "any kind of signifying relation." See Derrida 1974: 216–229; Laclau 1988: 252–257 (the quotes are on 254). Also see Foucault 1972: 31–39; White 1987: 185.

21. Gayatri Spivak presents another example of this phenomenon when she shows that in traditional India "widow sacrifice" and "female self-immolation" are acts of sexual violence which legitimate "rape as 'natural' and work . . . , in the long run, in the interest of unique genital possession of the female" (Spivak 1988: 303).

22. See Weeks 1977, 1985; Foucault 1978; Faderman 1981; Rubin 1984.

23. At least with regard to sex. Lévi-Strauss (1963, 1966) and other structuralists have developed the idea that it is an inherent human need to categorize and divide in order to understand. Indeed, the Maya divided things in various ways. They certainly developed ethnic and national divisions (although they did not understand ethnicity in the modern sense—cultural and not necessarily national difference, where one ethnicity can incorporate people from every class), and they did stress differences between various people based on sexual behaviors. Ramón Gutiérrez (1991: 3–36) has shown that the Pueblo of Arizona and New Mexico at the time of the Spanish conquest had

structured sexual acts, desires, fantasies, and fears based on certain taxonomic rules related to the ethnic and gendered structure of the society, but that these rules were not similar to those of the conquerors.

24. See Bleys 1995: 17–62; Trexler 1995: 38–63. Both of these groundbreaking works show ways in which colonial experience constructed ideas of an emerging European notion of sexuality.

25. Such taxonomies never have been so simple, and there has been significant slippage between categories throughout the modern period. Psychological theories regarding bisexuality abound. Many theorists have believed that one could be seduced into homosexuality and that situational homosexuality (e.g., in prison) was "normal." But as a whole the categories were created in order to be relatively absolute and to divide identities into normalcy and deviance. See Weeks 1977; Chauncey 1994.

26. The level of identity which was associated with the sinner and the "sodomite" is under debate, but it is clear that sodomites formed communities of their own kind, which certainly seems to contradict the idea that identity based on sets of sexual behaviors was invented in the nineteenth century. See Gerard and Hekma 1989; Perry 1990: 125–127; Bleys 1995: 82–99.

27. Spivak (1988: 271–280) critiques two of the pillars of postmodernism, Gilles Deleuze and Michel Foucault, for their notions of a transparency of desire. In this concept, according to Spivak, both Deleuze and Foucault promote a utopian sense of desire, interest, and agency among colonized peoples. She critiques these philosophers for placing desire within the body, making it libidinal, when Karl Marx had understood desire to be social. Indeed, Spivak argues, Foucault promotes the idea that various groups which we might term subaltern are able to speak for themselves, without the aid of the intellectual. As such, they express their own desires in a seemingly utopian fashion. While Spivak's critique of Foucault isolates a few texts from the broader body of his thought, which in places (see Foucault 1985 and 1986) includes a more flexible definition of power and its relationship with desire, her critique is well founded. Foucault's notion of alliance politics does ignore constraints on such politics among subaltern peoples. Moreover, Deleuze and Guattari (1983) critique an idealistic notion of desire, but their conceptualization of "desiring machines" promotes a desire not captured in the social mechanisms. Spivak promotes the concept that indeed desire is implicated in the powerful mechanisms of the creation of the West as Subject and its consequent erasure in the philosophies of Foucault and Deleuze (280).

28. Nietzsche 1956: 192–193; Arnold 1988: 393–396; Guha 1988: 63–66; Trexler 1995: 173–175.

29. Foucault argues in several places (e.g., 1977a: 19; 1980: 50–51, 68–70, 90–108) that power is about actions which control other actions, and that it never is inert. Nor, according to Foucault, does any individual hold power. Rather, it is displaced throughout the social field. Foucault here shows that power is not a static entity held by a monolithic bourgeoisie but rather is something which is initiated by the individual based on his or her place in the social and political hierarchies. The problem with Foucault's analysis is that, unlike a cultural Marxist approach (see Stern 1982), because power is so diffused, Foucault does not allow for resistance. It is unclear whether Foucault would have considered the acts of colonized peoples to be acts of power. Foucault says that power is only exercised over free subjects and only insofar as they are free

(1983: 221). The exact parameters of Foucault's concept of freedom are unclear, and it is plausible that Foucault would not consider colonial Maya people to have been free (or to have been "subjects" [see Klor de Alva 1992b]). Moreover, the power of the colonizer is somewhat more static than what Foucault's philosophy advocates. The colonizer asserts state power through various forms of exploitation which allow the separation of economic production from consumption. See Spivak 1988; Guha 1997: 63–72. The colonizer is able to assert power through state control, manipulation of local traditions, and cultural redeployment.

30. Power, of course, most often is institutionalized, made a part of tradition. Thus one does not necessarily consciously attempt to gain power over others. Rather, the production of ideology allows power to be maintained in the hands of one group, in this case the colonizers and their allies among the colonized. See Spivak 1988; Guha 1997: 80–95.

31. I have categorized these as sexual "acts," although certainly we would consider these to be not acts but rather fantasies. The realms of reality and fantasy are constructed phenomena. We do not know the nature of these sexual acts. Nor do we know if the Maya perceived them to be real or phantasmatic.

32. This, of course, does not mean that one cannot engage in valid and fascinating research on those norms based on the perceptions presented in these cases. See Stern 1995 for a reconstruction, based on criminal trials, of gendered culture in central Mexico.

33. Inga Clendinnen (1987), Nancy Farriss (1984), and Matthew Restall (1997) all have sought to understand this cultural matrix. Clendinnen has emphasized negotiation based on unconscious processes. Farriss instead focused on reactions to colonialist discourse itself. Restall emphasized indigenous survival. Despite these differences, however, all three showed the presence of a postconquest hybridization in which the various elements of culture and society were changed.

34. See Gutiérrez 1991; Herdt 1994a; Trexler 1995.

35. See Clendinnen 1982; Restall 1995b; 1997: 121–140. Also see Holmes 1978. On the relationship of gendered culture to the metaphorical gendering of the world and the cosmos in Native American societies, see Trexler 1995: 102–117.

36. Scholars must avoid idealistically positing utopian politics upon the Maya, just as they must avoid idealistically positing utopian sexual politics upon Native Americans as a whole. See Gutiérrez 1989; Trexler 1995.

37. See Hunt 1974; White 1987: 58–82.

38. See Nietzsche 1956: 209.

39. See Gruzinski (1993: 184–200 and passim) for a fascinating attempt at understanding the similar phenomena which occurred among the central Mexican indigenous peoples.

40. Lockhart 1991: 178–182.

41. Lockhart 1992: 5–9.

42. Depending on one's documentary focus, different conclusions may be reached. Miguel León-Portilla has concluded that despite the importance of the local city-state in Nahua society, there was a broader philosophical and ideal image of an "Aztec" nation. Lockhart sees Nahua society as made up of a group of essentially independent city-states. See Klor de Alva 1992a for a discussion of the different approaches. See

León-Portilla 1992 and Lockhart 1992 for detailed evidence supporting each approach. Philological research on the colonial Maya peoples probably has existed almost since the Maya began producing Maya-language texts in the Latin script. See Carrillo y Ancona 1887; 1890; Pío Pérez 1866–1877; 1868; Brinton 1882. Alfredo Barrera Vásquez, France Scholes, and Ralph Roys dominated much of the research into colonial era Maya-language documents in the early and mid twentieth century, while recent scholars to study this work include Victoria Bricker, Munro Edmonson, Matthew Restall, and Philip Thompson. See Roys 1931, 1939, 1940, 1943, 1957, 1965; Roys, Scholes, and Adams 1940; Scholes and Roys 1948; Barrera Vásquez and Rendón 1948; Barrera Vásquez 1957, 1965, 1984, 1991. See also Thompson 1978; Bricker 1981; Edmonson 1982a, 1982b, 1986; Restall 1995a and 1997. Also see Tedlock 1986, 1993 for two examples from Quiche; Hill 1989, 1992 for two examples from Cakchiquel. This is by no means meant to be an exhaustive list. I have only included those works which are the most relevant to this study.

43. Often both Marxists and poststructuralists define their theoretical approaches as in opposition to each other. Yet cultural Marxism certainly has much in common with some elements of poststructuralist theory. The cultural Marxist concept of hegemony and the related understanding of subaltern consciousness, both initially developed by Antonio Gramsci (1971), initiated a series of studies into "identity politics," a central field of study for poststructuralists. For applications of these connections to colonialism, see Spivak 1988; Guha 1997.

44. Gibson (1952, 1964) and Lockhart (1992: 14–58) both show that the alliances that existed in preconquest central Mexico were not only fragile but also based on the domination of many independent nations by a few.

45. Bhabha 1995: 33.

46. Bhabha 1995: 34.

47. Here defined as a system of domination whereby the people agree to be ruled by the particular ruling power. I do not mean to say that the Spanish did not attempt to establish hegemony. They did, and they partially were successful. However, force always was necessary to enforce colonial rule, and the development of hybrid forms of thought did not allow the Spaniards to let up in their use of force. See Rugeley 1996. The Indian situation was similar in this sense (see Guha 1997). Also see Stern 1982.

48. Nancy Farriss (1984: 320–351), using Church archives, shows that Maya religious values became mixed in a hybridized fashion. The colonial Maya developed interpersonal relationships that corresponded neither to preconquest Maya values nor to Spanish Catholic values. Inga Clendinnen (1987: 161–189) shows how colonialism formed new senses of guilt and identity in the Maya world. She also shows how these senses of guilt worked to challenge Spanish ideas of themselves and of the Maya. In Clendinnen's notion, the Spanish, in colonizing the Maya, created a distinct Other, which then served to reflect on values of the European Self.

49. See Butler 1993: 15 for "performative effects." See Irigaray 1985: 165 for "unrealized potentialities."

50. See Bleys 1995 for "geographies of perversion." See Spivak 1988: 297 for "white men are saving brown women from brown men." Also see DuBois and Ruiz 1990; Bhabha 1994: 73–76.

51. The exceptions to this were works which presented perceived sexual indiscre-

tions of indigenous peoples in the framework evinced by the European conquerors. No analysis was provided beyond statements of ways in which indigenous peoples' sexualities fit into contemporary Christian mores. See Guerra 1970 for an explication of these texts.

52. Gutiérrez 1991; Bleys 1995; Stern 1995; Trexler 1995. See Sigal 1998.

53. See the various essays in Murray 1995. The differences, however, particularly the notion of a homosexuality structured exclusively based on a strong dichotomy between active and passive roles, have been overstated. For example, it has been suggested that the active partner in the male homosexual act is practicing a normative bisexuality and attains significant masculinity from his sexual "conquest" of men (see Parker 1991; Lancaster 1992; Carrier 1995). This view has been challenged by Murray 1995 and Green 1999. Other scholars have also discussed similar topics. See below and Requeña 1945; Guerra 1970; Quezada 1974; Taylor 1978, 1985; Alberro 1980; López Austin 1980; Gruzinski 1982, 1985; Arrom 1985; Carrier 1985, 1995; Stone 1985, 1987; Trevisan 1986; Murray 1987, 1995; Silverblatt 1987; Strecker 1987; Paz 1988; Seed 1988; Lavrin 1989; Klein 1990; Parker 1991; Gauderman 1992; Restall and Sigal 1992.

54. See White 1978: 51–80.

55. See White 1978: 48–50; Jenkins 1991: 26.

56. See White 1978: 101–102.

57. See White 1978: 115–116.

58. I mark every place in which I develop this fictional genre. The fiction serves to explain, contextualize, and provide more material for deconstruction. See Irigaray 1985: 145–146 on this model of philosophical appropriation.

59. On translations, see Notes on Transcription and Translation.

60. Almost all of which were signed and dated by the notary. See Restall 1997: 229–250.

61. Restall 1995a: 11.

62. Restall 1995a: 11. Restall has been the first person since Roys to attempt to find all of the existing Maya-language texts. Scholars of the Maya owe him a great debt of gratitude for this.

63. There were a very small number of people, all men, in any Maya community who were literate. Although the first people to practice alphabetic writing were those of the ruling lineages, by the late eighteenth century few Maya leaders besides notaries and former notaries could write. The notaries produced all of the signed documents and likely wrote all of the anonymous ones as well. Yet the notaries were not the sole authors of most of these documents. Indeed, there was a long tradition of a corporate Maya production of documents. See Restall 1995a: 10–11.

64. See Restall 1997: 276–281; Sigal n.d.

65. Thus, unlike Stern 1995, I cannot reflect on the interpersonal social relationships of the subaltern people, and I cannot discuss the contestations of gender as a question of contingent versus absolute right.

66. The commoners cannot speak to us in any unmediated form. They represent a subaltern consciousness which can be uncovered only in relation to colonizers and Maya nobles. This consciousness was signified in the colonial documents, but it was filtered through colonial power relations. On the theoretical implications of subaltern consciousness, see Spivak 1988.

67. *Chilam Balam* is Maya for Jaguar Priest.

68. Those from Nah and Tekax substantially are irrelevant here, as they are calendrical and astrological (see Grupo Dzibil 1981).

69. Before the conquest such cultural material was preserved in hieroglyphic form. In fact, there were many similarities between the conventions of hieroglyphic writing and the writing in the Books of Chilam Balam. See Bricker 1989. Also see Alvarez 1974.

70. Based on what now is known about colonial Maya literacy, as well as the language, orthography, and some of the subject matter of the texts, the overwhelming evidence shows that the Books of Chilam Balam were written by local notaries and kept by the *cabildo*. On colonial Maya language change, see Restall 1997: 293–303. On the relationship of these changes to the Books of Chilam Balam, see Sigal n.d.

71. Roys 1965: vii.

72. Arzápalo Marín 1987: 10.

73. See Wood 1984; Lockhart 1992: 410–418; Restall 1997: 281–292.

74. See Barrera Vásquez 1965; Edmonson 1982b.

75. Restall 1997: 121–147.

76. Landa 1973; 1978.

77. See RGY; Cogolludo 1954; Villagutierre 1985. Note that I have not used criminal trials and only have used a few Inquisition documents. These documents tell many stories about sexual acts, but they are different types of stories, focused more on a social history of sexuality and less on cultural constructions of sexual desire. See Lavrin 1989; Stern 1995.

CHAPTER TWO

1. See particularly Roys 1943: 71–83; Farriss 1984: 131–139, 286–351; Clendinnen 1987: 139–160; Restall 1997: 98–165.

2. Roys 1943: 74; Thompson 1966: 262; 1970: 198–199; Hammond 1982: 277–278; Morley, Brainerd, and Sharer 1983: 468; Schele and Freidel 1990: 66.

3. Roys 1943: 73; Thompson 1970: 199.

4. For a more complete treatment of the gods, see Thompson 1970: 197–329; Hammond 1982: 273–283; Morley, Brainerd, and Sharer 1983: 468–480.

5. Roys 1943: 73–74; Thompson 1970: 209–233; Hammond 1982: 273–275; Morley, Brainerd, and Sharer 1983: 469–472; Coe 1987: 166; Schele and Freidel 1990: 366.

6. Thompson 1970: 235–241; Hammond 1982: 275; Morley, Brainerd, and Sharer 1983: 472; Coe 1987: 166; Schele and Freidel 1990: 113–115.

7. Roys 1943: 74–75; Thompson 1970: 276–280; Hammond 1982: 280; Coe 1987: 166.

8. She is, of course, discussed extensively in Chapter 5. See Thompson 1970: 241–249; Hammond 1982: 275–277; Morley, Brainerd, and Sharer 1983: 476; Schele and Freidel 1990: 366, 412–413. Many other gods were important, some perhaps more important to the people than the ones mentioned here. For example, the Chacs, the rain gods, today are the most popular, no doubt because of the effect they have on the harvest. The gods I discuss here are the ones mentioned most prominently in the documents that I use.

9. Roys 1943: 78–81; Thompson 1970: 167–175; Hammond 1982: 282–288; Coe 1987: 169–173; Schele and Freidel 1990: 200–203; Fash 1991: 92.

10. See Roys 1943: 71–75, 82; Thompson 1970: 183–184; Hammond 1982: 210–215; Clendinnen 1982: 429; Morley, Brainerd, and Sharer 1983: 484–496; Schele and Freidel 1990: 216–261; Fash 1991: 115–137; McAnany 1995: 64–110.

11. Roys 1943: 74; Thompson 1970: 191–194; Morley, Brainerd, and Sharer 1983: 492–496.

12. McAnany 1995: 66–84.

13. No doubt the body and brain's reaction to the pain and the amount of blood lost had much to do with these visions. See Roys 1943: 80–81; Thompson 1970: 174–175; Hammond 1982: 282–283; Schele and Freidel 1990: 66–71, *passim*; Fash 1991: 123–124, 128–129; McAnany 1995: 34–35.

14. McAnany 1995: 101.

15. Roys 1943: 80–82; Thompson 1970: 176–182; Hammond 1982: 282; Morley, Brainerd, and Sharer 1983: 484–487; Clendinnen 1987: 177–182; Coe 1987: 138–140; Fash 1991: 169–170; McAnany 1995: 107, 122; Stone 1995: 142.

16. See Schele 1983; Stone 1985; 1995: 146; Clendinnen 1987: 180–181.

17. Roys 1943: 75–76; Thompson 1970: 300–304; Hammond 1982: 282; Coe 1987: 166–169; Schele and Freidel 1990: 66–72.

18. Schele and Freidel 1990: 66.

19. Landa 1973: 60; 1978: 58.

20. On the five directions and sacred space, see Roys 1943: 75; Thompson 1970: 196; Tedlock 1992: 173–178; León-Portilla 1988: 56–90; Schele and Freidel 1990: 66–68.

21. Schele and Freidel 1990: 66. On the Maya sense of sanctity of time and on cyclical repetition, see Roys 1943: 84–86; Thompson 1970: 199; Hammond 1982: 289–294; Tedlock 1992: 88–131; Morley, Brainerd, and Sharer 1983: 548–563; Coe 1987: 173–176; León-Portilla 1988: 1–55; Schele and Freidel 1990: 77–84; Fash 1991: 30–31; Florescano 1994: 56–59.

22. On the male and female aspects of creation, see Roys 1965: xv; Thompson 1970: 200–201, 295–296. On gods changing genders, see Thompson 1970: 262–263, 273, 294–296, 304, 309. On the impersonation of the Moon Goddess, see Roys 1943: 78; Stone 1985; 1995: 145–146.

23. On gender parallelism in a different context, see Silverblatt 1987.

24. Thompson 1970: 172–173; Clendinnen 1982: 429.

25. Restall 1997: 149–150.

26. See Farriss 1984: 310–314. For Nahua society, see Lockhart 1992: 235–251.

27. See Bricker 1981: 103–115. It is important to note, however, as Rugeley (1996) has pointed out, that the Caste War did not mark cultural survival. The participants clearly considered themselves to be Christian, and their rebellion was not against Christianity per se. They rebelled against priests and other officials whom they believed to be abusive. They opposed the traditionally high fees that the priests charged. So they developed their own form of Christianity, a form that invoked the speaking cross. The Maya of Quintana Roo believed that they needed the Speaking Cross in order to engage in a successful revolt against Mexican authorities. The cross was worshipped in a sometimes similar way to Maya worshipping of preconquest gods: it was

given food, clothing, and other offerings. It represented the hybridity of postcolonial Yucatán. The Maya still understood the need for ritual offerings to the gods. Yet they did not conceptualize these gods in an anti-Christian or even un-Christian framework. Christianity instead was reinscribed with different meaning. See also Reed 1964; Bricker 1981: 87–118; Farriss 1984: 241–242.

28. Farriss 1984: 312–313.

29. Farriss 1984: 310.

30. Farriss 1984: 310–311; Restall 1997: 152–153.

31. Restall 1997: 154.

32. Farriss 1984: 321–323.

33. Farriss 1984: 321.

34. See, for example AA-Y's *libro de cofradía* for Hocaba.

35. Farriss 1984: 321.

36. Farriss 1984: 310–311.

37. Thompson 1970: 162–163.

38. Farriss 1984: 311.

39. Restall 1997: 153, 400 n.13.

40. Farriss 1984: 321.

41. Farriss 1984: 320–321.

42. In Nahua society, there was a similar phenomenon. The worship of the saints was perhaps the most important Christian belief to the Nahuas. They vigorously sported saints in their houses, developed community saints, and showed the representation of saints in subcommunities. Such broad effects showed that the Nahuas had strong reasons for adopting the saints. See Lockhart 1992: 235.

43. Restall 1997: 161–163.

44. Farriss 1984: 237, 335–343.

45. Farriss 1984: 265–266, 329.

46. Farriss 1984: 266–270.

47. Farriss 1984: 325–326.

48. Farriss 1984: 233–237, 266, 339–342; Restall 1997: 150–152.

49. Farriss 1984: 287–293.

50. Farriss 1984: 313.

51. Restall 1997: 162.

52. AGN-I: 69, 5, 275, 1187, 2, 59–60; AGN-BN: 21, 20, 2–8. See Restall 1997: 162–164.

53. AGN-I: 69, 5, 199. See Restall 1997: 162.

54. TI: 7r, 8r, 15r; Restall 1995a: 51, 57, 97. See Restall 1997: 158.

55. CBI: 44r–48v.

56. Farriss 1984: 322–323.

57. Restall 1997: 160.

58. See Farriss 1984: 321–326.

59. Restall 1997: 155–158.

60. Clendinnen 1982: 433.

61. Farriss 1984: 290–291.

62. Clendinnen 1987: 187–189.

63. Restall 1997: 148–149.

64. See Roys 1931, 1965; Thompson 1970: 163–164, 169; Farriss 1984: 297; Arzápalo Marín 1987.

65. Thompson 1970: 162–163; Farriss 1984: 313, 320, 323.

66. Stone 1995: 65.

67. See Clendinnen 1987: 112–115. In these goals, he did not differ from the Franciscans, including Bernardino de Sahagún, of central Mexico. Yet while Sahagún engaged in extensive work in Nahuatl, allowing his Nahua aides to "speak" on paper, Landa produced just one work in which he provided an analysis of Maya history and traditions discussed with him by his aides. Sahagún "strove to create space between the conversion process and the ethnographic project" as "he endeavored to separate description from interpretation" (Klor de Alva 1988b: 43–46). Yet Landa freely intermixed interpretation and description, and he saw his ethnographic research and writing as part of the process of religious instruction.

68. Restall 1997: 98–100.

69. Restall 1997: 100, 105–106. See also Hammond 1982: 184.

70. Maya nobles in the Classic period appear to have lived in much more elaborate houses: large, multiple-court residential compounds. See Schele and Freidel 1990: 491 n.58.

71. Farriss 1984: 178.

72. Farriss 1984: 178–179.

73. Restall 1997: 106–107.

74. Fash 1991: 77–114; McAnany 1995: 125–156.

75. McAnany 1995.

76. Although, no doubt, there were leaders who would have tried to do so if they had the power. Further, in central Mexico, the Mexica had plans to colonize the Maya area.

77. Restall 1997: 28–29, 47–50, 87–97, 117, 131–133. Farriss (1984: 137) disagrees: "The Yucatec Maya had about 250 patronymics, which may have reflected some kind of lineage division, since the Maya asserted that everyone bearing the same patronymic belonged to the same 'family.' However, we lack evidence for any functionally significant kinship organization beyond the extended family." The evidence in the Maya documents (much of which came to light after Farriss's book) seems more clear. Political ties were connected with lineage. Inheritance was constructed around the larger lineage group, not just the extended family. The Books of Chilam Balam and the Maya chronicles/titles contained much information about the lineage group.

78. Restall 1997: 117–118.

79. Farriss 1984: 133–134; Restall 1997: 99–100, 117.

80. Farriss 1984: 132–133; Restall 1997: 122–130. Restall accurately notes that the household itself was seen as male property. While women certainly dominated the household, as men very often were not there, the men were seen as household heads.

81. Clendinnen 1982: 433; Farriss 1984: 213.

82. See Farriss 1984: 169–170; Boloympoyche census in AA-Y, *Estadística: Matrícula de los vecinos e indios*, 1815.

83. Clendinnen 1982: 428; Coe 1987: 158.

84. Clendinnen 1982: 434–435; Coe 1987: 158.

85. TI: 14r–14v; Restall 1995a: 90–92; Restall 1997: 100.

86. Farriss 1984: 176–177; Restall 1997: 130+134.

87. Restall 1997: 130–131, 397–398 n. 29.

88. Farriss 1984: 189–190. Here Farriss questions how effective the prohibitions on cross-cousin marriage could have been.

89. Clendinnen 1982: 428; Farriss 1984: 134.

90. Farriss 1984: 134–135.

91. Clendinnen 1982: 428–429.

92. Clendinnen 1982: 433; Farriss 1984: 169–170.

93. See Restall 1997: 207.

94. Clendinnen 1982: 434; Farriss 1984: 173.

95. Farriss 1984: 172–174.

96. Farriss 1984: 137.

97. Clendinnen 1982: 434.

98. Roys 1943: 25; Morley, Brainerd, and Sharer 1983: 231.

99. Thompson 1970: 283. While the ceremony to which Thompson refers was from outside of Yucatán, the Books of Chilam Balam did compare the child to an ear of corn.

100. Roys 1943: 25; Morley, Brainerd, and Sharer 1983: 231–232; Coe 1987: 158.

101. Restall 1997: 41–46.

102. See AA-Y: *libro de Tepakan:* 2r.

103. Roys 1943: 25; Thompson 1970: 166; Morley, Brainerd, and Sharer 1983: 232.

104. Roys 1943: 25; Landa 1973: 44–47; 1978: 42–45; Morley, Brainerd, and Sharer 1983: 232–234. Coe (1987: 158), however, says that this rite was performed only every few years, and all children between three and twelve years old were included.

105. Roys 1943: 26. See Clendinnen 1982: 435; Morley, Brainerd, and Sharer 1983: 233–234.

106. Thompson 1970: 167–169.

107. Farriss 1984: 97–103, 335.

108. Farriss 1984: 171–172.

109. Probably a reference to Jesus, this term is particularly problematic. "*in yvmen*" could translate as "I am my father," or "I am my lord," or "my father," or "my lord." All of these translations have technical flaws, but I am convinced by my gloss of all of the songs that the proper translation is a religious one. Barrera Vásquez (1965: 54) has the same translation, but Edmonson (1982b: 184) has "Oh alas, I am my father."

110. Edmonson (1982b: 184) has "that time passed."

111. Edmonson (1982b: 184) has "when I was wet and dripping." Barrera Vásquez (1965: 54) has the same translation as mine.

112. *Dzul* translates as "stranger, foreigner." It also was used to mean "Hispanic person" during the colonial period. In this context it could mean any of these things.

113. SD: 53; Barrera Vásquez 1965: 54; Edmonson 1982b: 184.

114. Farriss 1984: 189–190.

115. Landa 1973: 31; 1978: 29.

116. Burkhart (1989: 15–25) and Gutiérrez (1991: 75–81) found the same tactic in Franciscan education in other areas.

CHAPTER THREE

1. On the preconquest era, see particularly Fash 1991: 160–172; McAnany 1995: 125–156. On notions of Self and Other after the Spanish conquest, see especially Restall 1997: 13–19. Also see Farriss 1984: 117–146; Clendinnen 1987: 190–192.

2. See Said 1978: 31–49; Spivak 1988; Gruzinski 1989a: 174–175; 1993: 14–20; Bhabha 1994: 123–138.

3. Bhabha 1994: 112–116.

4. See McAnany 1995: 131–134, 143–144; Restall 1997: 13–40.

5. Following recent gender and sexual theorists, I use "gender" and "sexualize" as verbs (where appropriate). This is done in order to stress that the gendering and sexualizing of various cultural elements is an active process. See Irigaray 1985: 133; Sedgwick 1990: 27–36; Butler 1993: 5–16.

6. Although, of course, it was more complex than this, as the Franciscan attempts at establishing a separation between colonizer and colonized showed.

7. Desire, as presented in the documents, particularly in the historical Books of Chilam Balam, was seen as something which flowed through society. On the theoretical implications of desire as a flow, see the somewhat problematic discussion in Deleuze and Guattari 1983: 36–41.

8. Desire among the modern Maya remains viewed as a powerful force. See Sullivan 1989: 109–123.

9. The question of what it means to be a person is one of the most basic cultural concepts, and this fits well with the idea of a cultural matrix. This concept is a central building block of culture. In other words, it is people attempting to define themselves that makes a culture a culture. George Marcus and Michael Fischer describe the process this way: "Perhaps the most effective focus for descriptions that would deal with the ways in which cultures most radically differ from one another is a consideration of conceptions of personhood—the grounds of human capabilities and actions, ideas about the self, and the expression of emotions" (1986: 45). They are not considering colonialism in this analysis, but the basic idea is that cultural processes create radically different ideas of what it means to be human.

10. This is not to suggest either that Maya society was simply a warrior society or that Spanish society was deeply religious. In both cases, the cultures developed symbols of what it meant to be a person. The warrior and the sinner were two of the most important symbols.

11. On the theoretical implications, see Nietzsche 1956: 209; Foucault 1977b.

12. On Maya warfare during the Postclassic period, see Thompson 1970: 302; Morley, Brainerd, and Sharer 1983: 159–167; Farriss 1984: 139–142; Quezada 1993: 21–28.

13. See, for one of many examples, Lewis 1981.

14. Webster 1976, 1977.

15. See Trexler 1995: 1–81.

16. Trexler 1995: 60–81.

17. See Stoler 1995: 36–49; Bleys 1995: 17–62; Trexler 1995: 142–155; Sigal 1998.

18. See Guerra 1970; Bleys 1995: 45–50; Trexler 1995: 64–81.

19. Bleys 1995: 45–50.

20. Trexler 1995: 47–55.

21. Bleys 1995: 36–50.

22. Bleys 1995: 63–81; Stoler 1995: 26–49.

23. Those who wrote contemporary written reports of the Spanish conquest, sometimes from a personal perspective and sometimes from the accounts of others.

24. For a general treatment of the chronicles, see Prescott 1936. For a treatment of the chronicles of Yucatán, see Means 1917; Chamberlain 1948. For a treatment of sexual behavior in the chronicles, see Guerra 1970. For references to the chronicles themselves, see below.

25. An Arawak term used by the Spanish to describe indigenous rulers.

26. Mártir de Anglería 1944: 200. See also Díaz del Castillo 1989: 50; Las Casas 1985: 482, 518.

27. Díaz del Castillo 1977: 2.

28. Lockhart and Schwartz 1983: 436.

29. Trexler 1995: 38–63.

30. Trexler 1995: 92.

31. Gutiérrez 1991: 176–206.

32. On the similar case of the Mexica, see Klein 1990; Clendinnen 1991: 87–152.

33. Edmonson 1982a: 45.

34. I have quoted a large part of this text in order to give the reader the narrative context. This text was intended to show how a Maya discourse on warfare was arranged.

35. Musen Cab was a god of bees.

36. Edmonson (1982a: 45) translates *citbil* as "remote," while I have translated the term as "father." Either translation could be correct, but Maya language testaments regularly use the term to describe the Christian God as father.

37. *Chee* can be either trees or wood.

38. From *canhel*, "serpent." This referred to the year-bearing deity, a preconquest god who reigned over the calendrical cycle. Landa (1973: 63–65; 1978: 62–63) stressed the centrality of the name *can*, also meaning "four." Edmonson (1982a: 46) takes the meaning of *can* literally, producing a translation of "the four yearbearers." Also see the explanation in DM part 1: 296.

39. Ho Sabac represented five lords or priests, probably referring to the Maya notion of five directions. The name translated literally as "Five Black Dye." Edmonson claims that this meant that "the Itzá party won. The first five (i.e., the directional) priests of the Xiu were eliminated" (1982a: 46).

40. *Inah* could have translated as either "seed" or "semen."

41. Landa (1973: 63–64; 1978: 63) declared that Bolonzacab was an important god. He was described to Landa and other Spaniards as an eternal being, and he may have been associated with (or a part of) Itzamna. See Hammond 1982: 275.

42. In other words, the Xiu were sacrificed (Edmonson 1982a: 46).

43. "Skin" comes from *madzil*, which the dictionaries translated as "skin of a fruit or grain." An alternative translation was "cuticle" (DM part 1: 509). I believe this case referred to human skin. Edmonson (1982a: 47) translates the term as "membrane."

44. The priests, connected with baptism.

45. Edmonson (1982a: 51) translates *che* (translated here as "tree") as "throne."

46. Edmonson (1982a: 51) translates *sauin* (translated here as "deceit") as "envy." Either translation is correct.

47. CBTi: 14v–15v; Edmonson 1982a: 45–54.

48. See Landa 1973: 52–53; 1978: 51.

49. Perhaps a metaphor for Christianity.

50. Edmonson suggests either adultery or sodomy, but only by implication (1982a: 52).

51. Also spelled *nacom*. A key priest who engaged in human sacrifice had the same title, but the two were different people.

52. He may have been forbidden to engage in all sexual acts, including those with men, boys, and animals. Landa did not elaborate on this point.

53. Landa 1973: 51–53; 1978: 50–51.

54. See Clendinnen 1982: 428, 439 n.12.

55. In Spain, the broken sword was a symbol of the dishonored man. Moralists preached against "effeminate soldiers." Perry 1990: 7, 127.

56. León-Portilla 1963: 76.

57. León-Portilla 1963: 77–79. Also see Garibay 1940: 112; León-Portilla 1992: 172–185. For the broader context, see Garibay 1964–1968; León-Portilla 1992.

58. Hassig 1988: 128–130. Also see León-Portilla's analysis (1963: 163–164).

59. Stone 1995: 144–146. See also Kerr 1990.

60. DM part 1: 570.

61. CBK: 27.

62. The word "judgment" was repeated, written once in Maya (*xot kin*) and once in Spanish (*juicio*).

63. Because of the context, I have translated the phrase *mehen cahob* as "inhabitants" instead of its literal translation as either "community children" or "child communities." While I at first believed this term to be a translation of "dependent communities," Matthew Restall pointed out to me that the current version is a more likely translation. Roys (1967: 162) and Edmonson (1986: 78), however, believe "little towns" and "descendant towns," respectively, to be the appropriate translation.

64. Roys (1967: 162) does not translate the term *maya cuzamil maya patan*. The use of the descriptive category Maya was relatively unique in these documents. This appears to mark the text as late, although it also may have registered a complaint that the Spaniards were treating all of the people as one group, terming them "Maya." The lack of an earlier cross-peninsula identity has been documented in Restall 1997: 13–19.

65. CBC: 100; Roys 1967: 162; Edmonson 1986: 77–78. Roys translates the last term (flower) as "carnal sin." See below.

66. As was shown in the remainder of this text. See CBC: 100; Roys 1967: 162–163; Edmonson 1986: 77–79.

67. Edmonson (1982a: 61) translates *ich* (which I have translated as "face") as "person." I believe he misses the bodily metaphor.

68. See above note. Edmonson translates this as "person on high."

69. A powerful regional leader. See Restall 1997: 64–65; Sigal 1997.

70. CBTi: 18v; Edmonson 1982a: 61.

71. For a more complete analysis of Christian sin, see Pelikan 1985.

72. Landa 1973: 47; 1978: 45.

73. See Clendinnen 1987: 108–109, 119.

74. See Clendinnen 1987: 69, 118.

75. Landa 1973: 58; 1978: 56.

76. One notes that this probably was not in fact the case, and that those who were in charge of counting time for the Maya likely altered the numbers slightly in order to allow particular rulers to continue, or in order to account for others who were killed or deposed. See Florescano 1994: 58–64.

77. Landa 1973: 58; 1978: 56.

78. Landa 1973: 53–55; 1978: 51–52.

79. See Thompson 1970: 175.

80. See Klor de Alva 1991. On the Maya and the Inquisition, see Farriss 1984: 334.

81. See Gruzinski 1989b.

82. See Burkhart 1989: 88–91.

83. See, for example, CBC: 13–15; Roys 1967: 77–79; Edmonson 1986: 107–111.

84. The *halach uinic* was certainly the closest to a god in this regard. See Chapter 9.

85. Burkhart 1989: 28–31.

86. Clendinnen 1987: 190–192.

87. Clendinnen 1987: 127.

88. Clendinnen 1987: 72–92.

89. Scholes and Adams 1938, vol. 2: 415–416; Landa 1973: 32; 1978: 30; Clendinnen 1987: 73. See also Farriss 1984: 291.

90. Scholes and Adams 1938, vol. 2: 416.

91. Scholes and Adams 1938, vol. 1: 170.

92. Scholes and Adams 1938, vol. 1: 169–171.

93. Scholes and Adams 1938, vol. 1: 24–68.

94. Scholes and Adams 1938, vol. 1: 78–82; Clendinnen 1987: 204–207.

95. See Scholes and Adams 1938, vol. 1: 171 for Landa's commentary on this topic.

96. Clendinnen 1987: 88–92.

97. See Beltrán de Santa Rosa 1895: 6.

98. See Cogolludo 1954.

99. See Chapter 2; Farriss 1984: 293–300.

100. Edmonson translates this sentence as "he will gather lust in the land."

101. CBTi: 18v; Edmonson 1982a: 62.

102. DM part 1: 392–393.

103. See Chapter 7; Roys 1965: xv; Thompson 1970: 260.

104. For more information on adultery, see Chapter 4.

105. There are many examples of sermons in a collection edited by Joaquín Ruz (1846). See particularly the sermon on penitence and conversion (vol. 1: 31–41) and that on confession (vol. 2: 51–65). Also see the correspondence describing some of these problems (vol. 1: 3–11).

106. CBTu: 2.

107. On this type of displacement, see Deleuze and Guattari 1983: 200–203.

108. See Nietzsche 1956: 199–202; Deleuze and Guattari 1983: 190–191.

109. In an 1822 catechism, Ruz stated that the Maya understood many of the concepts related to sin and that they could answer the questions correctly (Ruz 1822: 121–124).

110. This extends to issues such as property, land tenure, gender, and sexual desire. See Clendinnen 1987: 190–192; Kellogg 1995: 213–219.

CHAPTER FOUR

1. See Stern 1982: 135–137 and Kellogg 1995: 4 for similar points regarding Andean and Nahua peoples.

2. Restall (1997: 331) translates *tutuchci u cepob,* "stiff penises," as "erections." Although Restall's interpretation probably is correct, throughout this petition I have used literal translations.

3. Restall (1997: 331) translates *ueyob* as "girl friends."

4. Restall (1997: 331) interprets *macehual* as "Maya." As he points out earlier in his book, *macehual* ("commoner") had come to stand for the entire Maya community by the end of the colonial period.

5. AGN-I: 1187, 2, 59–62. I am grateful to Kevin Terraciano for finding this document in an AGN catalog and passing it on to Matthew Restall. It was initially translated by Restall, Lockhart, and Marta Hunt, but I am responsible for the above version. Another version of the transcribed and translated document can be found in Restall 1997: 330–331.

6. Restall 1997: 141–147 has significant overlap with the first part of this chapter. The two analyses actually complement each other (and I encourage the reader to consult Restall's book), although the emphases are different since Restall is discussing Maya society more generally, while I am focusing on sexual desire.

7. As do the documents surrounding this case in the Inquisition files. I surmised that the document was related to conflicts within the Church before I knew of the other documents. Now I can say that the petition related to conflicts between one Franciscan friar and these four priests. I have ascertained this through conversations with Matthew Restall, and I thank him for this information.

8. DM part 1: 782.

9. Several translations for sexual intercourse apparently existed in Maya, but this author chose none of those represented in the dictionaries. DM part 2: 78.

10. See Sullivan 1989: 176.

11. Nietzsche 1956: 235.

12. DM part 1: 921. We can see that sexual matters may have been confused in translation as, without context, we might have seen *uey* as a nonsexual reference from one person to another.

13. The women had sinned and required confession, another implicit request of the petition. See Gruzinski 1989b: 100–101.

14. DM part 1: 42–43.

15. From *ix cacbach,* translated as *puta.* DM part 1: 284.

16. Pencuyut may have translated as the "fornicating coyote," "the lustful coyote," or the "sodomizing coyote." The coyote could have represented either Spaniards or

Nahuas in Maya thought of the time. Such a community does exist (it is in the Mani region), but the choice of it may have represented a particular strategy designed to denigrate this woman and the priests.

17. See Restall 1997: 13–19.

18. Indeed, here one runs up against one of the problems of gender binarism. It seems plausible that women in the community could have been seen as insiders. The women in the petition clearly were constructed as outsiders. I cannot then essentialize the category "woman" cross-culturally, but rather must comprehend the differentiations that any particular culture has developed. Here Maya constructions of ethnicity and nation, based on the individual community, were central to understanding the differentiation between insiders and outsiders.

19. AGN-I: 1187, 2, 6–161. Matthew Restall, personal communication with the author.

20. Anderson, Berdan, and Lockhart 1976: 166–173; Restall 1997: 251–266. While it seems likely, based on the large number of such complaints, that these statements had a basis in fact, here it is more important to note the nature of the petitions.

21. Restall 1997: 160–165.

22. Phelan 1970: 44–45.

23. Phelan 1970: 69–70; Klor de Alva 1988b: 83–88.

24. Landa 1973: 26–28, 29–31; 1978: 24–26, 27–29; Farriss 1984: 87, 162. An *encomendero* was the recipient of an *encomienda*, a grant of indigenous labor and tribute. He or she was a member of the local economic elite.

25. Farriss 1984: 92.

26. See Phelan 1970: 44–45; Gutiérrez 1991: 67.

27. Gutiérrez 1991: 70.

28. Gutiérrez 1991: 70.

29. Gutiérrez 1991: 67.

30. Quoted in Gutiérrez 1991: 67–68.

31. See CD: 23C; RB: 42–44; Roys 1965: 16–17; Arzápalo Marín 1987: 298–300.

32. AGN-I: 1187, 2, 62.

33. See also Stern 1982: 115–119; Kellogg 1995: 214–215.

34. See Farriss 1984: 320–351.

35. See Kellogg 1995: 4.

36. See Spivak 1988; Gruzinski 1993: 184–200; Bhabha 1994: 193; Guha 1997: 100–108.

37. See Stern 1982; Spalding 1984 on the Andes; Spivak 1987 on India; Lockhart 1992; Kellogg 1995 on the Nahuas of central Mexico; Terraciano 1994; Stern 1995 on the Mixtec of Oaxaca; Stoler 1995 on the Dutch East Indies.

38. Anderson, Berdan, and Lockhart 1976: 167–169. Translation by Anderson, Berdan, and Lockhart.

39. Probably representing the *alcalde* (councilman) who signed the petition, Juan Vicente. It also was signed by Miguel López. Anderson, Berdan, and Lockhart 1976: 167, 173.

40. Anderson, Berdan, and Lockhart 1976: 171–173. Translation by Anderson, Berdan, and Lockhart.

41. I draw here from Restall. He compares the same documents. See Restall 1997: 262–263.

42. This over-literal translation comes from my desire to point to the parallel structure involved in the term "to give," *dzaic*.

43. *U pakic u keban*, from *pak keban*, was translated in the colonial dictionaries as "fornicate" (DM part 1: 626). This term appears to have come from *pak*, "sow," and *keban*, "sin." Restall (1997: 264) translates the term as "recompense him with their sins."

44. Note the use of *gobernador* instead of the Maya term, *batab*. The Maya alternated uses of the two terms.

45. AGN-I: 69, 5, 275–276; Restall 1997: 263–264.

46. In almost all Maya-language petitions, the bulk of the text was comprised of reverential phrases directed toward the various Spanish officials, including a strong expression of faith in the ability of the addressee to do what was requested of him. In this case the petitioners stated that they knew that Inquisition commissioner fray Hernando de Sopuerta was dedicated to the community and would come to their aid.

47. Although several of the communities recanted. Restall 1997: 265.

48. See Stern 1995: 228–251.

49. Morley, Brainerd, and Sharer 1983: 243.

50. RB: 44–46; Roys 1965: 17–18; Arzápalo Marín 1987: 299–301.

51. In this, they were similar to the Pueblo peoples. See Gutiérrez 1991: 64–72.

52. See Farriss 1984: 90–93.

53. James Lockhart, personal communication with the author.

54. Hunt 1974; Farriss 1984: 96–114.

55. Farriss 1984: 190.

56. For the importance of engaging in discourse over changing bodily and sexual definitions, see especially Foucault 1986: 39–68. Also see Foucault 1978 and 1985; Butler 1990; Laqueur 1990.

57. The same could be said of the Nahuas of central Mexico. See Lockhart 1992: 442–446.

58. Dover 1978; Boswell 1980; Foucault 1985: 185–225; Keuls 1985: 274–299.

59. On the relationship of bodily terminology to gender, sexual desire, and political power in colonial Maya society, see Sigal 1999.

60. DM part 1: 88.

61. RB: 122; Roys 1965: 42; Arzápalo Marín 1987: 357–358. Also see Chapter 9.

62. DM part 1: 686–687.

63. Note that I could translate *ah penob* as "carnal sinners, lustful sinners" or even "villains." (DM part 1: 687). I have used "fornicators" to establish consistency and because I believe this to be the most accurate translation in the context.

64. Other elements of the petition presented problems of translation and interpretation. I also find that Fabiana Gómez provided Maldonado with her vagina. This may or may not have suggested some form of prostitution. The colonial dictionaries translated the Maya word *och* as "provide" and suggested that it carried the image of providing food for someone for his or her sustenance. Here the author felt comfortable using the word for a woman providing her vagina to a man, perhaps implying some relationship between a woman serving a man his food and a woman providing sex-

ual service for a man. Nonetheless, any analysis of the term clearly demands further context.

65. See Nietzsche 1956: 235; Foucault 1977b.

66. See also Burkhart 1989: 150–159.

67. Landa 1973: 53; 1978: 51–52.

68. Landa 1973: 37–38; 1978: 35.

69. Landa 1973: 56–57; 1978: 54–55.

70. Landa 1973: 42–43; 1978: 41.

71. Such a criticism of the Spanish population fit into an extensive genre whereby the Franciscans (and even more so the Dominicans and Jesuits) strongly criticized Hispanic morality in general. They then asserted the relative "innocence" of the Indians. They were attempting to get the Spaniards to give the various Church orders more control over the indigenous populations.

72. The crown asked local Spanish officials to write about regional politics, economics, and history, including a description of indigenous laws and customs.

73. RGY I: 164.

74. For example, RGY I: 72–74, 164, 182, 200.

75. For example, RGY I: 165, 200.

76. See Jakeman 1952.

77. Jakeman 1952: 38–39.

78. RGY I: 165.

79. RGY I: 72–73, 124, 183, 200, 216, 270, 306, 363, 377–378; RGY II: 139.

80. Cogolludo 1954 I: 329.

81. Cogolludo 1954 I: 331.

82. Cogolludo 1954 [1688] I: 331–335.

83. CBTi: 18v; Edmonson 1982a: 62.

84. Edmonson translates this phrase as "there was lust." I can translate *pen* as lust, but the dictionaries gave *cech* several meanings, including "you who are" and many meanings related to deception. Several dictionaries translated the entire phrase *pen cech* as "excessive" or "abundant."

85. DM part 1: 279.

86. See Chapter 3.

87. From *ich can si ho*. Edmonson (1982a: 62) translates the metaphor as "Heaven Born Mérida."

88. CBTi: 18v-19r; Edmonson 1982a: 62–63.

89. *Y al ix kuk y al ix yaxum* Edmonson (1982a: 62) translates as "Of the quetzal born, of the blue bird born," meaning essentially the same thing as my interpretation. Edmonson, not writing about gender, does not emphasize that the quetzal and the blue bird were represented as female.

90. This was a sexual reference.

91. Excessive, *pencech*, was written as *pentacech*.

92. CBK: 27.

93. "*Pen cech cal pach banban coil coil than*" CBK: 27.

94. This sense of desire also is connected by the modern Maya to a specifically sexual desire. Sullivan 1989: 110.

95. CBTi: 16r; Edmonson 1982a: 20.

96. The last pre-Spanish attempt at unifying Yucatán under one rulership. Note that the leadership of Mayapán fell significantly before the Spanish conquest. Here the two events were conflated.

97. There were many other examples of the same type of lust, suggesting a desire for sex and destruction. See CBC: 20, 88, 91, 95, 100; Roys 1967: 83, 149, 153, 157, 162; Edmonson 1986: 148, 119, 142, 213, 78.

98. Such a concept of desire is familiar to the contemporary Yucatecan Maya people. Anthropologist Paul Sullivan notes that leaders of the Maya of Quintana Roo in the 1930s, in a lengthy exchange of correspondence with Sylvanus Morley, stress to him their desire and love of him. They engage this loaded terminology in an effort to secure an alliance with Morley in their struggles with Mexican authorities. The representation of desire and love (both in their own words and those of Morley) stood as a strategy which the Maya leaders sought to exploit for particular gains at a time when they saw war as imminent (Sullivan 1989: 109–112). The Maya, of course, did not see their relationship with Morley as a sexual one, and the language used was part of a tradition of honorific address used in an asymmetric genre of speech and writing.

99. See McAnany 1995: 111–124.

100. See Restall 1997: 3. Farriss 1984: 57–67 makes a much more detailed and complex argument about demography. It is plausible that significantly less than 90 percent of the population died off, but, whatever the numbers, they were large enough to have an effect on Maya concerns with lineage.

101. Note that the preconquest Maya also found lineage to be vital. See McAnany 1995.

102. CBC: 68; Roys 1967: 127; Edmonson 1986: 197. This was intended as a riddle. There was some confusion as to whether she had a "bell" or a "collar." Roys does not translate the last sentence.

103. Farriss 1984: 247–250.

104. The petition was dated 1569, but the date appears to have been added recently. Nonetheless, the language and orthography of the petition betray a sixteenth-century origin. Restall 1995b also discusses this case extensively.

105. Restall (1997: 134, 144) translates *u kati ti lolob* as "he wished it in vain."

106. DT: 33; Restall 1997: 134–135, 144.

107. DM part 1: 392, 623–626.

108. Rape, connected with lust and destruction, was in CBC: 95; Roys 1967: 157; Edmonson 1982a: 213.

109. The Maya had some success in using sex to gain power in this way. In many senses, this Maya notion of power appears to contradict Foucault's sense of power as a monolithic entity that cannot be challenged through sexual expression. See Foucault 1978: 3–13; 1980: 183–193.

110. Nietzsche 1956: 193; Deleuze and Guattari 1983: 198–200.

111. Farriss 1984: 192–198.

112. See Bhabha 1995.

CHAPTER FIVE

1. See Farriss 1984: 147–223; Restall 1997: 87–120.

2. Duality was an extremely important concept in Mesoamerican religion and society in general. These concepts have been discussed extensively elsewhere, and I will comment on them below. On Maya religion see Thompson 1966: 262–270; Hammond 1982: 273–288; Farriss 1984: 293–300; Schele and Freidel 1990: 64–95; Fash 1991: 120–124. On Nahua religion and society, see Clendinnen 1991: 236–263; Lockhart 1992: 15–28 and 206–209; Gruzinski 1993: 146–183.

3. Thompson 1966: 262; Schele and Freidel 1990: 66–67.

4. See CD: 16–23.

5. Thompson 1939; 1966: 262–263; 1970: 241–249; 1972: 47–52.

6. Thompson 1972: 47.

7. See SD: 83; Barrera Vásquez 1965: 84–85; Edmonson 1982b: 177–179.

8. Thompson 1970: 242; Schele and Freidel 1990: 366, 502 n. 44.

9. Schele and Freidel 1990: 412–413.

10. Although one may suggest that Itzamna was the head of this patriline, he played a distant role as the creator god. His figure never was linguistically associated with the head of the patriline across Yucatán. However, Itzamna clearly was seen after the conquest as still heading a male line of gods, and thus as having significant power. See RB: 150; Roys 1965: 51; Arzápalo Marín 1987: 378.

11. See Hammond 1982: 275–277.

12. Hofling 1989: 67, 68, 70. From CD: 16–17B, 21B, 21–22C (Almanacs 39, 44, and 51). The transcription and translation are Hofling's. Note that, as he uses modern orthography, his method of transcription is different from mine.

13. This is not to suggest that the preconquest Maya had a gender parallelism equivalent to the Andean, Mixtec, Nahua, and Zapotec cases. As will be shown in the next chapter, political power was heavily skewed toward a male line, probably more so than in the other four societies. However, in Maya society there existed a gender parallelism in the religious and ritual structures, where gods, blood, and ceremonies could all be classified as structures with complementary gender roles. On the Andes, see Silverblatt 1987. On the Mixtec, see Terraciano 1994: 392–427. On the Nahuas, see Kellogg 1995: 85–120. For comparative work on the Mixtec, Nahuas, and Zapotecs, see Stern 1995; Sousa 1998. Stern, however, points out that late colonial gender parallelism was not well marked in Morelos (a Nahua and Hispanic region) and was mixed with patriarchy in Oaxaca (a Mixtec and Zapotec region).

14. CD: 16C.

15. Thompson 1972: 57.

16. Thompson 1972: 57.

17. CBN: 39; EBM: 207–209; RB: 4–14.

18. CD: 13B.

19. CD: 21C.

20. Stone (1985: 23) maintains that these pictures clearly were intended to be sexual when one considers the fact that, to Maya women, virtually any engagement in physical contact with men was seen as sexual. These pictures were intended to represent creation and reproduction.

21. CD: 17C, 18C.

22. See, for example, CD: 16B, 16C.

23. Thompson 1970: 366–373; 1972: 47.

24. Thompson's insistence that the Moon Goddess was punished for her transgressions is based in a strictly Western reading of the texts. The Moon Goddess's power was very strong throughout the Classic and Postclassic periods. By having sexual intercourse with the various male gods, the Moon Goddess was pictured as the ultimate mother. She was the head of the matrilineal group. Nobles needed the Moon Goddess in order to prove their nobility. The Moon Goddess symbolically represented a variety of extremely powerful attributes. Yet, given Maya notions of excess, she was seen as a goddess who was at once both excessive and powerful. While contemporary mythology may engage in extensive condemnations of the Moon Goddess, one may ask if that contemporary mythology has not been influenced by the Virgin/Whore dichotomy introduced by the Spaniards.

25. CD: 22C.

26. Unfortunately, the accompanying hieroglyphic text has yet to be deciphered. See Hofling 1989: 70.

27. See particularly Farriss's description of the relationship between Kukulcan and Jesus (Farriss 1984: 303–306).

28. RB: 65; Roys 1965: 23; Arzápalo Marín 1987: 316. It is important to note that the Ritual of the Bacabs is a very complex text to translate. I am not convinced that I currently have the methodology for a fully accurate translation, but in each case I am convinced that the meaning of the text as a whole comes across in my translations. I have, of course, used all the previous translations available to me. I will alert the reader to any discrepancies in translation which would have an effect on my analysis of the text. In general, my translations are closer to those of Ramón Arzápalo Marín, who was able to interpret more of the obscure language. Ralph Roys, usually so reliable, did not render this document into a form that is entirely valid and understandable. Roys translated the first portion of this text, "four days he ruffles the red wooden trough; four days he ruffles the red lake."

29. Roys (1965: 70) and Arzápalo Marín (1987: 418) both translate these terms for birds as relating to prophecies.

30. Unknown types of birds.

31. *Aban* is literally "weed" in modern Maya. I have found no applicable definition in the older dictionaries.

32. A type of tree. This literally translated as "bone cure."

33. Literally, "tortoise bone."

34. Literally, "bone tree."

35. Roys (1965: 70) mistook the pronoun and translated this term as "his symbol." Symbol and sign were alternative translations for this term.

36. Roys (1965: 70) and Arzápalo Marín (1987: 418) translate *kax* as vine. I believe forest to be the better translation as the moon traditionally had been associated with night and the cover of forest. Roys realizes that this is a pun on the term.

37. *Oxlahun ytzen*, literally "I am the thirteen resin," comes to mean holy shaman in modern Maya. The number thirteen was a sacred number (representing the number of gods in the heavens), and in many cases it could signify the sanctity of a particu-

lar act or actor. The *ytz* comes to mean "sorcerer" in modern Maya (DM part 1: 272), and it seems likely that the colonial peoples believed something similar. Roys (1965: 70) translates the term as "supreme resin," and Arzápalo Marín (1987: 418) translates it as "thirteen sprinklings [of water]."

38. RB: 210–211; Roys 1965: 70; Arzápalo Marín 1987: 418–419.

39. See CBC: 42; Roys 1967: 98; Edmonson 1986: 152.

40. Farriss 1984: 287–314.

41. See Gutiérrez 1991: 46–94.

42. Lockhart and Schwartz 1983: 116–118; Lockhart 1992: 203–260.

43. One of the exceptions was an obscure (and late colonial) citation of the Christian God as the creator of Maya gods. RB: 215; Arzápalo Marín 1987: 421–422. Roys does not translate these late colonial texts.

44. All of these were written in a different hand than the rest of the texts. RB: 20, 63, 237; Roys 1965: 162, 164 (Roys misidentifies the terms "Jesus, Mary"); Arzápalo Marín 1987: 279, 315, 437.

45. "*Tu kaba Dios yumbil y Dios mehenbil y Dios espiritu santo . . .*" RB: 15, 211, 221; Roys 1965: 6, 70; Arzápalo Marín 1987: 276, 419, 427.

46. These "x"s probably were stylistic devices. I have left them untranslated.

47. Roys speculates that this signified a constellation.

48. "Virgin" came from *suyi*. Virgin in Maya was *suhuy* (see below). The relevant translations of *suy* related either to natural whirlpools or to some sense of sacrifice (DM part 1: 747). These do not appear to fit with the context as well as the translation of *suhuy*. "Virginity" is the translation Arzápalo Marín (1987: 415) uses. However, I am unsure of its accuracy. Roys (1965: 68) translates *suyi* as "all around."

49. RB: 205–206; Roys 1965: 68; Arzápalo Marín 1987: 414–415.

50. CBTi: 14v–15v.

51. RB: 194–206; Roys 1965: 65–68; Arzápalo Marín 1987: 408–415.

52. The only mention of virginity in this part of the text was as a place where the semen was hidden (a very provocative suggestion, but, since that particular translation is rather tentative, I will not comment on the significance any further).

53. See Kellogg 1995: 114–116.

54. Roys (1967: 150) translates *u kakal na Diosi u xiuil xitel* (which I translate as "the fire house of God, erecting and decorating") as "the public house of God, the widely extended."

55. Roys (1967: 150) translates this phrase interpretatively as "fair complexioned boy," believing this to be a reference to Jesus.

56. CBC: 89; Roys 1967: 150; Edmonson 1986: 128–129.

57. A diagram of concentric circles with the communities placed in their appropriate spots accompanied this text.

58. Roys (1967: 126) did not translate *u uil* (which I have translated as "of the moon"). Edmonson (1986: 195) translates the term as "the moonphase of the moon." It is clear that it referred to the moon.

59. CBC: 67; Roys 1967: 126; Edmonson 1986: 195–196.

60. See Fash 1991: 156–157. It also related to postconquest land markings. See Restall 1997: 189–193.

61. Literally, as in Barrera Vásquez (1965: 38) and Edmonson (1982b: 180), "core of their breasts."

62. Literally, "because, you understand, it is for the removal of your female virginity to the one who loves."

63. Ah Kulel referred to a governmental official, perhaps a lieutenant of the *batab*, perhaps a courtesan. See Fash 1991: 160–165; McAnany 1995: 152.

64. Edmonson (1982b: 180) translates *ah tan caan che* as a name, "Half Tall Tree."

65. Edmonson (1982b: 180) translates a *u* in this phrase as "moon," giving him the translation "ladyship of the moon and blossoms." I, like Barrera Vásquez (1965: 38), believe the *u* to have been a possessive marker.

66. As Barrera Vásquez (1965: 38) shows, this appears to have come from *lokba-yen*, "maiden." The *k* was missing. I find no other relevant translations of *loob ayen*. Edmonson (1982b: 180) translates the phrase as "intercessor." While this would be a neat fit in the text, we would have to believe that the term came from some form of *booy*.

67. Edmonson (1982b: 180) guesses that the "M" will spell out María or Mary.

68. *Zuhuy Kaak* may have referred to a particular god (Barrera Vásquez 1965: 39). The *u*, "moon," had no grammatical markers on it.

69. From *Ix Kanleox*, a god of maize whose name literally translated as "she of the precious leaf bud" (Barrera Vásquez 1965: 39).

70. From *ttootmuch*. *Ttoot* had to do with the growth of plants. *Much* was "frog." The translation "rain frog" comes from Barrera Vásquez 1965: 39 (in a footnote); Edmonson 1982b: 181.

71. *Peet ne*, from *peten*, "country." Edmonson (1982b: 181) translates this as "forests."

72. *Chak me*, from *chakan*, "field."

73. Perhaps a play on words, *dzitpich* could mean "split tree," thus making it a synonym for Dzitbalché. Dzitilpich could be an alternative name for the same community, or perhaps a subgroup of Dzitbalché.

74. SD: 37; Barrera Vásquez 1965: 38–39; Edmonson 1982b: 179–181.

75. Beverley 1992: 221.

76. Brading 1991: 658–659.

77. Seed 1988; Lavrin 1989; Gutiérrez 1991.

78. Mary was first represented only based on the context, as Maya writing often referred to her as *cichpan suhuy*, "beautiful virgin."

79. Edmonson (1982b: 182) translates *hopbal* (which Barrera Vásquez and I translate as "light up") as "its start." He believes that a glottal stop on the *p* is missing.

80. Barrera Vásquez (1965: 50) writes the pronoun "we." He, as will be seen, is correct, but there was no first-person plural pronoun in the Maya text. Edmonson (1982b: 182) writes "one."

81. According to Barrera Vásquez (1965: 51), the *chukum* is a particular type of plant native to Yucatán. Edmonson (1982b: 182) translates the term as "first flower."

82. *Lol v dzvl* appears to have referred to the flower *udzubpek*, known as the dog jasmine flower (Barrera Vásquez 1965: 51; Edmonson 1982b: 182). The word *dzul* also translated as "foreigner" or "Spaniard."

83. . . . *milah* could have referred to any type of blossom. Edmonson (1982b: 182) believes that it may refer to the "tangleflower."

84. *Hiib took* referred to a particular type of stone. *Hiib* appears to have referred to some type of crystallized formation. *Took* referred to flint or the hardness of a particular element. Edmonson (1982b: 182) translates this as "quartz and flint."

85. *Lvch* may have been a vase used in the process of spinning cotton.

86. *Peedzilil*, "weight," is unclear in this context. Barrera Vásquez (1965: 52) suggests that it may refer to some sort of artisan's instrument.

87. *Xoot* appears to have come from *xoth*, which referred to the actual act of spinning the cotton. Edmonson (1982b: 183) translates this as "fresh conch," but he questions his translation.

88. *Niicte ha*, literally "flower water."

89. *Kiliiz*, literally translated as "old man." The context suggested that this was a reference to antiquity or the humanity of the old days.

90. *Bvvdz ek*, literally "smoking star," signified a comet. The Motul Dictionary referred to a comet which appeared in 1577.

91. SD: 49; Barrera Vásquez 1965: 50–52; Edmonson 1982b: 181–183.

92. Both Barrera Vásquez (1965: 51) and Edmonson (1982b: 181) agree that this song referred to an old ceremony related to group sexual activity.

93. DM part 1: 570.

94. It also could be a metaphor for warfare, human sacrifice, and piercing. See Chapter 3.

95. See Barrera Vásquez 1965: 51; Edmonson 1982b: 181.

96. McAnany 1991: 64–74.

97. The comet was a smoking star in the Maya and Nahuatl languages, relating it to the brilliance of the moon.

98. See Gruzinski 1993: 184–200; Bhabha 1994: 251–252. This is not to say that there were not significant changes. The concepts were altered and placed in a new framework which radically changed their meanings.

99. Thompson 1970: 243.

100. Edmonson (1986: 146) translates *paat* (which Roys and I translate as "declare") as "expect."

101. Edmonson (1986: 146) translates *cicuntab* (which I translate as "happiness") as "announce."

102. CBC: 18; Roys 1967: 82; Edmonson 1986: 145–146.

103. See Farriss 1984: 306; Schele and Freidel 1990: 66–70; McAnany 1995.

104. Edmonson (1986: 211) translates *auat* (which Roys and I have translated as "cry out") as "argue." He thus develops a different set of sentences, the last one beginning, "It was argued that what was heard . . ."

105. CBC: 94; Roys 1967: 155–156; Edmonson 1986: 211.

106. Roys 1967: 155.

107. Edmonson (1982b: 178) has "loved."

108. Edmonson (1982b: 178) has "wildflowers."

109. Barrera Vásquez (1965: 84) has "pure and white."

110. *Zvhvy* translated as "virgin, maiden" (see below). This may have referred to the clothes or to the woman. Edmonson (1982b: 178) has "Oh virgin spirit."

111. SD: 83; Barrera Vásquez 1965: 84–85; Edmonson 1982b: 177–179.

112. DM part 1: 883.

113. The concept of virginity played a role in the conquest of Andean and Nahua societies as well. In Andean society at the time of the conquest, women's virginity was used to allow the Inca leaders to gain some connection with people from other Andean societies in the empire. The Incas would take a few young noblewomen out of their communities in order to serve the Inca king and the Cuzco elite. An agent of the Inca would go to the various communities in the empire in order to select these women. The young girls he chose would then fill the ranks of a community of women designed to be connected to the gods. Some of them eventually became wives for the high Inca nobility. Others were to remain celibate for their entire lives (Silverblatt 1987: 82; Mac-Cormack 1991: 65–66). This institution could cement alliances between Cuzco and other communities in the empire. The virginity of these women thus was used for a particularly political end. This strategy of virginity was even clearer when one considers that the Andean people had no strict controls over women's sexual behavior in general. The chronicles said that premarital sex was very commonly accepted among the people of the Andes (Silverblatt 1987: 102). This contrast existed because the Incas had little political reason to control the sexual behavior of women outside of the institution mentioned above. Among the Nahuas of central Mexico, there was a significantly different cultural appropriation of virginity. Although the Nahuas do not appear to have approved of lifelong celibacy, Alfredo López Austin claims that women had to be virgins at the time of marriage or they would face an unenviable fate. A woman's virginity was compared to a "jewel." In metaphorical terms, her virginity was considered her prized possession. When she was married, her virginity became public knowledge. If she was not a virgin, the feast which took place on the sixth day after the wedding would be served with broken vessels. If she was a virgin, the vessels would be unbroken. Such a ceremony (if it really was enacted) would serve as a major tool to keep women from giving up their virginity (López Austin 1980 vol. 1: 334–335, 345).

114. DM part 1: 333, 738.

115. Of course, I can metaphorically extend this into the construct of *Marianismo*, stating that women must ideally be both mothers and virgins. However, this construction does not appear to have taken hold in Mexico as a general phenomenon until the nineteenth century.

116. *Ueyul al* I have translated as child of a mistress. The colonial dictionaries translated this term as "bastard child from the mother" (DM part 1: 921). Arzápalo Marín (1987: 409) translates the term as "*femenina oculta.*" While his context is correct, I can find no justification for the specific translation. Roys (1965: 65) translates the entire phrase, *in heɔcunt yokol ueyul al*, as "over the *ueyulal.*"

117. Perhaps some unknown plant. Otherwise this phrase translated as "the thin virgin."

118. RB: 195–196; Roys 1965: 65–66; Arzápalo Marín 1987: 409.

119. RB: 157–160; Roys 1965: 53–54; Arzápalo Marín 1987: 383–385.

120. Thompson 1966: 282.

121. RB: 161; Roys 1965: 54; Arzápalo Marín 1987: 385. Here, and in all the texts where I discuss the "vagina's mother" and the "penis," Roys's translation differs from mine and Arzápalo Marín's. Roys does not translate the terminology but instead refers

to it as "curses." While the implication is correct, the specific terminology warrants analysis. Roys also does not interpret the double entendres in many parts of this text. Roys translates the above narrative as "Curses on your sting. The virgin needle would be your strength, which you took to enter into your sting. Suhuy-kak ("virgin fire" [goddess]) would be your strength . . ." Arzápalo Marín's translation is consistent with mine. I believe my translation to be justified. Roys's "curses" actually translate as "You! The vagina's mother." His "on your sting" also is a double entendre and means "on / with your penis." The translation of the term *chich* depends on vowel length. If the vowel is pronounced as a short vowel, this translates as "grandmother." With a long vowel, the word would translate as "strength." Unfortunately, the text does not refer to vowel length, but given the context of the other texts in this document, "grandmother" fits best.

122. The one significant difference between Arzápalo Marín's translation and my own is that he translates *suhuy* as "sacred." As I am arguing here, his translation is in many ways more valid than mine, but mine is valid (at least for the postconquest Maya) and necessary here for the sake of clarity.

123. Thompson 1939: 137.

124. See Farriss 1984: 131–146; Gosner 1992.

125. No doubt many nobles did believe that society would cease to function and all would be lost.

126. However, see Herdt 1994a: 255–260.

127. Of course, this would have been the same for any group with sexual goddesses. When they were conquered and Christianized, they would begin to see Mary as a sexual goddess. Moreover, her complex relationships with God, the Holy Ghost, and Joseph would seem to assert that she had to be promiscuous.

128. White 1978: 91–94.

CHAPTER SIX

1. See McAnany 1995: 126–131; Restall 1997: 90–92.

2. See Sigal 1999.

3. Early archaeologists had thought that this was a practice introduced by the Toltecs at Chichén Itzá, but it is now clear that sacrifice was a traditional Maya event. See Hammond 1982: 282; Fash 1991: 130; McAnany 1995: 122.

4. Hammond 1982: 282; Coe 1987: 170–171; Fash 1991: 129.

5. McAnany 1991: 122.

6. Roys 1943: 27.

7. Schele and Freidel 1990: 189–191; Fash 1991: 149.

8. McAnany 1995: 107.

9. Coe 1987: 171; McAnany 1995: 61–63.

10. See Clendinnen 1987: 72–92.

11. Farriss 1984: 290–291.

12. Farriss 1984: 340.

13. SD: 21; Barrera Vásquez 1965: 22–23; Edmonson 1982b: 202. The text for that song stated that the entire book was written in 1440, before the "white people" arrived. However, as the other songs have shown, that would have been impossible. The date

may have referred specifically to the origins of this particular song, it may have been an attempt to assert that the songs contained ancient wisdom, or it simply may have been a mistake.

14. Barrera Vásquez 1965: 14.

15. *Kolom che* translated literally as either "broken tree" or "clefted stick."

16. Edmonson (1982b: 203) translates these stanzas as "Oh lads! Stout fellows! Men! Shield bearers!"

17. Literally, "that they enter in the middle." I agree with Edmonson (1982b: 203) that this is a call to come forward.

18. Here Edmonson (1982b: 203) translates *kolomche* as "Little Arrow Dance," probably a good interpretation.

19. Edmonson (1982b) translates *ciichcelen* as "gallant."

20. This is a metaphor which referred to happiness, an alternative translation for *dzunun*. The narrative suggested that this person, about to be sacrificed, no longer needed to be content with mere earthly happiness. The hummingbird also was a representative of the Sun God.

21. Edmonson (1982b: 203) believes that the missing section referred to the "bluebird" as the bluebird and hummingbird often were placed together.

22. Edmonson (1982b: 203) translates *ciichcelem ceeh* as "Handsome Deerman." He believes that the *ciichcelem* was supposed to refer to a man, but it actually referred to some sense of masculine beauty.

23. From Chac Mol.

24. Barrera Vásquez (1965: 28) relates *kambvvl* to a yellow bird, but its literal translation was, as in Edmonson (1982b: 203), "yellow bean."

25. Literally, as in Barrera Vásquez (1965: 26) and Edmonson (1982b: 204), "not evil is the treatment of you."

26. Barrera Vásquez (1965: 26) translates this passage as "beautiful maidens will accompany you on your passage from town to town." Edmonson (1982b: 204) translates it as "beautiful are the girls joined with you in your appearances as you come along."

27. Edmonson (1982b: 204) translates this as "keep your mind upon whatever may happen to you."

28. *H'ol pop* translates as "head of the community," but it is literally "head mat." Edmonson (1982b: 204) translates the term as "Head Counsellor," an interpretation which may be correct.

29. Or, as in Edmonson (1982b: 204), the lord of Campeche.

30. The *nacon* was a title that referred to two different people: a war leader and a priest who engaged in human sacrifice.

31. From *cahaloob*.

32. SD: 25; Barrera Vásquez 1965: 26–28; Edmonson 1982b: 201–204.

33. The difference in the two translations (both are mine; Landa did not translate the term) came from the two different terms used. The Songs of Dzitbalché used *kolomche*, while Landa used *colomche*, coming from *colom* ("defense") and *che* ("wood/tree").

34. Landa 1973: 39; 1978: 36.

35. See Clendinnen 1987: 68.

36. They may have been women who died in childbirth.

37. Edmonson (1982b: 206) has "so his strength may suffer."

38. Edmonson (1982b: 206) has "holy."

39. SD: 75–76; Barrera Vásquez 1965: 77–78; Edmonson 1982b: 205–207.

40. We also see Spanish influence in the form of the songs. Rather than having a cellular structure similar to their Nahuatl counterparts, these Maya songs appear to have contained beginnings, endings, and clear stanzas. See Lockhart 1992: 392–400.

41. DM part 1: 807.

42. Sullivan 1989: 176.

43. These rituals have been a topic of conversation for many academics, as they were for the Spaniards. See Thompson 1966: 278–285; Morley, Brainerd, and Sharer 1983: 484–487; Schele and Freidel 1990: 205–209.

44. Kukul Can was the famous Mexican god, Quetzalcoatl.

45. *Tu lacal yal u mehen:* this phrase referred to the children of the nobility or the children who knew their lineage.

46. Edmonson (1982a: 19) translates *pactic* as "folded."

47. Edmonson (1982a: 19) translates *tumtic* as "renewal."

48. Edmonson (1982a: 19) translates *lai hunpel cu yubil* (which I have translated as "this was one mantle") as "this was one more seat and mantle."

49. Or, as in Edmonson (1982b: 20), "little flints." This signified that he was successful in creating a war and maintaining alliances with the military orders.

50. *Ma ya cimlal* literally translated as "death without pain." Note that it also could have translated simply as "Maya death." This was a reference to human sacrifice.

51. CBTi: 16r; Edmonson 1982a: 19–20. *Kintunyabil* could also be translated as "summer."

52. See Clendinnen 1987: 176–182.

53. Commoners were sacrificed quite a bit, so the difference between ideology and reality is apparent.

54. See Stoler 1995: 64–69. Foucault himself appears to have understood this point and suggested that the creation of the concept of sovereignty in this period was related to the creation of race.

55. Nietzsche 1956: 192–193.

56. Nietzsche 1956: 194–198.

57. Deleuze and Guattari 1983: 200–222.

58. As related particularly strongly in Clifford 1986: 1–26.

59. See White 1978: 81–83.

60. See Fash 1991: 168–170.

61. Butler 1993: 187–222.

62. See Sigal 1997.

63. See DM part 1: 9, 14, 516–517; Restall 1997: 123.

64. Spanish *hidalgo* came from *hijo de algo,* "child/son of something," meaning the child of someone of importance (the Spanish language gendered the term male). Nahuatl *pilli* was the same word used for child (Lockhart 1992: 102). The Maya case was the only one of the three that gave a sense of a parallel gender structure within nobility.

65. Stoler 1995: 62–73.

66. Dreyfus and Rabinow 1983: 133–142.

67. On the European context, see Stoler 1995: 73–88. On national distinctions and the relationship to colonialism and desire, see Chatterjee 1993: 18–24; Bhabha 1994: 239–241; Stoler 1995: 88–94.

68. On other colonized groups, see Chatterjee 1993: 46–54; Bhabha 1994: 142–144.

69. See Anderson, Berdan, and Lockhart 1976: 189.

70. McAnany 1995: 22–63.

71. Restall 1997: 48.

72. Restall 1997: 90–92.

73. McAnany 1995: 116.

74. See TI: 18v; Restall 1995a: 116–121.

75. Roys 1940: 35.

76. Roys 1940: 35.

77. Landa 1973: 41–42; 1978: 40; partially quoted in Roys 1940: 35.

78. Which was often, both before and after the conquest. See Farriss 1984: 199–223; Jones 1989.

79. See Farriss 1984: 136–138.

80. Roys 1940: 37–38.

81. The word *chibal* related to descent from the father's lineage, while *dzacab* and *naal* related to descent from the mother's lineage, although the documents show that these terms were used inconsistently, at least during the colonial period. Roys 1940: 38; DM part 1: 133, 873.

82. Roys 1940: 35.

83. See Restall 1997: 41–46.

84. CCa: 31.

85. The Nahua naming patterns kept evolving through the three stages of cultural contact that took place during the colonial period. These evolutions allowed for significantly more differentiation of social status and also apparently allowed for a greater variety in women's surnames. However, women's appelatives seemed to become the place in which the Nahua naming system allowed for little variety. See Lockhart 1992: 117–130.

86. Roys 1940: 41; Farriss 1984: 137; Restall 1992: 296–297.

87. See Stern 1995: 189–204.

CHAPTER SEVEN

1. While this story obviously is fictional, it is based largely on the penis-piercing rituals described in CBC, RB, and Schele and Freidel 1990: 89, 111, 149, 202, 233, 281, 286.

2. Hammond 1982: 282–283; Schele and Freidel 1990: 64–71, 275–286; Fash 1991: 92, 100, 123, 148–149; Love 1994: 48; McAnany 1995: 34–35, 44–45.

3. Stone 1987: 37.

4. Schele and Freidel 1990: 68–69.

5. McAnany 1995: 44–45.

6. Eric Thompson (1970: 184) stated that women were not allowed to attend many of the public religious ceremonies. However, preconquest iconography clearly showed

that women did attend many of the most important ceremonies, seated separately from the men. Further, Inga Clendinnnen showed that women were responsible for the important domestic shrines (Clendinnen 1982: 428).

7. McAnany 1995: 44.

8. Schele and Freidel 1990: 68–70; Fash 1991: 148–149.

9. Stone 1985; Fash 1991: 123.

10. It is this type of description that makes Schele and Freidel very controversial figures among scholars who study the preconquest Maya. While I do not intend to comment on this controversy, I use this description because it elucidates some of the connections between gender, sexuality, and bloodletting. The central points, that Lady Eveningstar let blood through her tongue during this ceremony and that Bird-Jaguar figured in this act, are represented clearly in the hieroglyphs. Further, as I noted in Chapter 1, I find the use of fictional representations in historical discourse to be important as it allows us to understand some elements of culture and society.

11. Schele and Freidel 1990: 279.

12. Schele and Freidel 1990: 279–280.

13. McAnany 1995: 43–45.

14. See Lacan 1988: 272. "It is in so far as the woman is in a symbolic order with an androcentric perspective that the penis takes on this value [creating narcissistic depression based on the reflection of her image in men]. Besides, it isn't the penis, but the phallus, that is to say something whose symbolic usage is possible because it can be seen." Also see Butler 1993: 197.

15. Furst 1976: 183; Clendinnen 1982: 430.

16. Clendinnen 1987: 180–181; Gutiérrez 1991: 29–30.

17. Eric Thompson connects bloodletting to the maintenance of the sun. The sun could recover strength and rise during the day only if he was given blood at night. This blood would have been obtained through human and animal sacrifice and bloodletting rituals. Success in warfare allowed the people of the community to offer the blood of the enemy's nobles. The warriors obtained special privileges by keeping the sun and the other gods happy through ritual sacrifice. Thompson 1966: 113.

18. Roys (1965: 4) translates *olom* (which I have translated as "lineage") as "clotted blood." Arzápalo Marín (1987: 271) translates the term as "torrents of blood." *Olom* translated literally as either blood or lineage (see DM: 605).

19. Arzápalo Marín sometimes translates *chab* (which Roys and I translate as "creation") as "coitus." Indeed, this was an alternative translation for the term, a point that I make in my analysis.

20. RB: 7; Roys 1965: 4; Arzápalo Marín 1987: 271–272.

21. DM part 1: 399.

22. DM part 1: 605.

23. As Arzápalo Marín (1987: 271–272) interprets the passage.

24. For the translations, see DM part I: 267–268.

25. Literally, "for not seeing from the womb of a woman," this was a phrase meant to signify menstruation.

26. Literally, "he, the jicama."

27. EBM: 18; Sotuta Manuscript, T-LAL: 44v.

28. Clendinnen 1982: 430; Farriss 1984: 287; Stone 1985: 26–27; Clendinnen 1987: 181.

29. Kellogg 1995: 164.

30. Kellogg 1995: 162–165.

31. Kellogg 1995: 88–91.

32. Hammond 1982: 290–292.

33. Miswritten both times: the glottal stop on the *ch* was missing. Yet the context appears to necessitate the term *chah*. (See Arzápalo Marín 1987: 287.)

34. *Olom*, as in above, also means "lineage."

35. A type of grain.

36. RB: 28; Roys 1965: 10; Arzápalo Marín 1987: 287.

37. Arzápalo Marín 1987: 270; DM: 121.

38. See RB: 8, 45, 116, 120; Roys 1965: 5, 17, 40, 41; Arzápalo Marín 1987: 272, 300, 353–354, 356.

39. "Vagina" was written as *xu*. It was from *xub*. Note that this terminology was different from the *pel* discussed below.

40. *Fel u na* came from *pel u na*, "the vagina's mother."

41. Roys (1965: 46) skips the section between "the nine gods, the thirteen gods" and "how is the cutting," translating that entire section as "curses upon him!"

42. RB: 135; Roys 1965: 46; Arzápalo Marín 1987: 367–368. Also see below.

43. Roys 1965: xv.

44. Lacan and the Ecole Freudienne 1982: 83; Butler 1993: 195–197.

45. Clendinnen (1982: 428) asserts that women were excluded from bloodletting rituals. Her evidence is based specifically on Landa, who misinterpreted the rituals.

46. Schele and Freidel 1990: 89. This process is well documented in the texts from Palenque, codices, and cave art. See Thompson 1966: 69–70, 101; Stone 1985, 1989, 1995; Schele and Freidel 1990: 66–72, 232–235.

47. Fash 1991: 92, 123–124.

48. McAnany 1995: 34–35.

49. Schele and Freidel 1990: 281.

50. Schele and Freidel 1990: 272–274. Also see Hammond 1982: 202–204; Coe 1987: 185.

51. See, for example, Landa 1973: 39–41, 55–56; 1978: 37–40, 53–54.

52. Landa 1973: 49; 1978: 47–48. Emphasis added.

53. Landa 1973: 65–70; 1978: 62–68; Clendinnen 1987: 193–194.

54. This was a metaphor common to several of the incantations. I do not know its meaning.

55. *Som chi* and *som pul* were names. *Som chi* would have meant "forceful mouth." *Som pul* would have meant "forceful throw."

56. "Great Four Lordship."

57. RB: 42–44; Roys 1965: 16–17; Arzápalo Marín 1987: 298–299.

58. Hanks 1990: 121–122.

59. Lacan and the Ecole Freudienne 1982: 74–85.

60. "Seizure" is from *tan sil*, which should be *tancasil*. The context of the full text shows this translation to be correct.

61. RB: 60; Roys 1965: 22; Arzápalo Marín 1987: 312.

62. Suggesting that Roys's interpretation of *chab* as the masculine principle in creation is correct.

63. See Roys 1965: 22; Arzápalo Marín 1987: 312.

64. "The Closed Heart."

65. This appears to be some obscure reference to lineage. Perhaps the patient taking his or her name was a cross-reference to the very end of the incantation, which stated that the scorpion sting and certain sexual acts represented the genealogy of the mother and father.

66. The dictionaries stated that the Maya word used here (*pel*, written as *fel* in this text) was a derogatory slang word for vagina. In every case that I have found the word used, it does have a derogatory feel. I thus agree with the interpretation that the dictionaries gave. However, at this point I do not understand the nature of the derogation, and I thus simply have translated *pel* without its derogatory aspect. Throughout these texts, Arzápalo Marín translates the term with the epithet *coño* (cunt).

67. Roys (1965: 54) has "curses on your stinger." See below.

68. Both the cave and the crater were represented as female. The ground and underground areas were associated with female attributes, and the cave was considered female in preconquest Maya thought. See Stone 1995: 41.

69. RB: 160–162; Roys 1965: 54–55; Arzápalo Marín 1987: 385–386. Roys translates this text significantly differently. He does not interpret the double entendres. Nor does he translate much of the document, because he believes it simply related to the concept of "curses."

70. DM part 1: 92.

71. Although the context of ritual humor could allow us, as Westerners, to imagine the castration implicit in such a text. On a Western notion of a castration "complex," see Freud 1962: 23–24.

72. See Stone 1985.

73. The cave is a common metaphor for the vagina in Mayan thought (See Bricker 1973: 149–150). The cave also was connected with sexual excess in several ways. See Stone 1985: 28; Strecker 1987: 35; Stone 1995: 143–146.

74. See Stone 1985.

75. DM part 1: 92.

76. Lacan and the Ecole Freudienne 1982: 83.

77. DM part 1: 564.

78. From *ix yal*, which represented her as the daughter of a woman. As will be shown, this reference intended to empower the women in the ceremony, not to denigrate the daughter.

79. See, for example, CBC: 30; Roys 1967: 90; Edmonson 1986: 173.

80. Which can prohibit a discourse around incest. See Freud 1950; 1962; Lévi-Strauss 1963.

81. Farriss (1984: 190) points out that the Christian clergy did complain that "the colonial Maya . . . had fairly relaxed taboos on incest. The practice of father-daughter incest was supposedly common and, even more scandalous, had no shame attached to it. As the Maya—again, reportedly—explained it: 'The father planted the seed and he

harvests the first fruit.'" Nonetheless, the clergy cannot be trusted on such a topic. Further, Farriss does not mention mother-child incest.

82. Note that there is no simple way to devise a difference between transsexual and transgender in the Maya universe. There was no information on the original body of the patient. Nor was there any picture of her or his body at any point. Transsexuality in the Western world has to do with the relationship that one has to "sexual reassignment surgery." Transgender identity is based on the crossing of gender boundaries and the claiming of an identity at odds with a person's supposed "sex." Both terms are contested terrain, and neither can fit into simple definitions in Western thought, much less be transferred easily onto the Maya. See Butler 1990; Garber 1992; Bornstein 1994.

83. Laqueur 1990: 7.

84. Roscoe 1994: 342.

85. See Herdt 1994b.

86. See Trexler forthcoming.

87. This is from the Florentine Codex. It is quoted in López Austin 1980: vol. 2, 276–277. Translation from the Nahuatl by López Austin.

88. Sahagún's interpretation and López Austin's gloss of Sahagún could both be incorrect here. As I note above, translations of sexual terminology manifest huge problems, particularly in a colonial situation. See Kimball 1993.

89. The Nahua case requires further analysis and context. Could Sahagún's Nahua aides have been discussing symbolic representations? Could they have been discussing particular elements of ritual discourse? Were they relating a Nahua element of disgust toward hermaphrodites and lesbians? Were they attempting, without much success, to translate Mesoamerican ideas of duality from one system of cultural meaning to another? Or were they simply telling the Franciscan friar what he wanted to hear?

90. Lacan and the Ecole Freudienne 1982: 84.

91. Butler 1993: 196.

92. Butler 1993: 89.

93. We should be careful not to idealize Maya gender definitions. The notions represented here still prioritized intercourse and penetration. As Gayatri Spivak points out in a different context, these notions fail to symbolize either the possibilities for female sexual pleasure or a libidinal economy that suggests a liberatory potential (Spivak 1987: 150–153).

94. Lacan and the Ecole Freudienne 1982: 164–165.

95. Hanks 1990: 86.

96. RB: 128, 135–137, 145, 153; Roys 1965: 44, 46–47, 49, 52; Arzápalo Marín 1987: 362, 367–369, 375, 380.

97. Roys (1965: 56) has "curses."

98. RB: 166–167; Roys 1965: 56; Arzápalo Marín 1987: 389.

99. Arzápalo Marín 1987: 362.

100. See Bricker 1973.

101. The second term may be translated "bloodletter" as well.

102. Roys (1965: 46) has "curses on the snake."

103. RB: 134–135; Roys 1965: 46; Arzápalo Marín 1987: 367. Roys has this last line as "the unique enemy of man. the unique enemy of Anom."

CHAPTER EIGHT

1. Such a sense of equality would have been alien to the Maya of this period. Inga Clendinnen's point is insightful: "Yucatec Maya women certainly remained separate from men, and were subordinate to them. Males systematically took precedence over females: males controlled public ritual activity and the whole public sphere, while women moved in what we designate the domestic zone. But to say women were separate and subordinate is not at all the same thing as to say they were segregated and subjugated, and were regarded, and regarded themselves, as inferior. Males were equally if differently bound, by the duty of the younger to the older, of the lower to the higher rank. Nor did social authority enhance 'independence': lords were doubly bound by their duty to commoners and priests, priests by their duty to men and to the gods. Within that conceptualization of the world differentiation of function, as of status, was understood in terms of interdependence. Men and women moved in largely separate zones, but those zones were linked by multiple bridges of mundane and ritual action expressive of that interdependence, and within them each group could move with equal assurance" (Clendinnen 1982: 431).

2. Lacan 1988: 272.
3. Lacan 1977: 284–286.
4. Deleuze and Guattari 1983: 51–56.
5. See Sigal 1997.
6. Lacan 1977: 290–291.
7. See Guattari 1996: 83.
8. See Lyotard 1993: 114–121.
9. See Malinowski 1927; Lévi-Strauss 1966: 252–254 for attempts at using psychoanalysis within the confines of ethnography. Also see Devereux 1978: 177–215 for the concept that ethnography and psychoanalysis are complementary.
10. See particularly Herdt 1994a: 255–294, 311–316.
11. See Freud 1961, 1962.
12. See Klein 1928; Freud 1962: 85–96.
13. See Freud 1962: 91–94.
14. See Freud 1961; Marcuse 1962.
15. Freud 1962: 61. The girl's penis envy, however, is significantly different from the boy's castration complex. Here Freud understood that the girl's psychosexual development was not a mirror image of the boy's, but still he attempted to force it to fit into such a model. For an intriguing critique, see Irigaray 1985: 25–34. See also Rubin 1975; Grosz 1990.
16. Freud 1962: 91–94.
17. Lyotard 1993: 1–6.
18. Deleuze and Guattari 1983: 106–113.
19. Foucault 1978: 17–49.
20. See Lacan 1977: 1–7; Lacan and the Ecole Freudienne 1982: 137–148.
21. Lacan 1977: 1–7, 141–145; 1988: 178–186.
22. Lacan and the Ecole Freudienne 1982: 79.
23. See Butler 1993: 57–92.
24. Lacan and the Ecole Freudienne 1982: 79–80.

25. For an overview of these debates in Lacanian thought, see Brennan 1993.

26. See particularly Foucault 1972, 1977a, 1977b, 1980, 1985, 1986; Deleuze and Guattari 1983; Butler 1990, 1993; Lyotard 1993; Guattari 1996.

27. For an analysis of this situation, see Spivak 1987: 197–221; 1988.

28. Note here that I do not argue that there is no natural body. Nor do I argue that there is no natural order of things. Some of the more "radical" constructionist approaches appear to argue that the body is not a material entity. This theoretical approach, which suggests that the body is nothing beyond the discursive, has been critiqued effectively by others. Here I argue that the body, in order to enter the human imagination, necessarily is socially constructed. As the body enters the imagination in Western culture, it may be encoded with a particular gender, which then leads to sexual object choices.

29. Butler 1993: 2.

30. This is most clear in an analysis of the AIDS crisis. At the same time as a very "natural" disease breaks down the body and its immune system, thereby killing massive numbers of people, the very bodies that AIDS destroys are constructed in a heterosexual/heterosexist matrix as diseased bodies not because they contain a particular virus or a particular set of "natural" diseases but rather because those bodies and the identities that they signify are viewed as immoral and unnatural. See the analysis of this position in Watney 1987.

31. See Spivak 1993: 46–51.

32. Irigaray 1985: 142–151.

33. One cannot underestimate the massive discursive shift which took place as the Maya senses of writing and history were changed. The movement from one system whereby history was viewed in a cyclical manner to another system in which history was viewed as linear entailed significant alterations in Maya mental processes. The change from a system of writing that demanded the interpretation of specialists to one in which every element of the story was written on paper was no less of a change. See Gruzinski 1993: 184–200; Florescano 1994: 100–183; Mignolo 1995: 125–216.

34. Deleuze and Guattari 1983: 184–192.

35. Lacan 1977: 288–289.

36. The subject appeared to be male but then later became female. The immediate preceding statement referred to the pain of the first man, and this text seems to have symbolized a critique of the mother by the son.

37. Roys (1965: 42) has "progenitress" instead of "lust," despite the fact that these texts consistently referred to lust when they used the term *cool.*

38. A play on words: Roys (1965: 42) and Arzápalo Marín (1987: 358–359) do not translate the terms, so they discuss the *ix buhumil* serpent, the *ix cuyum* serpent, etc. However, the terms were double entendres.

39. The child may have been illegitimate (she was termed *al*, which translated as "child of a woman"). She was called the *al* of both the mother and father, suggesting that the father played a lesser role in the child's development, implying illegitimacy. This also may have been a way of "feminizing" the father.

40. A play on words: If I adjust the glottal stop slightly, making *Ix Ma'tzil Ahau* (the apostrophe representing the glottal), the translation may become "she, the virgin queen."

41. RB: 123–124; Roys 1965: 42; Arzápalo Marín 1987: 358–359. Roys does not translate these last terms.

42. Thompson 1966: 294.

43. Klein (1990: 8–9) also shows that snakes represented particular goddesses in Nahua thought.

44. Literally, "the flower seizure." The flower here represented eroticism in a phrase that was repeated throughout much of the Ritual of the Bacabs. See below for a more extended analysis of erotic seizures.

45. The seizure is termed *co*, an ambiguous term which could refer either to "lust" or to "insanity." Arzápalo Marín and I choose "lust" because of the context. Roys chooses "madness."

46. *Olom*. Again, this is either lineage or blood.

47. RB: 6–7; Roys 1965: 4; Arzápalo Marín 1987: 271.

48. Lacan 1988: 259–260.

49. Behar 1989: 197.

50. See Silverblatt 1987: 159–196 on the penetration of European witchcraft into indigenous Andean society.

51. Cecelia Klein (1990), discussing the connection between warfare and femininity among the people of Tenochtitlán, says that for them, femininity served as a construct which could play a variety of roles in warfare. The woman playing her proper, moderate role would help win a war. The woman playing an improper, excessive role would be condemned in the discourse around the war.

52. On the penetration of captives, see Trexler 1995: 64–73.

53. Similar to the chronicles from Yaxkukul and Chikxulub. See CCa, CCh, and CY. See Restall 1997: 276–293.

54. CCa: 13.

55. See, for example, Hall 1983.

56. Stone 1995: 63.

57. The implication that the male slaves were sexualized would not have approximated a homosexual identity, even if they engaged in sexual activity specifically with their masters. All commoners and even some nobles, if captured in warfare, could become slaves. The commoner would have been valued linguistically and socially as this slave. The association thus was not with a sexual identity or even with particular sexual acts. Rather, the slave was feminized in a particular gendering of captives. In none of these texts do we find any clear delineation of a homosexual identity.

58. Arzápalo Marín (1987: 288) has "eradication."

59. *Hunuc can ahau kin lic u chabtabal hunac ah kinam* was a play on words intended to insult the god Hunuc Can Ahau. He created the disease, the great pain, through the "greatness," from both *hunuc* and *hunac*.

60. Roys (1965: 11) says that the *dzulbal* was a ceremonial hut "named for trees, but then associated with the lineage cults."

61. The avocado (*on*) and the flower (*nicte*) were intended symbolically to represent male and female genitalia. *Ton*, which the dictionaries translated as "penis," was one reference point here. The avocado also meant testicle in Nahuatl. *Nicte* formed a parallel construction to *ton* and thus represented female genitalia, as *nicte* could be trans-

lated in this manner. Arzápalo Marín translates the selection as "the male member and the female member."

62. *Dzunun nicte* also referred to the "hummingbird flower," suggesting another metaphorical representation of women's sexual desire (DM part 1: 874, 893).

63. A native Yucatecan plant.

64. *Ac* no doubt was from the masculine agentive *ah*, making this "He, the man of air."

65. RB: 30–32; Roys 1965: 11–12; Arzápalo Marín 1987: 288–290.

66. Ciudad Real 1984: 328v; DM part 1: 570.

67. Although the dictionary was anonymous, it seems likely to have been written by the Franciscans.

68. On the relationship of various metaphors to sexual behavior, see Hanks 1990: 119–123.

69. Lacan 1977: 4–6; Butler 1993: 91.

70. Irigaray 1985: 133–146.

71. See Chapter 4. AGN-I: 1187, 2, 59–62.

72. The author was using the derogatory word *pel*.

73. The Other, to Lacan, represents the person put into a relationship with the subject, who is fundamentally narcissistic. The subject relates to the Other only as the subject sees him- or herself through his or her image in the mirror. Lacan 1977: 1–7.

74. Lacan 1977: 187–189.

75. In many ways this represented an anxiety which Lacan would suggest stemmed from the castration complex. However, if we reject the transhistorical narrative of the castration complex, we still may suggest that the fear of excess sexual behavior destroying society represented a Maya tradition which was supported by a Mesoamerican imaginary that demanded adherence to the ideal of moderation in all aspects of life.

76. I do not mean to oversimplify the concept of Maya fantasy. Different people had different fantasies. Some collective fantasies, however, were represented in Maya ritual discourse. These fantasies certainly did not signify reality for all or even most of the Maya people. The fantasies did signify a relationship between shamans, nobles, and commoners which presented a collective attempt at fantasizing about the cosmological world. It is this relationship type of fantasy that I seek to discuss here.

77. Sullivan 1989: 66; Fash 1991: 36–37; Jones 1998: 334–335.

78. See Perry 1990: 127; Stepto and Stepto 1996.

79. Were these people actually women? Were they transsexuals? Were they transgender? Should we call those, who, like Erauso, chose to live as a man, male? One issue with these questions is cultural specificity. For Erauso, we have no knowledge of his/her internal makeup, of his/her thoughts or feelings. Certainly Erauso was someone who wished to cross genders for particular purposes, and thus can be considered a predecessor of the modern transsexual. But s/he had neither the options nor the limitations of female-to-male transsexuals of today. Nor did Erauso have the cultural background or knowledge to be able to discern many of these issues. Treating Erauso as if s/he were male, I think, erases the fact of transsexuality from the historical imagination. Yet, treating Erauso as if s/he were female also erases transsexuality. This is why I have chosen to use the rather awkward sequence of pronouns.

80. See Garber 1992: 93–117.
81. See Bornstein 1994.
82. See Butler 1990 and 1993.
83. See Whitehead 1981; Williams 1986; Roscoe 1988 and 1991.
84. See Whitehead 1981; Blackwood 1984.
85. See Gutiérrez 1989.
86. See Guerra 1970; Trexler 1995.
87. Trexler 1995: 64–117.
88. Klein 1990: 5–6; Kellogg 1995: 102; Trexler 1995: 68–71.
89. See Chapter 9.
90. The letter is found in the Archivo General de las Indias, but I have not been able to consult the original. It is cited in Jones 1998: 499 n.45. The passage reads, "Lord, the perversity of the miserable people reached such a point [that] next to one of their principal temples they had a walled-around large house of very decorous construction solely for the habitation of acquiescents, into which entered all of those who wished to have their sodomitic copulations, especially those who are very young, so that they could learn there, these ministers of the Demon wearing women's skirts and occupying themselves only in making bread for the priests and in their obscenities." Translation by Jones.
91. This is not to say that the Maya may not have dressed male slaves as women. There is no ethnohistorical evidence one way or the other for these figures. On the other hand, see Williams 1986: 131–151. He asserts that the Maya of Yucatán did have a similar role, but his evidence is virtually nonexistent. Unfortunately, Williams mistakes the most Westernized of Maya occupations for a sign of preconquest Maya cultural survival. See Sigal forthcoming.
92. Schele 1983; Stone 1985: 25; Fash 1991: 36–37.
93. Stone 1995: 143.
94. Bricker 1973: 215.
95. Stone 1985; 1987; 1989: 327–328; 1995: 143–146. See also Strecker 1987. In 1985, Stone argued that other pictures in this cave, which Strecker was to argue represented masturbation, in fact were depictions of autosacrifice. But after rethinking the evidence and reading Strecker's article, she argued in response that there was significant evidence of masturbation in Maya art and that perhaps Strecker was correct about one of the pictures. Moreover, Stone made an important point that there were very vague boundaries between the concept of fertility/sexuality and the concept of sacrifice in the Maya world. On this topic, see Chapter 7.
96. Lacan and the Ecole Freudienne 1982: 74–85.
97. *Siyan* is intepreted as *sian*, "enchantment." While *siyan* itself could have meant "story," the texts which used this term all suggested some sort of enchantment. Here the curer attempted to enchant the spider. One could easily use the other translation, "Words of the story of spiders."
98. Pun on *yamtunil*, from *amtun*, meaning "garden." It also could have meant "spider of stone."
99. *A uach*, "your penis," was used throughout these texts as a double entendre. In a different context, *ach*, "penis," could also have meant "sting." Roys (1965: 53) translates it as such.

100. "Ugliness" is from *kas*, written here as *ka*. Roys (1965: 159) translates the term as "gall" or "bitterness." Arzápalo Marín (1987: 384) does not translate the term.

101. Arzápalo Marín (1987: 384) interprets this section differently. To him, the shaman was attempting to decipher the signs.

102. RB: 157–160; Roys 1965: 53–54; Arzápalo Marín 1987: 383–385.

103. See Hanks 1990: 121–122.

104. See Hanks 1990: 110–112; Restall 1997: 125.

105. Note that the Maya also made fun of Christianity by appearing to stutter. After all, the *am*, "spider," was not that different from the sacred term "amen." Maybe the narrative took its ritual strategy as an attempt to make fun of Christianity.

106. Herdt 1994a: 244–246, 255–272.

107. Bricker 1973: xiv–xv.

108. Bricker 1973: 219–224.

109. Bricker 1973: 29.

110. Bricker 1973: 30.

111. Bricker 1973: 30. On another type of ritual statement with sexual import, see Gossen 1974: 257–258.

112. Hanks (1990: 86) notes that the modern Maya use double entendres to get across all kinds of sexual ideas.

113. Lacan and the Ecole Freudienne 1982: 83.

114. Butler 1993: 72–88.

115. See Irigaray 1985: 133–146 on the necessity in masculine discourse to make people, particularly women, imagine the phallus to have immense power.

116. See Butler 1993.

117. See Foucault 1978; Deleuze and Guattari 1983.

118. White 1978: 81–100.

119. On the importance of this process of transsexualization in understanding change, specifically in postmodern Western societies, see Baudrillard 1993.

CHAPTER NINE

1. Brasseur de Bourbourg 1857–1859, vol. 2: 67, 77, 173. Cited in Bleys 1995: 122.

2. Thompson 1970: 20–21.

3. Díaz del Castillo 1989: 7–8.

4. RGY vol. 1: 165.

5. Bleys 1995: 122.

6. On the creation and maintenance of a homosexual identity in the modern West, see Weeks 1977; Foucault 1978.

7. See Gutiérrez 1991; Herdt 1994a; Trexler 1995.

8. Bleys 1995; Sigal 1998.

9. Landa 1973: 54; 1978: 52. Cited in Trexler 1995: 132.

10. Perry 1990: 123–27. The regulations were less applicable to female homosexual behavior. In a study of criminal trials in early modern Seville, Perry found just two cases of prosecutions against female homosexuality, both involving "the use of false genitalia." We also can see the limited effects of Christian prohibitions in fifteenth-century Florence (Rocke 1996).

11. Perry 1990: 125–36.

12. Perry 1990: 125.

13. Trexler 1995: 45–46.

14. Trexler 1995: 40–41.

15. On the Spanish subculture, see Perry 1990: 126–127; Trexler 1995: 58–60. On Mexico, see Gruzinski 1985, forthcoming.

16. See Trexler 1995: 40–43.

17. Edmonson (1982a: 107) translates *u mehen tzintzin* (which I have translated as "the child of the anus") as "the sons of sodomy."

18. CBTi: 9v; Edmonson 1982a: 107. The final term, "anus buggers," I derived from Edmonson's "ass buggers." The translation is an interpretation of *coc xul*, and the most likely direct translation is "to lacerate the end." Edmonson interprets this as a metaphor for "ass buggers," and I believe he is correct.

19. Molina 1992 part 2: 153.

20. This story should not imply that the Maya really believed that sodomy could result in a child. The statement represented a connection made by the Maya between sexual excess and the social health of the society. In other words, the authors said that this particular excess led to or gave birth to a breakdown of the social contract, which then led to the destruction of society.

21. Stone 1989: 327. However, also see Brady 1988.

22. Lacan 1988: 119–120.

23. In addition, connections I have not discussed existed with regard to vegetable and animal sacrifice and tattooing.

24. AGN-I: 1187, 2, 59–62.

25. I thank Matthew Restall for pointing this out to me. AGN-I: 1187, 2, 6–161.

26. "*ɔocan va a kebanchahal yetel uinic tan a tuclic y chuplal yanech?*" From *Modo de confesar en lengua Maya Tixcacal Cupul*, manuscript, photographic reproduction located in the Tozzer Library, 1803: 247. University of Pennsylvania Library, bound as last part of *Colección de pláticas doctrinales y sermones en lengua maya* (by various authors, copied in Mérida, 1868).

27. Although this was changing as the modern period was beginning.

28. DM part 1: 271, 807.

29. Although the word was less ambiguous than the English term. *Top* could not refer to divisions between male and female.

30. DM part 1: 687.

31. Though note that the confessional manual did not use the term *pen*.

32. DM part 1: 115.

33. DM part 1: 807.

34. Later dictionaries further clarified the phrase *ah top chun*. New definitions included *ah topehen* ("he who has carnal acts with men's children") for pederast, and *ah top lom chun* ("he who originates wounding carnal acts" or "he who wounds the anus with carnal acts") or *ah top lom it* ("he who has carnal acts wounding anuses") for sodomite; DM part 1: 807. All of this may have referred simply to the Christian obsession with sexual mores which had developed since the thirteenth century. See Boswell 1980.

35. CBC: 79; Barrera Vásquez and Rendón 1948: 72; Roys 1967: 141; Edmonson 1986: 61. Edmonson translates this as "Kak U Pacal, the sodomist," but he admits Kak

U Pacal and Tecuilu usually were treated as two lords associated with Mayapán. Barrera Vásquez and Rendón believe that *tecuilu* came from a different term which translated as "brazier."

36. Fray Alonso de Molina translated *tecuilonti* as the active partner in sodomy. The passive partner was translated as *cuiloni*. Molina 1992 part 2: 93, 16.

37. "*Tu kin yan tzintzin coc xul tu kin yan tzintzin bac toc,*" CBTi: 6r; Edmonson 1982a: 84.

38. CBTi: 15v; Edmonson 1982a: 52.

39. Of course, this could be an oblique reference to oral sex. Without further evidence, though, I am not willing authoritatively to suggest that conclusion.

40. Scholes and Roys 1948: 91.

41. Trexler 1995: 74.

42. López Austin translates the phrase *cuiloni* as "sodomite."

43. The text was from the Florentine Codex. The translation (except for the first term) is by López Austin. Quoted in López Austin 1980 vol. 2: 274. See also Kimball 1993.

44. See Karttunen 1985: 4–14.

45. DM part 1: 271, 686–687.

46. Trexler 1995: 68–71.

47. Foucault 1980: 96–100; Trexler 1995: 64–81.

48. This was the last text in the entire manuscript, and thus was likely to be a late colonial text. However, it clearly represented the time immediately before the Spanish conquest and was probably a text that was handed down for some time.

49. The children, marked by *al*, showed that "strength" here was represented as female. Roys (1967: 168) has "thrice weighed down is their strength." Edmonson (1986: 76) has "thrice-born is thy strength."

50. While the context clearly suggests this translation (which Barrera Vásquez, Rendón, and Roys support), Edmonson instead translates this as "Those who constantly rise to be baptized—Those who raise quarrels."

51. CBC: 107; Barrera Vásquez and Rendón 1948: 202–203; Roys 1967: 168–169; Edmonson 1986: 76.

52. Nacxit was one name used for Quetzalcoatl. *Xochitl* was "flower" in Nahuatl. See Roys 1967: 83.

53. See Thompson 1970: 21, 46; CBC: 19–20; Roys 1967: 83; Edmonson 1986: 148.

54. Trexler (1995: 81), looking at this same passage, asserts that the Maya "showed their rear ends" to the Spanish conquerors. While the implication is correct, Trexler is relying on an older translation.

55. CBC: 106.

56. Avendaño y Loyola 1696: 43r. Cited in Thompson 1970: 46.

57. See Jones 1998: 334–335.

58. From *ɔam chektahech* I have derived "submerge." The whole phrase was translated as such in the colonial dictionaries. What's more, both *dzam* and *chek* had sexual connotations. *Dzam* connected with the idea of impregnating someone, while *chek* was a word describing some generalized sexual activities.

59. Arzápalo Marín translated *tu ca cobol a na tu ca cobol a yum* (which Roys and I

have translated as "the genitals of your mother and the genitals of your father") as "into the prostitute of your mother, into the whore of your father." He is interpreting genitals as a metaphor for prostitution.

60. RB: 122; Roys 1965: 42; Arzápalo Marín 1987: 357–358.

61. See Chapter 2.

62. Lacan 1977: 1–8; Butler 1993: 57–91.

63. The four *bacabs* themselves represented the world. See Morley, Brainerd, and Sharer 1983: 465–466.

64. Trexler (1995: 88–95) shows that other indigenous societies had a similar attitude toward male passivity. The passive himself was denigrated, but the sodomitical act was seen as necessary.

65. Note here that I am not saying that the phallus itself is or ever was attached to any *body*. The phallus was a part of the shaman's power, and a part of the power of the parental gods. It was in some way attached to their identities, but not necessarily to their bodies.

66. One thinks of the unaltered intersexed/hermaphroditic individual raping a man, but the text was too unclear to assume this to be the case.

67. Something reiterated many times in writings related to the epidemics after the conquest. See RGY.

68. For a more extensive analysis of this topic, see Sigal 1997.

69. See below: Zuyua was represented as unintelligible, foreign language. It probably was linked with the Toltecs or the Itzá.

70. Solís Alcalá (1949: 151, 365) translated *zuyua* as "confusion" or "figurative language."

71. All of my citations are from the Chumayel, which is the more readily available text. The Tusik text paralleled the Chumayel. For some citations from the Tusik text, see Sigal 1997.

72. Roys (1967: 89) has "This is the examination which takes place in the katun which ends today." What Edmonson and I have translated as "questions and answers," Roys consistently translates as "examination."

73. Roys (1967: 89) has "ruling men" instead of "people and lords."

74. CBC: 29; Barrera Vásquez and Rendón 1948: 209; Roys 1967: 89; Edmonson 1986: 170. Edmonson translates the last phrase as "whether the lineages of the lords or the officials of the lineages are cited correctly."

75. See Frank 1991: 69–79.

76. See Hanks 1990: 114–119 for a discussion of asymmetric genres of speech. Also see Frank 1991: 69–79.

77. See Sigal 1997. Girls did not face the same testing, for they did not play a direct role in the political hierarchy.

78. While scholars have interpreted these rituals as involving sitting *batabob* (see Barrera Vásquez and Rendón 1948: 204–219; Roys 1967: 88–98; Edmonson 1986: 168–193), it is highly improbable that these *batabob*, very powerful political leaders, would have attended a ceremony where they were required to serve the *halach uinic* in such a degrading way. Allan Burns's interpretation that these were simply humorous anecdotes also is problematic, for there are no other extant cases of this type of humor in these documents, which were presented as very important and serious historical

texts. While portions of Burns's arguments are convincing (these rituals served to entertain and humor members of the communities), the evidence related to the Chilam Balam genre showed that these rituals could not have been intended only as humorous anecdotes. See Burns 1991. Burns (1983) also discusses sexual banter in modern Yucatán.

79. *"Ti yx culan yax balam yokol kin u kik u kikele suyua u naataal,"* CBC: 29; Barrera Vásquez and Rendón 1948: 209; Roys 1967: 89–90; Edmonson 1986: 172.

80. *Kik* was "blood"; *kikel* also could be "semen."

81. For an explanation of the idea of a phallic signifying economy, see Lacan and the Ecole Freudienne 1982: 74–85.

82. From *ex*, which was translated only in modern dictionaries, although it was present in many colonial documents. This was clearly a term that developed into "trousers" in the postconquest era. See DM part 1: 921.

83. CBC: 36; Barrera Vásquez and Rendón 1948: 211; Roys 1967: 94; Edmonson 1986: 183–184.

84. See Keuls 1985: 275.

85. CBC: 38; Barrera Vásquez and Rendón 1948: 215–216; Roys 1967: 96; Edmonson 1986: 187.

86. Lacan and the *Ecole Freudienne* 1982: 85.

87. See Deleuze and Guattari 1983: 154–166.

88. Edmonson (1986: 199) has "guardians of the fields of girls."

89. Edmonson (1986: 199) has "I will cheer up the girls."

90. CBC: 68; Roys 1967: 128; Edmonson 1986: 199.

91. Foucault 1978: 135–137; 1980: 90–92.

CHAPTER TEN

1. For Latin American examples, see Joseph and Nugent 1994; Radding 1997; Vaughan 1997.

2. See Restall 1997: 305 for a similar argument.

3. See also White 1978: 51–80; 1987: 58–82.

4. In this, my goals and methods are similar to those of Bleys (1995) and Trexler (1995), both of whom are attempting to understand connections between gender and sexual desire among colonized peoples. Both also are very interested in colonial discourse.

5. See Stern 1995: 299.

6. See Clendinnen 1982: 430–431.

7. See the indirect critique in Stern 1995: 285–294.

8. See Kellogg 1995: 111–119.

9. See Trexler 1995: 64–81 on the feminization of enemies. See López Austin 1980: 309–312 on the relationship between sexual behavior and the survival of society.

10. See Andrews and Hassig 1984: 78–80. There have been no studies on the Nahuas which have determined the extent of this symbolic structure.

11. Gutiérrez 1991: 3–36.

12. See Bhabha 1995: 33–34.

13. Gruzinski 1993: 229–268. See also Klor de Alva 1982.

14. Kellogg 1995: 213–219.

15. Lockhart 1992: 429–436. Here I have described analyses of the Nahuas because the Nahua case was better documented, and thus historians have been able to analyze change, colonialism, and hybridity more effectively. As shown throughout this book, however, Farriss (1984), Clendinnen (1987), and Restall (1997) have all made similar points regarding the Maya. The Nahua situation provides a fruitful ground for comparison.

16. Though Maya acculturation was much slower than that of the Nahuas.

17. See Foucault 1978: 57–59.

18. Lyotard 1993: 127.

19. Foucault 1978: 59–73.

20. See the critiques in Spivak 1987: 197–221; Bhabha 1995: 34.

21. Deleuze and Guattari 1983: 216.

22. See Spivak 1988: 220; Bhabha 1994: 171–172.

ABBREVIATIONS

AA-Y   Archivo del Arzobispado (Secretaría)—Yucatán, Mérida, Yucatán.

AGN-I   Archivo General de la Nación—Inquisición, Mexico City, Mexico.

CBC   The Book of Chilam Balam of Chumayel, published in facsimile as Gordon 1913.

CBI   The Book of Chilam Balam of Ixil, facsimile located in T-LAL.

CBK   The Book of Chilam Balam of Kaua, copies located in T-LAL.

CBN   The Book of Chilam Balam of Nah, published in facsimile as Grupo Dzibil 1981.

CBTi   The Book of Chilam Balam of Tizimin, published in facsimile as Fontes Rerum Mexicanarum 1980.

CBTu   The Book of Chilam Balam of Tusik, photographic copy located in the University of Washington archive's Ralph Roys papers.

CCa   Calkiní Chronicle, published in facsimile as Maya Society 1935.

CCh   Crónica de Chikxulub, located in T-LAL.

CD   Códice de Dresde, published as Fondo de Cultura Económica 1983.

CY   Crónica de Yaxkukul (1769 copy), located in T-LAL.

DM   *Diccionario Maya*, published as Barrera Vásquez et al. 1991.

DT   Documentos de Tabí, located in T-LAL.

EBM   *The Ethno-Botany of the Maya*, published as Roys 1931.

RB   El Ritual de los Bacabes, published in facsimile as Arzápalo Marín 1987.

RGY   *Relaciones histórico-geográficas de la gobernación de Yucatán*, published as de la Garza et al. 1983.

SD   Songs of Dzitbalché, published in facsimile as Barrera Vásquez 1965.

TI   Testaments of Ixil, located in the Colección Carrillo y Acona of the Centro de Apoyo a la Investigación Histórica de Yucatán, Mérida, Yucatán.

T-LAL   Latin American Library, Tulane University, New Orleans.

BIBLIOGRAPHY

Alberro, Solange, et al. 1980. *Seis ensayos sobre el discurso colonial relativo a la comuni-dad doméstica: Matrimonio, familia y sexualidad a través de los cronistas del siglo XVI, el Nuevo Testamento y el Santo Oficio de la Inquisición*. Mexico City: Instituto Nacional de Antropología e Historia.

Alvarez, María Cristina. 1974. *Textos coloniales del Libro de Chilam Balam de Chumayel y textos glíficos del Códice de Dresde*. Mexico City: Universidad Nacional Autónoma de México.

Anderson, Arthur, Frances Berdan, and James Lockhart. 1976. *Beyond the Codices*. Berkeley and Los Angeles: University of California Press.

Andrews, J. Richard, and Ross Hassig, eds. 1984. *Treatise on the Heathen Superstitions That Today Live among the Indians Native to This New Spain, 1629, by Hernando Ruiz de Alarcón*. Norman: University of Oklahoma Press.

Arnold, David. 1988. "Touching the Body: Perspectives on the Indian Plague." In Guha and Spivak 1988.

Arrom, Silvia. 1985. *The Women of Mexico City, 1790–1857*. Stanford, Calif.: Stanford University Press.

Arzápalo Marín, Ramón. 1987. *El ritual de los Bacabes*. Mexico City: Universidad Nacional Autónoma de México.

Avendaño y Loyola, Andrés de. 1696. *Relación de las entradas que hizé a la conversión de los géntiles Ytzaex*. Manuscript copy located in the Tozzer Library at Harvard University.

Barrera Vásquez, Alfredo. 1957. *Códice de Calkini*. Campeche: Biblioteca Campechana.

———. 1965. *El libro de los cantares de Dzitbalché: Una traducción con notas y una intro-ducción*. Mexico City: Instituto Nacional de Antropología e Historia.

———. 1984. *Documento n.1 del deslinde de tierras en Yaxkukul, Yuc*. Mexico City: Insti-tuto Nacional de Antropología e Historia.

———, and Silvia Rendón. 1948. *El libro de los libros de Chilam Balam.* Mexico City: Fondo de Cultura Económica.

———, et al. 1991. *Diccionario Maya.* 2d ed. Mexico City: Editorial Porrua.

Baudrillard, Jean. 1993. *The Transparency of Evil: Essays on Extreme Phenomena.* London and New York: Verso.

Behar, Ruth. 1989. "Sexual Witchcraft, Colonialism, and Women's Powers: Views From the Mexican Inquisition." In Lavrin 1989.

Beltrán de Santa Rosa, Pedro. 1895. *Declaración de la doctrina Cristiana en el idioma Yucateco.* Mérida: Librería de Espinosa.

Beverley, John R. 1992. "On the Concept of the Spanish Literary Baroque." In Cruz and Perry 1992.

Bhabha, Homi K. 1994. *The Location of Culture.* New York: Routledge.

———. 1995. "Signs Taken for Wonders." In *The Post-Colonial Studies Reader.* Bill Ashcroft, Gareth Griffiths, and Helen Tillin, eds. New York: Routledge.

Blackwood, Evelyn. 1984. "Sexuality and Gender in Certain Native American Tribes: The Case of Cross-Gender Females." *Signs* 10: 27–42.

Bleys, Rudi C. 1995. *The Geography of Perversion: Male-to-Male Sexual Behavior Outside the West and the Ethnographic Imagination, 1750–1918.* New York: New York University Press.

Bornstein, Kate. 1994. *Gender Outlaw: On Men, Women, and the Rest of Us.* New York: Routledge.

Boswell, John. 1980. *Christianity, Social Tolerance, and Homosexuality: Gay People in Western Europe from the Beginning of the Christian Era to the Fourteenth Century.* Chicago: University of Chicago Press.

Brading, D. A. 1991. *The First America: The Spanish Monarchy, Creole Patriots, and the Liberal State 1492–1867.* New York: Cambridge University Press.

Brady, James E. 1988. "The Sexual Connotation of Caves in Mesoamerican Ideology." *Mexicon* 10/3: 51–55.

Brasseur de Bourbourg, Charles Etienne. 1857–1859. *Histoire des nations civilisées du Mexique et de l'Amerique-Centrale durant les siècles antérieurs à Christophe Colomb.* 4 vols. Paris: A. Bertrand.

Brennan, Teresa. 1993. *History after Lacan.* New York: Routledge.

Bricker, Victoria. 1973. *Ritual Humor in Highland Chiapas.* Austin: University of Texas Press.

———. 1981. *The Indian Christ, The Indian King: The Historical Substrate of Maya Myth and Ritual.* Austin: University of Texas Press.

———. 1989. "The Last Gasp of Maya Hieroglyphic Writing in the Books of Chilam Balam of Chumayel and Chan Kan." In Hanks and Rice 1989.

Brinton, Daniel G. 1882. *The Maya Chronicles.* Philadelphia.

Burkhart, Louise M. 1989. *The Slippery Earth: Nahua-Christian Moral Dialogue in Sixteenth-Century Mexico.* Tucson: University of Arizona Press.

Burns, Allan. 1983. *An Epoch of Miracles.* Austin: University of Texas Press.

———. 1991. "The Language of Zuyua: Yucatec Maya Riddles and their Interpretation." In *Past, Present and Future: Selected Papers on Latin American Indian Literatures.* Mary H. Preuss, ed. Culver City, Calif.: Labyrinthos.

Butler, Judith. 1990. *Gender Trouble: Feminism and the Subversion of Identity.* New York: Routledge.

———. 1993. *Bodies That Matter: On the Discursive Limits of "Sex".* New York: Routledge.

Carrier, Joseph M. 1985. "Mexican Male Homosexuality." *Journal of Homosexuality* 11: 75–85.

———. 1995. *De los otros: Intimacy and Homosexuality among Mexican Men.* New York: Columbia University Press.

Carrillo y Ancona, Crescencio. 1887. *Compendio de la historia de Yucatán.* Mérida: Librería Católica.

———. 1890. *Estudio filológico sobre el nombre de América y el de Yucatán.* Mérida: Impr. Mercantil.

Chamberlain, Robert S. 1948. *The Conquest and Colonization of Yucatán, 1517–1550.* Washington, D.C.: Carnegie Institution.

Chatterjee, Partha. 1993. *The Nation and Its Fragments.* Princeton, N.J.: Princeton University Press.

Chauncey, George. 1994. *Gay New York: Gender, Urban Culture, and the Making of the Gay Male World, 1890–1940.* New York: Basic Books.

Ciudad Real, Antonio de, ed. 1984. *Calepino Maya de Motul.* 2 vols. Mexico City: Universidad Nacional Autónoma de México.

Clendinnen, Inga. 1982. "Yucatec Maya Women and the Spanish." *Journal of Social History* 15/3: 427–442.

———. 1987. *Ambivalent Conquests: Maya and Spaniard in Yucatán, 1517–1570.* Cambridge, Eng.: Cambridge University Press

———. 1991. *Aztecs: An Interpretation.* Cambridge, Eng.: Cambridge University Press.

Clifford, James. 1986. "Introduction: Partial Truths." In *Writing Culture: The Poetics and Politics of Ethnography.* James Clifford and George E. Marcus, eds. Berkeley and Los Angeles: University of California Press.

Coe, Michael D. 1987. *The Maya.* London: Thames and Hudson.

Cogolludo, Diego López de. 1954. *Historia de Yucatán.* 3 vols. Campeche: Comisión de Historia.

Cruz, Anne J., and Mary Elizabeth Perry, eds. 1992. *Culture and Control in Counter-Reformation Spain.* Minneapolis: University of Minnesota Press.

De la Garza, Mercedes, et al., eds. 1983. *Relaciones histórico-geográficas de la gobernación de Yucatán.* 2 vols. Mexico City: Universidad Nacional Autónoma de México.

Deleuze, Gilles, and Félix Guattari. 1983. *Anti-Oedipus: Capitalism and Schizophrenia.* Minneapolis: University of Minnesota Press.

Derrida, Jacques. 1974. *Of Grammatology.* Baltimore: The Johns Hopkins University Press.

Devereux, George. 1978. Ethnopsychoanalysis: Psychoanalysis and Anthropology as Complementary Frames of Reference. Berkeley: University of California Press.

Díaz del Castillo, Bernal. 1989. *Historia verdadera de la conquista de Nueva España.* Madrid: Quinto Centenario.

Dover, K. J. 1978. *Greek Homosexuality.* New York: Vintage Books.

Dreyfus, Herbert L., and Paul Rabinow. 1983. *Michel Foucault: Beyond Structuralism and Hermeneutics.* Chicago: University of Chicago Press.

DuBois, Ellen, and Vicki Ruiz. 1990. *Unequal Sisters: A Multicultural Reader in U.S. Women's History*. New York: Routledge.

Edmonson, Munro. 1982a. *The Ancient Future of the Itzá: The Book of Chilam Balam of Tizimin*. Austin: University of Texas Press.

———. 1982b. "The Songs of Dzitbalche: A Literary Commentary." *Tlalocan* 9: 173–208.

———. 1986. *Heaven Born Mérida and Its Destiny: The Book of Chilam Balam of Chumayel*. Austin: University of Texas Press.

Faderman, Lillian. 1981. *Surpassing the Love of Men: Romantic Friendship and Love between Women from the Renaissance to the Present*. New York: Morrow.

Farriss, Nancy M. 1984. *Maya Society under Colonial Rule: The Collective Enterprise of Survival*. Princeton: Princeton University Press.

Fash, William. 1991. *Scribes, Warriors, and Kings: The City of Copán and the Ancient Maya*. London: Thames and Hudson.

Florescano, Enrique. 1994. *Memory, Myth, and Time in Mexico: From the Aztecs to Independence*. Austin: University of Texas Press.

Fondo de Cultura Económica. 1983. *Códice de Dresde*. Mexico City: Medio Siglo.

Fontes Rerum Mexicanarum. 1980. *El Libro de Chilam Balam de Tizimín reproducción*. Graz, Austria: Akademische Druck.

Foucault, Michel. 1972. *The Archaeology of Knowledge and The Discourse on Language*. New York: Pantheon Books.

———. 1977a. *Discipline and Punish: The Birth of the Prison*. New York: Vintage Books.

———. 1977b. "Nietzsche, Genealogy, History." In *Language, Counter-Memory, Practice*. Oxford: Basil Blackwell.

———. 1978. *The History of Sexuality. Vol. 1: An Introduction*. New York: Vintage Books.

———. 1980. *Power/Knowledge: Selected Interviews and Other Writings, 1972–1977*. New York: Pantheon Books.

———. 1983. "The Subject and Power." In Dreyfus and Rabinow 1983.

———. 1985. *The Use of Pleasure: The History of Sexuality, Vol. 2*. New York: Vintage.

———. 1986. *The Care of the Self: The History of Sexuality, Vol. 3*. New York: Vintage.

Frank, Arthur W. 1991. "For a Sociology of the Body: An Analytical Review." In *The Body: Social Process and Cultural Theory*. Mike Featherstone, Mike Hepworth, and Bryan S. Turner, eds. Newbury Park: Sage Publications.

Freud, Sigmund. 1950. *Totem and Taboo*. New York: W. W. Norton.

———. 1961. *Civilization and Its Discontents*. New York: W. W. Norton.

———. 1962. *Three Essays on the Theory of Sexuality*. New York: Harper Collins.

Furst, Peter T. 1976. "Fertility, Vision Quest and Auto-Sacrifice: Some Thoughts on Ritual Blood-Letting among the Maya." In *The Art, Iconography, and Dynastic History of Palenque, Part III: Proceedings of the Segunda Mesa Redonda de Palenque*. Merle Greene Robertson, ed. Pebble Beach: Robert Louis Stevenson School.

Garber, Marjorie. 1992. *Vested Interests: Cross-Dressing and Cultural Anxiety*. New York: Harper.

García Canclini, Néstor. 1995. *Hybrid Cultures: Strategies for Entering and Leaving Modernity*. Minneapolis: University of Minnesota Press.

Garibay K., Angel María. 1940. *Llave de náhuatl: Colección de trozos clásicos con gramática y vocabulario, para utilidad de los principiantes*. Mexico City: Otumba.

————. 1964–1968. *Poesía náhuatl.* 3 vols. Mexico City: Universidad Nacional Autónoma de México, 1964–1968.

Gauderman, Kimberly. 1992. "Father Fiction: The Construction of Gender in England, Spain, and the Andes." *UCLA Historical Journal* 12: 122–151.

Gerard, Kent, and Gert Hekma, eds. 1989. *The Pursuit of Sodomy: Male Homosexuality in Renaissance and Enlightenment Europe.* New York: Harrington Park Press.

Gibson, Charles. 1952. *Tlaxcala in the Sixteenth Century.* New Haven: Yale University Press.

————. 1964. *The Aztecs under Spanish Rule.* Stanford, Calif.: Stanford University Press.

Gordon, G. B., ed. 1913. *The Book of Chilam Balam of Chumayel.* Philadelphia: University of Pennsylvania Museum.

Gosner, Kevin. 1992. *Soldiers of the Virgin: The Moral Economy of a Colonial Maya Rebellion.* Tucson: University of Arizona Press.

Gossen, Gary H. 1974. *Chamulas in the World of the Sun: Time and Space in a Maya Oral Tradition.* Cambridge, Mass.: Harvard University.

Gramsci, Antonio. 1971. *Selections from the Prison Notebooks.* New York: International Publishers.

Green, James N. Forthcoming. *Beyond Carnival: Male Homosexuality in Twentieth-Century Brazil.* Chicago. University of Chicago Press.

Grosz, Elizabeth. 1990. *Jacques Lacan: A Feminist Introduction.* New York: Routledge.

Grupo Dzibil. 1981. *Manuscritos de Tekax y Nah.* Mexico City: CEiD.

————. 1982. *Manuscrito de Chan Cah.* Mexico City: CEiD.

Gruzinski, Serge. 1980. "La conquista de los cuerpos." In Alberro et al.

————. 1985. "Las cenizas del deseo: Homosexuales novohispanos a mediados del siglo XVII." In *De la santidad a la perversión o de la porqué no se cumplía la ley de Dios en la sociedad Novohispana.* Sergio Ortega, ed. Mexico City: Editorial Grijalbo.

————. 1989a. *Man-Gods in the Mexican Highlands: Indian Power and Colonial Society, 1520–1800.* Stanford, Calif.: Stanford University Press.

————. 1989b. "Individualization and Acculturation." In Lavrin 1989.

————. 1993. *The Conquest of Mexico: The Incorporation of Indian Societies into the Western World, 16th–18th Centuries.* Oxford: Polity Press.

————. Forthcoming. "The Ashes of Desire: Mexican Homosexuality in the Middle of the Seventeenth Century." In Sigal forthcoming.

Guattari, Félix. 1996. *The Guattari Reader.* Gary Genosko, ed. Cambridge: Blackwell.

Guerra, Francisco. 1970. *The Precolumbian Mind.* New York: Seminar Press.

Guha, Ranajit. 1988. "The Prose of Counter-Insurgency." In Guha and Spivak 1988.

————. 1997. *Dominance without Hegemony: History and Power in Colonial India.* Cambridge: Harvard University Press.

————, and Gayatri Chakravorty Spivak, eds. 1988. *Selected Subaltern Studies.* New York: Oxford University Press.

Gutiérrez, Ramón A. 1989. "Must We Deracinate Indians to Find Gay Roots?" *Out/Look* 1: 61–67.

————. 1991. *When Jesus Came, the Corn Mothers Went Away: Marriage, Sexuality, and Power in New Mexico, 1500–1846.* Stanford, Calif.: Stanford University Press.

Hall, Jacqueline Dowd. 1983. "The Mind That Burns in Each Body." In Snitow, Stansell, and Thompson 1983.

Hammond, Norman. 1982. *Ancient Maya Civilization.* New Brunswick, N.J.: Rutgers University Press.

Hanks, William F. 1988. "Grammar, Style and Meaning in a Maya Manuscript: Review of *Heaven Born Mérida and Its Destiny: The Chilam Balam of Chumayel,* Munro Edmonson." *International Journal of American Linguistics* 54: 331–364.

———. 1990. *Referential Practice: Language and Lived Space among the Maya.* Chicago and London: University of Chicago Press.

———, and Don S. Rice, eds. 1989. *Word and Image in Maya Culture: Explorations in Language, Writing, and Representation.* Salt Lake City: University of Utah Press.

Hassig, Ross. 1988. *Aztec Warfare: Imperial Expansion and Political Control.* Norman: University of Oklahoma Press.

Herdt, Gilbert. 1994a. *Guardians of the Flutes: Idioms of Masculinity.* 2nd ed. Chicago: University of Chicago Press.

———, ed. 1994b. *Third Sex, Third Gender: Beyond Sexual Dimorphism in Culture and History.* New York: Zone Books.

Hill, Robert M. 1989. *The Pirir Papers and Other Colonial Period Cakchiquel-Maya Testamentos.* Nashville: Vanderbilt University Department of Anthropology.

———. 1992. *Colonial Cakchiquels: Highland Maya Adaptations to Spanish Rule, 1600–1700.* Fort Worth: Harcourt Brace Jovanovich.

Hofling, Charles. 1989. "The Morphosyntactic Basis of Discourse Structure in Glyphic Text in the Dresden Codex." In Hanks and Rice 1989.

Holmes, Barbara. 1978. "Women and Yucatec Kinship." Ph.D. dissertation, Tulane University.

Hunt, Marta. 1974. "Colonial Yucatán: Town and Region in the Seventeenth Century." Ph.D. dissertation, UCLA.

Irigaray, Luce. 1985. *Speculum of the Other Woman.* Ithaca: Cornell University Press.

Jakeman, M. Wells. 1952. "The 'Historical Recollections' of Gaspar Antonio Chi." *Brigham Young University Publications in Archaeology and Early History* 3: 1–45.

Jenkins, Keith. 1991. *Re-Thinking History.* New York: Routledge.

Jones, Grant D. 1989. *Maya Resistance to Spanish Rule: Time and Resistance on a Colonial Frontier.* Albuquerque: University of New Mexico Press.

———. 1998. *The Conquest of the Last Maya Kingdom.* Stanford, Calif.: Stanford University Press.

Joseph, Gilbert M., and Daniel Nugent, eds. 1994. *Everyday Forms of State Formation: Revolution and the Negotiation of Rule in Modern Mexico.* Durham, N.C.: Duke University Press.

Karttunen, Frances. 1985. *Nahuatl and Maya in Contact with Spanish.* Austin: University of Texas Department of Linguistics, Texas Linguistic Forum 26.

Kellogg, Susan. 1995. *Law and the Transformation of Aztec Culture, 1500–1700.* Norman: University of Oklahoma Press.

Kerr, Justin. 1990. *The Maya Vase Book: A Corpus of Rollout Photographs of Maya Vases.* 2 vols. New York: Kerr Associates.

Keuls, Eva C. 1985. *The Reign of the Phallus: Sexual Politics in Ancient Athens.* Berkeley and Los Angeles: University of California Press.

Kimball, Geoffrey. 1993. "Aztec Homosexuality: The Textual Evidence." *Journal of Homosexuality* 26/1: 7–24.

Klein, Cecelia. 1990. "Fighting with Femininity: Gender and War in Aztec Mexico." Paper delivered at conference on "Gendering Rhetorics," SUNY Binghamton.

Klein, Melanie. 1928. "Early Stages of the Oedipus Complex." *International Journal of Psychoanalysis* 11: 167–180.

Klor de Alva, J. Jorge. 1982. "Spiritual Conflict and Accommodation in New Spain: Toward a Typology of Aztec Responses to Christianity." In *The Inca and Aztec States, 1400–1800: Anthropology and History.* G. A. Collier, R. I. Rosaldo, and J. D. Wirth, eds. New York: Academic Press.

———. 1988a. "Contar vidas: La autobiografía confesional y la reconstrucción del ser nahua." *Arbor* 515–516: 49–78.

———. 1988b. "Sahagún and the Birth of Modern Ethnography: Representing, Confessing, and Inscribing the Native Other." In Klor de Alva, Nicholson, and Quiñones Keber 1988.

———. 1991. "Colonizing Souls: The Failure of the Indian Inquisition and the Rise of Penitential Discipline." In *Cultural Encounters: The Impact of the Inquisition in Spain and the New World.* Mary E. Perry and Anne J. Cruz, eds. Berkeley: University of California Press.

———. 1992a. "Nahua Studies, the Allure of the 'Aztecs,' and Miguel León-Portilla: An Introduction." In León-Portilla 1992.

———. 1992b. "Nahua Colonial Discourse and the Appropriation of the (European) Other." *Archives de Sciences Sociales des Religions* 77: 15–35.

———, H. B. Nicholson, and E. Quiñones Keber, eds. 1988. *The Works of Bernardino de Sahagún: Pioneer Ethnographer of Sixteenth-Century Aztec Mexico.* Austin: University of Texas Press.

Lacan, Jacques. 1977. *Écrits: A Selection.* New York: Norton.

———. 1988. *The Seminar of Jacques Lacan Book II: The Ego in Freud's Theory and in the Technique of Psychoanalysis, 1954–1955.* New York: Norton.

———, and the Ecole Freudienne. 1982. *Feminine Sexuality.* Juliette Mitchell and Jacqueline Rose, eds. New York and London: W. W. Norton.

Laclau, Ernesto. 1988. "Metaphor and Social Antagonisms." In Nelson and Grossberg 1988.

Lancaster, Roger. 1992. *Life Is Hard: Machismo, Danger, and the Intimacy of Power in Nicaragua.* Berkeley and Los Angeles: University of California Press.

Landa, Diego de. 1973. *Relación de las cosas de Yucatán.* Mexico City: Editorial Porrua.

———. 1978. *Yucatán: Before and After the Conquest.* Trans. by William Gates. Baltimore: The Maya Society.

Laqueur, Thomas. 1990. *Making Sex: Body and Gender from the Greeks to Freud.* Cambridge, Mass.: Harvard University Press.

Las Casas, Bartolomé de. 1985. *Historia de las Indias.* 3 vols. Hollywood, Fla.: Ediciones del Continente.

Lavrin, Asunción, ed. 1989. *Sexuality and Marriage in Colonial Latin America.* Lincoln and London: University of Nebraska Press.

León-Portilla, Miguel. 1963. *Aztec Thought and Culture: A Study of the Ancient Nahuatl Mind.* Norman: University of Oklahoma Press.

———. 1988. *Time and Reality in the Thought of the Maya.* 2nd ed. Norman: University of Oklahoma Press.

————. 1992. *The Aztec Image of Self and Society: An Introduction to Nahua Culture.* Salt Lake City: University of Utah Press.

Lévi-Strauss, Claude. 1963. *Structural Anthropology.* New York: Basic Books.

————. 1966. *The Savage Mind.* Chicago: University of Chicago Press.

Lewis, Herbert S. 1981. "Warfare and the Origin of the State: Another Formulation." In *The Study of the State.* Henri J. M. Claessen and Peter Skalnik, eds. The Hague: Mouton.

Lockhart, James. 1991. *Nahuas and Spaniards: Postconquest Central Mexican History and Philology.* Stanford, Calif.: Stanford University Press and UCLA Latin American Center.

————. 1992. *The Nahuas after the Conquest: A Social and Cultural History of the Indians of Central Mexico, Sixteenth through Eighteenth Centuries.* Stanford, Calif.: Stanford University Press.

————, and Stuart Schwartz. 1983. *Early Latin America: A History of Colonial Spanish America and Brazil.* New York: Cambridge University Press.

López Austin, Alfredo. 1980. *Cuerpo humano e ideología.* 2 vols. Mexico: Universidad Nacional Autónoma de México.

Love, Bruce. 1994. *The Paris Codex: Handbook for a Maya Priest.* Austin: University of Texas Press.

Lyotard, Jean-François. 1993. *Libidinal Economy.* Bloomington and Indianapolis: Indiana University Press.

MacCormack, Sabine. 1991. *Religion in the Andes: Vision and Imagination in Early Colonial Peru.* Princeton, N.J.: Princeton University Press.

Malinowski, Bronislaw. 1927. *Sex and Repression in Savage Society.* Cleveland: Meridian.

Marcus, George E., and Michael M. J. Fischer. 1986. *Anthropology as Cultural Critique: An Experimental Moment in the Human Sciences.* Chicago: University of Chicago Press.

Marcuse, Herbert. 1962. *Eros and Civilization: A Philosophical Inquiry into Freud.* New York: Vintage.

Mártir de Anglería, Pedro. 1944. *Décadas del Nuevo Mundo.* Buenos Aires: Editorial Bajel.

Maya Society. 1935. *The Maya Calkiní Chronicle.* Baltimore: The Maya Society.

McAnany, Patricia. 1995. *Living with the Ancestors: Kinship and Kingship in Ancient Maya Society.* Austin: University of Texas Press.

Means, Phillip A. 1917. *A History of the Spanish Conquest of Yucatán and of the Itzás.* Cambridge, Mass.: Peabody Museum.

Mignolo, Walter D. 1995. *The Darker Side of the Renaissance: Literacy, Territoriality, and Colonization.* Ann Arbor: University of Michigan Press.

Molina, Alonso de. 1992. *Vocabulario en lengua castellana y mexicana y mexicana y castellana.* Mexico City: Editorial Porrúa.

Morley, Sylvanus G., George W. Brainerd, and Robert J. Sharer. 1983. *The Ancient Maya.* 4th ed. Stanford, Calif.: Stanford University Press.

Murray, Stephen O. 1987. *Male Homosexuality in Central and South America.* New York: GAU-NY.

————. 1995. *Latin American Male Homosexualities.* Albuquerque: University of New Mexico Press.

Nelson, Cary, and Lawrence Grossberg, eds. 1988. *Marxism and the Interpretation of Culture*. Urbana and Chicago: University of Illinois Press.

Nietzsche, Friedrich. 1956. *The Genealogy of Morals*. New York: Doubleday.

———. 1967. *The Will to Power*. New York: Vintage.

Parker, Richard. 1991. *Bodies, Pleasures, and Passions: Sexual Culture in Contemporary Brazil*. Boston: Beacon Press.

Patch, Robert W. 1993. *Maya and Spaniard in Yucatán, 1648–1812*. Stanford, Calif.: Stanford University Press.

Paz, Octavio. 1988. *Sor Juana*. Cambridge, Mass.: Harvard University Press.

Pelikan, Jaroslav. 1985. *Jesus through the Ages: His Place in the History of Culture*. New Haven: Yale University Press.

Perry, Mary Elizabeth. 1990. *Gender and Disorder in Early Modern Seville*. Princeton, N.J.: Princeton University Press.

Phelan, John Leddy. 1970. *The Millennial Kingdom of the Franciscans in the New World*. Berkeley and Los Angeles: University of California Press.

Pío Pérez, Juan. 1866–1877. *Diccionario de la lengua Maya*. Mérida: Imprenta Literaria de Juan F. Molina Solís.

———. 1868. *Códice Pérez: Extractos de varios ejemplares del "Chilam Balam"*. Manuscript copy located in the Tozzer Library at Harvard University.

Prescott, William. 1936. *The History of the Conquest of Mexico and the History of the Conquest of Peru*. New York: Modern Library.

Quezada, Noemi. 1974. "Erotismo en la religión azteca." In *Revista de la Universidad de México* 28/2: 6–19.

Quezada, Sergio. 1993. *Pueblos y caciques yucatecos, 1550–1580*. Mexico City: Colegio de México.

Radding, Cynthia. 1997. *Wandering Peoples: Colonialism, Ethnic Spaces, and Ecological Frontiers in Northwestern Mexico, 1700–1850*. Durham, N.C.: Duke University Press.

Reed, Nelson. 1964. *The Caste War of Yucatán*. Stanford, Calif.: Stanford University Press.

Reiter, Rayna R., ed. 1975. *Toward an Anthropology of Women*. New York: Monthly Review Press.

Requeña, Antonio. 1945. "Noticias y consideraciones sobre las anormalidades sexuales de los aborígenes americanos: Sodomía." *Acta Venezolana* 1: 43–73.

Restall, Matthew. 1995a. *Life and Death in a Maya Community: The Ixil Testaments of the 1760s*. Lancaster, Calif.: Labyrinthos.

———. 1995b. "'He Wished It in Vain': Subordination and Resistance among Maya Women in Post-conquest Yucatán." *Ethnohistory* 42: 577–95.

———. 1997. *The Maya World*. Stanford, Calif.: Stanford University Press.

———, and Pete Sigal. 1992. "'May They Not Be Fornicators Equal to These Priests': Postconquest Yucatec Maya Sexual Attitudes." *UCLA Historical Journal* 12: 91–121.

Ricard, Robert. 1966. *The Spiritual Conquest of Mexico*. Berkeley: University of California Press.

Rocke, Michael. 1996. *Forbidden Friendships: Homosexuality and Male Culture in Renaissance Florence*. New York: Oxford University Press.

Roscoe, Will, ed. 1988. *Living the Spirit: A Gay American Indian Anthology.* New York: St. Martin's Press.

————. 1991. *The Zuni Man-Woman.* Albuquerque: University of New Mexico Press.

————. 1994. "How to Become a Berdache: Toward a Unified Analysis of Gender Diversity." In Herdt 1994b.

Roys, Ralph L. 1931. *The Ethno-Botany of the Maya.* New Orleans: Tulane University.

————. 1939. *The Titles of Ebtun.* Washington, D.C.: Carnegie Institute.

————. 1940. "Personal Names of the Maya of Yucatán." *Contributions to American Anthropology and History* 6: 31–48.

————. 1943. *The Indian Background of Colonial Yucatán.* Norman: University of Oklahoma Press.

————. 1957. *The Political Geography of the Yucatán Maya.* Washington, D.C.: Carnegie Institute.

————. 1965. *The Ritual of the Bacabs.* Norman: University of Oklahoma Press.

————. 1967. *The Book of Chilam Balam of Chumayel.* Norman: University of Oklahoma Press.

————, France V. Scholes, and Eleanor B. Adams. 1940. "Report and Census of the Indians of Cozumel, 1570." *Contributions to American Anthropology and History* 30: 2–30.

Rubin, Gayle. 1975. "The Traffic in Women: Notes on the 'Political Economy' of Sex." In Reiter 1975.

————. 1984. "Thinking Sex: Notes for a Radical Theory of the Politics of Sexuality." In *Pleasure and Danger.* Carol S. Vance, ed. Boston: Routledge.

Rugeley, Terry. 1996. *Yucatán's Maya Peasantry and the Origins of the Caste War.* Austin: University of Texas Press.

Ruz, Joaquín. 1822. *Catecismo histórico ó compendio de la istoria sagrada, y de la doctrina cristiana.* Mérida: D. Canton.

————. 1846. *Colección de sermones para los domingos de todo el año, y cuaresma, tomados de varios autores, y traducidos libremente al idioma Yucateco.* Mérida: Jose D. Espinosa.

Said, Edward W. 1978. *Orientalism.* New York: Vintage.

Schele, Linda. 1983. "Human Sacrifice among the Classic Maya." In *Ritual Human Sacrifice in Mesoamerica.* E. P. Benson, ed. Washington, D.C.: Dumbarton Oaks.

————, and David Freidel. 1990. *A Forest of Kings: The Untold Story of the Ancient Maya.* New York: William Morrow.

Scholes, France V., and Eleanor B. Adams. 1938. *Don Diego Quijada: Alcalde Mayor de Yucatán, 1561–1565.* 2 vols. Mexico City: Antigua Librería Robredo.

Scholes, France V., and Ralph L. Roys. 1948. *The Maya Chontal Indians of Acalan-Tixchel.* Norman: University of Oklahoma Press.

Sedgwick, Eve Kosofsky. 1990. *Epistemology of the Closet.* Berkeley and Los Angeles: University of California Press.

Seed, Patricia. 1988. *To Love, Honor, and Obey in Colonial Mexico: Conflicts over Marriage Choice, 1574–1821.* Stanford, Calif.: Stanford University Press.

Sigal, Pete. 1997. "The Politicization of Pederasty among the Colonial Yucatecan Maya." *Journal of the History of Sexuality* 8: 1–24.

————. 1998. "Ethnohistory and Homosexual Desire: A Review of Recent Works." *Ethnohistory* 45/1.

————. 1999 (forthcoming). "An Ethnohistory of Colonial Maya Bodies." *Colonial Latin American Historical Review.*

————. Forthcoming. "Gendered Power, the Hybrid Self, and Homosexual Desire in Late Colonial Yucatán." In *Actives, Passives, and Beyond: Male Homosexuality in Colonial Latin America.* Pete Sigal, ed. Chicago: University of Chicago Press.

————. n.d. "Passing Time: Methodology and Authorship of the Books of Chilam Balam." Unpublished manuscript.

Silverblatt, Irene. 1987. *Moon, Sun, and Witches: Gender Ideologies and Class in Inca and Colonial Peru.* Princeton, N.J.: Princeton University Press.

Snitow, Ann, Christine Stansell, and Sharon Thompson, eds. 1983. *Powers of Desire: The Politics of Sexuality.* New York: Monthly Review Press.

Solís Alcalá, Ermilo. *Diccionario español-maya.* 1949. Mérida: Editorial Yikal Maya Than.

Sousa, Lisa. 1998. "Indigenous Women in Central Mexico and Oaxaca." Ph.D. dissertation, UCLA.

Spalding, Karen. 1984. *Huarochirí: An Andean Society under Inca and Spanish Rule.* Stanford, Calif.: Stanford University Press.

Spivak, Gayatri Chakravorty. 1987. *In Other Worlds: Essays in Cultural Politics.* New York: Routledge.

————. 1988. "Can the Subaltern Speak?" In Nelson and Grossberg 1988.

————. 1993. *Outside in the Teaching Machine.* New York: Routledge.

Stepto, Michele, and Gabriel Stepto, eds. 1996. *Lieutenant Nun: Memoir of a Basque Transvestite in the New World, Catalina de Erauso.* Boston: Beacon Press.

Stern, Steve J. 1982. *Peru's Indian Peoples and the Challenge of the Spanish Conquest: Huamanga to 1640.* Madison: University of Wisconsin Press.

————. 1995. *The Secret History of Gender: Women, Men, and Power in Late Colonial Mexico.* Chapel Hill: University of North Carolina Press.

Stoler, Ann Laura. 1995. *Race and the Education of Desire: Foucault's History of Sexuality and the Colonial Order of Things.* Durham and London: Duke University Press.

Stone, Andrea J. 1985. "The Moon Goddess at Naj Tunich." *Mexicon* 7: 23–29.

————. 1987. "Commentary." *Mexicon* 9: 37.

————. 1989. "The Painted Walls of Xibalba: Maya Cave Painting as Evidence of Cave Ritual." In Hanks and Rice 1989.

————. 1995. *Images from the Underworld: Naj Tunich and the Tradition of Maya Cave Painting.* Austin: University of Texas Press.

Strecker, Matthias. 1987. "Representaciones sexuales en el arte rupreste de la región Maya." *Mexicon* 9: 34–37.

Sullivan, Paul. 1989. *Unfinished Conversations: Mayas and Foreigners between Two Wars.* New York: Knopf.

Taylor, Clark Louis. 1978. "El Ambiente: Male Homosexual Social Life in Mexico City." Ph.D. dissertation, UC Berkeley.

————. 1985. "Mexican Male Homosexual Interaction in Public Contexts." *Journal of Homosexuality* 11: 117–136.

Tedlock, Barbara. 1992. *Time and the Highland Maya.* Rev. ed. Albuquerque: University of New Mexico Press.

Tedlock, Dennis. 1986. *The Popol Vuh.* New York: Simon & Schuster.

————. 1993. *Breath on the Mirror: Mythic Voices and Visions of the Living Maya*. San Francisco: Harper San Francisco.

Terraciano, Kevin. 1994. "Ñudzahui History: Mixtec Writing and Culture in Colonial Oaxaca." Ph.D. dissertation, UCLA.

Thompson, J. Eric. 1939. "The Moon Goddess in Middle America, with Notes on Related Deities." In *Carnegie Institute Publication 506*. Washington, D.C.: Carnegie Institute.

————. 1966. *The Rise and Fall of Maya Civilization*. Norman: University of Oklahoma Press.

————. 1970. *Maya History and Religion*. Norman: University of Oklahoma Press.

————. 1972. *A Commentary on the Dresden Codex: A Maya Hieroglyphic Book*. Philadelphia: American Philosophical Society.

Thompson, Philip. 1978. "Tekanto in the Eighteenth Century." Ph.D. dissertation, Tulane University.

Tozzer, Alfred M. 1977. *A Maya Grammar*. New York: Dover Publications.

Trevisan, João. 1986. *Perverts in Paradise*. London: Gay Men's Press.

Trexler, Richard. 1995. *Sex and Conquest: Gendered Violence, Political Order, and the European Conquest of the Americas*. Ithaca, N.Y.: Cornell University Press.

————. Forthcoming. "Gender Subordination and Political Hierarchy in Prehispanic America." In Sigal forthcoming.

Vaughan, Mary Kay. 1997. *Cultural Politics in Revolution: Teachers, Peasants, and Schools in Mexico, 1930–1940*. Tucson: University of Arizona Press.

Villagutierre, Juan de. 1985. *Historia de la conquista de Itzá*. Madrid: Historia 16.

Watney, Simon. 1987. *Policing Desire: Pornography, AIDS and the Media*. Minneapolis: University of Minnesota Press.

Webster, David. 1976. "Defensive Earthworks at Becan, Campeche, México: Implications for Maya Warfare." In *Middle American Research Institute, Tulane University Publication 41*. New Orleans: Tulane University.

————. 1977. "Warfare and the Evolution of Maya Civilization." In *The Origins of Maya Civilization*. R. E. W. Adams, ed. Albuquerque: University of New Mexico Press.

Weeks, Jeffrey. 1977. *Coming Out: Homosexual Politics in Britain from the Nineteenth Century to the Present*. London: Quartet Books.

————. 1985. *Sexuality and Its Discontents*. New York: Routledge.

White, Hayden. 1978. *Tropics of Discourse: Essays in Cultural Criticism*. Baltimore: Johns Hopkins University Press.

————. 1987. *The Content of the Form: Narrative Discourse and Historical Representation*. Cambridge, Eng.: Cambridge University Press.

Whitehead, Harriet. 1981. "The Bow and the Burden Strap: A New Look at Institutionalized Homosexuality in Native North America." In *Sexual Meanings: The Cultural Construction of Gender and Sexuality*. Sherry B. Ortner and Harriet Whitehead, eds. Cambridge, Eng.: Cambridge University Press.

Williams, Walter L. 1986. *The Spirit and the Flesh: Sexual Diversity in American Indian Culture*. Boston: Beacon Press.

Wood, Stephanie. 1984. "Corporate Adjustments in Colonial Mexican Indian Towns: Toluca Region." Ph.D. dissertation, UCLA.

Edmonson, Munro, 45
Erauso, Catalina de, 200, 289n79
erections, 66
essentialism, 187–188
ethnicity, xiii, 142; and blood, 138; and
exoticism, 39; and flowers, 51; and
human sacrifice, 140–141; and interracial sexual relations, 68; and lineage,
143–145, 186; and the phallus, 194;
and power, 113–114; and preconquest
Maya, 40, 252n14; and self-identity,
39–45, 247, 253n23; and sexual desire, 42–43, 65, 68–69, 74–75, 119,
225, 247–249, 253n23; and sodomy,
215–216, 226–228; Spanish concept
of, 42–45; and warfare, 40, 140–141,
143–144, 225, 239–240; of women,
65, 68–69, 74–75, 113–114, 268n18.
See also "Other"; race
ethnohistory, 11, 242, 249
Eve, as compared to the Moon Goddess,
101
excess, 86–88, 91–93, 225, 247, 289n75;
and festivals, 82; and flowers, 51; and
slavery, 190, 193–194; terminology
of, 80–81, 86–88, 193–194
exoticism, 39

family: 31–38; and gender roles, 31; and
household, 18, 31–32; and lineage,
32. *See also* lineage; marriage
fantasy, 289n76; and blood rituals of
women, 153–155; and gender transformation, 164, 168–169; and penis
piercing, 151–152, 160–161, 165,
168–169, 174, 179, 182, 183, 209; and
the phallus, 161, 166, 186, 200, 209–
210, 244, 248–249; and sexual intercourse with the gods, 209–210, 232,
244; and transsexuality, 169, 173–174,
179–182, 183, 200, 207, 209, 232,
244, 248–249. *See also* fear
Farriss, Nancy, 25, 27, 28, 32, 71, 251n5,
256n48, 261n77, 284n81
Fash, William, 202
fear: of gods, 232; phallic, 170, 244,

248–249; of rape, 232; of slaves, 192–
193; of sodomy, 232, 244; of women,
206. *See also* fantasy
femininity, 121–123, 182; and blood,
151–152, 157–158, 160, 165–166,
244–245 (*see also* menstruation); and
disease, 205; and dualism, 197; and
gods, 45; and human sacrifice, 141,
148; and lineage, 148; and the male
slave, 193–194; and Maya community
power, 76; of Maya warriors, 45–47;
and the moon, 59; and night, 59; of
the "Other," 40; and passive role in
sodomy, 224–227; and the phallus,
177, 185, 191–192; and power, 125,
157, 160, 170, 180, 183, 207, 244; and
rape, 44; and transsexuality, 202–204;
and the vagina, 177; and virginity,
125, 245; and warfare, 40, 42, 44–
45, 240, 288n51. *See also* gender;
masculinity
fiction, 3, 14, 150–151, 155, 213–214
Fischer, Michael, 263n9
flowers, 244; and blood, 50; and conquest, 49–52; and excess, 51; and
the "Flower Katun," 45–49; and the
flower seizure, 191–192; and the
Moon Goddess, 119; and Nahuas, 50;
and penetration, 51–52, 139, 244; and
the phallus, 190, 194–197; and poetry, 50, 118, 122; and ritual, 50; and
sex, 50–51, 88, 116–119, 191–192,
194–197, 226; as symbols of death,
47, 49–50, 52; as symbols of duality,
49–52; as symbols of human sacrifice,
49; as symbols of life, 47, 49–50, 52,
88–89; and virginity, 111–115
Foucault, Michel, 143, 187, 239, 247–
248, 253n18, 254nn27,29
Franciscan friars: and children, 37–38;
and critique of colonialism, 82–84,
270n71; eroticism of, 72–73, 77–79;
and ethnographic project, 30; ideology of, 65, 67, 69–73; and production
of dictionaries, 80–81, 123, 196; and
relationship with Jesus, 72, 77; and

114–115, 129, 168, 179, 211, 220,
232; and gender, 95; and gender
transformation, 168–173, 178–179;
of human sacrifice, 135, 137–141;
humor, 180, 206–208, 235–239; and
Moon Goddess, 106; and politics,
232–239; and sexual desire, xiv, 202–
204, 227–232, 242, 248–249; and
spectacle, 135, 137; and transsexuality,
200, 202–205, 210–212, 248–249;
and Virgin Mary, 110–111
Ritual of the Bacabs, 15–16, 80, 95,
104–108, 123–125, 157–160, 164–
169, 179–181, 190–191, 195–196,
204–205, 208, 210, 219, 222, 228,
242, 273n28
Rivas, Manuel Antonio de, 70
Roys, Ralph, 35, 145, 158, 160
Rugeley, Terry, 259n27
rulership: and blood, 147–148, 150–151;
and human body, 129–130, 185; and
human sacrifice, 131, 135, 141; and
lineage, 147–149; and transsexuality,
210

sacrifice. *See* blood; human sacrifice
Sahagún, Bernardino de, 175, 261n67
saints, Catholic, 24–26; and *cofradías*,
25; and Maya gods, 24–27; as representatives of community, 24–25
Schele, Linda, 152, 162–163, 202
scorpions, 169–173
semen: and blood, 164–168, 184, 233,
244, 247; and creation, 47–48, 107–
108, 167–168, 247; and curing, 165–
167; and evil, 168; and power, 165–
167, 182, 245; and ritual, 107–108,
164–168, 182; and Virgin Mary, 107–
108
sexual acts, 9; and "orgies" during festivals, 82, 117–119; between people and
gods, 7, 9. *See also* sexual desire; sexual
terminology; *specific acts*
sexual desire, xiv, 122; and blood, 138–
139, 148, 157–158, 169–173; and
commoners, 89–90; construction of,

xv, 7, 185–189; as creator, 41, 159–
160, 167, 218; as destroyer, 41, 51,
88–90, 217–218; discourses of, 6–8,
214, 241; and the flower song, 118;
and human sacrifice, 133–134, 148;
and lineage, 143–145, 148; and Maya
narratives, 86–93; and penis piercing,
151, 165, 169–173; as powerful force,
41, 74, 91–93, 101, 167, 239–249;
for Saint Francis, 73; and sexuality, 7,
10, 214, 241; and sin, 7; and Spanish
narratives, 81–86; and Spanish politics, 44; and the state, 92–93, 248;
and warfare, 42–49, 133, 242. *See also*
sexual acts; sexual terminology; *specific
acts*
sexual terminology, 7, 66, 79–81, 138–
139, 193–194, 220–222, 254n25. *See
also* sexual acts; sexual desire; *specific
acts*
sexual violence. *See* rape
shamans, 166; and idolatry, 29; and
Moon Goddess, 105–106; and penis
piercing rituals, 162, 166, 206, 209;
sexual acts of, 213, 228–232; and
transsexuality, 200, 210; and Virgin
Mary, 121
sin, 53–62, 78, 94, 139, 142; and Catholic control, 53; and creation of the individual subject, 60–61; and fate, 54–
55; and free will, 53; and identity, 41;
and illness, 54; and Maya moral codes,
56, 80–81; Maya notion of, 53–55;
and Maya politics, 58–59; and metaphor, 40–41; penalties for, 54–55,
58–59; and rape, 90–91; and sodomy,
221; and Spanish concept of sexual
desire, xiv, 7, 215, 221
slavery, xiii; and human sacrifice, 22; and
the phallus, 190; and sexual desire,
190–195; and warfare, 40
social constructionism, 7–8, 187–188,
287n28
sodomy, xiii, 65–66, 70, 80, 85, 202,
213–240, 247, 254n26, 290n90; and
destruction, 217–218, 223, 226–227;

and deviancy, 43; and fear of gods, 232; and insanity, 226–227; and Maya ethnicity, 226–227; and power, 8–9, 214–215; punishment for, 85, 216–217; used as insult, 217, 223–227; use of in Spanish discourse, 42–44, 215–216; and warfare, 42
Songs of Dzitbalché, 16–17, 95, 242; "Anoint Yourself Well with the Fat of a Deer," 136–138; "The Broken Tree/Clefted Stick," 131–134; "Flower Song," 116–119; "I Love You," 122–123; "Orphan Song," 36; "We Are Going to Receive the Flower," 111–115
Spanish conquest. *See* colonialism
spectacle: and blood sacrifice, 163; and human sacrifice, 135, 137
spiders, 165–166, 204–205
Spivak, Gayatri, 187–188, 210, 252n1, 253n21, 254n27, 285n93
Stone, Andrea, 194, 203, 220, 290n95
strategic inversion, 73–79, 91, 192, 242
Strecker, Matthias, 290n95
subalterns, 252n1, 257nn65,66
Sullivan, Paul, 271n98

testaments, Maya, 28
Thompson, J. Eric, 101, 125, 191, 273n24, 282n17
time and space, Maya notion of, 23, 45–46
transgender identity, 200–204, 285n82, 289n79
transsexuality, 174–182, 244–245; and curing, 167; and femininity, 194, 202–204; and the floating phallus, 174, 177–179, 181–182, 183–212; of gods, 96, 102–103; and identity, 200–204, 285n82, 289n79; and masculinity, 177–178, 197; in ritual, 169–173, 183, 191; and unconscious, 197; use of in Spanish discourse, 42–43, 200–201
transvestism: in the Maya world, 200, 202–204, 220–221, 290nn90,91; Spanish penalties for, 200–201, 216–

217; use of in Spanish discourse, 42–44, 200–201. See also *berdache*
Trexler, Richard, 42, 201–202, 216, 231

unconscious, 10, 179, 186–187, 197, 204, 237, 248; and hybridity, 11–12, 246
underworld, Maya, 22–23, 47, 55, 171

vagina: and insults, 180–181, 284n66; and menstruation, 151, 157–158; as represented in ritual texts, 160, 165–166, 169–170, 179–181, 205, 208; as signifier, 178; symbolism of, 151–161, 178, 244
virginity, 95, 116, 122, 136–137, 170, 241, 247, 277n113; and Catholicism, 19, 78, 242; and curing, 123; and human sacrifice, 125; and Moon Goddess, 100, 205; and power, 124; terminology of, 123–126; and Virgin Mary, 95, 111–115, 242
Virgin Mary, 94, 106; in Books of Chilam Balam, 108–111; as Catholic saint, 25; and curing, 121; and disease, 120; and fire goddess, 121; and gendered power, 28, 108, 128; giving birth to Maya gods, 121; as goddess, 106, 119–123, 242; as hybrid figure, 62, 95, 115, 242; and lineage, 114–115; and Maya shamans, 121; power of, 109, 111, 114–115, 128; in Ritual of the Bacabs, 107–108; as seen by Maya commoners, 128; in Songs of Dzitbalché, 111–115; and virginity, 95, 111–115, 120, 242. See also Moon Goddess; Virgin Mary Moon Goddess
Virgin Mary Moon Goddess, xvi, 1–3, 17, 62, 95, 110–111, 115–123, 126–128, 149, 189, 241–242, 246–247, 252n1

warfare, 94, 151, 162, 244; and ethnicity, 40, 140–141, 143–144, 239–240; and flowers, 49–52; and gender, 42–52,